POWER OF SCANDAL:
SEMIOTIC AND PRAGMATIC IN MASS MEDIA

JOHANNES EHRAT

Power of Scandal

Semiotic and Pragmatic in Mass Media

UNIVERSITY OF TORONTO PRESS
Toronto Buffalo London

© University of Toronto Press Incorporated 2011
Toronto Buffalo London
www.utppublishing.com
Printed in Canada

ISBN 978-1-4426-4125-9

Printed on acid-free, 100% post-consumer recycled paper with vegetable-based inks.

Toronto Studies in Semiotics and Communication
Editors: Marcel Danesi, Umberto Eco, Paul Perron, Roland Posner, Peter Schulz

Library and Archives Canada Cataloguing in Publication

Ehrat, Johannes, 1952–
Power of scandal : semiotic and pragmatic in mass media / Johannes Ehrat.

(Toronto studies in semiotics and communication)
Includes bibliographical references and index.
ISBN 978-1-4426-4125-9

1. Scandals in mass media. I. Title. II. Series: Toronto studies in semiotics and communication

P96.S29E37 2011   302.2′4   C2010-906758-4

University of Toronto Press acknowledges the financial assistance to its publishing program of the Canada Council for the Arts and the Ontario Arts Council.

 Canada Council Conseil des Arts
for the Arts du Canada

 ONTARIO ARTS COUNCIL
CONSEIL DES ARTS DE L'ONTARIO

University of Toronto Press acknowledges the financial support of the Government of Canada through the Canada Book Fund for its publishing activities.

Contents

Preface ix

Acknowledgments xv

1 A Theoretical Approach to the Nature of Media Scandal   3
   1.1 How Scandal Research Tends to Treat the Achievement of Media Scandals   4
   1.2 Scandal as Logic: Ideal and Sanction   9
   1.3 Scandal as Industrial Product and Institutional Practice   15
   1.4 Media Scandals and What They Are Not   18
   1.5 Video-Truths   25
   1.6 Comprehending Media Scandals from Media   33
   1.7 Publicity Narrative as Precondition of Scandals   40

2 What Is Publicity, the Public Sphere?   48
   2.1 Publicity as Methodological Construct   50
   2.2 Publicity as Simulacrum   54
   2.3 Publicity and Meaning as Subsistence   59
   2.4 Semiotic as Theory of Formal and Concrete Meaning   70

3 Semiotic of Publicity   76
   3.1 Publicity as Teleology   78
   3.2 Legitimacy   83
   3.3 Public Opinion as Historical-Cultural Role Relation   88
   3.4 Public Opinion as Theatre   91
   3.5 Public Opinion Operates by Constructing the Role of Enunciation Instance   97

4 Publicity in Media Theory 103

    4.1 Media – Functional or Semiotic? 104
    4.2 Is There a Need for a Separate Semiotic Media Theory? 122
    4.3 Signs of Society 126
    4.4 Functions of the Three Correlates in the Media Sign 147
    4.5 Technological Determination or Sign Process: The Case of Televangelism 157
    4.6 Godcasting: Meaning Apparatuses of Religious Self-Display 170

5 From Jubilation to Scandal 180

    5.1 Religious Meaning outside of Public Opinion 181
    5.2 Television Studies and Aesthetic Form 185
    5.3 Media Construction of Religious Space and Time 188
    5.4 The Call Forward 195
    5.5 Witnessing 199
    5.6 PrayTV Yields to PreyTV: Acts of Televangelist Authority 204
    5.7 Primordial Scandal Religion 210

6 Judgment: Bringing into a Scandal-Position 215

    6.1 Scandal Technique 216
    6.2 Investigative Journalism and Objectivity 222
    6.3 Metatexts: Simplifying Sanctions in Public Opinion Texts 236
        6.3.1 Metatext I: The Permission to Act 240
        6.3.2 Metatext II: The Scale of Self-Realization 242
    6.4 Deduction of Classes of Scandal 249
        6.4.1 Scandal of Destination 251
        6.4.2 Scandal of Action 254

7 The Course of the Scandal Pro-Gram 257

    7.1 Media Scandal Methods 258
    7.2 Event: How Destination in the Shanley Story Created the Scandal 260
    7.3 The Role Structure of the Shanley Story 268
    7.4 Two Discursive Scandal Constructions 276
    7.5 Reality: News Practice between Reality Determination and Satirical Alienation 280

8 Effect and Reality of Scandal 291

    8.1 Scandal as Objectivity Effect 292

8.2 Objective Scandal Effects   294
8.2.1 Scandal as Effect   297
8.3 Critique of Subjectivity Approaches and Functionalism   303
8.4 Scandal Effect as Semiotic   307
8.5 Institutions as Pragmatic Predetermination of Purpose   311
8.6 Delegitimization of an Institution as Purpose of Media Scandals   374

9 Conclusion   323

Notes   333

Bibliography   379

Index   403

Preface

What is public opinion? Or better: What is it not?

It is not *my* opinion; it is not *yours*. It is not even the opinion of both of us, be it as agreement, or as sum, or as least common denominator. Furthermore, it is not even the opinion of everyone. Public opinion, scandals, are in reality what 'All' think about someone or something.

What public opinion polls turn into the object of their research is not public opinion. It is at best a statistical abstraction, as selected by the researcher, of the opinion of some who are thus selected to stand for all (cf. Bourdieu 1980).

Instead, public opinion is the opinion of All. It is what *I* think that *All* think, it is what *you* think that *All* think, and it is what *all* think that *All* think. But no one thinks that anyone will ever be able to find out what all think.

Public opinion is amateur sociology *en miniature*. All of us indulge in it, and when we do, we encounter the same problem as professional sociologists when they reflect on their activity (Schutz 1973, I:118–39). That problem is, How are we to understand All? Clearly, All is not an object in the world out there, but one that is intrinsically related to ourselves as pragmatic subjects. Schütz, when discussing Weber's central tenet, made this cognitive status of society a mainstay of his theory, with consequences we will discuss later.

Which does not mean that public opinion is merely an idea. Indeed, it has a strong influence on which actions can be performed, and how. The idea has real effects.

We have just noted that scandals are what All think about someone. All recognize for themselves the right to sanction someone, but they can act only as All. A scandal introduces a small but significant difference into All: that we are different from the one who is being sanctioned. In other words, 'This is the bad one – and we are the good ones.'

Religion has a special relationship with public opinion. The two are natural enemies of sorts, and they battle on the field of authority. Public opinion directs human actions by determining goals for them. God, as the point of reference of religion, has a practical influence over the life of believers when He is sought as a transcendental goal, as a source of the good. At the same time, God is jealous (קִנְאַת 2 Kings 19:31) and does not tolerate other gods next to Him (אֱלֹהִים אֲחֵרִים 2 Kings 17:7), not even public opinion's divine voice (cf. *infra*). In a religious media scandal, one god tries to prevail over another in a struggle of proxies.

Methodologically, it would have had a certain 'natural' appeal to approach the subject of religious scandals as a collection of historical events in the course of which religion, and not some other grand idea, happened to be the bone of contention. This would have meant 're-narrating' religious scandals – that is, painting narrative panoramas so as to illustrate various facets of the subject. A number of studies have taken this 'natural' approach for political scandals, sex scandals, and so forth. For religion – in particular regarding the abuse scandals in the United States – such treatments of the subject have already flooded the market. Our interest is much more theoretical and general as opposed to event-oriented. Our method, therefore, is not narratable, a history of [whatever] in disguise.

The first four chapters of this book amount to a vast theorizing effort. They develop initial insights from observations of media scandals; they then reflect on theories of meaning from which communicable public meanings can be deduced; this then leads to a semiotic theory of publicity.[1] Finally, we test our results against the media theories of Habermas and Luhmann.

In chapter 1 we reflect on the phenomenon of scandals and examine how various theories grapple with it. This will serve as a platform from which to uncover dimensions that are not obvious and that point to deeper inquiries into broader and more general fields.

Chapter 2 approaches one of these fields: the peculiar nature of the object itself, that is, the public opinion phenomenon. As a means to grasp an idea so intangible, we propose two fundamentally different figures of thought: *simulacrum* and subsistence. Simulacrum is a figure of thought that makes the intangible familiar as a 'simile' to the experienced. The substance, or subsistence, figure procedes from the familiar experienced to intangible principles 'under which' they are thought to 'subsist.' This discussion of ideal objectness provides an opportunity to debate with, among others, Habermas, the author of one of the best-known approaches to public opinion. In order, however, to avoid a narrow Habermasian exegesis, we will be casting a wider net. The goal here will be to comprehend opposite approaches that address in fundamental ways the nature of communicable meaning *in se*, and how communication relates to the idea of society. Without clear ideas about where meaning comes from and how it is constructed, all elaborations about public meaning (and one of its chief condensation points, scandal) would be left dangling. We have judged that it would be more useful to introduce central semiotic concepts gradually into the various debates (i.e., instead of tabling a treatise of semiotic from the ground up). This has the advantage that semiotic as discussed in this book will be immediately connected with concrete theory problems (and thereby will be less abstract than it so often is). Besides, a general introduction to semiotic has already been presented by the present author in an earlier book (Ehrat 2005a).

In chapter 3, the idea and concept of sign will bear fruit for a novel understanding of publicity. Being a product of meaning and not a tangible object, its concrete mode is uniquely the process of a sign. That said, we must avoid disconnecting public meaning from reality, as if meaning production had to mean that the real should not play a part in production. Furthermore, publicity is a particular *kind* of sign process – one that produces teleology as both narrative text and legitimacy. While there are many conceptualizations of narration, ancient and modern, the 'linguistic' strand that leads to structuralist and semiological theories has become dominant. Its latest incarnation, semionarratology,[2] conceives of narration as dependent on an act of enunciation. Since, despite various attempts at amalgamation, semiotic does not share most basic assumptions, this draws us into an unavoidable debate, while at the same time offering a semiotic alternative. After investigating the logic and semiosis of teleology and of legitimization, we will consider the cultural and historical forms of public opinion. Though an outgrowth of precise historical contingencies, publicity is nothing new; rather, it is modelled on a pattern of spectacular meaning that can be traced back to antiquity. Conveniently, our theatre model of public opinion will summarize a model of meaning that is a spectacle, or θεωρία in Greek.

Chapter 4 debates at length some key assumptions of Luhmann's systems theory. Here, the central topic is media theory. Semiotic is inherently aware not just of media but of all varieties of sign. The bone of contention with systems theory thus arises at the level of principles. Do signs have a function? What is their business, not only in the classical Peircean domains of a cognitive grasp of the possible, existent, and necessary being, but also in a narrower sense of the being-in-society? Again, this provides an occasion to develop the semiotic of society and immediately connect the results with a concrete social media being. Here we will test a preliminary analysis of a fascinating phenomenon of public opinion, one that encroaches on religion (and *vice versa):* televangelism.

In chapter 5 we strive for a theoretical clarification of the central mechanism of meaning. Systems theory tries to conceive of this mechanism as function. Does this hold more explanatory power than a theory of the real that hinges on the triadic concept of the sign? The strength that systems theory claims for itself is that it offers a comprehensive theory of society, referred to non-ontically as the 'society of society' (Luhmann). Albeit without the same premises, we will be testing the potential of semiotic in the same area: the challenging but central matter of the theoretical concept of society. This chapter will go on to practical considerations, towards the core issue, which is the encroachment of public logic on forms of religious presentation. This brings us to televangelism, which as we will see, once the 'sign of society' sheds its light on it, is more than an aesthetic form, or an instance of 'television form.'

Chapter 6 looks briefly at religion as it appears *before* it becomes an object of public opinion; we then examine the transformations that occur at the point where religion decides to appear as 'public.' Televangelism is again the classic illustration of the transition from privately religious to publicly religious. This provides an occasion to describe in terms of semiotic processes the structural pillars of televangelist shows. At this stage the bedrock conflict with public opinion becomes evident, as a sort of primordial 'scandalicity' of all things publicly religious.

Chapter 7 examines the 'techniques' of narrative scandal production. Which narrative apparatus needs to be established to produce the specific meaning (pro-gram), which becomes a scandal when turned into a series of events? We will be guided in this and in further analyses by the now famous early coverage of the child sexual abuse (from now on 'CSA') scandal in the *Boston Globe*. This will lead us to consider professional practices, such as investigative journalism and the 'industrial' production of objectivity. An important result of a semiotic analysis is the concept of metatext, of which there are two kinds: the legitimization of power and the realization of the Self. From there we can deduce purely theoretically all classes of scandal.

In chapter 8, we observe the process arising from the program. The most important aspect to be unearthed at this stage is the construction of the event, both as a narrative and as a logical step in a processual whole. With regard to this theoretical scaffolding, we will concern ourselves mainly with describing one concrete series of events in the CSA scandal.

Chapter 9 turns to the central question of reality. What is *real* in a scandal? Initially we dismissed the simplicist idea that 'real facts' cause scandal. Instead of causes, we investigated formal, mainly narrative elements that determined almost perfectly the meaning of scandal. But reality is intrinsic to that meaning, so that theory must find other than naive ways to integrate the real. With the aid of metatexts, it is possible to view society as an institutional reality, not in the sense of rawly, physically real, but as *organized* as reality. In this domain, scandals unfold by forcing real changes on institutions; that is what happens when one social institution affects other institutions. But before effects, there must be causes, and there must be more weight behind scandal causes than mere 'indignation.' We will examine how turning the experiential real into a problematic real is key to turning the former into a cause of institutional effects.

When we return to our object of study, scandal, it will be clear that increasingly it has come to define the practice and theory of journalism *tout court*. Scandal is so ubiquitous and such a mainstay of the press that we find it even at the zenith of journalism. Periodically and worldwide, we stumble over 'gates.'[3] Yet as industry products, scandals seem to contradict certain aspects of the ideal of objectivity, which, by the way, was invented by the Anglo-American press (after Chalaby's well-known albeit somewhat extreme thesis). The ideal of objectivity has given way to more sober characterizations of the news industry's products, but it still serves its purpose. The press's self-justifications inexorably seem to involve an appeal to this ideal. In our analyses of the scandal-igniting articles in the *Boston Globe* (around CSA), we will come across some fascinating conflicts: troubled relationships with sources, the public relations efforts of law firms. In this vein, problematic relationships arise when the scandal target is religion, which somehow seems to be above the tribunal of public opinion.

In prevailing approaches to communication studies, it is astonishing how little attention is paid to the media themselves. Mainstream sociology situates 'scandal' on the audience side. Scandal as the product of an industrial text thus appears as a mere abstraction: the scandal's root is genuinely observable only as an operation of public opinion. The 'qualitative,' 'active audience' approach in cultural theory does not account for the media's quality. It is thus confined, outside the medium, to a social aggregate 'readership,' from which it reconstructs 'normal' expected scandal-instigated reactions. Here, the 'real' scandal takes place in the everyday world of the spectators, as an indignant emotion, a social interaction, a mind frame. Alternatively, scandal is approached from a starting point in real-life events, and media scholars see their task as following the events' straight or meandering paths through the media. This approach is quite common, yet it explains nothing. These events owe their scandalicity to basic operations that judge them to be scandalous – which, however, are not self-explanatory. Media are neither transmission belts nor transparencies – they produce meaning in their own right and with their own means. It is not helpful to mix the various factors of the genesis of scandals. This only hides the decisive contributions of the journalistic construction.

Scandal is not a real event as reported in the press; it is a press report of a real event. In other words, it is through public opinion that a real event becomes scandal. Public opinion is not anybody's opining, nor is it any statistical measure of it; rather, it is narrative meaning production, and this has always been so.

Acknowledgments

Even before they meet the readers' eyes, *habent sua fata libelluli*. While this book was being written and prepared for publication, it seemed to me that my object of study exploded before my eyes. Scandals of the kind on which this study focuses were bursting like bubbles, one after another, in very different places. However diverse these events, they all seemed as if they were being run by one and the same book of rituals, titled The *Sexual Abuse of Children by Priests*. It was almost as if I was writing a play while it was being performed on stage. This scenario has become a well-established *topos*, a true commonplace. One could become defensive, apologetic, or sarcastic when dealing with this matter. However, the public outrage, much justified, proved also to be very helpful and continues to have a strong impact. While the abuse all was carried out by individuals, the scandal targeted the institution, and the institution reacted. Did the Church react to the real suffering of human beings or to prodding by the media? The more I understood the nature of public opinion in this study, the more I understood this as a moot question: institutions are almost immune to individuals; only other institutions can force them to change. In that sense, the current crisis serves as an illustrated volume of our descriptions. So much for the real-world setting of the topic and the vital personal interest of this book ...

I shared an interest in this subject with a number of people, to whom I want to express my gratitude. My students, in particular my doctoral students from so many countries, motivated me to expand my purview. To them, to their questions and research, I owe a sense of the real. My colleague and friend in London, Maria Way, volunteered to correct the manuscript's language and style. She gave generously of her time and energy. Humanities editor Richard Ratzlaff at University of Toronto Press was extraordinarily kind to me and helpful. The travail has been longer and more excruciating than we thought and hoped, but in the end what counts is the baby (which seems now to be 'wrapped in dry cloth' as Germans use to say).

For this book, and for my work among the refugees of Dzaleka, Malawi, I received much moral and financial support from family and friends, for which I acknowledge here my gratitude.

Abysmal evil exists that should be a scandal but is not. When we gauge events by the measure of human suffering, we are perpetually astonished by the diverse ways in which human beings react. Some of these ignored events merit being treated as scandal, but directly yield to the logic of retribution – eye for eye, rape for rape, massacre for massacre.

While I was correcting this manuscript, I had the privilege to accompany as an educator, priest, and friend many women, men, children, in this sea of misery and violence, with stories as dramatic as only life and death can be in Africa.

I dedicate this study to those in St Mary's and St Étienne in the Dzaleka, Malawi, refugee camp, who hold fast to the only treasure that survived with them: their faith.

Kitabu hiki ni kwa ajili yenu kaka na dada zangu ambao mmekataliwa na watu wenu na nchi zenu na bado mnakumbana na matatizo ya kimaisha kuishi Dzaleka.

Ninahuzunishwa na hali ya wasichana na wanawake ambao wamekumbwa na vitendo vya ukatili visivyoelezeka. Ingawa mmeepushwa kuuwawa, wengi mmepoteza familia zenu.

Mungu wa amani na baba wa huruma awe nanyi nyote!

POWER OF SCANDAL:
SEMIOTIC AND PRAGMATIC IN MASS MEDIA

1 A Theoretical Approach to the Nature of Media Scandal

Not every scandal is really a scandal. What those with vested interests call 'scandalous' often does not have a scandal's power. It is, therefore, advisable to separate the wheat from the chaff. Not every piece of 'negative press' generates impact, just as not every successful public relations stunt has sustainable effects. Many mini-scandals, moreover, are products of an industry striving to have celebrities talked about by any means. Under the rules of this 'fame game,' tacit agreements exist between PR agencies (celebrity handlers) and the tabloid press; indeed, the two have an out-and-out symbiotic/parasitical coexistence. Clearly, then, how to define a scandal is not a moot question; rather, it is central to any theoretical grasp. This will be discussed in section 1.1. Then in section 1.2 we will discuss the following: the characteristics of media scandals from the perspective of both victors or victims; the pivotal factor of how the Ideal Subject and the Ideal Object of value are constructed; and how judgments or sanctions are passed. Note that none of these operations can occur in isolation as individual operations; rather, all are supported by the scaffolding of industrial practices, which depend on cultural patterns of logic that have roots even in ancient rituals, as in the (architectonic, social, meaning) form of the ancient theatre. This is evident in the narrative form that scandals take, which we introduce and discuss at length in section 1.3.

The 'materiality' of media scandals is relevant not simply because of the pragmatic of its production. Section 1.4 contends that 'scandal' in its (original) religious sense had a different meaning from the social and *a fortiori* from the media setting. Notwithstanding the semantics at hand here, there is no continuum of scandal meaning from the Torah to the

4   Power of Scandal

yellow press. Media scandals, it follows, are best understood without semantic cross-fertilization.

Is television the best medium for scandal? In section 1.5 we will see that television has, if nothing else, the strongest potential to ward off doubt, for partisan constructedness kills scandals. Should television not ascertain an objectivity of the points of accusation, the objective ἁμαρτία, television scandal production would remain a merely subjective affront.

How are we to develop a radically media-oriented theory of scandal? Is it possible to develop such a theory without referring contantly to general human action as an *explanans*, as the source of all morality and punishment? In section 1.6 we resort to unconditional narrativity, independent of real human acting but logically imitating and transforming it. We never act an event in the same fashion as we narrate it, though in narrative hindsight we believe that we did so. One and the same action, however, can be recounted in many different tales. Publicity's mediality consists precisely in its being that determinate, recognizable form of narrating, supported by a multisecular cultural model.

That model is epitomized as publicity. Publicity is narrated, but not each time from scratch. It is a base narration, which then breaks itself down into subdiscourses. The latter, however, still provide normativity in a narrative manner as a matrix of comprehension for every event that within its frame is told as a new event story. Normative narration, we argue in section 1.7, has its own truth conditions, which recognize reality through the link of norms.

1.1   How Scandal Research Tends to Treat the Achievement of Media Scandals

It is no trivial exercise to make it clear what impact true scandals have. Some scholars have established a conflict relation between scandals and 'dominant moral standards.' McRobbie and Thornton (1995, 560), for instance, discuss at length *'moral panic'* (559), which is a topic of media sociology. But are scandals actually connected to moral sentiments? Would it not suffice to investigate the narrative production of a scandal's 'inner moral' as a pure textual product? How should one conceptualize the influence on the mass media of actually lived ethical norms, on the evidence provided by that most moralizing media genre, scandal? How can this be done plausibly? It certainly is not enough that indignation seethes in real-world readers, listeners, or spectators; yet that is the impression left by Lull and Hinerman (1997, 10f). Many situations are sure to generate indignation, and that indignation is bound to be class- or interest-specific. But this is not a reliable marker for scandal, which does not depend on a real receiver. Rather, it needs an imaginary one, which exists – as 'The Reader' – only in the minds of the news staff as the target for whom they produce.

One sociologizing definition is quoted often: 'A media scandal occurs when private acts that disgrace or offend the idealized, dominant morality of a social community are made public and narrativized by the media, producing a range of effects from ideological and cultural retrenchment to disruption and change' (Lull and Hinerman 1997, 3). This, however, needs to be reformulated by adjusting the relations of its elements as follows: 'A media scandal occurs when through media publication and narrativization an act is constructed in such a way that it can be subjected to a sanctioning judgment of an instance of public opinion, which is also constructed; these constructions will then have effects, as acts of negative sanction, on the social institutions and social actors concerned.' The term 'construction' need not suggest that this is fiction. We will be using 'construction' in its semiotic sense, where constructivity – as much as degenerativity – is the normal and necessary characteristic of every further interpretation. Signs 'grow' when a new interpretation adds new meaning. In this sense, the scandalicity of scandals is a meaning surplus value over and above the meaning that regulated the original conduct or behaviour. This additional meaning needs to be analysed independently because it is not explained from the meaning underlying the conduct that is acted. Even though this conduct is the object of scandal, in order to achieve a more concise grasp of the scandal itself, we will for the time being disregard the pragmatic meaning of the conduct methodologically. In a broader pragmatic context, of course, scandal is related to conduct.

A methodological delimitation of scandal from conduct should prevent us from viewing scandal only as an extension of behaviour. In particular, media scandal risks losing its characteristic specificity if we treat it as essentially the same as normal acting. The disadvantage of Lull's morality-based approach lies not in its supposed realism but rather in its implied *ceteris paribus*. That the moral sentiment of a real-world actor should be essentially identical to the narratively produced indignation in media scandals ignores important principle-based differences. A precise semiotic analysis will have to show that the respective meanings in media scandal and scandalous behaviour are not only different but also of a different nature. This differentiation will also be useful in terms of the moral sentiment itself, which cannot be explained cognitively through simple narrative techniques. The semiotic – that is, the pragmatism – of sign-regulated moral conduct is certainly a worthy subject matter in itself. Even so, it is certain that the cognitive-logical generality (the Third Correlate in the sign relation) is not predetermined narratively-teleologically (we will return to this in more detail). Rather, it is related in a unique way to direct experience, the Second Correlate. In this particular context of moral sentiment, taking offence at something (σκάνδαλον in the original biblical sense of the term) will determine meaning in a radically different way than does the narrative confection of media scandals. There are good reasons, then, to renounce attempts to refer to the moral sentiments of real readers, or to dominant moral ideas, and then to deduce from those sentiments the nature of media scandals. Lull and Hinerman (1997, 18f) – from a semiotic point of view – in this regard misunderstand the 'use of symbols,' as if in both social interaction and personal experience the use of something else would be added. Instead, the real social interaction itself is the real symbol.

The industry that produces scandals *en masse* must certainly entertain a rather different view on all this. Much of the producers' self-justification enters the product itself, and this must be relevant to the scholarship on media scandal. Should we accept the apologetic self-righteousness of scandal 'manufacturers,' who maintain that society should thank them for ensuring that malefactors cannot suppress uncomfortable truths? Only through their efforts, they contend, can politicians and the courts be jarred into action. The targets of these endeavours would see things quite differently, of course. From their perspective, scandals are devised merely for prurience's sake. The power of scandal is almost impossible to resist, even through the courts (i.e., the damage cannot be fixed even if the plaintiff wins the case).

So is scandal a matter of individual perception? Of the side on which one stands? Is perspective a key characteristic of scandal *in se*? In these regards, scandal would seem to eliminate the possibility of neutral ground. Society enjoys this *tertium comparationis* through the legal system, before which all conflict parties are initially equal, as well as through the democratic polity, where there is no dictatorship of the majority but where a third party – the sovereign people – can bring about change at any time. Such mechanisms are lacking in scandal, which is closer to more atavistic forms of justice such as lynchings, kangaroo courts, character assassination, and 'sound popular sentiments.'

Here our interest is in scandals *per se*. How do they function? How are they produced, and how avoided? But let us first ask this: What actually makes them scandals? It is part of the trade of scandal mongering to suggest that the difference is in the object[1] – that there is something specific that is uncovered only through scandal. But this is a patent self-promotion – one that shrouds what is common to many text genres of the same orientation. A muted police report and a red-headline media scandal can have exactly the same object and can report on exactly the same historical-factual event. Nevertheless, they are worlds apart from each other. There is something specific to scandal. What makes a scandal a scandal, and a police report a legal document? By which means does a scandal become this extra object, which we experience as its surplus value, its prurience, which alone is capable of luring us out of our reserve and lets us react, and which makes us expect that others react in the same way?

There can be a scandal about anything.[2] *But* scandal cannot be 'done' in just any way – one has to know how to produce it. This is not to suggest that the matter, the 'stuff,' of scandal can be arbitrary, that it can be imaginary or invented, because an important aspect of a scandal is that it be 'right.' The material content of what is 'right,' though, can be whichever part of the product. That is why it is important that true, hard, indisputable facts be reported. However, 'everything' (being correct) is not the thing that is 'right.' Those hard facts grow into more than just facts; the facts brings their truth as dowry into the story that is being narrated – a story that therefore must set Aristotle's poetic beginning, middle, and ending in ways that narrators want and find plausible. So, while a scandal story needs facts, it needs them for purposes that are not justified from those facts. For the same facts, there exist other purposes. Police reports use facts for proofs, to the extent the procedural code allows for their only purpose: deciding what is lawful.[3]

This suggests something unique about scandal, which relates to how it produces surplus value: scandal is not specific in its object. Rhetoric generally amplifies or dampens, but it still concerns itself with reality claims. Scandal, by contrast, involves transformation – its purpose is to modify actors. Our first observations on mass media scandals can remain impressionistic, but eventually we need to be able to support them with a strong theory if we are to understand them thoroughly. Also, we need a strong theory in order to observe the underlying mode of scandal operations. Only then will we be able to grasp the unique nature of religious and church scandals. Even practical communication strategies (public relations, crisis management, spin control) rely on theory.

When it constructs reality, what does scandal actually achieve? What can we glean about its nature from what it accomplishes? Once we answer these questions, we will be able to distinguish scandal from rhetorical argumentation, or αὔξησις. So let us next try to answer them, even though approaching the problem in terms of reality construction will place us onto a collision course with certain scandal theories.

The conflict arises largely from the fact that theories such as Tumber and Waisbord's (2004a, b) focus on comparing scandal with reality. Yet as we will see, questions such as the following are false problems: How faithful to the real, and truthful or 'objective,' is a scandal? Or (in terms of Berelson's reflexion hypothesis) what social realities does scandal uncover? ing the social reality. Tumber and Waisbord, following Lowi, reductively reify scandal as the publication of corruption,[4] thereby establishing a relation to what everybody expects from the behaviour of a few selected, privileged role players. But in doing so, they lose sight of the proper 'achievement' and dynamic of scandal. In light of the increased frequency of media scandals – especially religious scandals – this approach inevitably leads to the impression that more scandals are taking place because our social world is going to pieces, and vice versa – that our social world is going to pieces because more scandals are taking place. At the least, media scandals have this social effect: they produce real crises. Yet even though we are constantly hearing about financial scandals, sex scandals, and so on, this does not imply that more cases of economic criminality are coming before the courts, or that psychotherapists are having to treat more problems of individual morality. Clearly, then, only a radical methodological rupture will enable us to understand the real structure and dynamic of scandals.

Scandals always have two sides: that much can be conceded to Tumber and Waisbord. This arises from the principles of scandal construction. The impression of perspectivity, discussed below, is readily demonstrable as a textual mechanism. These authors' examples of corruption generally indicate that every scandal functions as a relation of the power holder to the powerless (i.e., between those who can *do* and those who can only judge what *was done*). This relation, though, does not refer to real, political, economic power; rather, by its very nature it is purely symbolic (some would say 'symbolically generalized'). It can thus refer even to celebrities, who apart from their celebrity have no 'real' power at all. Beyond this symbolic interlinkage between the expectations of the powerless and the responsibility of the powerful, the specific nature of scandal is *not* to be identified with criminality or any other social reality.[5]

It is highly instructive to switch sides for a moment – that is, to consider how the legal system treats social existence and all its conflicts. Here, the 'material' of scandal reveals itself to be difficult to sustain, despite public pressure on the legal system. For the actors in a scandal are rarely perpetrators or offenders in the legal sense. Scandalous conduct, if it is litigable at all, normally does not hold up to censure by courts of law. The megascandal popularly known in Italy as Tangentopoli[6] engulfed almost all of Italy's political class but led to almost no final court judgments, despite the criminalizing term, which suggested that the offence of bribe taking (*'tangente'*) had occurred. The deliberate similarity between sanctions in the media and judgments in criminal trials is not a fantasy product but has a real potential to disrupt the orderly court of law procedures. The legal system, which arrives at its findings at a much slower and more controlled pace, refuses to tolerate this sort of interference – at least sometimes, in some places. In England, budding media scandals have been killed for the sole reason that the matter was *sub judice*. The 1948 Belcher scandal, which threatened the government, was presented at a Tribunal of Inquiry and thus became a pending case. Media reports and parliamentary debate were therefore forbidden until the final court ruling came out.[7]

Even more dubious is the idea that scandals have inundated us today because the public has become more critical, owing to 'accountability mechanisms.'[8] The Renaissance, with its tales of lust and gore among the powerful, should put paid to that notion. Those scandals astound us to this day – indeed, they make today's scandals pale in comparison.

1.2 Scandal as Logic: Ideal and Sanction

Scandal cannot be ignored by anyone, including the victim, who has a different perspective on the same event. They are logical products, in which the participants pass through a logical process, because scandals follow a logical course.

In terms of their construction, scandals have two stages, which follow a logical though not necessarily temporal sequence. First, a scandal constructs an ideal; second, it passes a sanction. Scandals are never natural events of elementary justice in, for instance, the style of a tragedy with its excess, its overmeasure of punishment, which must be accepted by tragic nature. This misalignment of offence with chastisement is thus called 'tragic.' By contrast, the ideal that has been violated must first be furnished in an explicit way if one intends to stage a media scandal (which is quite literally a *mise-en-scène*). Logically speaking, ideals are pragmatic purposes, aims of action, and thus a collection of pragmatic values. Values are 'idea'; they are never factual reality. But an idea must be presented by someone, since nowhere can it be seen as a *fact*. Even though one can refer to it as object of an action, objectivity of this sort is not a bivalently true/false *vis-à-vis*, not a state of affairs. For example, 'presidential dignity' as a value (i.e., not a fact) was truly/falsely attributed to President Clinton but had its origin in an institutionally represented purpose of action. Presidential conduct must be brought into a negative relation with the pragmatic purpose 'sexual self-determination' before a 'Zippergate' can result. Instead of an objective fact, this is an instance where a purpose of an action had first to be presented ('put before our eyes'). This can be done through a variety of semantics – wishes, desires, longings, and so on. A pragmatic purpose must be, or ought to be, but is not.

At the same time, and by the same token, the presentation of an ideal subject of action takes place, together with the presentation of a pragmatic object as value. Purpose and subject of the action must correspond – otherwise the performance will fail owing to lack of competence. Whoever the concrete acting human subjects are, they are already greater than themselves whenever they are executing the ideal that is the basis of the scandal and all its conduct judgment. Then, ideal pragmatic competences are immediately affixed to it; and these ideals are nothing less than a collection of personality traits corresponding to the ideal object of conduct. As much as it is possible to reify the object instead of referring to the ideal purpose of conduct, one can personify the actor. In reality, however, both obfuscate that everything is deduced from a pragmatic purpose, which someone has presented as an ideal.

Are scandals really so complicated? In common parlance, acting means that someone *does something*. However, Peirce's Pragmatic Maxim shows that this becomes much more complex when one conceives of action as conduct. This makes acting 'conscious' – that is, controlled by an idea, which is a rule and therefore of a general nature. Only this allows us to communicate about acting; only in this manner does action have meaning; only thus can it be grasped, criticized, and discussed fully as this meaning. Through meaning, much more is grasped in action than is visible now, before, or in the future, because as meaning, it grasps only the whole, all – not the sum total. This is a general rule. In the normal course of action, meaning does not catch the actor's eye. Once one can no longer tacitly presuppose meaning, the entire structural scaffolding of acting becomes apparent. Then meaning must be searched – as, for example, in the situation of an unexpected discovery of something hitherto unknown, or as in scandal, where meaning is externally imposed. We will have to investigate the nature of such meaning and of such imposition. But generally speaking, meaning is communicated as teleological or as purpose, and 'from the end' this meaning presents itself as an ideal.

With scandal, then, interpretation takes a decisive and specific further step: the ideal, which includes the ideal subject competence, enters into a comparison relationship with the performance of the scandalizing actor subject and thus becomes the ground for sanctioning. This can also take place as a comparison of two universes. One is, in the ideal conduct, the universe of the object of conduct (which amounts to a parallel world, as it were). The other is the real world interpreted as object of a scandalous conduct. Those who represent the scandalous universe as pure reality also construct a narrative pragmatic universe – one, however, that is located in 'the reality' (of performance). For now, this *aperçu* of the logical operations of which scandal consists must suffice; but we will have to investigate in detail this rather complex production of meaning as narrative logic. In the present context, we merely aim to emphasize the meaning-generating presence of the ideal, which in turn causes the necessary, implicit or explicit parallelity of two universes and two pragmatic subjects.

The Clinton–Lewinsky scandal ('Zippergate') illustrates ideality and its mode of functioning very well. In keeping with the logic of scandal, a 'construction of credibility' fulfils the function of ideal, in a number of versions that vary with positions in a 'culture war' (Langman 2002, 502). In this particular ideal, a highly determinate kind of word of honour ('take my word') is only possible, as this sort of credibility, in mass media. However, Clinton constructed his own ideal before he could bring it into position for his own defence and before he could be measured against it in any sanction.[9] Over and above his personal reputation for being telegenic and convincing through his conversational style, all bearers of political office must be inherently credible to their office: 'everything they say is true' (according to the ideal of public office). Ideality of conduct in office is predetermined (and conferred to a concrete subject of conduct through an elaborate process of legitimatization).

Conversely, once an office bearer has been legitimized, any need to proffer arguments, or to use rhetorical means of persuasion, ceases. The ideal already owns its bearer (and such an aura of trustworthiness is a godsend for holders of political office). Luhmann defines this aura of power as 'symbolically generalized,' a functional communication that dispenses with the need for argumentative justification. Outside the ideal's aura, contrary to all rhetorical evidence, there are only interminable discourses in politics – that is, areas of interests, which can only be enforced through majorities against other areas of different interests. It matters nothing how rational such acts of power are. The classical 'significant tautology,' or mantra, lies in this: 'A majority is a majority!' Small surprise that parliamentary debates are struggles – more precisely, eristic discourse (struggle to be right *per fas et nefas*) – rather than forums in which the better argument is expected to win. Even the courts have their own form of conduct resisting the force of argument – that is, in the principle of *stare decisis*. If the ideal comes into force, however, it changes the epistemic object: an ideal act of an office bearer (no longer a politician) is a 'solution' – that is, something correct, an objective solution reached under professional criteria, *lege artis* necessary and compelling. No longer is this an advancement of particular political interests, something undecidable epistemically, a lesser evil to be weighed, matters where in an eristic way one can only be right (but not *in* the right).

The ideal, then, appropriates its object *and* its subject. It does not involve subjects achieving their ideal. Scandals correspond to this construction as they can concern only object or subject, but not the ideal itself that the media scandal has constructed in the first place. This appears to contradict the evidence of journalistic procedure. Here, an investigative journalist first finds a *corpus delicti* or a smoking gun, then the culprit. The juridical semantic (of which many variants so often appear in journalistic texts) can dispense with explicit references to laws, because crime always presupposes a law that defines it. This same antecedence of formal rules is not given with media scandals, not even as ethical principle. Journalism continues to pretend that it merely needs to refer to general principles. Actually, these principles need to be invented in the first place, must be postulated as plausible, and must be included in the story. Helpful in this construction effort are scandal precedents – that is, schemata for scandals that have a recognized place in the industry and that have achieved a status of easy genre recognition and recall. Despite this scaffolding, invention of the ideal remains the central part of a media scandal; only then can it seek its object and subject.

Let us focus now on the ideal of political office, which is so pivotal to Waisbord's scandal research (Tumber and Waisbord 2004a, b; Waisbord 1994, 2002). An object of conduct in harmony with the ideal of good office is an adequate, 'good problem solution.' In a media scandal, conversely, a subject is sanctioned when the conduct at hand involves private over ideal interests, or individual advantage, or bribes or the intention to bribe. While sanction only concerns the subject, the object of media scandal can be seen in incompetence (there was once a 'Dan Quail effect' in the United States, and in Italy a certain politician goes by the *epitheton ornans* 'Burlesconi'), in lack of will or resolve, or in indiscipline, alcoholism, dishonesty, and so on. For the political ideal construction, the following derivative sequential order of logical operations obtains:

ideal	universe	subject
ideal construction →	object of conduct →	personality traits
(+) trust →	objective problem solution →	infallible competence
(−) scandal →	egotistic solution →	incompetence

Regarding the religious ideal construction – its object of conduct and especially its subject – the same conditions apply in a stricter and more complex form. In this field, a media scandal is patently not as free as a social scandal (a word that has entered profane usage from biblical language: regarding σκάνδαλον, see § 7.4 and n227). Regarding the construction of the ideal in particular, there is a crucial difference between the media of public opinion and a religious destination of conduct. It is not difficult to imagine the misunderstandings and confrontations generated by this difference of nature – which we will call the 'primordial scandal' of religion and the Church when we investigate it in detail (§5.7). Public opinion seeks to avoid such a conflict – most of the time, however, by fitting religion into a mimetic cohabitation under its own roof. While the ideals of public opinion and of religion are specific, they still need to be constructed. Yet under conditions of cohabitation, it is public opinion itself that constructs the ideal for religious scandals. Cohabiting confers on ideal religious subjects the miraculous provision of human propriety – that is, those subjects must obey a purely ethical normativity (in lieu of the almost miraculous possession of infallible competence in politicians), and not a religious one.

Once the constructed nature of ideals has been recognized, there is nothing 'natural' left in media scandals. Though public opinion dominates the scene, its ideal is no less constructed. This, in the main, is shown in situations where the predetermination of an ideal purpose of conduct enters into conflict with another ideal, either one that comes from within the same society, or – much more virulently – one that comes from beyond the boundaries of cultures. Religion – admittedly not another culture – is nevertheless not as perfectly integrated into public opinion as politics. While both ideals are products of media text construction, they are not without effects in the social reality, and they enter – with those who are at the receiving end of behavioural competence, qualified by the same ideal – into a cooperative relation. That can be involvement either as accomplice or of reciprocal dependency. As if by the touch of a magic wand, a politician becomes an office holder; a sinner becomes a moral shaman. This will be demonstrated more clearly, and in much more detail, when we analyse media scandals involving televangelists, abusive priests, and power-abusing bishops. All of these roles are loaded; but through public opinion, they are differently loaded than in past configurations.

Historically, there is little resemblance between a bishop in his public media role today and a bishop in the era of encyclicals. It is only that the media of public opinion have turned today's bishop into a mouthpieces of public morality. Some centuries ago, a bishop's specific role was related to territorial domain and estates. A bishop was expected to behave according to the standards of his estate, not necessarily in a moral way. Later, the bishop's role was radically altered so as to include moral exemplarity. As an unintended consequence of this, the bishop's role now falls under the judgmental authority of the tribunal of public opinion, which created it in the first place. The logical subtlety of this alteration is evident in a historical comparison of modes of church criticism – for instance, between the baroque pasquinades[10] and our contemporary scandal press. Of greater interest, however, is to analyse the swing of the judgment (the very meaning product of the scandal press) from a positive into a negative one. What is a religious actor doing, especially when endowed with an institutional church role? Since the press needs to tell a story, it can only narrate an actor when it builds a pragmatic purpose into such a role; through this it makes an action understandable, but it implies an ideal pragmatic competence. This idealization/ ideality of the responsibility of religious conduct constitutes a *litotes* of being sinner; the scandal then amounts to the double *litotes* 'not-not-sinner,' but here caught red-handedly. It is a sort of affirmation, which is not a simple 'yes,' but a reaffirmative 'indeed.' On this point, the religious public ideal is clearly different from the public ideal of political office bearers, whose profile tends towards sound omnipotence.

Our analysis of the media of public opinion will show that they prefer to outsource into a separate instance of destination whatever must be thought and said about the normative in human conduct. This makes the construction of an ideal much more practical and practicable and makes it possible to turn ideals into professional norms and industrial practices. Thus, higher destinations see the light of day, formulated as ideals, provided that the destinator himself is an instance situated upstream of conduct. A functional model exists in certain roles built into ancient theatre. Just as moral authority is separate from the place of action, so a theatrical stage is separated from the rule, which then comes under the author's ownership. Authors make that role media-visible merely as ideality, but – distinctly from ancient theatre – without the help of divine transcendence.

1.3 Scandal as Industrial Product and Institutional Practice

What we have presented as a sort of argumentative logic is the practice of an entire industry. Perhaps, when decorating their argumentative product, they are trying to obfuscate this, but there continue to exist plenty of traces of actual rhetorical labour[11] in professional rules, ethics, trade standards, codes, and so on. This rhetorical effort, and the textual analysis of the product itself, can be methodologically reconstructed by treating it as a type of argumentation.

Looked at in the cold light of day, the press as a whole – both as product and as practice[12] – is oriented towards themes rather than facts. There are only a limited number of themes (i.e., 'hot topics'), which have a certain lifespan, with the survival rate always limited by media specifics. It will come as no surprise that press archives and Internet news databases collect and store these news stories as themes. Some use the court metaphor 'dossier' (*Neue Zürcher Zeitung*), some 'archives' (*New York Times*), some the theatre metaphor 'spotlight'[13] (*Boston Globe*). As a rule, a thematic order means a chronological order, which is a narrative one. This archive order tells one story (corresponding perfectly to Aristotle's *Poetics*) with one action, one time, and one place (all of which constitute a pragmatic spatiotemporality, not a physical one).[14] That said, the day-by-day output continues to tell merely several stories in instalments. So a unifying force is required, one that reorganizes chronological into pragmatic time and in this way causes a 'sense of an ending' (as Frank Kermode conceptualized) from the beginning.

Yet present-day journalistic genre formats are not unique merely by being narration: they have developed a quite specific form of it. One distinctive attribute of this form is the 'inverted pyramid,' which began to gain acceptance as an industrial practice in the United States after the Civil War. It came to prevail over the chronological sequential order of narrating, which until then had been accepted as natural. Today, it helps readers recognize the genre immediately as a journalistic one. This transformation has had its major impact as a technique of argumentation and rhetoric, in that weighting through textual placement amounts to thematic weighting. We will take a more detailed look at other formal characteristics of the genre, which has become journalistic industrial practice and thereby had consequences for rhetoric. In the end, all of this resulted in the finished rhetorical product called 'journalism,' which is able to hide its *faux* naturalness behind professional standards and 'codes of ethics.'

Media history, as a history of rhetoric, has yet to be written from the perspective of how modes of argumentation developed. Literary form has not itself been a goal of journalism; that said, the literary form that journalism has taken is a form of reality construction and so a form of reality. It should not surprise us that this embryonic reality constitutes this industry's ecology: power and accumulation of material goods. Other realities could certainly be observed, but they must remain more or less exotic in reference to the core relation, its reality proper. The fact that this industry has since divided itself into news, advertising, and entertainment subindustries sheds even clearer light on the form of reality construction taken as a whole; in no way, however, does this constitute a disintegration of a homogeneous universe. At this point, it would be too easy to become ensnared into a sort of ontology (looming, for instance, in the manner of radical constructivism). After all, nowhere is it more obvious than here that journalism is a matter of rhetorical forms, of choices in argumentation. The matter at hand, then, is not an experiential world that produces its apperception, but a rhetoric that argumentatively produces its proper universe. However, journalism is but one rhetoric, along with and in competition with others. Furthermore, it has had its own historical development, meaning that its rhetorical-argumentative operations are easier to reconstruct as historical events. There is no good reason for us to regard the industry's present developmental state as natural; better, instead, to examine how that present state has come about as a result of rhetorical options and logical determinations. What we call the 'press' today did not begin when printed paper sheets were sold, and it will not end with the rise of the Blogosphere.

Of special interest for our purposes is the history of certain subforms of the journalistic genre – in particular, the history of scandal. Media scandal as presently practised led to a unification of quasi-ontological diversification. In the present praxis, news facts glide into the *peripeteia* of entertainment, adorned with the unreal gloss of advertisement. Scandal in itself has become a proper media industry, an industrial biotope with diversified roles and interests. Celebrities hire agents known as 'celebrity handlers' to build up and modify their public persona (and to destroy those of their competitors) (Salmon 2005), in order to enter the Hall of Fame through the 'right' scandal. Scandal, then, is a bartering in the marketplace of mutual interest of press and celebrity. Even political power is becoming more and more inseparable from the correct handling of scandals. Spin doctors and investigative journalists build up or damage political careers. Those politicians who have the most friends in the press enjoy the longest political lives.

Antecedent to the scandal biotope is the scandal form, which also provides narrative unity, since labelling a photograph or story as scandal in effect generates a unity over time, turns instalments into the one scandal story. This is the exact opposite of facts – and the only really hard, indubitable facts are, perhaps, stock quotations, which lack both purpose and end until someone gathers them together from the perspective of a market crash or bank failure. Only then does the confusing flow of news become a story. It follows that when the universe, on which we 'all' entertain one public opinion, appears to us as unified, we owe this to the red threads of narrativity that permeate and weave together what we then receive as an impression of development. In this way – out of nothing, as it were – a 'case' comes to light.

At what point does our present rhetorical praxis as industrial product become relevant to scandal? The Big Bang of a scandal is always presented as a discovery. Thus it appears not as the construction of an ideal, but rather as an 'ever new case' of an old, well-known object and the usual subjects, according to the type of scandal (cf. *infra*). This discovery, however, is only then filled with movement and put into motion if one succeeds in transforming it, through the constructed ideal, into a process of judgment. The writing of stories, as much as the writing of history, first brings forth the description of an action, but action understood as a goal that is realized through this action. Purpose is so central to this logic that it functions, even when it is not realized, as an ideal – when it becomes a goal that, in a counterfactual conditional, action would have aimed at though in reality it has not done so. Pure news developments – news understood in the sense of one event following another – do not exist (except, for example, as stock tickers). News must head for crises and then seek their *dénouement*. A stream of novel events can become a crisis then, and only then, when someone is found who can be saddled with the responsibility for those events. Governments become saddled with the responsibility for the weak or strong course of the economy, for example. In the process, subjects modified in accordance with the ideal and ideal objects are quite literally installed on stage, a true *mise-en-scène*.

Scandals are why the readership must be kept informed and, *per extensionem*, why a given society cannot dispense with its watchdogs, be they chained or loose. Scandals are also why 'situations,' to which one remains glued, develop, and why papers and newscasts must constantly be coming out with no end in sight. Scandal, or being-responsible-for, creates a unified universe. At this point a general view may suffice for the industrial argumentation praxis; below, the really interesting details will lead us into a detailed description of some media scandal cases.

1.4 Media Scandals and What They Are Not

The word 'scandal' has Indo-European origins, which means it has a Sanskrit root.[15] In St Paul's letters (Galatians 5:11; cf. 1 Corinthians 1:23), and Christian theology as a whole thereafter, σκάνδαλον τοῦ σταυροῦ, *scandalum crucis* (see §7.4) played a central role, and as a result the term scandal became shorthand for any sort of offence. This linguistic, etymological basis cannot, though, serve as the basis for our understanding of scandal as a media product. Burkhardt's (2006) borrowing of some of his principal categories for the analysis of media scandals from the semasiology of the term must fail. First, the concept is rooted in very old literary strata of the Old Testament. For example, the stumbling block (מִכְשׁוֹל) placed in the way of blind people in Leviticus 19:14, *offendiculum* in the Vulgata translation, in the LXX was first translated into Greek as σκάνδαλον; but so was another similar Hebrew term. Even if the Hebrew term had been translated consistently into an identical

Greek term (which is not the case at all – see Isaiah 8:14, Jeremiah 6:21), it would be a blunder to assume that it continued to mean the same thing. Second, a major change had to take place when Christ himself became the σκάνδαλον. The 'rejigging' of the term meant that his person brought many to sin, or to stumble in a metaphorical sense. One would have to go into too much detail to explain the transformation even of the concept of sin. The term's third and final meaning shift came about when it was again recontextualized in the moralistic literature. Those who try to approach this term as a coherent theological theory will find it riddled with inconsistencies. It would be absurd to try, as it will become obvious quite quickly how terms are built into new contexts that result in radical changes to their meaning. Especially when boundaries of such different languages are crossed, base metaphors, from concrete object to abstract concept, are quickly lost (here: Hebrew stumbling rock substituted by stick of a trap, which is the ground of the Greek metaphor). Moreover, neither base metaphor nor the various abstract concepts explain what is occurring in media scandals.

One must object to *ceteris paribus* approaches. Most such comparisons with biblical, psychological, or societal models misrepresent scandals as morally offensive occasions, as psychologically traumatizing events, or as social sanctions. Yet the media operate differently: they do not occasion the damnation or castigation of stumbled sinners; as text products, they do not have the same effects on the human psyche as direct human communication; and they never reach the sphere of religious experience, which they could indeed hurt. All of these misguided comparisons call for a twofold caution against misunderstanding understandings of mediated understanding:

1. Scandals are not facts; they are *more than* facts. There *are* no scandalous or non-scandalous facts, only facts that catch a scandal's interest and those that scandals choose to ignore. There exist states of affairs that the media do in fact turn into scandals. That said, to become included as reality in a scandal is, as we shall see, an important function. Conversely, no scandal can be reduced to mere factual reality without loss of meaning. The analysis of media scandals does not inevitably lead to Nominalism or, even worse, Radical Constructivism. Unfortunately, questions of objectivity tend to obstruct analyses of media scandals. Until we return to the subject of journalistic objectivity in an explicit discussion, we will avoid those traps by presupposing for argument's sake that all facts are true that scandal

stories assert to be true. Let us also presuppose that those very facts can or could be proven as true statements in the discursive context of a juridical, historical, or other verification. Verificatory discourses such as these turn facts into effective and final judgments of law, or historical effects, or psychotherapeutic anamneses, or simply moral sins, depending on the respective argumentative procedures. Let this assumption (not prejudice, though) for the time being be valid for Zippergate, for homo- or paedophile abuse by priests, for the adulteries of televangelists, for compliance to murder by Argentinean military chaplains, for Rwandan nuns participating in genocide, and so on. But at the same time, we must also exclude from scandal any insinuation of juridical, therapeutic, moral, historical, administrative, or disciplinary verification. Our only contention will be that constructions of media scandals also function without juridical, historiographical, psychoanalytical, or religious proofs. Their function is autarkic and in their own right.

Maintaining that scandals function without being (juridically) true does not imply that the facts that are used in the scandal story are not true. In our analyses of CSA stories we will stick to the scandalization itself and leave the truth question alone. Even the victims' narratives, before they turn into accusations (as their narrative goal), are not homogeneized – they are as complex as life itself. As such testimony of authentic suffering they merit the utmost respect and compassion. These lines are written in an African refugee camp, in a sea of stories of gang rape, the contracting of AIDS by sexual abuse, genital mutilation, humiliation, and murder. This sheer endless and boundless human misery is absolutely true and suffered, though it will realistically never have a chance of becoming a basis for some sort of human justice. If someone were to succeed in turning some of these victim stories into media scandal stories, one would not only change their narrative nature, but also their pragmatic reality even when using a selection of the same facts. The analysing and criticizing of scandal stories can safely be disconnected from facts they incorporate in the narrative, as scandal construction is neither based on, nor does it follow logically from, facts. To uncover and dissect the logic of scandal construction is not to minimize the veracity of any fact. Scandals are not true or false, they just function or not.

2. Offensive conduct or social scandals[16] are quite different from media scandals. Our interest here is limited to the media scandal as epis-

temic object. This leads to a peculiar binary judgment: scandalous, or normal. A media judgment does not send anyone to prison, or a couch, or a confessional, nor does it cast anyone from office. This is because it has different sanctioning means. Interpersonal sanctions in a social scandal, be it in a village, or at court, or in high society, have a different essence and use other instruments.[17]

It is safe to assume that in a social context, scandal processes lead to an even more complex anthropological or ethnographical description than do media scandals. The mass media are not a village scaled up to megadimensions (*pace* McLuhan). In this book, at any rate, because the method would have to be so different, no social scandals are investigated. How exactly we define a social scandal can thus be left open, yet even here it holds that a real scandal is more complex by magnitudes than a narrated social scandal. For the latter, there already exists a *genus litterarum*; it is more difficult for the former to identify any rules and patterns of conduct. Compared to social scandals, all 'text scandals' probably show the media in an unfavourable light as being impotent and without any real power. For media scandals at any rate, reality is as much a question as the effect problem. Preceding this, the main interest concerns first the media form. Such an interest, so specified, in the media form of judgment can be compared to the discourse analysis of, say, the code of criminal procedure, which has its own peculiar forms of reality production for what is absolutely legal and what is not. What is – or what can become – scandalous in the mass media? Through what means does it become so? From what is it set apart?

This thematic concentration, and the resulting distance from the rest of social reality, enables us to grasp the astonishing argumentation effect that the mass media are capable of mustering in a scandal. It explains, in short, what makes people both angry and self-righteous. A surplus value effect such as this is no longer explainable purely as a rhetorical αὔξησις (or in Eco's simile, 'blowing up & narcotising'), where it is merely a matter of blowing up the claim of a state of affairs (in the sense of a *quaestio facti*). When media 'do a scandal,' instead, a full-blown program takes its course. Before this course is set in motion, the logic of the program – anticipating the main points of our detailed discussion below – generates a temporal sequence, constructed through narration, where readers/spectators are attributed their roles and where social proceedings outside the media are simulated. Despite such simulation of the social, the media scandal cannot be explained as

(1) social scandal.[18] The reason is that no conduct is expected so that an actor can violate it and no general public reacts by rejection. This does not imply, however, that media scandals once they are produced cannot serve the very real interests of political stakeholders. Media scandals are not a moot literary exercise; rather, they are an instrument of power, which the media then use in their own peculiar way (cf. §8). Nor is the media scandal explainable as (2) a psychological scandal in a feeling of indignation or rage (or in the religious sense of the biblical term, i.e., offence), for the element of psychic trauma is lacking (and so is the offence of religious awe).

These premises put this approach at variance with the bulk of scandal studies in communication, political, and social sciences. From our perspective, there is a glaring neglect of the mediation of the media, of the media form and its construction. Our research interest, and the methods corresponding to the object as described above, must not reduce communication sciences to a sort of literary theory without practical relevance. Conversely, one cannot buy practical bearing by extrapolating simply from other, socially relevant communication situations that are also labelled as scandal. Calling everything scandal is no proof that all scandals are produced the same way. For the study of media scandals, is it necessary to look first at at societal morals, as some scholars believe? Is this supposed to clothe the media's literary products with social reality? One could, of course, reduce the moral constraints operant in a society to the constraints inherent in its normative discourses. This, however, would again place the cart before the horse, by leaving these discourses without a collective moral experience – at which point, of course, morals would amount to the discourse of public opinion. Doing so would not simply level morality to a literary construct and empty it of any real experience (how this can be theorized will be discussed later); it would also overlook the nature of the difference between the two. Social life will always consist of rules that capture the expectations of cooperation. These laws can be encapsulated in the definition of objects, but they also consist of pure normativity. In the first case, a word such as 'chair' really means a final causality, like 'something on which to sit in order to interact as power holder.' In the second case, we find all instances of rules, ranging from laws to decent manners. What all of these cases have in common is that sanction is always real. Public opinion, however, is merely the appearance of sanction, which is in force only for the media and for all actors in the media's narrative universe; but this does not concern media consumers or society at large. The latter are subject to possible sanctions of another nature. This essential difference is squashed by Lull and Hinerman (1997, 10): 'A media scandal [...] when private acts ... disgrace or offend the idealized, dominant morality of a social community.' Also, we must strongly doubt them when they tell us: 'Scandal serves as a term to delineate a breach in moral conduct and authority' (Lull and Hinerman 1997, 3). The morality of a media scandal is quite autarkic, made for in-house purposes. After being utilized in one media scandal, *ad hoc* moralities can become disposable goods if they are not recycled into scandals with similar patterns. In principle, however, all producers of media scandal are free either to construct their own ideality or to simulate patches of social morality.

This difference in nature has practical importance, because its existence guarantees that there exists the possibility of resisting, of ducking away from, of subverting in the everyday, the pressure of public opinion, as Certeau describes (1980).

When we confuse morality with the narratively constructed moral of a tale, the result is grave methodological penalties. Instead of acknowledging the autonomous nature of media scandals, Hondrich (1989), for one, merely applies social scandals *ceteris paribus* to mass media. What he describes as outrage hasbears no relation to media-produced representations of outrage, except that the latter simulate the former. Outrage and its representations differ both in their genesis and in their effects, however. There is a certain tendency among 'empirical' communication scientists to apply their psychological methods to media objects. What they pretend to describe empirically is 'the public's outrage' – a bizarre effort in more than one account. First, they must 'feed' their respondents media-generated materials (scandals) that exist only in the media universe and that are not experiences (or that are literary 'experiences' at best). Second, since surveys, albeit the method of choice, are costly and time-delayed (and therefore measure remembrances of past 'outrages'), only extremely rarely can they be used to access the 'real public.' The 'outrage' represented in the media universe is, as a consequence, readily accepted as a substitute for the inaccessible real outrage in the real world. 'For determining public outrage,' write Esser and Hartung (2004, 1047–8), 'a number of devices are at hand. One's assumptions about the public, one's feelings for it, can help to guess its extent, but one can never be sure. Party organizations might send messages from the people, but they may be biased. Everyday contacts may tell a politician something about the people's reactions, but many of them live in a world apart. Surveys can be done, but they cost time and money. As all these methods have their limits, we can assume that the mass media frequently serve as a proxy – or more formally speaking, as a functional equivalent – for the public in scandal communication'). In short, the media should not be treated as arbitrary stimuli. By their form, they produce meaning as a universe, in which the author, but also the recipient, are present in text-transcending roles. They also determine how they establish their relation to the social reality.

How are we to prove the difference between social and media scandal? What counts here is how the various media contribute in different ways to the communicative act.[19] All communication is mediated by a medium, be it language (some oversimplify by calling it 'propositional'), or by speech act or some other linguistic pragmatic device, or by symbolic generalization. Each mediation by a medium is a different type of sign relation that imposes different types of interpretation. For instance, it is impossible to lie 'in black and white.' Thus, printed and written communication allows for false statements that any quantity of statements contrary to the first one can criticize; these collections of statements are epitomized as the 'library' idea (as the collection of 'authorities' in the plural). Lies, for their part, presuppose a shared universe of discourse, here and now, between two speakers. The mass media and their different interpretation rules change that equation again. How do the mass media 'lie,' then? Neither in the manner of liars, nor in the deferred, 'un-final' mode of print.

Every society has rules of deviance as well as contingent sanctions. This is easily acknowledged; harder to see is that the various media come with their own taboos as well; also, that they produce such deviance as is proper to their nature – deviance that is possible only through *this* medium and no other. Society, it follows, does not regulate deviance in a simple, straightforward way. Otherwise, it would no longer be possible to practise gossip as 'gossip column' in the tabloid press, or (the oral mainstay) 'rumour' as reality TV news. Thus a family scandal[20] in a social context is not identical in meaning with the TV series *Dynasty*, which originated a new form of scandalicity with family roles, or with the news product 'Cleveland scandal,'[21] the anti-scandal scandal in the British press.

Financial or economic scandals (such as Enron and a number of other, lesser cases), courtroom scandals (the O.J. Simpson trial), and political scandals (starting with Watergate, the mother and icon of investigative journalism[22]) are all media-generated effects. One might say, conversely, that without the mass media, these realities would not have come to light, though today it is no longer possible to separate media from social reality as a result of to their multiple commingling. Without question, judiciary scandals existed before the genesis of the bourgeois and mass press; but they came about differently, were disputed differently, and had to seek a different sense of justice in a different social consensus.

That media scandals resemble social scandals is certainly desirable because of the simulation. There is, therefore, no need to deny such similarity. It is desirable, for instance, that Monica Lewinsky appears as a modern 'Susanna' and that President Clinton resembles a 'dirty old man,' as in the biblical story of Daniel. It is only that this effect obfuscates the entire dynamic of this media scandal. Typically, the mass media construct the typical meaning by narration. Narrating, however, always functions on the basis of a purely pragmatic-ethical probability, which anchors it to a quite determinate social morality. The media, as a consequence, must presuppose this narrative plausibility and apply it.

There are good reasons to use the term 'media scandal' in the singular: it suggests that there exists only one media scandal, regardless of the actors who populate it. It is likewise plausible to treat religious scandal as a unified form. Both terms conceptualize coherent phenomena and do not serve as umbrella terms for a variety of phenomena. This coherence does not apply, however, to the univocal use of the term 'scandal.' A media scandal with actors taken from the inventory of religious roles differs in essential ways from a religious scandal, and this is not a matter of degree or domain. A religious scandal takes place in a universe of divine awe, which certain human behaviours can upset, in turn disturbing other persons. By contrast, a media scandal with religious roles will always follow the general pattern of media scandals. Here, in the media universe, there is no relation of reverence and awe between human beings and God. What *does* arise is the power abuse of actors playing religious roles, in precisely the same fashion as this can be enacted by political, juridical, mundane, and other actors. The secure recognition value of media scandals is the very basis of their marketing and consumption.

1.5 Video-Truths

Scandal is precisely the surplus value over and beyond facts. Yet truth is not substitutable in the production of scandals. So it is worth exploring whether this production can tap television's truth potential in a manner particular to scandal. That this is so seems to be a commonly accepted fact. Small wonder, then, that the film title *Sex, Lies, and Videotape* (Soderbergh) inspired a number of headlines and titles especially relating to works concerned with sex scandals in audiovisual media (Anon. Editorial 1998; Cannon 2002b; Felling 2002; Knox 1999). According to Lull and Hinerman (1997, 17): 'Because visual media can best capture the essence of a transgression by reducing it to a clear and understandable image, TV, newspapers, magazines, and on-line graphics are the best conveyors of the narrative (who could forget Nicole Simpson's bruised and bloody face on international TV, for instance, or the Duchess of York stepping out of her lover's swimming pool onto the front pages of the tabloid press?).' Yet this still does not explain the reason for this inspiration.

As I have argued elsewhere, audiovisual media indeed have a very particular truth relation to reality (Ehrat 2005a, 435–57 et passim). Ultimately, if these media want to emphasize truth in a particular way in their enunciation, they must rely on functionally – or logically presuppose – a common knowledge. That knowledge consists in the directness of the photographic relationship between moving image and reality in front of the film material. One can refer to this technological and logical configuration as cinematic apparatus, which is built around this basic relationship, whether it is realized on celluloid, through electronic circuits, or as a simulation of these on a computer. Does this make photographic moving images uniquely true (i.e., since a manipulation would have to involve a deceit of perception, which is almost 'tamper-proof')? Postulating the photographic genius for truth – or at least for authenticity – goes back to Bazin; yet we would be oversimplifying if we were to attribute percept qualities solely and especially to audiovisual media. Correctly understood, all signs share this attribute. Every sign relation starts as a percept. This makes sense once we recognize that percepts are more than mere apperception – namely, they are perceptual judgments. As judgments, however, their unique feature is to be absolutely certain. This distinguishes all other judgments from percepts. Therefore, a percept cannot be interpreted critically: it will eventually be replaced by another percept should it reveal itself to be inadequate. Only when more than one percept is at hand can a sign relation critically compare them. But this is then already another sign – or another cognition, which concerns itself with the grounds of this deception in perceiving. It is no longer the perception itself.

Percepts alone do not go very far to explain the extraordinary impression of authenticity in audiovisual media, for it is not impossible to notice the manipulation of moving images. Yet even here, previous knowledge of the conditions of production is necessary. Among these conditions, the most important are three: (1) The construction principles of the camera, leading to insights into the meaning in which the perceived is framed, that certain effects of optical depth and sharpness of focus arepossible. (2) Non-continuity, leading to the possibility of montage and editing in a temporally arbitrarily serialized order. (3) The technical separation of the channels of perception, which enables a disparity and segregation of sound and image and allows an arbitrary composition of foreign sound material with arbitrary images. As a rule, however, some media-specific constraints stay in force – in particular, the asymmetry of time in both the moving image and the sound. Both consume time. Manipulations in this area immediately destroy the audiovisual impression. Should this be the desired outcome, the result would be an artistic experimental film, video art, animation film, or computer game. Then, however, no privileged truth relation would obtain. Indeed, that such a relation can exist is proven by the impossibility of negation through images in audiovisual media. An animation video, on the other hand, is perfectly capable of simply making objects disappear. Film's inability to negate brought it the reputation of being especially apt for all 'documentary' purposes. In the language realm, it is the copula 'is' by which a proposition determines something existentially as a fact, or by which an attribute is attached to a state of affairs. Nothing comparable is found in purely audiovisual signs. Despite this apparent lack, films can also affirm something or describe it, beyond language.

A fascinating example of film and language being constructed as a contradiction – even more explicitly, as redundancy – is *Je, tu, il, elle* (Akerman 1974). Other examples exist of films attempting to lie. Lying is especially difficult when it must be done without with a twinkle in one's eye (i.e., without the support of the rhetorical figure of *ironia*). We find the reason for this not in the image as such, but again in our knowledge of the production process. Only then can we see in film a coherent universe of space and time, provided that we know how photography existentially relates a mundane object to the material that records it. As soon as we suspend this knowledge, so disappears as well the impression of spatiotemporal reality. In animation films, cartoons, and (more recently) computer-generated quasi-realistic moving image products, no such spatiotemporal universe surfaces as an effect, but merely a pragmatic universe of a story. The same effect, however, also arises in a Punch and Judy show – at least in the eyes of the young beholder. In a quite different way, the film camera can stand as a synecdoche for the existential relation.

Most films, however, are lying with truth. The true facts of the camera become the artfully knitted lie of the teleology of narrative actions. *Rashômon* (Kurosawa 1950) has demonstrated this procedure masterfully, though in the form of a game of confusion. In this game, of course, there is no prospect of ever establishing the story's truth as a reconstruction of the correct pragmatic purpose of the true facts. Such a purpose is much clearer in *Sex, Lies, and Videotape* (Soderbergh 1989), where lies are part of the self-representation – that is, of identity for social purposes. At least the rationality of this latter purpose can be reconstructed.

From a semiotic[23] viewpoint, it is not surprising that such a specificity of audiovisual material enters directly into the triadic sign relation as the First Correlate. Through this entry, the remainder of the sign relation is also determined for all subsequent interpretations. The interesting question is, then, how exactly does the audiovisual Representamen in the First Correlate determine the nature of narration in this medium in such a way that it differentiates specifically and significantly television journalism from its print sibling? Concretely, must narrative teleology be constructed differently with moving images? The asymmetry of time persisting in the movement of the image does not by necessity lead to a purpose. The essence of this medium merely imposes a consecutive one-after-another. One object, identical with itself, is first in one state, and second in another state – and here Peirce returned to the ancient exemplification of the drunk and sober Philip (CP 3.93). A logical contradiction would result (following the principle of the excluded middle) if one quality were to be attributed and not attributed at the same time. This contradiction is resolved only when one introduces an ordering from a first to a second state, and this order then becomes a temporal series, thus falling under a law governing its serialization. Philip, then, can either get drunk, or he can sober up (if one has grasped as a law the effects of alcohol). Through this law, images are brought into a series towards a goal. In such logical progression, the order in which these images are shown is no longer important (if one takes into account audiovisual discontinuity).[24]

Such laws do not result automatically from a temporal serial order. Nevertheless, audiovisual serial order can exercise a suggestive power on the logical order. When it obfuscates the lack of a general law, the logic of *post hoc ergo propter hoc* can be used creatively, albeit incorrectly. Especially in audiovisual media, showing the pure temporal course can create a style for representing an inevitability of precisely this course of events: 'It had to happen like this!' This saves the *auteur* the trouble of offering an explicit reason for this course of events. Most often, though, run-of-the-mill narrative television and normal commercial films declare that reason more than clearly. They provide teleological reason for a temporal course of events through psychological motivation: of a murderer, of lovers, of vengeance, of retaliation, and so on. Yet already the temporal serial order is, if not a reason proper, then a strong clue to possible reasons. The latter must, however, still be sought because they are not contained in the pure course of events. This is proven by experimental films, which impede the declaration of a teleological purpose, thereby producing the impression of an aimless back and forth. In principle, such a film should offer the possibility of beginning at any point in time – that is, it could just as well be an infinite loop as it could be in real time. Yet it is precisely these 'difficult' films that make especially manifest, by which point the spectator has lent reason to the course of events. In other words, it is from thence onwards that the course becomes directed towards a goal, that it becomes the course of 'something.'

Regarding the supposedly natural link between audiovisuals and reality, suffice it to mention just one constraint. The elapsing of time encourages us to seek rationales for that elapsing. The elapsing is calling for a goal, as it were, but without being able to deliver it through proper means. At this point, the artistic character of production comes into play, and this is what radically separates cinema from the experience of a real outside world. It is not always possible to 'read' laws into the nature that surrounds us; to a considerable extent, we have no choice but to live in the physical world without cognizing. With an artificial product or artefact, however, we always suppose that there is a purpose behind its production; from this it follows that there must be a predetermined purpose to be cognized. As a sign process, audiovisual objects are quite unlike linguistic ones; yet this difference does not apply to the necessity for teleological predetermination. Precisely for this reason, it is possible to narrate audiovisually.

If it is possible to narrate, however, then it is possible to narrate (for) the purpose of sanctioning. This makes television scandals possible. Yet the asymmetry of the temporal course of events is also available to the specifically audiovisual construction of teleology as a suggestion of some 'naturally' predetermined purpose. Owing to this 'natural' immunity from lies, it would seem that scandal, precisely because it uncovers something that has been concealed, should function much better on television than in print media. One has merely to show it, as it were – which can mean only that it is suggested. In language-dependent media, conversely, one can exploit language's ambivalence in order to achieve, through figuration, an equivalent of *post hoc ergo propter hoc* logic.

Attempts to tame by regulatory means this audiovisual potential usually remain stuck, either because of the barren demand for it, or because the impressions of regulatory bodies are entirely subjective. Legal clarifications in, for instance, the context of libel or defamation cases, must usually rely solely on the language used in audiovisual media. This is logically consistent with, and adequate for, a temporal medium, given that mere suggestions of teleology become realities only in the mind of the beholder. The result, time and again, is the broadcast of scandalously true images. Among what are (one hopes) the most extreme examples, are the beheadings of American and Iraqi hostages in the wake of the Iraq War in front of live cameras. The emotional impact of these images is beyond doubt. That impact is strengthened by additional television-specific attributes of the sort that also build on temporal asymmetry. Examples: the live broadcast effect suggests an especially rigid link between production and reception (even when the actual diffusion takes place on the Internet as a video clip). This strong suggestion of freedom from manipulation is framed in the double sense of the word: pictorially as camera frame cut-out, and temporally through introduction and commentary in the framework of a newscast.

In these audiovisual procedures, the scandalous 'proper' emerges from a full-blown narrative teleology: here, with extreme instruments, the veil is torn away from the 'shameful' object. Yet what is seen can look rather different in different contexts. For much of the world, the ugly grimace of terrorism is unveiled; for the other side, the veil presumably had been covering the toothless impotence of 'Satan' (i.e., *vulgo*, the U.S. Army). This merely shows that teleologies are never so rigidly connected to the pure temporal course of events that they cannot also be replaced by another, different teleology.

'True confessions': There is a further potential for scandalization that is specifically audiovisual; indeed, it is so engrained as an industry practice that it can actually become naturalized as a genre convention. The index of authenticity also plays a key role here, the only difference being that it does not lean on temporal asymmetry but rather on the optical apparatus. The camera becomes a confessional because it has an extraordinary capacity to show the authentic in confessions, especially in close-ups of facial mimetic. In a certain way, this practice finds its counterpart in the print media's journalistic exposés. As soon as audiovisual media appropriate scandalous objects, a strongly determinate form of representation is quite often, and quite prominently, used. These are confessions, from victims as well as offenders and from witnesses in general.

Attributing an industrial genre character to confessions must not lead us to the false conclusion that it is the representation's genre pattern that makes claims regarding factual truths. This is neither positively nor negatively the case. Which facts exactly are stated, or negated, can only be discovered through close examination. That proof is, however, especially difficult in audiovisual media for a number of reasons. First, there are specifically audiovisual ways to produce confessions as a genre. For that scope, there is of course no need for the language statement 'this is a confession': the camera itself shows something as a confession – and not as a lie – without any need to maintain this explicitly. The second reason, then, relates to the confession genre as such, which suggests authenticity in that it takes the formal features of a tribunal, as Jauß has shown clearly in literary traditions starting with Jean-Jacques Rousseau's 'Confessions' (Jauß 1977).

Indeed, the genre is well oiled in the present media industry, but it is also ambivalent. Semiotic analysis, while concerned with bivalent, existential, dyadic truth relations, clearly strives for more. Generally speaking – and we will come back to this analysis in greater detail – its main concern is to predetermine a purpose, a pragmatic goal, as rule and therefore as a triadic law. Yet the dyadic truth relation gains from this as well, though logically speaking, it is the simpler of the two. This gain consists in the fact as such. Facts cannot be argued; furthermore, they rely on the undeniable and final authority of the true/false existence of something. This existence is always relative to an enunciator, or to the universe of discourse common to oneself and one's opponent. Just as, for example, the demonstrative pronoun 'this' reveals itself to be only true or false (and only this) relative to me and to you, proponent and opponent, the camera, too, can establish an existential relation to something (else). This happens much more easily than it would have had it taken place through language. In both cases, only the dyadic existential relation between an *aliud* and – on the other side – our universe of discourse is semiotically important. The camera's authenticity (masterfully exploited in confessions) relies entirely and always on this existential relation, which always looks directly on a first person ('me') with a second ('thou'). For the same purposes, where language must use demonstrative pronouns ('this is ...') in order to establish truth values in the first place, a camera merely needs to look. In absolute terms, the most effective look is a counter-look. If a simple camera shot can represent itself as a simple look, what it sees is also true – with final authority.

The camera's built-in truth, moreover, prepares the ground for logical extensions of authenticity such as 'confessing' and (even more so) 'unmasking.' Both comprise variants and anomalies to the degree that they have succeeded in prevailing as industry practice or as genre. Investigative journalism – whether one calls it so or by a less noble name – is built on, among other features, facticity (Mindich 1998; Schudson 1978, 2001; Tuchman 1972). Television, then, reveals itself to be a congenial medium for the showing of 'something' as being 'true' because of the apparent bi-univocal – and for this reason also tamper-proof – relation between image and reality. Despite this appearance, here too the image is already a Representamen or sign aiming at the pragmatic purpose of a possible interpretation (i.e., one possible interpretation). Because there is a finality to interpretation, it imposes a choice on all sign users. Those concerned about such *mise-en-image* are able – indeed, obligated – to mould their experiences into the representational form of audiovisual authenticity. Language does not exhibit the same 'natural' marks of authenticity as the camera. Mimicries and gestures in all their subtleties for exemple, are fully effective only when captured by the *vis-à-vis* of a camera. That said, even a camera's representations must be believed deliberately. They must be *convincing* (corresponding to Habermas's therapeutic discourse); they must convince me of an alter ego's state of interiority, (made) accessible by definition only (by/) to this representing subject (in an interpretative effort). Whatever the authentic human suffering behind it, it is not accessible independently of its form of representation (of interiority).

In scandal production, this audiovisual genre of 'confession' has been widely used, albeit quite often in the form of involuntary or reluctant confessions: someone cannot prevent the showing of the truth about oneself against one's intentions. This calls to mind the exposure model of scandal, which can be highly effective. For eample, a Canadian production, *The Corporation* (Achbar and Abbott 2003), and various 'mockumentaries' (e.g., Michael Moore's films; see Moore 1989, 2002,

2004), are quite specifically audiovisual forms of scandal truths. They are supported decisively by the rhetoric of an exposure discourse, coherently maintained overall through voice-off, voice-over, and diegetic sound. That discourse argues the normative yardsticks of the public opinion judgment. The person bearing the discourse then enters, as agent provocateur within the staged event. Everything else, including the camera work, serves the sole purpose of exposing the reaction of the targets in order to unmask them.

1.6 Comprehending Media Scandals from Media

As object, scandals in the media and in merely social settings are different and so must be treated differently. This raises a methodological question: How are we to investigate the production of scandals in the media, and not in some social substrate? Unfortunately, analyses of media taken in isolation remind us of ill-fated approaches in structuralism. On the other hand, analyses of real-world social interaction as the real basis of media reflexivity most often reflect an empiricist dogma. The real task, instead, is to connect media with outward reality without suppressing the qualitative properties and specific rules of either side. What might sound like a contradiction in terms is certainly not easily achievable, but semiotic-pragmatic theory opens excellent possibilities for solving this double problem.

The connection between media and reality has often been raised, but no satisfactory theory is available. Following the old reflection hypothesis,[25] media were extrinsically an improper mirror of the intrinsic proper reality. This hypothesis falls back on societal behaviour as the explanatory ground for media phenomena and thus 'steals' the contribution owed to the media sign. Our method calls initially for a reversal of the cause–effect relation – and in this way reverses *explanans* and *explanandum* – in order to grasp the autonomous life of the sign. Once this has been analysed, the relation to factual reality in the way specified by the sign will expose itself. In this field, many follow their naively 'realist' reflexes and proceed methodologically as though media were only a reflection of a premedia interpersonal communicative reality (a representation as reflexive as a mirror picture, which amounts to a surveillance camera model of communication).[26] It is, of course, precisely this impression of 'objectivity' that the media themselves like to promote. They have strategic reasons for doing so – it makes them less vulnerable to attack, as if 'the world' itself (and not the papers) were full of scandals, as if scandals were facts and not universes constructed solely through certain logics. The real world itself, however, is 'only' full of facts, which logical rules – most of them under the semantic cover of concepts – then synthesize in order to generate necessary cognitions. These then have the capacity to control behaviour as it develops in the real world. Only through these general rules beyond facts can scandals impose themselves – *after*, of course, they are able to construct pragmatic goals through logic of the *post hoc ergo propter hoc* type. It is precisely this logic that constitutes narration. The medium's intrinsic character is such that, in principle, it is different from the merely factual real before being narrated. Therefore, comparing media with reality does not do justice to the transforming achievement of the medium. Those who cannot acknowledge the achievement of narrativity are fated to presume a simplicistic relation between story and facts. That adequation is never materially reached, however. We are left merely with the hope that gradually narration will reflect facts, as a minimum requirement for any narrative 'about.' On the other hand, this obfuscates the genuine generative achievement of narration.

In rejecting facile reflection theses, we do not dispense with these warranted questions: How does the real world enter narratives? Must narrative media scandals not also be part of human social behaviour in general? Do they not take place in our common social world? Is this not reason enough to seek an empiricist solution to the problem of the relation between media and the real? Media would then merge with the empirical world, and their nature of meaning would cease to be an object of separate attention. Yet is a natural mediatization also emerging from social reality? One would expect the linkage between media and reality to show most clearly at the one pivot of human interface between the media universe and the real world – that is, where source and organ, informant and journalist meet. In the empirical framework, here is the social genesis of the tale, where the social reality generates narration.

Not surprisingly, attempts have been made to anchor media scandal relations as empirical, real-worldly, to interpersonal real relations, ones that differ by nature from the scandal construct. The central figure in the genesis of a media scandal – on the side of the object of scandal – is the informant (also referred to, variously, as the whistle-blower or the mole). On the media side, the central figures are journalists in possession of 'contacts' (reminiscent of secret agency conspiracies). Conflict constellations can arise in two different directions: if the source is called 'public relations,' then reporters are in a conflict of expectations; if, on the other hand, the source is called 'whistle-blower,' then the conflict is in someone's own backyard. Regarding both, those who behave according to the respective expectations are referred to as 'loyal,' whereas those who do not respect those rules must appeal to a 'higher loyalty.' But the semantic here betrays a reason for the act, because loyal (i.e., *legalis*) designates those who act according to a law (i.e., a rule that is the *modus operandi* of an institution). In these conflicts, therefore, rules enter into conflict with one another and not with people. Because rules can be predicted precisely, institutional behaviour can also be calculated – and of course be strategically exploited for personal motives. Since pragmatic subjects rarely subject all of their pragmatic goals of behaviour to institutional rules, or are regulated by more than one institution, the loyally regulated conduct – which is also institutional conduct – can only be relatively coherent (as for whistle-blowers).

In this context, what by its essence is an institutional conflict is representable as an individual pragmatic subject's interiority, or personal motive. But would such representation pierce through to a reality outside the medium? In our context, is it apposite to call this treason? Except in terms of metaphorical licence, certainly not, because such treason would not be possible if there were no rules of institutional loyalty. Subjective feelings of confidence or treason are rooted in institutional rules; thus only this confidence, this mutually dependent relationship, can suffer damage (Liebes and Blum-Kulka 2004). *Mutatis mutandis*, the same order applies to the institutionally regulated journalist–source relation euphemistically described as 'public relations.'

The more general problem of how reality finds its way into media is not answered by this human interface. The subjective feeling of a personal relationship is at best only one of many intermediate articulations between social reality and media representation. That articulation is ruled by institutional logic – the precise construction of which will be the focus of our interest later – but further logical determinants between reality and media obtain. Between these two ends – story and reality – a number of decisive logical steps of interpretation have been achieved. Each step constitutes a possibility, according to its degree, of determination and manipulation. These steps are logical, however, and not necessarily in temporal order. Taking, for instance, Liebes and Blum-Kulka's description of malfunction of trust that at the same time is a function of public opinion, which she considers to be the true scandal (*'whistle blowing – betrayal by an insider'*): not only does this overlook the proper achievement of narrative transformation, but it also obfuscates a narrative (and not an acoustic or musical) achievement at the 'source' with the story-telling whistle. In this case, the pragmatic goal is set by the informant, and journalists accept it because it fits well with their institutional purpose. (This subject will be considered again under the concept of 'metatext.')

Each logical step between real life and scandal story, each degree between effective action and narrative action, is a specific achievement of interpretation. One can schematize these steps or degrees roughly in this order (which leaves the nature of the interpretation involved open):

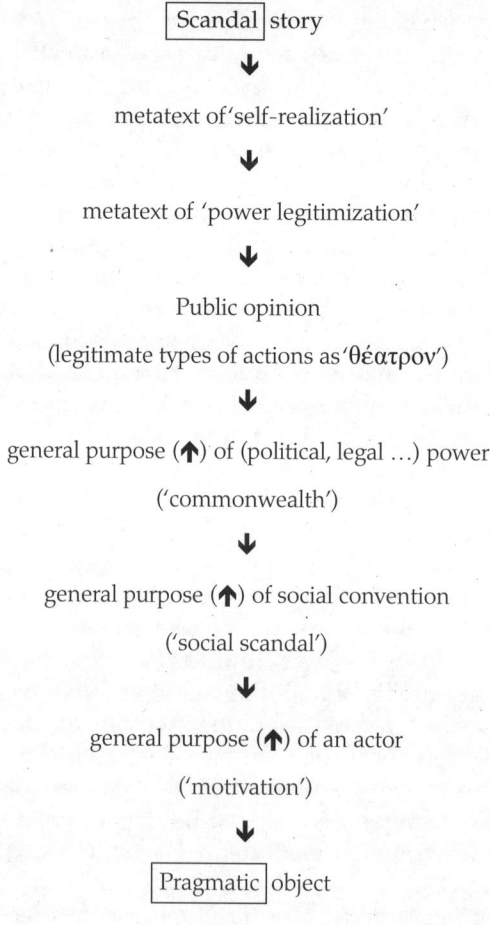

Since interpretation or representation is behaviour towards cognition, the interpretation of action is also action towards action. The logical layers starting with the mass-media product 'scandal story' and ending with the pragmatic execution of an act could certainly be refined *ad libitum*, especially at the interface of power and public opinion. At the bottom, the first actors, whom all other representations signify, provide a goal for their action should they want to represent it to themselves and everyone else. As illustration (we will come back to this case in greater detail), we mention the 'qualms' expressed by Shanley as he represented them in his diary. By controlling one's action, one has supplied an interpretive general rule that turns a non-specific 'doing something' into 'sleeping, or reposing, or lazing ...' One offers this very same rule as interpretation aid to the general public if one is asked explicitly (an implicit interpretation is the inner dialogue of a subject identity). The schema renders both interpretation directions with arrows, with the up-arrow always meaning the rule and the down-arrow directing interpretation to the object.

Actors in an organization that administers power must interpret their actions according to the rules of the institution's pragmatic purpose. Whistle-blowers are different only in that they interpret their own organizational institutional actions with a negative valuation and represent that valuation in this key to public opinion. For instance, Shanley prided himself on the many public distinctions and awards he had received for the care he extended to runaways and young homosexuals. The negative valuations, on the other hand, were all those complaints lodged with Shanley's archbishop, against which he had to defend himself time and again at a very early stage in his career. Both interpretations could become journalistic sources: the former as personal promotion or public relations, the latter as whistle-blower. If this relation were to become a social scandal, it would constitute a conflict between two interpretations, one subjective, the other institutional, and not between action and news story. In normal circumstances, the symbiotic entanglement of journalists with their sources (whom they pretend to control) is nearly total and leaves little space for personal interpretation.[27] This makes access to sources more difficult; it also discourages sources (who are, in reality, more properly speaking self-representers) from taking an interest in representation, which might be ignored by the journalist. Scandal can, therefore, only originate from opponent-representers, be they internal or external to the organization, whose interest in representing can thus be gratified. Since, however, this source group is rarely the actors group with their own action motive, sources are found on the side of alternative interpretations. Evidently, these are in conflict with the actors' interpretation.

If the action is an *inter*action, both parties have motives for action, which of course they represent to different general publics. In the case of the Boston CSA scandal, motives of action that conflicted among themselves led to conflict representations in court. This, however, is an instance pronouncing on both representations in the name of positive law, which is a still higher general public.[28] When events are transformed into scandals, two effects are produced: (a) an abstract meaning process of supposing an ideal to events as their pragmatic purpose; and (b) a sort of 'social ontological' role differentiation between tribunal and actor, court and stage.

The double interpretation in both directions indicates that rules are in force at higher degrees. These higher rules are quite different from pragmatic rules. They are known neither in motivation interpretations nor in social scandals. The media universe proper is only comprehensible through its proper construction means. Traditional media theories cannot do justice to this phenomenon. So, no 'uses and grats' help us understand scandals. Nor do scandals give rise to media effects in the sense of an instance that engineers a scandal in order to provoke an effect. In the best case, such theories produce an anthropomorphizing media effects theory in the form of a scandal conspirator theory (Liebes and Blum-Kulka 2004). This, however, does not provide much explanatory power, even when conspiratorial intent can be proven in an actor. It does not explain how scandal – even an intentional one – can be produced.

Methodology poses a problem if the object of study is indeed scandal as such, and not its psychological impact or its political use. Under a strictly empiricist model, the result can become parodic. This transfers scandal as an independent variable into the measurable world, as if scandal existed as a simple fact. Only this approach permits us to measure scandal before and after its impact as an dependent variable (e.g., which empirical effects show up in subjects and between subjects?). Common sense declares one arbitrary fact effective cause of some other fact (since everything must have its sufficient reason, following Leibniz); any change of state is then interpreted as causality. However, this approach does not allow us to comprehend anything of the complex progress from a before to an after, which is all of scandal's fascination.

What the medium accomplishes, however, is primarily narrativity.

A Theoretical Approach to the Nature of Media Scandal 39

The core relationship to the real world is established through stories. With this object of study, therefore, only a comprehensive narrative method can explain what happens in and through media.[29] It would not even suffice to analyse propositions about real states of affairs (ordered as a theory covering empirical data) as links connecting language and world. It is insufficient because scandalized real social subjects do not face propositions that state facts or states of affairs (given that these subjects have no unmediated access to the fact itself). Moreover, every method that treats scandal as no more than a state of affairs will eliminate its most essential part. In this context, journalistic 'objectivity' as practice is deceptive. A method that strives for a substantial grasp of the production of scandal cannot base itself on the use of factual propositions sifted into news stories in the 'serious press' to achieve the objectivity effect.[30] Notwithstanding factuality, this criterion does not preclude constructing narrative ideals. These alone can set in motion the logic of scandal, but facts have no logical relationship to ideals. Thus, scandal is not in the misdeeds, nor in statements of misdeeds, but in their negative idealizing as 'corruption.' Only stories can convey corruption, which is already beyond statements of factual events. Therefore, the epistemic object of scandal is a story, which does not exist as a fact, because story is teleology. Kant rated the cognitive potential of teleology among the 'metaphysical appearances.' They pretend to be cognition even though there can be no experience of a *telos*. The nature of the epistemic object media scandal is sometimes not seen. Also, the true site of its production is rendered blurry in this definition. Jiménez (2004, 1008–9) tells us:

> Political scandal is a lively social reaction of indignation once there is a public awareness of the occurrence of a particular behaviour carried out by an actor holding – or who can hold in the future – a public office invested with social trust. But not every behavior of a political agent causes a scandal; only a subset of them does, and the boundaries defining this subset are cultural boundaries. That is, to determine what behavior of a politician – publicly spread and interpreted – may provoke a scandal is something that depends on the cultural framework where such behavior is made meaningful.

Here the veritable producer of scandal is culture, but it is left unclear how culture can cause indignation. Even if the extremely fuzzy concept of culture in this definition is cloaked with a little order in the form of three zones of acceptability (black, grey, white), this does not tell us how and why something is in one and not in the other zone – that is, how something becomes a scandal or not.

> This being so, for a scandal to happen, it is either about one of those extreme cases that have just one and always the same meaning – belonging to the black zone – or it depends on the way certain behaviour is interpreted at a particular moment. This interpretation depends also on institutional and temporal factors. (ibid.)

From our analyses it is impossible to assume, with Jiménez, as a precondition for scandal, that the political forces are unanimously outraged. On the contrary, it is *public opinion* that has the ability to create the impression that 'all' feel the same, even if this is effectively only the staged feeling of an élite or of a group with vested interests. This has been described extensively in a media scandal involving Michel Friedman, the famous confrontational TV host and member of the German Jewish Central Council (Burkhardt 2006), for instance.

Methodological questions about the genesis of media scandals are not to be skipped over. Once it is recognized in principle that all reality construction in media is in fact narrative,[31] there are methodological consequences. Thus, only those methods capable of treating the rhetoric and poetics of mass media reality construction can be contemplated as methods for analysing the phenomenon of media scandal. Semiotic and discourse theory, for instance, rank among these as much as semionarratology, but so does the pragmatic tradition, as it might be considered to subsist in critical theory or in ethnomethodology.

1.7 Publicity Narrative as Precondition of Scandals

Media scandals are nothing other than the motor of a logic, which is the ongoing construction of an ideal (see §1.2), from which arise events that can then be sold as scandals. This is quite unlike scandals that develop in the purely social domain. What villages and Royal or Imperial courts have produced in scandals is of a quite different nature: gossip and scandalous demeanour presuppose certain mimetic processes among those who physically take part in the interaction. If mass media were to 'report' on social scandals, they would be creating a new product. Yet gossip and social scandal represented narratively as rules of a general nature are too boring, because it is precisely the 'buzz' of an interactive scandal that cannot be conveyed in a medium. Consequently, media construct their best scandals by their own means. They can produce much more interesting scandals with products of their own making – for instance, stars, monsters, celebrities (who are not the same as socialites), politicians, criminals, or even those nameless oddballs or nerds under the *faits divers* rubric.

A scandal's logic differs according to whether society or mass media produce it: at play is the logic of norms in the former, of ideals in the latter. The *tertium comparationis* for social behaviour, the pivot and linchpin from which all behaviour is compared, is no longer an ideal but a norm, which is then rendered plausible with considerable effort. Social norms are antecedent to every social action – depending on the theory, they are either pre-existent or preconstructed. However normativity is reflected, the object is, always, a real conduct of real subjects within the real constraints of the physical and social world. Mass media then must abstract from all of this in constructing their meaning.

Norms are more than ideals; moreover, they are of a different nature and are justified and justifiable in a quite different manner. When explaining ideals, it might suffice to treat them as textual constructs or within a broader framework as logical implications of a determinate text genre; a norm, by contrast, requires a quite determinate relationship to reality. Norms, by definition, do never exist (yet), but just as much as values, they are beyond mere existence. Kant, consequent to his transcendental premises of being, concluded that such values have no use for cognition. But he also acknowledged them for ethical behaviour as pragmatic values, to which he conceded a generality *sui generis*. Peirce, in the wake of Kant's pragmatism, applied his Pragmaticism to the entirety of being, including cognition and aesthetic. As cognitive behaviour, cognition is subject to normativity, as is every other behaviour. Its norm is therefore antecedent to any concrete cognizing. From this he developed the idea of Normative Sciences, which constitute a level of reflection *below* experience or of cognizing thought but *above* phenomenology after the latter has completed its task of taking into account whatever appears as mental content. Thus, semiotic as much as logic[32] – the most comprehensive Normative Science – classifies all possible thoughts in abstract. Norms, it follows, are the pragmatic linkage between signs and reality in their essentially different modes of being.

Just as norms require the relation to modes of being real, the scandal ideal needs a coherent form of 'rightness,' without which it cannot orient itself towards anything but its own construction. The practical consequence for media is that they cannot found their meaning on experience, be it the producers' or consumers' experience. The representation is capable of representing experience but cannot itself take place with the means of experience – it can only do so through pure symbols, or even texts. Those who reconstruct media sense within the existential experience of those who are involved – and this is true for all social psychology approaches to scandal, as already mentioned – are in reality enriching it with a further dimension. Mass media's meaning is not comprehensive of living experience and human existence, though it is possible to enrich it through the further step of interpretation with experience. Here, Peirce speaks of constructive respectively degenerative signs.

This logical separation of experience and ideal should not be mistaken as the radical separation of experience from the social as we encounter it in the phenomenological tradition. 'Reconstructive' social philosophers like Schütz, Berger, and Luckmann recognize two levels of meaning. Besides the subjective sense, rooted in subjective intentionality, they assume another sense, beyond the subjective, in a sort of 'social' rationality (Schütz et al. 2003 Bd. 2). One can object that by their own phenomenological method, they cannot reconstruct where this second level originates. It certainly cannot be the collection or sum of subjective senses. Even Heidegger had still to differentiate two levels: one of authenticity, the other of the vulgar. Despite its being 'always mine' (*je-meinig*) as existential experience, as it belongs in the sphere of my quite solitary being-towards-death (*Dasein zum Tode*), time also exists as *public* time in the *now*. Ricoeur succeeded in building his theory of narrated time on this vulgarization of time. *De facto*, this materially amounts to what Schütz called the 'objective sense,' the social part of intentional acts.

For the world relationship, the two separations share as a consequence that the object of mass media meaning is not identical to the meaning of experience. Experiential action is oriented by pragmatic norms, and one of the three norms constitutive of experience is bivalent truth (true/false; what Peirce calls Ethic). In contrast to experience, however, media narrativity is oriented towards its self-constructed ideal of a pragmatic purpose or goal of action. In this, there are no further constraints other than those self-imposed by the ideal. This construction must also generate – for instance, as narrative – the pragmatic in its own world of action, a separate universe. This world of action is the public world, publicity. (Note well that as mentioned in note 1 of the

Preface, we use this term in its broader and more common sense, as defined by the *Oxford English Dictionary:* 'The quality of being public; the condition or fact of being open to public observation or knowledge.' This, too, is quite open to philosophical perspectives, such as what Heidegger would have labelled *vulgus*. 'Public sphere' translates Habermas's key term '*Öffentlichkeit*' only partially and should be taken in the sense of publicity; 'publicness' sounds awkward.) It must be the public world because it is precisely no longer the physically real world. Only the latter is a corrective to experience; only the latter imposes itself on cognition from the outward sphere. This public world must be previously shared by all *without* being a possible object of cognition. In addition, this world does not know of any reality constraints. According to these – as in the sense of Peirce's Pragmatic Maxim – actions must be feasible (counterfactual conditional) within the boundaries of social and physical reality. Instead of narrative teleology, mere plausibility suffices. Hyperbolically, in the universe of publicity there is no essential meaning difference between films like *Wag the Dog* and a president managing crises – except of course for the built-in indices of reality or of fiction.

Obviously, one could object that this cannot be true for every narration. Are there not also true narrations? Where can the truth of narratives be grounded? There can be no doubt that a quite naive realism exists – for example, in those proverbially true stories that some films pretend to contain (i.e., 'based on a true story'). It is pointless to respond to such objections, for obvious reasons. However, there are serious interlocutors in the documentary camp, since many documentary films indeed make truth claims – or at least they flaunt their own authenticity. Even in the broader philosophical context, some approaches treat narration not so much from the perspective of its construction, but more as an inquiry into the origin of its truth. Ricoeur, as mentioned, undertook to integrate narration into the horizon of human existence. In the process, he attributed to narration a derived truth (cf. Ehrat 2005a, 346–60). In this vein, Weinrich at some point mentions the anecdotal evidence of the Hopi, for whom the narrated world is more essential than the existing real world. For phenomenological-existential approaches, such as Ricoeur's, it is self-evident that this truth has nothing in common with facts or other mirror theories. How the real world is mirrored in the narrative, on the other hand, is of central concern for analytical philosophy interested in film or more narrowly in cinematic narration. The illustrations chosen for this concern in theory deal with recognition characteristics of the real horse in a film horse (cf. ibid., 192–206).

Beyond this philosophical context, there are the debates in science theory and cognitivism, which target the cognitive object of historiography. For classical historians like Ranke, it was self-evident that the task of historiography should be nothing other than *'er will blos sagen, wie es eigentlich gewesen'* (to tell how it actually happened) (Ranke 1824, Vorrede); in order to arrive at the historical facts themselves, he and the historicist school needed to employ historical-critical 'police' methods. Such an optimistic view of methodology has since evaporated; and in postmodernism and the Paris School of *historiographie non-événementielle* (Veyne 1971), the approach has veered towards the opposite. This debate is still quite lively, and we will return to it in the context of Hayden White's narrative historiography.

At first sight paradoxically, pragmatic semiotic is in both camps: realism *and* narrative construction. This is because critical realism *and* constructivity of the sign process are both explicitly parts of this theory. Fortunately, this saves it from the vicious alternatives of naive realism and nominalism. If the nature of narrative construction in general is understood well, it becomes clear that, properly speaking, there *are* no true narrations. But this does not exclude those narrations from containing true facts. It is just that *how* these facts are built into a narration is determined by the pragmatic purpose as predetermined by the narrative, and no longer by facts. This purpose need not be as obtrusive and conspicuous as the moral in a fairy tale. Our analyses will show how such a goal or purpose can be predetermined in an almost 'natural' manner, similar to the unobtrusive naturalness shown for audiovisual truth (§1.5). Furthermore, this opens perspectives for genre development based on the criterion of the ways in which narrative goals are set and how teleology is constructed. There is a continuum from the most explicit to the most subtly implicit predetermination of purpose, without constituting through this variation a change in the teleological nature of narrativity. A factual report, even by a direct eyewitness, is a report, and thus more than a collection of facts – especially if this is imitated when a newspaper story prints this report in an insert box as an eyewitness story, or when reality TV runs a clip of the same report, apparently devoid of any auctorial intervention, almost as if it is telling itself.

Every narrative possesses a single irrepressible connection to the factual reality. This is the anchorage in the real act of enunciation, which can be conceived as an implicit statement such as 'I tell you now this story ...' 'I, you, now, this' are the anchors to the real world. The rest appears only through a teleology. However, one must distinguish strictly between text and narration, because texts can also contain phrases that in no way pertain to narration. It is even possible to drill holes in the teleological narrative universe. For example, by applying it linguistic instruments the text can drill holes through an anodyne use of adjectives, which constitute a valuation. Other sign classes (e.g., audiovisual) must invent analogous instruments. This sort of hole in the narrative logic is insinuated by the use of the demonstrative pronoun 'this,' since 'this' presupposes a common universe of discourse between a proponent and an opponent. Comprehensibility and validity are limited to precisely this one universe. 'This' is true or false – in other words, a fact. Facts are also incorporated into news stories, which is possible without problems once the text has been configured to two logics. The truth of stories, of history, can now be qualified in the sense that the story of history can contain truths without being in itself a true fact. In logic terms, one can express this more clearly by speaking of two universes of different nature.

Discussion about media scandals, therefore, always refers not to the empirical but to the public world. The media universe relates to the real universe of the life world almost as if it were a parallel universe within which media scandals are staged. To accomplish this, it does not even require a clear concept of what constitutes a public sphere. Habermas can critically reconstruct it; with Luhmann, one can see it as the result of a system selection. Important in this context is merely that media do not construct a further life world connection. Mass media do not create objectness (in a phenomenological manner, 'protensionally') as an act correlate of a subject or of a collective subjectivity (in the concepts of A. Schütz). Such an imputation would quite misunderstand their real mode of operation. The specific way that media relate to their object possibly at some stage could also be reduced to some sort of subjective *vis-à-vis*, not the least because for phenomenology *per definitionem* everything must be reducible to the subject. Doing so, however, eliminates that which is specific to mass media, through the application of the all-purpose sieve of subjectivity. This eliminates also the possibility of comprehending why the mass media–constructed world is unparalleled. This universe is not simply one of the sectors of the life world in its meaning context of the one continuous unquestioned horizon.[33]

In this book the media world, or universe, will be termed *publicity* or *public sphere*, interchangeably. For the time being there is no need to clarify whether this universe is seamlessly inserted into the universe of the 'life world horizon,' or whether (and if so, how) it relates to the physical world of facts or states of affairs. Methodologically, at least, it in enough to assume a parallel universe; we need not first clarify the relation to other universes. In other words, it is important that this question be left open – that we assume one uniform universe into which media are fitted based on *ceteris paribus* arguments ('because there can be only one world').

Even if we bracket the empirical truth-capable where-question, we still have the what-question: What is publicity, what are its qualities? The simple answer – that it is the public sphere – *nemine contradicente* – is not an empirical fact; one can neither apperceive nor experience it through sensory means. Furthermore, no one can show it: 'Here it is!' It is taking place, though, all the while – 'in our heads,' as it were. No one has ever seen it, yet everyone behaves as if it does indeed exist. Publicity 'is' not something objective, substantial; it becomes a given only as a function. In this manner, however, it guides human comport; it regulates in the same way that transcendental ideas regulate thought within the framework of Kantian Idealism.

It is not the case, though, that the public world is mere invention, or *ficta*, drawn from the *facta* of the real world. First, the idea of sheer 'reality' is relatively novel and exists only in nominalistic philosophical contexts (the empirical, non-mental sort, viz., what contemporary humanity takes to be real). Then, however, a world image or *Weltbild* always existed and exists, and it should be coherent in the main. Likewise, there was not always a public sphere in the same way as it determines our contemporary lives and behaviour. The manner of its development as bourgeois culture also determines and defines privacy, its opposite. Complementary, they constitute two different modes of communication. Yet this was not always so. Today it is very difficult to imagine, and only in a negative mode, that the identity of a person could have been at the same time a personal and a social identity, private and at the same time public. Victor Turner's theory of liminality describes this unified identity in premodern societies, whereas Weber's demythologization thesis explains the decomposition of the compact world image through the impact of modernity. Weber allows us to see modernity's resulting fragmentation as different but contradictory world images, as rationalities in the plural. In this vein, one can conceive of the public world, object of public opinion, similarly as a universe with a coherent rationality. A public sphere is a rather recent phenomenon, an outgrowth of the victorious advent of the bourgeoisie. This artefact of media history, a contingent being, the phases in the delivery of the public sphere, will contribute to our understanding of this ephemeral phenomenon (see below).

2 What Is Publicity, the Public Sphere?

To address publicity as a logical and epistemic problem is one thing; to approach it as a historical explanation of contingent events is another. What does it mean to cognize the 'public,' and how is this done? What does this involve, and which operations must take place? Publicity does *not* exist for the purpose of creating a universe parallel to the empirical one, though this is an unavoidable by-product. The public sphere is staged primarily for the purpose of publicly putting forward an opinion. This does not consist of opining whatever; it is not in the first place an uncontrolled belief in whatever state of affairs, corresponding to Schütz's life world. Rather, one 'has an opinion on ...' – that is, on actors and their pragmatic objects.

The duty to have an opinion on actions is remotely cognate to epistemological critique, where cognition ascertains itself on its own operations. In a strict sense, though, there can be no epistemology of actions-guiding interest or motive. The sole remaining control is a sort of vicarious pragmatic. Only by means of vicariously acting subjects can one make the correct judgment. Action is staged in the public *theatrum mundi*, which is mounted precisely for this sole purpose. On social subjects acting in the real world, no such judgment is feasible, for their goals and interests diverge, beyond any control. In order to pass a pragmatic judgment that is more than merely formal, cognition of a purpose of action is necessary. It is solely the public sphere that predetermines that purpose. From real subjects' actions it is impossible to obtain purposes that are generally and validly recognizable. Only one's own personal subjective pragmatic interest can be seen by oneself. Yet it is not valid generally – only for one's own self.

A general pragmatic (which then could perhaps give rise to more than a formal, substantial ethic) is impossible; but a pragmatic of generality *is* possible. In the real world, we do not act generally. It would certainly be a stroke of genius if we were able to describe conduct *in se* as comprehensible and binding for everyone – if there were such a thing as general action. In its stead, there are long-standing cultural practices. To accomplish a practice, we need not have present all of the factors of pragmatic logic for concrete acting. It is sufficient to construct generality or action in general, through exemplary actors performing important actions. In this general pragmatic, publicity serves the purpose of a pragmatic legitimization of what can be done, of that to which one is empowered, of what constitutes power. Legitimization of power is thus the *raison d'être* of public opinion, as Geiger's classical sociology stated: 'In less enlightened times humble subjects subjected themselves to the orders of an authority instituted by God and bowed in front of a tradition that "always has been like this." The contemporaries, having grown up in the imagination sphere of democratic self-determination, baulk at this way of being pushed, and their protestation looks behind the impersonal system constraining their self-determination and freedom of movement, the persons responsible for leading this system, the power holders' (my tr.).[1] Getting a grip on those in power, however, is not feasible through interactive control of behaviour; this can only be accomplished in the symbolic space of the legitimization of their power. This space is the public sphere.

Publicity is not the narration itself but merely its teleology, which allows us to see a reality *sui generis*. Like a phoenix, this other reality rises from stories about primary realities. In identifying idiomatically public opinion with publicity, semantics has led some astray (see Donsbach 2006): publicity is not 'something'; rather, it is a meaning product. It exists purely as meaning. Habermas was compelled to reconstruct this class of meaning within a framework provided by meaning-in-general. Of course, it is not to be assumed that his 'fundamental pragmatic' reconstruction is the only possible one or even the best. There are reputable alternatives for determining social or even public meaning from a theory of meaning in general. Only the shallow empiricist, for whom public opinion is reduced to this or that event of an opined opinion, can escape from this necessity.

So that we do not have to discuss every single isolated meaning theory, let us arrange them in classes. Because we are dealing with a non-experiential cognitive object, only an indirect cognition comes into question. Abstractly, one can differentiate two modes of conceptualizing: either (1) media-produced publicity is thought as a simulacrum of meaning in general, or (2) concrete meaning subsists. For instance, when meaning is explained as a speech act – as sentence or text grammar – this is a different class from an explanation from consciousness, which makes something meaning-full owing to its other. This is the most abstract way of sketching an object that exists only as a theory construct and not as experience. (The second section of this chapter discusses the *simulacrum*, the third the subsistence class of explanation of the non-object publicity.) It is subsistence thinking when concrete meaning is deduced from the absolute I or from the authenticity of existence. Simmel's 'social *a priori*' indicates its transempirical relation even in the name, as does Habermas's Ideal Speech Situation.

The names given to these abstract classes may sound a little bizarre if we do not situate them among the multisecular challenges of philosophy. One such challenge is how to consider a physical object as simultaneously a meaning object. *A fortiori*, will that be the case with an object that no one maintains is tangible but that nevertheless stands between all of us as a regulative of meaning? How is it possible for meaning to uncouple itself from the concrete object? How can it function as a merely invisible meaning? Is this not similar to the meaning of 'phlogiston' or 'unicorn,' which Peirce's Pragmatic Maxim unmasks and dissolves? In very practical terms – returning to section 1.5 about video truth – here meaning is not exhausted by the fact that a thing is shown (which could be rendered completely by 'this man exists at the time of taking the picture'). Beyond the visible object on screen, a powerful man is shown who justifies his power in his way of showing. This is not evident but begs an explanation.

In section 1.7 we came to see the *clou* of semiotic as a theory of meaning. By explaining meaning as form, the idea of the sign mediates being and substance (De Tienne 1996). The interstice is the domain of the *accidentia*, of which the abstract forms are the three categories. Every concrete meaning can be grasped in the triadic relation of the sign, but this is far from saying that what is formally possible is also actually produced. Here the culturally contingent comes into play, which means the unforeseeable. While publicity in a logical-formal sense is particular class of meaning – that is, sign (see chapter 3), it is by the same token a historical event, a contingently developing cultural form, one that also can be described historiographically.

2.1 Publicity as Methodological Construct

An obvious objection to such an overtly theory-driven approach to publicity is encountered in empirical theory-adverse practice. For instance, some assume that 'humans, although they are different from other "objects" of the sciences, can still be described by the same methodology, based on the same epistemology as, say the objects in physics or chemistry' (Donsbach 2006, 443). Here, though, the problem is placed before the problem – that is, it does not acknowledge the non-empirical nature of the object. This goes beyond the lamented disciplinary identity crisis of communication sciences. Those who take this approach acknowledge the existence of a plethora of theories that contradict one another; even so, the methodology they choose amounts to a declaration that the object is empirical and measurable. In practical terms, therefore, this constitutes a way of thinking about the public sphere and public opinion. Without really reflecting on the nature of the object, some empirical thinkers talk of the 'public,' of opinion and sphere. It seems they do this merely to gain a comfortable abstract collective term, one that stands for what they consider to be the really real: opinion. Public opinion, in this sense, would then be what empirical subjects are opining. For subjective opining to become public, it first must be turned into an aggregate. The belief is that if this cannot take place through elections, or consumer or other social behaviour, then the social sciences can turn it into a statistical aggregate. There is, of course, more behind this attempt than mere method. Following its most prominent proponents, materially one could even see an implicit ontology here, as a theory of both being and society. To the degree that this can be relevant to our subject, we will return to this point later.

Regarding public opinion proper, suffice it to say that public opinion undoubtedly transcends subjective, individual opinion. No subject opines publicly; whereas it is possible to represent certain kinds of ideas as those shared by all. Everyone who grasps such ideas correctly must comprehend them as not his or her own ideas in contradiction to the ideas of others. Rather, these are non-discriminating ideas, the ideas of all. But how is it feasible to attach an all-quantifier to a subjective opinion? How this can be achieved is a cultural and historical question that will be addressed separately below. The practical effect of this all-quantification is clear, and that it *be* clear is the desired aim of the operation. By this quantification, something acquires the status of a truth – that is, everyone must treat it as always and by necessity valid. If one can maintain this of something that oneself opines but does not know, then a further turn becomes convenient: the shifting from logical to numeric all-quantification. Concretely, this shifts us from necessary knowledge to the opinion of all, from generality to allness. Notwithstanding that this is not exactly what statistical aggregation performs, it can still easily be interpreted in this sense by opinion research. The statistical aggregate is a determinate procedure for abstracting from singularities. Its total, the population, is therefore precisely *not* a validity for all and everyone. This is clearly evinced by the irreversibility of such reduction; put another way, from the aggregate one cannot infer backwards to any individual in the collection. Yet this is precisely possible in the case of a logical all-quantifier. The practical effect called 'public opinion' is, therefore, clearly different from and more than a statistical aggregate.

The nature of publicity as an object of study is such that it requires a methodology different from the one we follow for tangible empirical objects. Thus we use 'public' sphere conservatively and without ontological prejudice in a technical sense as a determinate kind of text. For this text, moreover, the historical term 'public opinion' applies perfectly well. In semiotic analysis, this text reveals itself as a determinate logical constellation of determinate role logics, in a pure logical universe, as it were, purposely constructed. Today this universe is that of the mass media – as soon as they present themselves as an enunciation instance. As a cultural practice, publicity is more than what in a society is simply self-evident.[2] Despite being public, the self-evident does not need the support of a refined practice such as publicity, which only acquires its precise sense through this cultural practice.

In choosing a research design that takes its point of departure from the text as the datum most immediately graspable, we need not confine ourselves to mere intratextual mechanisms. An adequate method must be capable of bridging the hiatus between real experience and the otherness of the meta-empirical object, publicity. This necessarily involves questions that address the framework of society as well as objective reality. This connection and the relations of interdependency can be described as life world[3] – which already brings us to one of a number of possible solutions.

In the case of public opinion, the interlacing of object and medium must not be disentangled. Even so, some scholars attempt to do so methodologically by extracting data from the rest. In doing so, they may think they have gained direct access to reality *in se*. Less radically than this strictly empiricist approach, others have attempted to at the very least salvage an empiricist core from the propositional form or from speech acts. In attempting this, however, they still presuppose a 'real' reality, which they then compare to the propositional version of the state of affairs, thereby verifying or falsifying it. But this method is fundamentally flawed because it surrenders before the complexity of the object.

Non-reductive methods struggle with difficulties of their own when recognizing and methodologically acknowledging this interlacement – when acknowledging, in other words, that publicity does not exist without signs and exists only 'as language.' Such a peculiar object nature inevitably produces a methodological dilemma. Since one cannot possibly investigate the object by its own means, one has to search for an outside point of comparison, for a purchase on something other than language. But what could be the other of signs, or of language, if there exists no direct access to reality *in se* that is not already mediated through signs? This other cannot be another thing (factor, variable, event, mental state); it can only be a relation to otherness that serves the purpose of explaining publicity. According to the type of otherness – to which an analysis of the object publicity (and other objects of meaning) establishes a relation – there are two methodologically different accesses: *simulacrum* and subsistence.[4] These abstract relational categories will become explicit through a discussion of their major representatives.

These two concepts merely designate the type of relation of something to its other: here, the relation of public meaning – which is the object to be explained – to meaning as such. The nature of 'being public' is not evident in itself. It can be explained only from the qualities, the *what*ness, of the other – according to the nature of the relation through which they are connected to each other. How one grasps meaning *in se* is, however, a philosophical choice. It can be orientated towards experience of reality, or it can be derived from social convention or from the limited number of possibilities for acting.

How do *simulacrum* and subsistence differ as relations of otherness? If subsistence designates this relation, it refers with this image to something other that is at the basis of something; from this ground stems its essence. The term *simulacrum*, for its part, suggests the idea of a 'manifestation' (Greimas), or, as in systems theory, of co-principles.

Both concern themselves in their own way with the co-presence of two unequal meanings; both explain the dependence of the one on the other. It is only the kind of logical dependence that is different. In a naive view of one of the theories, the difference would of course take on diverse accents. Following the argumentation of systems theory, for instance, the difference that really matters is between action-based and system-based theories. This is tinged with the system theoretical way of polemically constructing its adversaries, for the theory problem is shared by both – that is, How can the meaningful 'something' be explained through something else? It is not ultimately relevant that this explanation can be executed as an explanation of action, because something and its other constitute a logical difference, whereas 'action' can be found on both sides. It is only that on each side it means 'something' else. Pragmaticism, for instance, explains action under the control of meaning not by some transcendental idea or metaphysical speculation about being, but through action and its prerequisites.

The logical difference is quite important and also of practical consequence. Debates between 'materially' close theories are aroused by the fundamental diversity of both approaches. Ricoeur, for instance, has a theory of public action based on the representation of action in Aristotle's *mythos*. His theory would agree with much of Greimas's Narrative Grammar, even in some fundamental tenets, were it not for this ultimate radical diversity in the foundation of publicity. In Ricoeur, this foundation lies in an existentially grounded temporality of action ('in the act of reading,' constituting a subsistence type of meaning derivation); in Greimas, instead, it lies in a generativism-based meaning production. This generativism, however, does not refer to innate ideas but rather to the social imaginary, which is impossible to transcend by means of further questions. This, then, constitutes a pure *simulacrum* of meaning organization.

Furthermore, on this point there is no difference between theory and empiricism. Theory – 'speculation' in Latin – is contemplation. What can be observed is antecedently constructed as object and is therefore an emanation of a theory without which the object of experience could not be contemplated. Is the context of social life contingent on theory or independent of it? There is no need to argue this, for in practical terms it would mean that one would have to be in possession of a theory of the social before one could attempt to act. Theory has always a more reduced complexity, or a greater generality, than mere practical acting.

2.2 Publicity as Simulacrum

A complex reality is only accessible as epistemic object of inquiry once it has been rendered 'methodologically artificial,' as artefact. 'Simul' in this endeavour is not meant in the sense of 'similar to'; rather, it means, generally, similitude as form: whatever 'is,' is always of the same form and therefore similar – simul-ontology. Quite explicitly, systems theory addresses the artificial character of the reduction of complexity. Semiology, furthermore, acknowledges what we have called methodological artificiality, whereas Saussure explicitly excludes *parole*, spoken words, from his purview because this method cannot grasp them. A semiotically informed pragmatic, with its realist implications, favours the critical understanding of similitude. However, what we have brought under the common umbrella of *simulacrum* is not an exclusive offshoot of our perspective, since for both semiology and systems theory radical philosophical critiques already exist. These critiques elucidate that both constitute a type of ontology, since they explicate themselves as theories of being, in their respective ways. While Luhmann muses about ontological premises for his systems theory (1984b, 1997), Scheibmayr (2004) attempts a severe challenge. Deleuze (1973) accomplished a similar result for structuralism, semiology, and other likewise differentially structured theories.

Both subspecies – systems theory and semiology – are based on levels. For its part, structuralist thought developed a theory of roles. This development occurred beyond a lexically oriented semiology – namely, by means of the comprehension of enunciation instances, that is, textual reflections of a situation of communication. This corresponds to structuralist homology, which in these instances can be applied equally to texts and sociality. In texts, they are verifiable in any case as narrative grammar. How this functions as a methodology we will see later.

In systems theory, on the other hand, the drop in the level of complexity is built into the system boundary as the difference between system and environment. It has been argued that this theory is barely capable of operationalization – in other words, that it cannot be applied systematically to what can be observed empirically (cf. Saxer 1983, 95). Such criticisms relating to an empirical deficit are understandable in view of the peculiar objectual nature of publicity. At any rate, the public sphere, in principle, is an 'autopoietic' system; in other words, it reduces complexity and is differentiated from other systems by its own system behaviour. We will debate systems theory at length in another context, when we discuss its semiotic alternative (see §4.1 below).

Comprehensive theses are sustainable only with the support of a methodological instrument supported by sufficiently good reasons. Semiology talks of meaning production instead of social reality. What are the methodological presuppositions for this concept? Does a method have to abandon the claim to reality in order to grasp the 'other' as meaning? From a social science perspective, one interesting version of semiology is semionarratology, also known as the *Paris School*. It identifies the core of all meaningfulness in the concept of action rather than in physical reality.[5] There is a special twist, however, to the semionarratological idea of action, relating to how it ties action to language. But this is an unequal connection: language is the meaningful proper, and action is the 'other.'

Beyond semionarratology, there are other sociologies that are not oblivious to language (Schütz, for instance, introduces language when action turns into a type of action within the life world). That said, nowhere else has every single aspect of meaning been deduced so uncompromisingly from the sole form of language. At this stage there is no deduction of what the social reality must be. In semionarratology, much as with the structuralist model, language predetermines the framework of what meaningful behaviour can possibly be; linguistic structure then determines language. The only requirement is the capacity to be narrated – that is, textuality. It would be wrong to surmise that narration is a confinement narrower than rationality in sociological action theories. Quite the contrary – it widens considerably the field of the possible or the feasible. In traditional action theories, actions count as rational if, in their purposiveness, they are orientated towards the marginal utility of economic action. Everything beneath that threshold is irrational or less means–end rational (see Joas 1999, 291ff).

All 'comprehending' sociologies share action as explanatory device; pragmatism, phenomenology, and structuralist semionarratology do *not* use this core concept in a univocal sense. Semionarratology rescinds from action all points of reference in reality and only admits language. It is possible to act, just as it is possible to form sentences; sentences require linguistic rules solely in order to function properly. The problem of meaningless enunciations does not even surface, because such sentences are never needed. Through meaningless sentences, no enunciation can establish the basis of all narrativity, the *contrat fiduciaire*[6] with its two illusions, the *illusion énonciative* and the truth-telling *illusion référentielle* (under «*carré de véridiction*»). This corresponds perfectly to what Deleuze has shown to be the 'primacy of praxis' before the formal structure in structuralism (cf. Deleuze 1973). What is enunciated in a society as praxis also must bring forth veridicality or truth telling; otherwise it cannot function.

Belief formation has traditionally been the domain of media effects theory, which is derived largely from social psychology. Compared to the effects in this definition, such a research agenda appears as a totally different problem in semionarratological communication sciences, liberated as it is from reality constraints. Now it can no longer select raw reality as its 'other,' as traditional media effects research does. There a communicator and audience research come together in the 'text' itself and in the fiduciary contract. Furthermore, polysemy, the diversity of reading modes in media recipients, is meant as a principle,[7] for the instance of enunciation can endow the text with textual ambivalence, which it is possible to investigate directly at the source itself. Even so, it is possible to glean this effect also from an empirical audience; but this is not the best way, and from a semionarratological perspective it is not necessary to find the reasons for these alternative readings, since they are contained in the text.[8]

All methods that trace their history back to structuralism can easily be charged with being anti- or at least non-empirical. In fact, here it is impossible to ignore the contribution of theory. Methods that declare themselves empirical hide their theory behind the null hypothesis. This is not the place to review and debate theories of science; but as far as social science methods are concerned, we are safe in saying that much. No serious and informed participant in that debate today argues that social science theories are exclusively or even mainly supported by or founded solely on data. That said, once we admit that pragmatic criteria lie behind the choice of a theory, there looms the danger of infinite regress or arbitrary choice (cf. Hesse 1978). Structural, semiological theories, instead, openly declare their claims to universal meaning. As a consequence, their science-theoretical claims, as special cases of meaning in general, can only be appreciated from within this framework. Deleuze (1973), however, has shown how problematic this is and rightly identifies transcendentalist presuppositions in structuralism, the openly adopted basis of which is the radical concept of meaning as binary differentiation: meaningful is whatever is different. In reality, meaning is held together by a third vanishing point, which is no longer meaning-full and in which all differences are one. Deleuze calls this the difference-less *objet X*, Mana, Phallus, that is, the ultimate system without a further environment as difference.

If semiology were to reflect on its ultimate presupposition, it might become aware of the triadic (i.e., not really binary) nature of its meaning-generating relations. Deleuze alluded to the triad but did not draw any logical conclusions from it. Peirce, however, long ago placed the triad at the centre of his semiotic, having deduced this centrality from more fundamental general facts. But difference is not lost in the triadic mediation, where it remains as the basis of critical comparison. It is not without reason that the Third Correlate in Peirce's sign function is called the Interpretant, which means that a difference's (dyad's) Interpretation (triad) produces something new, that is, more general; but though new, it is derived from the comparison itself. Semionarratology does not logically reflect this; here generativism in a sense takes the functional role of a triad and of generality.[9]

Semiology, though it functions solely in terms of structuralist ontology, accurately accounts for the sign nature of language. As theory it is so designed that it is a sensible choice for turning language into an object proper. Peirce had earlier achieved the same (but better, as we shall see) result in a quite different manner with his first sign trichotomy (Qualisign, Sinsign, Legisign). From this perspective, the purely differential treatment of the linguistic object was infelicitous. In defence of semiology, it may be that pure differentiality originally served the functional purpose of preventing contamination by extralinguistic reality and translinguistic mentalism. Syntax is also reductively conceived as a serial axis of elements. Not surprisingly, semionarratology explicitly attempts to underpin syntax with predication logic (Greimas 1970b). Typical of semionarratology, this is realized through levels of depth. Supposedly, this generativism explicates the syntactically binding forces through pure difference, or at least difference that is as pure as possible, because only superficially can the syntagmatic structure of meaning be deduced from the structure of sentences. Indeed, on the deepest level, at least three binary differences explain the propositional structure. First, *phoria* is differentiated into dysphoria and euphoria (explaining the basic impulse to act). Second, enunciates are differentiated into those of being and those of doing (in both cases, disjunctive or conjunctive object possession by a subject: grammatical and pragmatic subject are identified). Third, the double differentiated modalities of doing and of being (Greimas 1970b, 1983b) are comparable to modal verbs, which subject merely hypotactical sentences to further differential conditions. The deepest of these conditions are thought of as anthropological constants, expressed as *phoria*, and realization levels of action, starting from virtuality to actuality.

Peircean semiotic is capable of passing from the sign to behaviour. It cannot and need not eliminate anything that semiology isolates owing to the purity of the linguistic object. Being is relational, not a being-in-itself (either as *Ding an sich* or as *a priori* judgments), and this logical relationality becomes real in cognitive conduct. It follows that being is always *cognized* being (because it is meaningless to address being before its being-cognized) and thus relational being.

2.3 Publicity and Meaning as Subsistence

There is a second class or method for achieving a theoretical grasp of the intangibility of meaning. It also works with levels, but the relationship between those levels is different in nature from the *simulacrum*. Here, the subject is meaning proper *vis-à-vis* derived; the higher level in this relation we can call – in a somewhat diffuse sense – subsistence.[10] Public meaning, publicity, is still no object 'proper' and can be analysed only with the help of its determinate other. Now the point of comparison arises from an origin of meaning, instead of from identifying and describing the other of publicity in the differentiality of language, or in the system. As figure of thought, 'origin' implies a meaning-substance, as it were, meaning *in se*, almost as an *ens realissimum*. All concrete, actually changing meaning relates to its origin as its unchangeable ground (Aristotle, Cat. 3b16, might call this ὑποκείμενον). Through meaning *in se*, public meaning is now classified as *accidens* of a substance, and this constitutes its explanation.

Meaning overarches everything; furthermore, it is *in* everything, in a certain way. However, could this being-in be (known) as substance? Assuming that such meaning *in se* is knowable (each theory has its own unique way of revealing it), the only relevant question is how to present actual meaning as it is used. Meaning *in se* is viable as an explanation of actually used meaning if a theory has no other way of explaining the sudden appearance of meaning. How, then, does meaning appear – that is, become public and communicable? Figures of substance thought are much more traditional than thinking in *simulacra*, prevailing more in ontological contexts of being and its changeability. Idealism, the zenith of this figure, brings it into the context of the Subject, the absolute I. In the wake of the linguistic turn, however, the absolute I yields in many various ways to the collective I (if one can say this). Peirce argued that meaning *in se* as collective I exists just as little as the *Ding an sich*, because it cannot be experienced. No one doubts, however, that the manifold of the meaningful indeed exists. In terms of public opinion, this figure turns it into a sort of opinion *in se*, as it evidently does not coincide with subjective opinion. But how can it be shown that it is more than this? For this, substance affords thinking 'derivation,' in that thinking of something as derived refers back to (or indicates) its absolute point of reference, and, staying within this image, 'indication' can operate to diverse vanishing points. Of what kind that 'indication' establishes its indicative relation, then, differentiates among various theories.

The meaning-creating relation to meaning *in se* – or, in this context, to authentic meaning – is present in an especially marked version of a tradition of thought. It shows its effects in the social sciences even in the postmodernist vein. Adorno (1964) gave it the notorious *epitheton ornans* 'jargon of authenticity' (*Jargon der Eigentlichkeit*): theory inspired by Heideggerian existentialism. By necessity, this figure of thought had a strong influence on the question of meaning and could not fail to have one also on the production of public meaning (as mentioned, in passing, above). Ricoeur's narratology stands vicariously for this type of theory, where the ground for the possibility of all common experience lies in the fact that 'all' is in time and in the context of time. Ricoeur derives all publicity from authenticity; most authentic of all, however, is 'originary' time, the time of existence, which has its origin as a whole one from death. Death is common to all, but despite being authentic time, it is still only mine (*je meinig*), and as a consequence is not narratable.[11]

The originary mode of sociality is the 'being-with,' an originary given. An adumbration of this originary being-with can be spotted in Schütz's 'unquestioned horizon of the life world,'[12] where meaning *in toto* is also present in an ungraspable form in the form of an in-between. Often this term becomes inflationarily connected with constructivism, because via the Schütz link and his integration of Mead, it has finally landed with Berger and Luckmann, who titled their book precisely 'social construction' (Berger and Luckmann 1967). However, this cannot be compared to the radical constructivism that is endemic in the systems theory orbit. The epistemological and ontological premises here are quite different. In this sense, Schütz's social phenomenology is not constructivist – though it is true that it remains firmly anchored in the philosophy of consciousness[13] with its attempt to comprehend communication as a medium of meaning. Before every content of consciousness comes the unthematic unquestioned life world (the Husserlian sense of this concept has already been discussed), which must be a common one. Schütz and Luckmann (1975, 137) comprehend this as the totality of knowledge supply, which determines a non-problematic social universe of action.

The bridge to the other, however, is not easy to construct, in keeping with the Heideggerian relation between the authentic and the vulgar.

In Ricoeur's narratology, the public temporality of narration had to imitate or replicate the authentic originary time of the *Dasein*. In Schütz, who wis not a Heideggerian, this bridge functions only by means of an auxiliary construction. Despite his reputation as the father of the sociological concept of life world, there can be no doubt how much he still owes to Weber's conceptual apparatus, such as means–end and rationality. In his 1932 work *Der sinnhafte Aufbau* (Schütz et al. 2003, II), it is rationality, not subjectively constituted meaning, that is the real communicative bridge between subjects who are methodologically solitary and isolated (regarding this point, subjective meaning is similar to Heidegger's 'always already mine' Dasein-towards-death). Actions can be coordinated only because and inasmuch as they are rational. However, this should postulate a foundation of meaning beyond subjectivity and (following Weber) not lean on any objective gauge against the experienced world. While world views (*Weltbilder*) are the unavoidable end result of this idealistic pragmatism, it is precisely because of the pluralism of world views that they do not qualify as suitable for substantial orientation. Rationality is the desubstantialized orientation for action, the pure form of a pragmatic reason, which as this *a priori* form provides connection among subjects. For this reason alone, there is no threat to theory in a decomposition of formerly compact world views in modernity. Quite the contrary, one could say that the 'irrationally' metaphysical world view in the singular – precisely because it was holistically religious – would not have allowed for any theory at all. Indeed, here the one world and the one legitimate regulation of actions constitute the totality of the theoretical. Simmel later drove this pragmatic social apriorism even farther, to the stage of the Social Form of socialization (*Vergesellschaftung*).

Evidently, this social idealism is incompatible with Pragmaticist realism. The contrast between these truly alternative programs of theorizing is even more explicit for the Pragmaticist scientific method proper. Its consequences were formulated by Peirce in his first article series on pragmatism in *Popular Science Monthly*. Only if we can still conceptualize the social without resorting to a Weberian desubstantialized acting in the pure form of rationality can we expect radically new perspectives for communication. This liberates intersubjectivity from two vicious alternatives, apriorism and convention. Luhmann's (1997, Bd 2) media theory shows clearly how onerous it can be – and how conspicuous the theory effort – to coordinate the acting of singular actors (respectively subjectivities) through sheer convention.

Simmel's social form is, in a certain way, an empty formula of social meaning *in se*. The generality of the social has its real presence in the individual subject. This is how Simmel answers the problem of the mode of existence of society. Society, then, is not a reality *sui generis* but a psychological state, a social form of the individual psyche. When transferred to the realm of what appears to be re-enactable psychologically, in the main the costs must be met by reflection. In this realm, the thorny question remains without a satisfactory answer: From where does this social form come? To whom is it owed? But for the social sciences, the convenience of being psychologically enactable insight from an agent's perspective comes at a cost: sociology in general becomes a form, an empty custom of perception.

Psychology continues to be attractive because it seems to be a sensible correction for problematic theorems. For Joußen (1990) a rediscovery of the social form is of interest mainly as a means to overcome the drawbacks of media effects research. 'Mass' being the unquestioned fundamental assumption in this kind of research, it is criticized as a self-fulfilling prophecy. Joußen's critique relates to an empiricism that isolated individuals and from which conclusions regarding society as a whole were then drawn by extrapolating from methodological abstractions. Effects research is based on a *ceteris paribus* argument, and this theory design is unreflected. By contrast, social form could provide the advantage that it reflects sociality in the individual.[14] Being an idealist, Simmel has no need to start from the positive existence of the entity 'society' – as Durkheim had to attempt. The reason for this is that 'society' takes place, as socialization, in the individual subject itself. In this it is deeply indebted to the philosophy of consciousness. But how is socialization supposed to operate? Simmel resolves this problem of foundation in a mixed mode, not by means of transcendental philosophy but primarily through social psychology. In other words, in the first place it is 'the image which a man gains from another through personal contact.'[15] Since no one is capable of exploring the other to the fullest, all of us are for others only 'fragments of ourselves.' This makes the need for completion to the whole almost mandatory, but we are never whole 'purely and fully.' We can grasp others as types, but this involves simplifications. Simplified thus, we can possess ourselves as an identity across all the contingencies of communication situations. That is, then, our sociality, but a sociality that is first and foremost the presupposition of individuality. The I, thus being less, is more; it gains 'through the gaze of the other.' Simmel calls this 'reciprocal effect' (*Wechselwirkung*).

In its abstract form, this concept is nothing other than the social form. In this way, Simmel can avoid taking sides for the individual against society, or the reverse. Reciprocal effect also means that giving the form of the societal does not determine the individual totally, but that beyond the social 'there still is something' ('*noch etwas ist*'; Simmel 1968, 26).

When we ask what exactly 'whole,' 'type,' 'reciprocal effect,' 'social form' are supposed to be, apart from their pseudo-cognitive function, we encounter distinctly Kantian ideas. Categorical-schematic concepts, *a priori* judgments, can never result from experience but must be in effect before any experience can take place; this means that a social *a priori* must be postulated, for only in this manner can the social become experience. Contrary to Kant, for Simmel this *a priori* can no longer be a category. He can only grasp it as a deficit of another, authentic experience – also referred to as the 'barter form' of the exchange value in its total monetary abstraction form. This allows us to refer to Simmel's theory of social meaning as a form of subsistence, even though the *explanans* is ultimately an empty form.

Habermas's theory of social meaning is also built on a reference to an Other of sorts. He discovers a reference to Reason in all human aspects, from reality to identity. In this understanding, media publicity constitutes systems constraints that confine what was a form of an originally free communication. Absent such constraints, free communication is capable of discursively satisfying three rational validity claims. But what, substantially, is validity? This fundamental question concerns Habermas's highly 'fundamental pragmatic' approach, to which we will return. To claim validities we must communicate in always different ways – that is, in ways distinguishable in their form of appealing to their respective rationalities. From these different forms of appeal, Habermas infers a difference in nature, multiplying the one *ratio* into many rationalities, which compete among themselves. This plurality is reducible to one common vantage point of meaning. In a formal, not-substantial way, meaning can be turned into discourse. A discursively describing system requires a relatively higher validity compared to the described world view. Whereas the highest validity is the competence of the Ideal Speech Situation itself, such procedure constitutes meaning *in se*, but only in procedural form. In its ideality it must be valid universally, of course (cf. Gerhardt 1979). These critical remarks are not merely philosophical ruminations on Habermas's *Fundamentalpragmatik*. They have strongly practical bearings on foundational debates in ethnography, which still have repercussions for certain theoretical aspects of ethnomethodology.

In social and communication sciences, Habermas is known mostly for his critical appeal, and much less for his ideal formalism. Though everything comes in the form of (coming to an) agreement, and not as being, agreement must still be reducible to validities capable of being negated in a clear and unambiguous way. Critical theory does not presume, however, that all of this takes place in normal everyday actions, because in this realm the unquestionable horizon of the life world prevails. Still, sectors of this horizon of meaning should provide the capacity for critically reconstruction. At a minimum, this would serve to prevent meaning bacchanals in the style of Baudrillard's postmodern media world, but also, on the other side, systems theory's restrictive corset of media functionalism.

Critical theory is critical insofar as it dissects the uncritical life world handed down from Schütz into strands of logic amenable to critical examination and, pragmatically, into action types. These untainted types contrast with the types alienated through media, where corresponding rationalities are no longer valid without restrictions. Habermas's reconstruction efforts lead him to speech act theory and generally to a strong orientation towards language; this is what the 'linguistic turn' stands for in his theory. Claims to three validities, different in nature and supplemented by a fourth (or, better, a 'zeroth': validity of well-formedness), by and large lean on the three types of locutionary forces[16] in Austin's speech act theory. The first validity, corresponding to the locutionary speech act, refers to the objective world and claims truth. The second, in the illocutionary speech act, refers to norms and claims normativity. The third, which claims authenticity, in perlocution refers to the veracious expression of my interiority, to which privileged access is granted to no one except the subject itself.

Habermas's linguistic turn does not prevent him from being fascinated with functionalist media theories (cf. McCarthy 1991, 152–80). Much like Parsons and his concept of medium, Habermas conceives of media as degrading a genuine, albeit ideal, communication as it comes under the influence of system constraints. From Parsons's functionalist perspective, a medium has to meet two criteria (see Habermas 1981, II:395ff): it must be exchangeable in any quantity, and it must be storable and measurable. It is no surprise, then, that the medium *par excellence* is money. Habermas finds critique easier when he extends the medium concept to other social exchange functions. For instance, when the same three criteria are applied, the power medium, if it is meant to ascertain the function of exchange for a social system's goal attainment, quickly stumbles into the problem of how to legitimize that goal. It is even less evident that the medium of influence, serving the integration of society, can dispense with coming to an agreement that addresses all contingencies. *A fortiori*, this applies to the medium value commitment, serving for the maintenance of patterns in the subsystem culture. Unlike the idea of a medium, coming to an agreement must rely on language, the non-reducible medium of meaning. Agreements must also be capable of failing and therefore cannot be stored. In Habermas's view, this saves the identity and irreplaceable role of agreement, with language, within a common life world. Media, then, he can only relegate to the role of the system idea that constrains the genuine meaning process.

Habermas's Speech Act deductions are understandable in two ways. First of all, what is the nature of validities originating from the form of language? Second, what is their nature when they originate in the world that imposes its laws on action – under the premise of speech acts interpreted as conduct in language? At stake is a fundamental choice between nominalism and realism, not just an interpretation subtlety. Despite its apparent subtlety, this juncture is decisive for the kinds of problems in which a theory subsequently allows itself to become involved. Habermas, while protesting against consciousness philosophy, lets himself be drawn into the old way of posing the problem of dualism, by means of the 'linguistic turn.' According to that perspective, the problem still consists (reconstructively) in (the validity of) ideas about the world – their other, a dyadic relationship over a hiatus (cf. Ehrat 2007). The bridge is the language in which a society 'acts' its projects – almost an *ens mixtum*[17] of sorts. This task – here formulated in a deliberately simple way – is the latent foundation of the entire theory of critical reconstruction. We will see in the context of a Peircean Pragmaticism that this approach to posing the problem is a faulty one,[18] or at least one that does not impose itself naturally.

Is the bridge of language merely a remnant of Heidegger's concept of 'being-with'? Husserl, in his Fifth Cartesian Meditation, still had to struggle to grasp intersubjectivity. As discussed earlier, this vacillation raised doubts in Schütz as to whether one could simply presuppose that the meta-individual existed. In a more abstract form, the problem trickled down to radical constructivism and Luhmann's systems theory. In their answer, both had to quickly provide in their theory designs the means to allow systems to enter into contact with one another. In principle, this is impossible over systems boundaries unless there are provisions for it in both systems. For Habermas, in the life world (substantially understood), there exist simply meaning (not in Luhmann's sense of the term) and language, and these serve as the ultimate foundations for the questioning of single contents of meaning; otherwise, no communication whatsoever could function.[19] What Habermas calls his fundamental pragmatism, therefore, is not in a real foundational sense the foundation of a theory; rather, it merely reconstructs what is already a given.

In his contrived attempt to avoid metaphysical thinking, Habermas exposes himself to the opposite risk: that a discourse exists that reason regulates, free of domination, needs to be proven in the concrete meaningful practice of communication, in discursive practice. The problem, in other words, lies in the nature of discourse. Is it sheer ideality, close to Apel's transcendental pragmatism? Or is it a factual reality, albeit limited to a few sectors of the horizon of life world? At any rate, he needs to preclude any 'knowledge of the whole,' be it a philosophy-of-history knowledge or a metaphysical one. It has to be precluded that the concrete reasonability of a discursive situation is classified as knowing reason *in se* and as a whole. On the contrary, communication (this empirical, historical social practice) must show autonomously which *telos* or goal it operates according to; otherwise it could not operate at all. Communicating, one presupposes to operate by following an idea of a purpose, according to its own ideality, and Habermas thinks this idea of a purpose can be deduced from the propositional form of empirical language. The argument infers from the linguistic rule to the regulation of language users. Expressed as counterfactual conditionals, propositional claims could not be utilized intersubjectively unless they were, in fact, grounding language. Even when it includes instrumental misuse in strategic communication[20] still presupposes the functioning of validity claims.

Despite this appearance of realism, teleological idealities that called for a quite different justification found their way, surreptitiously and latently, into the core of Habermas's system. It is evident in itself that reason inscribed in language is not always non-contradictory. Nonstandardized prescientific language is notorious for its ambiguities and contradictions. Moreover, there exist a plethora of culturally determined world views that can only manifest themselves in language and that follow quite diverse rationalities. Upstream of the analytically descriptive, one must find a way in which such world view–based language systems – and all are like this to a certain degree – can communicate with one another. Unless one wanted to postulate a bit naively a unified rationality, and thus were compelled to range cultures other than one's own as being more primitive (as happened in ethnology), a mere side-by-side comparison would be unsatisfactory – indeed, it would constitute a philosophical problem of how the limits of understanding can be grasped conceptually. The simplest solution remains to adhere to the principle of the universality of cognition and comprehension. Habermas, however, burdens himself with an additional onus. He bars himself from deducing universal comprehensibility as reasonable, on the grounds of the supposedly inevitable consequence that this must lead to metaphysical or at least aprioristic thought.

In spite of that precaution, such thoughts do indeed exist in his reconstructivism. As a first step, comprehension becomes agreement. This means the 'communicative liquefaction' (*kommunikative Verflüssigung*) of comprehension. Language remains the horizon that is in principle insurmountable in any reconstructive explanation of communication. Selectively, single debatable sections of that horizon can be delinked for the purpose of coming to a communicative agreement. The result, then, must be the ideal speech situation of a domination-free discourse. Unless this condition is met, the force of the better argument cannot prevail (cf. Habermas 1981, I:88). This comparativization of the argument contains Habermas's metaphysic *in nuce*. This is shown clearly from an analysis of how he (Habermas 1981, 45ff) adapts his source, Toulmin (Toulmin, Janik, and Rieke 1979), in this central question: How and where does a better argument originate, and how is it compellingly recognized as such? With Toulmin (1969), Habermas maintains:

a) There are rationalities only in the plural, and these exist exclusively in a historical and social form.
b) Through this concession, one can avoid, perhaps in the sense of an objective idealism, assuming one universal and total spirit.
c) Which rationalities there are is in the competence of a society. Institutions, too, can admit only certain reasons that in their context are rational and can ban all other reasons from their discourses. This effectively extends communicability by means of better arguments to rationalities that are constituted institutionally and that are potentially contradictory, within one society.
d) An argument is better or worse only in the context of the cognitive efforts of such institutions.

So far, this is no concession to, or admission of, autarkic relativistic rationalities. For this reason, one must explain why scientific rationalities are subject to the fruitful crises into which they are thrown from outside – that is, from a different rationality. This makes dialogue possible both in between and obliquely to rationalities. A collective enterprise of reasonability for humankind in its entirety must thus be presupposed. Within this global framework of reasonable argumentation, there are arguments that serve the global purpose and there are arguments that do a disservice to it. At this point Habermas has caught up with one central aspect of Pragmaticism – but without the realist component that was so central to Peirce. Habermas is thus unable to follow Peirce in ground-laying argumentations that justify his system further (such as phaneroscopy or the normative sciences), let alone to follow him in the 'Pragmaticist hope' (see §3.2). More is needed than simply to maintain that the global enterprise of reasonability exists. This includes the implication of reason in the comparative, and thus of a purpose worthy of the argument. Nevertheless, there is no reason to suppose that searching for this foundation has forcibly pushed Habermas into the Charybdis of metaphysic – were he to think in a semiotic framework. From semiotic a metaphysic can certainly be deduced – but not as the First Science.

The Pragmaticism of the late Peirce (especially)[21] could have constituted a non-apriorist justification. Habermas avoids precisely this kind of argumentation as much as Toulmin does. In its stead, he opts directly for an axiomatic basis of the production mode of such a global reasonability. The '3 Ps' – product (the argument), process, and procedure – are supposed to 'deliver' the consent of a universal audience for the purpose of helping it adopt the 'impartial standpoint of the reasonable judgement.' Again, this universal audience reminds us somewhat of (Apel's and) Peirce's *consensus catholicus* (Peirce, CP 8.13). Yet Peirce is fully aware that this global consent is factually unreachable. It cannot, therefore, be used as the adequate criterion for a concrete sublunary true cognitive conduct. Peirce does not claim to know anticipatively the ultimate adequate opinion. One reaches merely as far as the mechanic blueprint of the truth of true cognition, without ever being able to predetermine its contents. When Habermas examines the 3 Ps from the perspective of establishing criteria, he conceptualizes the last two of the Ps, in the main, as types of social or communicative behaviour, which condense into types of assertion forms (or, classically, into dialectic).

What hinders Habermas's fundamental pragmatism, in principle, from becoming a semiotic Pragmaticism? In the last resort, his dualism stands in the way of a triadic Pragmaticism such as Peirce's. Still underlying all his speech analytical and linguistic pragmatic endeavours is mind–matter dualism (or language – three universes) – a theory of society that reckons with reason (and that does not throw it overboard, as Luhmann does in favour of self-regulating systems). Nevertheless, Habermas cannot escape the Scylla of crude realism and the Charybdis of metaphysic or even a Hegelianizing philosophy of history. The procedural, his *trouvaille*, continues to rely on a quasi-metaphysic. Habermas has denucleated the substance down to the procedural; nevertheless, the relation to rationality remains a kind of subsistence.

Mead's theory of generalization also appears to be procedure – at least superficially. Yet in the same way, one could interpret it as a mirror of Simmel's restitution of the whole (*Ergänzung; see above*). A number of colligations to the Chicago School would favour such an interpretation, most directly through Robert Ezra Park's studies with Simmel. Both glances, however, are deceptive. A Peircean heritage really does pierce Mead's generalization – the 'generalized other' – mediated by Mead's teacher and colleague, Dewey. Mead, however, no longer formulates the problem in a semiotic key; he prefers the problem context of understanding the past and otherness. Instead of treating interpretation as prejudgment, as hermeneutics does, it is more adequate, historically and materially, to explain Mead in terms of his origins in pragmatism. For this reason, despite all the similarities, understanding in Mead is not a 'fusion of horizons' of two subjects as Gadamer conceives of it. Mead is ultimately not interested in the 'divinatory,' and therefore psychological, unification of one's own with an outside subjectivity.

It is interesting that for Mead, as much as for Simmel and Weber,[22] the problem of understanding the past is almost interchangeable with the other problem of understanding an alter ego. Clearly, this involves a kind of abstraction. For Weber, the particularity of the event is derived from, and tributary to, a generalizing comparison with 'what could also have been different.' Simmel abstracts the alter ego into a social transcendentalism of the form in order to render it understandable and communicable. Since entering into interaction with the other individual is not sociology's purpose in understanding the alter ego, the proper form of abstraction is that of an 'action *in se*,' which intends, therefore, the general – that is, the frame within which it is possible to act. An understanding of the general of action is therefore also a precondition of a historical understanding of the acted, or past action.

2.4 Semiotic as Theory of Formal and Concrete Meaning

The two figures of otherness, simulacrum and substance, cannot be the only conceptions of meaning, communicable and public. Somehow, the two need to be unified. It is not by chance that there are representatives of both approaches who resort to Peirce to various degrees, as authority or as resource. As a thorough realist, however, Peirce takes all his 'validity claims' from experience. This sort of realism has the potential to spoil the 'doctrine' of both figures of thought. Realism would not fit where *simulacrum* theories turn into mere formalism, and subsistence theories risk metaphysical assumptions. With semiotic Pragmaticism, a third element enters into the equation – raw reality, which is not there because the real world is there, but to serve as a corrective to the cognitive process. But where and how can cognition integrate raw reality? This question arises only in a realist context; and none of the theories discussed above – for their respective reasons – has tried to answer it, let alone succeeded. Being subject to, and capable of, experience is a methodological quality that is especially useful for the subject of public opinion. Among other reasons, it allows the inclusion of an actor's perspective into the method itself. Absent the actor, it is almost unavoidable that publicity will be taken as merely a transcendental concept – one without any cognitive value. Such a reduction in semiotic Pragmaticism is, however, rejected as a principle, for every sign usage contains a relation of continuity both with the general and with the possible. We will follow this thread in the following discussion, but not before picking up the fruits of the two methods: *simulacrum* and subsistence.

Our object itself is – we have found – an 'other' observable only in or at the non-other. This contrasts sharply with the natural observational attitude towards objects, which appear to be within direct grasp. The diverse nature of being object has far-reaching practical consequences for cognition; this in turn means that objectiveness can be generalized as a method for cognitive appropriation. These figures of being object thus correspond to two fundamentally different methods: descriptive (or historiographical), and formal. As what, how, and where are media phenomena observable? If the medium one can see with one's eyes is not the object one is looking for – if, rather, this object is merely somehow *expressed* by the medium – then we need a method of indirect observation. In a communication science framework, a *simulacrum* aims to obtain the general (cognition) by observing the historically contingent (e.g., television practice). To prevent arbitrariness, furthermore, it must aim to make this cognitive object falsifiable, if possible by the same method. These combined requirements are unthinkable without first assuming meaning as unquestionable and, more important, without formalizing meaning as an object in a way that makes it reproducible.[23] Whoever conceptualizes meaning must mean the *form* of meaning, and not its individual use – or even the sum total of all individual uses. This insight is in principle shared by semiology and semiotic, even if they draw radically different consequences from it. The central definition of the sign is its expression, on which all else hinges.

Why does meaning need to be grasped formally? The answer: because of universality, which is possible only in this way. Before having any content at all, if communication is to be possible, meaning must be at everyone's disposal as a form of access to, and appropriation of, the world. Whether the form is necessarily that of language, as semiology claims, cannot be ascertained except on the basis of a comprehensive theory of signs (more about this later). For the time being, much can be gained for this problem's solution by assuming that meaning is present as form, and not as a psychological condition (which is the tendency in the phenomenological tradition of social sciences). Moreover, a derived condition is that forms of meaning differ in their nature in order to produce differences in meaning through the manipulation of the form.

But what is a form through which we can produce a meaning as content? Is form merely an oblique approach to breaking down reality into principles, ἔργον/*actus* and ἐνέργεια/*potentia*, μόφη/*forma* and ὕλη/*materia*? Form as an ontological concept cannot escape these questions, but we concern ourselves here with the form of meaning, not the form of being that would amount to a recasting of Aristotle's hylomorphist ontology. Meaning, as a concept, does not attempt to penetrate deeper than the phenomena. Without the intervention of cognition, it would not be capable of analysing being in itself. Meaning takes the world as it presents itself and does not strive for a world *in se*. And there is another decisive difference from ontological formalism: we can experience meaning only as the *concrete content* of meaning. The form of meaning therefore (only) abstracts from the content and is not an unexperienceable form before all actual being. Two established models exist for this abstraction: by means of units, and by means of the global. The former takes its approach 'from below,' that is, from the smallest units that are the lowest limit of making a meaningful difference. With the latter, meaning is deduced 'from above,' that is, from global forms that regulate every concrete meaning. Because inquiry into global forms cannot be a particular science, like linguistics or structural poetics, no (syntactic or semantic) units and combinatory rules are identifiable where meaning takes its form. At the highest level of abstraction, an abstract global form is the concept of triadic sign relation. Concrete global forms grow historically and culturally. While the sign relation and its classifications represent them abstractly from a logical perspective, they are contingent and not transcendental. Once they have come into existence, though, they impose a predetermination on any meaning that is within their sphere of influence. By their very nature, it is difficult to theoretically grasp global forms, unless one intends to indulge in philosophy of history. Languages in the sense of *langue* are also global forms of meaning, provided one takes them as a world view of a society. This has become customary in global abstraction, which – as a tradition in the philosophy of language – goes back to Herder, Franz Boas, and Weber, with ramifications down to Habermas. Language can mean a concrete world view – for example, the ancient world – but even in that world view is still a general form of meaning. A metaphorical term, world view (*Weltbild*), is then used to be given to this global form. However, it is through the idea, as form, that one can differentiate various heterogeneous world views. Without the form idea, one would see only confusingly incongruent realities, each owning its own world, observing its environment in its own way. But not even radical constructivism is as relativistic as this. By exchanging 'view' with form as the leading concept, however, one obtains the possibility of an inquiry upstream of contingent world views: the inquiry on global meaning in its construction principles. Semiotic is precisely that kind of abstraction that is interested in constructing meaning. The idea of mere world views, by contrast, leads no further than perspectives relative to collective subjects, a sort of collective subjectivism.

From a historical and cultural perspective, some of these global forms of meaning can become so self-evident that the impression of choice vanishes and one of straightforward predetermining imposition prevails. In language use, one still can and must choose words, but a cultural form appears to take away even that possibility; we are historically born into it. In the realm of such quasi-automatically predetermined meaning, choices with relevance to meaning are a possibility merely in principle – for instance, the decision to recognize money as money such that all things then have 'their value.'[24] Later in this text we will come to view public opinion as such a decision, one that is full of consequences and that has enormous relevance to meaning. The concept of form within the framework of a pragmatic theory of meaning will then allow us to distinguish public meaning from other forms of meaning, such as the meaning of a religious institution. Publicity is conceived as a global pre-form of (universal) meaning. It is, however, an already formed meaning, and not a transcendentalist meaning *in se* (everything is meaning and as a consequence, meaning becomes a non-discriminating concept). In addition, this meaning does not impose itself as strictly necessary. Once 'it' is there, however, everything is subject to the polarization schema that is typical of it. Thus polarized thus, for example, everything in religion becomes either public or private. 'Sin' becomes private, whereas 'dishonesty' is reserved for public figures in the hierarchy (a run-of-the-mill *topos* of critical journalism). In a positive key, 'irreproachable impeccability' (or the demonstrative exemplarity of spiritual roles) is also a public equivalent of non-sin. Generally, once public opinion has been etablished, demonstrated faith and private beliefs within one's interiority become imposing alternatives, among which religious institutions have to choose.[25]

How can abstract form and historical contingency coincide? Abstract and concrete meaning are not mutually exclusive. Both concepts are mutually conditional, a necessary division of labour. In the Pragmaticist-semiotic form, this division presents itself as two different problems. As an ultimate consequence, this question relates to normative sciences and the simple descriptive sciences – 'ideoscopy' in Peirce's terminology. Form, as logical abstraction, can only mean rule. If global form is understood as the rule, it is then possible to describe, as a concretion or application of the general rule, further historical constellations of meaning. In our subject matter, this leads to the discovery and description of two megaforms of meaning in their difference from each other: the megaform of public opinion, and the megaform of an absolute monarch's divine right. The two are still relatively abstract, but at the same time they are historically contingent. For their respective historical epochs, both forms are self-evident, but by the same token, each is incomprehensible in the other epoch. In Montesquieu the abyss between the two forms of power can still be felt (we will discuss this later in detail). If power and order do not originate directly in God, however, the locus of religious institutions must change radically.

The formal method constitutes the main difference between semiotic and rationality-oriented theories. If publicity can be analysed as the global meaning it is, then the methodological grasp of it becomes decisive. Semiotic is, of course, not the only contender, especially since

Habermas popularized a procedural rationality in the theory of publicity. Among other things, he used it to characterize negatively systemic constraints on media. The preconditions of this approach and its consequences for methodology have already been discussed; later we will show how much more fruitful than rationality is an approach based on signs.

In public opinion, too, global meaning on the highest cultural level owes itself to a textual operation. A handy comparison with novels suggests itself here. The fictional universe of a novel is in itself compact[26] and coherent and has a single plausibility. It leans on an explicit act of uncoupling. In certain theories of literature this universe 'between two interruptions of communication' (Weinrich) is connected with the enunciation. That operation separates the universe of the narrator ('commenting') from the narrative universe ('narrating'), which in turn is inspired by, and modelled after, Gadamer's 'aesthetic differentiation/ non-differentiation' in the play. Analogically, public opinion is conceivable as a universe. The peculiarity of this universe is, though, that it is more parallel than alternative: we do not have to decide whether to be submerged into the narrative world, as is the case with playing a game or reading a novel. The text 'publicity' is a treatment of meaning in parallel from two worlds that are isochronous to each other but at the same time separated by the virtual orchestra pit of the *theatrum mundi*. If the guiding concept were 'rationalities'[27] instead of universes, the relationship to the producing operation through uncoupling would be lost.

Drawing practical methodological consequences from our analysis of the objectness of public opinion, we can now postulate the base threshold below which the object itself is not grasped. A method commensurable with this phenomenon must satisfy at least three requirements: (1) that it not address public opinion as a phenomenon of nature without meaning but rather by methodologically valorizing its essence as one exclusively determined by meaning; (2) that it analyse meaning as form, and not merely describe it historically; and (3) that it determine form operationally through functions and rules (and not as gestalt or as a given). After the critique of certain run-of-the-mill methods in communication sciences and a discussion of possible other candidates, we must make our choice. Peirce's theory of signs (or, in his own terminology, Speculative [i.e., theoretical] Grammar) satisfies these requirements of method, which thus can also be called the 'semiotic method' in the social sciences. Other methods may suffice as well, but we will not pursue them further. We will further develop our own method of analysis, as semiotical, around the object of public opinion. While the semionarratological method has been used for this subject, there is an advantage to the semiotic method: it is capable of being both formal and empirical.

One might object that one cannot learn anything new, nor cognize anything empirical, from a formal method. True, the form itself is merely an abstraction. However, the situation is somewhat special for objects such as ours, which are not objects of experience. Indeed, with all pure products of meaning, all cognition is actually comprehension. This is possible only with the help of a type, the comprehension of the typical. It is also true that this sort of comprehension is never surprised by novel experience in such a way, or to such a degree, that its previous theory of social meaning must be reversed. However, 'empirical' studies – which have, to this point, been described as 'sociology of variables' or as the 'variable paradigm' (Abbott 1997, 1149 and passim)[28] – present their results customarily as (foreseeably) surprising results. Social meaning is always already comprehended; this is the precondition of its functioning. This fact, too, must become part and parcel of the method. Yet it also must keep open the ways in which new theoretical insights can develop.

In taking this objection seriously, the problem consists in the universal claim to a method in which everything is already foreseen, both in principle and speculatively. Now it becomes a decisive factor that this method is only formal. 'Speculative' does not mean that formal meaning is not full of surprises once it becomes concrete meaning. *Formal* means merely the producibility of meaning (which must, however, be possible in principle), but this meaning can then take any shape. Which concrete shape it takes in single instances can only be described – without, however, sacrificing on the altar of meaning-blind objectivity that in describing one has already understood this meaning. Rightly, then, this methodology has entered the mainstream of social and communication sciences to various degrees. To us it allows the formal analysis of public opinion, a quite determinate meaning, as it enters in a quite determinate meaning, in determinate relations.

3 Semiotic of Publicity

Publicity, which in today's communications debates is still entangled in contingencies of the early Habermasian 'public sphere' (Habermas 1962),[1] is far from being a clear research concept. It is now incumbent on Pragmaticism and semiotic not only to take it out of the specific Habermasian context, but also to offer a better understanding of meaning as public. With reference to our discussion of theories explaining publicity from different origins in meaning *in se*, semiotic straddles both classes of meaning theories. While the challenge of strong theories of meaning *in se* is accepted, semiotic has the potential to address as well concrete manifestations of meaning.

Choosing between (two evil alternatives) either strong or weak theories, this claim must sound ambivalent, as if it is a requirement somehow that the two types of theories be mutually exclusive. A strong theory, such as Luhmann's functionalism, requires an explanatory power of everything and depends for this on a handful of fundamental premises. Weak theories indulge in banal realism by supposing that society *tout court* is an external reality from which we are to wrest a number of regularities, from which the rule is then hypothetically drawn. Most empirical theories are weak in this sense. These theories do not pretend to grasp the complex meaning nature of society and pretend to be merely practically useful; not even taken together as a totality can they claim to be a theoretical insight into how society operates. Their disdain for 'grand theory' obfuscates the lack of grasp for the object's specificity by referring to its bland realism as 'mid-level theory.' Semiotic must disappoint both sides. In keeping with its critical realism, semiotic cannot engage in either/or – that is, either experience or generality. From a semiotic perspective, strong theories explain too much when they explain the totality of everything. Worse, such theories already know everything, which protects them effectively from any surprises (in this context we encounter 'system re-entry,' the mantra of Luhmann's systems theory). Weak theories, conversely, have abandoned their attempts to venture into real explanations. Instead they have opted to hide explanation behind generality as being of a different nature than factual truth or the mere facticity of empirical events. The 'covering theory' idea pretends that explanation arises from the facts 'as by itself,' as hypothesis. From there, however, it could not originate because facts are precisely mere raw reality. As a consequence, these magical explanations of facts originate from an unreflected 'sound' common sense. Genuine hypotheses – such as in laws of nature – do not obfuscate their law character as logical (i.e., not factual). As a consequence, the relation between generality and facticity begs for an explanation, through an elaborate process of reflection, and cannot simply be assumed (as in strong theories) or embezzled (as in empirical theories).

Our semiotic investigation of publicity proves the ambivalence from both sides. Empirical research, in the sense of Popper's positivistic critical rationalism (Adorno 1969; Adorno, Perrin, and Jarkko 2005), is emphatically oriented towards experimentation with partial problems such as investigative journalism, media scandals, 'moral panics,' public opinion surveys, and so forth. It regards our first step – comprehending publicity as a teleological type of meaning – as superfluous or even as a nonsensical problem of totality. But this does not lead to an essentialist theory of society as a totality, if we apply Peirce's Pragmatic Maxim. We will be discussing this relevant point later in terms of the fake totality of publicity's teleology, which must latently pretend to grasp 'all.' We will show the origin of the patterning of public meaning in ancient theatre, whose logic of literal drama was then reutilized in the judging of public performance by a freshly invented public opinion in the eighteenth century. This problem of social cognition on the basis of the totality of society will necessarily be revisited in the next chapter during a discussion of Luhmann's media theory.

The semiotic way of generalizing (for example) publicity is based on formal reflection on the interplay in cognition between generality and concrete experience. Society is no exceptional cognitive object. Regarding the concrete operation of public opining, the need for a social generality will be demonstrated. Unlike the conduct pragmatically analysed in other instances as cognitive behaviour, in the case of publicity we are concerned with the conduct of others. More precisely, it is *my* behaviour towards the behaviour of *others* – *my* interpretation, in other words – that imputes my own purpose vicariously.

Signs play a central role in the relation between generality and facticity. This is the crucial and differentiating contribution of semiotic to a science of the social. But this presupposes the achievement of a comprehensive concept of the sign. Thus it excludes the possibility that signs can be treated as if they are things (and therefore facts). Unfortunately, this is the practice of many so-called 'semiotic' methods in the social sciences.[2]

3.1 Publicity as Teleology

Teleology: this is how semiotic conceptualizes publicity comprehensively. Its entire point as a 'strong theory' is that semiotic lays its ground first of all in action, as conduct or behaviour.[3] But signs are not an afterthought of pragmatism; rather, they are a logically abstracted explication of a comprehensive concept of action. These *principia* do not correspond at all to 'action theories' as animadverted by Schwinn (1998), be it Parsons's voluntarism, or intentionality in phenomenological and hermeneutic theories, or the concept of agency (Loyal and Barnes 2001). Criticism directed against psychologism, against linguistic pragmatic, against concepts such as Danto's 'basic action,' and the like, do not concern a semiotic Pragmaticism and will not be discussed further. All of these theories bypass the idea of the mediation in signs – which is the very point of Pragmaticism – including the far-reaching consequences of that idea.

Semiotic of publicity describes the specific in being public. A theory of meaning *in se*, but also of reality, is the general task of sign theory ('Speculative Grammar'). Any meaning results from cognizing an object, as case of a generality, represented by a quality or attribute of something. Therefore it must comprehend a rule (necessity), a concrete occurrence (existence, also past and future), and a concrete (sensory or other) quality attributed to that object. These three factors differ logically and on that basis relate to one another in order to constitute together what cognitive conduct based on real experience means. For reality, as a cognized reality, this implies that there are three different modes of being, not just a single fact (existence). A mere fact could not be cognized. It follows that no form of sociality can be unimodal or plainly existent. It is crucial that the idea of modal being accord with diversified functioning in social forms (§4.3 below). From such a sign theory, modal metaphysics and further fundamental sciences can also be derived, but this has no bearing on the modal logic of sign relations.[4] Speculative Grammar, which is neither an experiential science nor a derivation of metaphysics, endeavours to deduce in pure theory from very basic abstract principles every possible kind of meaning. The result is a classification. These principles are not metaphysical but cognitive. Every act of cognition, though a unity, can be abstracted into three logical steps (De Tienne 1996) called categories, but these can also be grasped in the different ways in which everything presents itself before the mind: there are three different modes discernible in a science Peirce called phaneroscopy (of which the last step is also an abstraction of the observed). Based on this trimodality, signs classify in multiples of three categorial differences. Each specific sign class[5] is first classifiable into three trichotomies reflecting its categorial composition, then also reflecting its type of 'relationing' as categorically determined. This becomes crucial for concrete use of the sign; indeed, it represents a fourth, traversal trichotomy (cf. Pape 1986, 46-52), though Peirce himself laboured to integrate both classificatory schemes to his ends (Short 2007). That concrete usage is not just the province of Speculative Rhetoric ('there is a purely logical doctrine of how discovery must take place') (Peirce CP 2.107, 'Baldwin's Dictionary of Philosophy and Psychology. Logic'). As a class of the establishment of a relation between this sign user and this object, it is also a further determinant for meaning as the categorial composition of the sign's material, reality relation and its logical appeal.

Furthermore, sign use can be represented as a social practice, or as a linguistic mark, or as a theory of argumentation (rhetoric). This is far better than an individual practical search for meaning, for sign trichotomies are concerned only with purely logical essence. Though logic was the determining aspect of Peirce's own investigations in semiotic, the category of Secondness (or in pragmatic parlance: because of the genuineness of living doubt) is the cause for the fact that use is so decisive for meaning. All of this requires that the rules of use be an object of inquiry. But this does not amount to 'applied semiotics'; indeed, it is complete semiotic – not a genitive-semiotic of publicity, but the concretion of meaning. Peirce's very fundamental theories can only provide the instruments. Their model character, however, does not preclude semiotic descriptions of this sign use.

With regard to publicity, its teleology is a proof that such signs are always and exclusively used for scientific cognition. Scientific use is possible, as demonstrated by the sign class containing 'Argument' as one of its correlates. Nevertheless, sign use can, indeed must, terminate earlier – for example, when a pure statement of facts is concerned; *or,* one can use signs in such a way that they predetermine an argument. At such times they state the ultimate goal for argumentation without admitting any further development of the argument. We will discover in the discursive practice that is commonly summarized as 'public opinion' that there is predetermination of such a goal. In this case, determination by means of a sign class is, in fact, rigid – that is, either true or false as a bivalent dyadic fact.

Public opinion refers to a practice, conduct, or behaviour that procures legitimacy. As a larger class, legitimacy existed before the bourgeoisie invented public opinion under the historically contingent conditions of the nascent civil society, because any behaviour is legitimate for which the authority of a rule is claimed. One supposes for this rule, however, that it satisfies, and is worthy of, general acknowledgment and assent. According to this kind of supposition, one can deduce a schema of classes of legitimacy, with or without historical realization. Peirce attempted precisely this in his article series 'Illustrations of the Logic of Science' in *Popular Science Monthly,* which in 1877–8 presented pragmatism for the first time. Among his seminal topics in that series were the four different classes of authority used to establish belief in opinions and settle doubts (CP 5.377). This recurs, though, as the fundamental topic of method. Today the customary context of these questions would probably be a theory of truth, which unfortunately is conceived in the dualistic framework of how mental and mundane units can be brought to coincide. In Peirce, however, this justifies his fallibilism as the unavoidable consequence of the interminable process of cognition, see Ehrat (2007) in more detail.

Public opinion always includes a relationship to rule, but this does not mean that semiotic should comprehend it exclusively as what sociology groups under 'normative theories.' Everything counts as a normative theory that constrains unforeseeable empirical social facts into the straightjacket of norms and that deduces from those norms to a greater or lesser extent. As long as the origination of norms in processes remains open, a description in terms of argumentation theory recommends itself. For Peirce, this incidentally constitutes the essence of the 'method of science.' Other social philosophies, however, do not have a high regard for those theories that belong to 'normative theories.' The objection here is that they do not really reach the social reality (see Henderson 2002) and that they grasp merely a certain perspective of action – for example, as rationality. While this position undoubtedly has its merits, it really does not concern a realist philosophy such as the semiotic Pragmaticism.

How 'is' value to be understood? In what does its mode of existence consist, since it does not exist *per definitionem* but is upstream of all (action) as purpose? Implying much less than surmised (e.g., Luhmann 1997), theorizing value does not necessitate an ontology, metaphysical thought, or hierarchical social structure. The only basic assumption for grasping the mode of value is that action be an object of theory only insofar as it is controlled action – otherwise, not.[6] As only this action is subject to the order of meaning, it is controlled by signs – therefore not by determinations of anthropology, metaphysics, or philosophy of history, or even of philosophy of consciousness. For that reason, semiotic concerns itself with precisely three dimensions: (1) the next interpretation of (2) the fact of a sign becoming doubtful, which (3) stands in the continuum of a final causality[7] – and not effective causality – in a chain of interpretations tending towards an ideal final point. The latter is not an idealistic interpretation, but a world totally and adequately interpreted in the infinite community of scientists in a *consensus catholicus* (Peirce, CP 8.13) of opinion. This compact formula renders the whole idea of semiotic; and we will endeavour to explicate it by public opinion. A genuinely semiotic theory of society, in consequence, cannot understand signs as objects (which is unfortunately the case with many so-called semiotic approaches in the social sciences).

Thus, public opinion is a sign process – albeit a unique and highly complex one. Early on, Peirce concluded that there is 'no cognition but in signs' (C.P. 5.250–3 'Questions concerning certain Faculties Claimed for Man' 1868). The consequences of this tiny formula were radical, for they entailed an antitranscendental, radically fallibilistic epistemology. For its part, cognition is not confined to science. Nothing prevents anything that is meaningful from being represented semiotically. This explicitly includes what does not correspond to the 'method of science' (Peirce, CP 5.384) in the sense of Peirce's *Popular Science Monthly* article 'The Fixation of Belief.' The modes of argumentation as practised in public opinion correspond more to one of the 'medieval' methods that Peirce expounds in that article. Public opinion never pronounces judgments in the opiner's own name – and with proofs – but always in the name of a higher authority. To show this in detail will be the purpose of our analysis of mass media scandals (starting at §5.7). Even so, much can be anticipated here: the surplus value of a scandal over and above a judicial procedure is not constituted by the opinion of the journalist or of the editorial staff; it consists in the fact that one speaks in the name of the ethical sentiments of 'all.' Since no one else exists – except the accused – outside of 'all,' every other judgment is rendered impossible: the *volonté de tous* (minus 1) becomes the *volonté générale* (to reuse Rousseau's terminology). That this rhetorical strategy works is evident in repair and correction mechanisms, which set in when the strategy is in danger of collapsing. Then the hour of opinion polls has come. In the case of the *Boston Globe*, Church scandal turned more and more into advocative (or advocacy) journalism, which culminated in the journalists' open demand for the resignation of Boston's Cardinal (see §7.4).

How, then, is the sign applicable to a non-perfect cognitive conduct such as the 'method of authority'? Is it not an almost existential condition for sign processes that their interpretation never comes to an end?[8] Following Peirce's amusing commentaries on the method of authority (CP 5.380 'The Fixation of Belief'), the price for this violence from a 'central authority' (CP 1.60 'Lessons of the History of Science') is high in order that the progression of interpretation (i.e., of the doubt/belief cycle) be upheld. Regarding public opinion, while it is unable to uphold the moral, the 'spiral of silence,' or political correctness in the long run, the sign relation (or 'method') will nevertheless function (as long as it functions). Considering that a theory of reality is derivable from the sign process, instability also applies to such reality constructions. Presupposing such sign-reality, and its continuation of/in a theory of argumentation, habitual or even industrial patterns of argumentation can be described.

Correlating the nature of publicity with the method of authority might suggest cultural pessimism and a devaluation of mass media. In other words, it might seem to be a degradation phenomenon of what *in se* should be perfect. This kind of criticism is as old as the catchword 'sophism.' It was useful for the Platonist polemic, where sophism stood for a mere *doxa*[9] instead of for truth. Similarly, Aristotle discerns a difference between persuasion (τὸ πιθανόν) and logical truth. This, however, is not the place for a new round in this perpetual debate. Nor does Peirce venture into devaluating less-than-scientific cognition. Similarly, we will be trying to understand publicity without valuation, as a type of meaningful cognitive conduct. Now it is typical of this type that it succeeds in representing an object without turning it into an object of experience – that is, into raw and directly experienceable reality. When we observe our way of talking about publicity, it seems that we do not mean something existent, something that has a bivalent truth (i.e., true or false). On the contrary, public opinion is hardly equipped with the resistance of a real. It owes its entire existence solely to an effort of representation (which, however, can or cannot be). The two framework roles – source and target, *who* represents and *for whom* – are therefore always part and parcel of the meaning and can never be eliminated entirely from what is represented.[10]

3.2 Legitimacy

Representation of whom for whom – does that suffice? A specificity sufficient for either publicity or public opinion must include the purpose for which this practice is predetermined or preordained: representation is legitimizing. In practical terms, this entails representing in such a way that in a factual reality – which in itself has no purpose – a purpose is cognized. A purpose is never true or false, but always before or in the future (which can also be a future dated back to the past – what Schütz termed *modo futuri exacti*). In this manner, the *idea* of an action is laid over the factual. That superposition is not what the Pragmatic Maxim intends by the pragmatic idea, as a cognitive behaviour of anticipating all conceivable practical consequences;[11] rather, it is intended as knowledge of how an action would or should end. In a cognate manner, Weber's concept of means–end rationality (*Zweckrationalität*) treats actions serving an end as legitimate, and those that serve no end as hindrances.

Legitimization is, under various names, a central or even crucial topic in the social sciences. We might go so far as to maintain that it is next to impossible to cognize society without somehow taking the path of rules. Rules being the result of various types of causality, not every rule is an expression of a goal; but in the social realm the nature of the object suggests goal-rules. Since under sublunary circumstances no one is in possession of the end of society, representing the social as oriented towards a determinate end constitutes a dangerous venture. After the crumbling of insinuated universal acceptance, such an end leads back to its proponent. Which raises this question: Before whom is the proponent's goal legitimated, or *for* whom? In functionalism, the legitimization of one's ends is at the core of the theory problem. Since by definition no system is allowed to disturb the self-reference of its neighbouring systems, entering into (even 'cognitive') contact with them is a matter of making oneself legitimate in the observer's eyes.

Observing others, and making oneself observed by others in the most favourable light, is important in order to avoid mutual disturbances or even blockades. But in Pragmaticism there are no autopoietic systems that can only observe their own functions. Pragmaticism is a deeply 'interpretive' (or better, *understanding*) sociology. Incomprehensible actions can never turn into conduct. At best, they may remain the singular volitional manipulation of an object, or singular imaginative actions. The question 'Legitimate before whom?' is more concerned with an essential aspect of understanding than with the alter ego towards which it is directed, as systems theory understands it. Here, in the absence of a general legitimizing instance, any observer with relevance to a system's behaviour is as good as others. In Pragmaticism, however, the concern is not with selecting a determinate Other from among an arbitrary number of others, as the one that observes the system. Questions regarding 'before whom' one is legitimated can be answered only with an instance – that is, literally, 'standing before' a higher judge. The instance is different in nature from the factual event, because it can only be of a general nature, beyond the mere factual.

The practical consequences of this apparently philosophical analysis of meaning are enormous. Let us take public relations as an example. Some communication science scholars define PR as functional communication between social systems that operate exclusively within the parameters of their own unique criteria and that observe their own environment in the mode and to the extent to which they themselves allow (Hoffjann 2001). Only this makes it a problem of system survival to observe other systems in one's own environment and to legitimize one's system operations before the 'outsider' system so as to avoid obstructions and disturbances of communication. In themselves, however, systems do not see anything from the proper perception of an outsider system. They 'understand' with *their own* proper operations, and only those that in foreign systems connect with *their own* system operations. Thus each individual system has to present itself to others in such a way as to be recognizable – even though, from their own perspective, these are misrepresentations. It is not difficult to imagine what kind of Babel of languages looms here – or, respectively, what 'complexity' is growing here, which must be 'reduced' by a higher (emerging) system in order to escape extinction. For this purpose emerges the mass media system of public opinion, which communicates legitimacy only by reducing complexity. In their substance, these are all misrepresentations that have the functional purpose of legitimization. Conversely, when public opinion withdraws legitimacy in a scandal, this happens always for the wrong reasons (as seen from the perspective of the system at hand). This reduces everything to the problem of viable representation.

Pragmaticism, by contrast, assumes no principles that see communication as consisting of blockades or problems. There is no reason to axiomatically assume that blind (tautological or paradoxical) systems take the place of continuity of mind; there are no environments relative to the system that take the place of raw reality; no systems emerge that reduce complexity to take the place of a cognitive continuum of interpretation.[12] In the eyes of Pragmaticist realism, system theory constitutes merely the paroxysm of nominalism. In practical terms, system theory has itself created the problem that an unlimited number of legitimizations are required between all possible combinations among different systems. Similarly, its solution is relative to the problem that is generated, which is how to reduce this complexity of legitimization to the medium of public opinion.

Pragmaticism needs only a single legitimization of controlled behaviour. Is this reason enough to raise the metaphysical suspicion that this one control will have to converge at an apex that legitimizes all? Luhmann would probably suspect this of Peirce, and if Peirce were Hegel, this suspicion might have some foundation. Actually, Semiotic permits one 'apex' of the Interpretant in the sign relation at hand. A cognitive conduct is capable of cognizing only because it succeeds in linking a generality with the relation between the outsider's factual reality and the possible. This is the definition of the sign relation. Similarly, through this procedure conduct attains its rules – that is, for itself and for similar cases.

For this reason, we can dispense with the requirement that subjects justify themselves before other subjects – that is, justify their own actions against other actions. Every conduct always already – ideally – includes humanity in its synchronic and diachronic totality (as Peirce explained in The Fixation of Belief). It is within the power of every concretely used sign to determine how much generality will be included in the relation – though the sign can never completely exclude generality. But at the same time, it is quite difficult to use an Argument-sign (the highest class of signs) where a necessarily true and therefore maximally general interpretation is taking place. One opponent with one case to the contrary would suffice to make the interpretation of the proponent incomprehensible. The proverbially incontrovertible (as one might object) '2 + 2 = 4' is *not* a general cognition because it is not an experiential cognition but merely hypothetical thought. Where experience enters the relation, though, this sign would have to comprise the totality of all experiences and, in addition, the proof of its own completeness (which is impossible).

The converse attempt to exclude generality completely would not function. This is important for the practice of public opinion. Some postmodern theorists seem to advocate a certain playful arbitrariness, where any legitimization is futile. Much less radical, but also less playful, is what Schopenhauer expounds as 'eristic dialectic.'[13] For him there are undecidable questions regarding which the only important objective is to be right, or to prevail. The lineage from Schopenhauer to Nietzsche and postmodernism is totally non-Pragmaticist, for in a functioning sign relation one Correlate is the general one and interprets the other Correlates. Why does our experience dispose of a generality at all (for facts, as much as for quality) and not just of mere positivity or arbitrariness? Peirce plases 'general experience' on an continuum, which guarantees that there are no completely non-cognizable singularities and that everything is accessible to cognition. Proof of this assumption, the proof of Pragmaticism (Roberts 1981), is hardly a trivial matter – but this is not the place to demonstrate it. Let us merely note that this is the single most important difference between pragmatic Semiotic and all other theories of social meaning. From a semiotic perspective, then, if public opinion were indeed any sort of functional legitimization one chooses, it would be as inaccessible to comprehension as it is in structural functionalism.

Misak goes so far as to identify a democratic principle of truth in Pragmaticism, and she is certainly right. In Pragmaticism, one is limited to the experienceable and must do without transcendental *a priori* validity. The only alternative to transcendentalism is research, which is guided solely by the hope that in the end the opinion will adequate itself to the reality. 'All of this requires a kind of radical democracy in inquiry. The differences of inquirers – their different perspectives, sensibilities and experiences – must be taken seriously. If they are not, inquiry is not conducted and reaching the best or the true belief is not on the cards' (Misak 1994, 745). This free play of inquiry can no longer apply to public opinion, though, because here the 'method of authority' obtains as long as this sign relation functions as public, and not as scientific, opinion.

How can an opinion function that is under the constraint of publicity? If cognitive behaviour is orientated towards truth, and if all other methods must apply force or even violence, how can public opinion, as sign relation, maintain itself as meaning? How can it succeed (at least to a large extent) in taking the place of a truth equivalent? This reminds us of mass media criticism as a 'colonization of the life-world' (cf. Habermas 1981, II:489–547) and of similar efforts in cognitive stylization. Would the mentioned democracy not be able to achieve every sign as radically public (something that public opinion decidedly is not)? For this sign does not lean on a convention of a contingent group; rather, it relies on general logic that is transcultural and time-transcending. This is just the hope in the long run, and as an ideal named science, and obviously no one possesses as knowledge about future development what this hope aims at. With regard to single signs or interpretations, however, common sense is all there is in that semiosis.

Every sign is used in concrete contingent circumstances; this also applies to the cognitive behaviour of science – and *a fortiori* to public opinion. In the case of the latter, however, what happens is an outright regression. As an example, let us take science journalism, the closest cognate to science. Not merely a plain description that is within easy grasp, it actually transforms science into something about which everybody can and should have an opinion.[14] This opinion does not even have to cognize, since opining is not to be attained cognitively through a better interpretation of the same object. In semiotic, the meaning effects of opining publicly are reconstructable formally, since it is within the power of interpretation or sign relations either to 'degenerate' (which means to become a less complex relation) or to 'construct' (an increase in generality, or ampliative reasoning). What is here expressed in terms of the logic of relations appears in consciousness in various forms: as aestheticization (e.g., of language in lyrics), as symptomization[15] (this symptom is here in lieu of a general law), or as 'trace.' The direction of the 'next interpretation' is not determined in advance, nor is it foreseeable – unless it is already a 'practice.' Only use determines the meaning of a sign; and before concrete sign use, semiotic is not more than Speculative Grammar or a theory of any possible use.

Signs – more precisely, triadic sign relations – necessarily partake in meaningful action in the real world. Semiotic pragmatic highlights a crucial difference from a Habermasian turning of communication into language (*Versprachlichung*): conduct comes before language. Signs are not before language. When Habermas turns language into a substitute for a transcendental foundation of society, he effectively distances society from the realm of experience. Language then finds itself upstream of experience. With this, the contingent cultural and historical structures of natural languages assume the status of absolute validity of logic. Semiotic, on the other hand, is a general theory and classification of all possible sign relations (called either Speculative Grammar or Logic by Peirce). This allows us to theorize that 'symbols grow,' as Peirce states in his Grand Logic[16] (Peirce, CP 2.302). Perhaps the core of the problem with Habermas is not even so much in the 'linguistic turn,' which he merely re-enacts, but with 'fundamental pragmatic' itself – that is, how it reconstructs action in a dualistic way.[17]

3.3 Public Opinion as Historical-Cultural Role Relation

Public opinion is comprehensible once its teleological nature is recognized. This makes it a matter of logic, the basic component of meaning. Since there are many kinds of teleological meaning, however, from the idea of evolution to narration as such, public opinion needs first to be differentiated in terms of its specific characteristics.

Public opinion is a cultural invention that does not exist in all cultures. Where it does exist, strong variations are to be expected. In light of this, it is risky to speak univocally of public opinion, as if it were the same everywhere. The pitfalls of univocality are often encountered in the social sciences. One such relates to the debate over development or modernization (vilified as *'desarrollismo'*). A study concerning African societies found that this desire to create public opinion overlooked that introducing modern media artificially from outside created disturbances in this society's entire system of communication, with falsifying effects (West and Fair 1993). Unfortunately, this debate has been largely ignored by scholars of intercultural communication. This discipline tends to reduce the problem to manageable person-to-person interactions and to delegate the wide cultural framework of all interaction to other disciplines.

Because of how its cultural and historical form has developed, public opinion can only partly be explained through logic; the rest must be described. The logical scaffolding, which also serves public opinion in the particular historical and cultural context of its invention, has generally been seen in a strong, if not exclusive, relationship with power and its rules. This mainly (i.e., not exclusively) means political power. Yet when we analyse this logical scaffolding in isolation, we notice that its suitability is much more universal than that – public opinion does more than legitimate political power. This presupposes, however, that the scholarship on public opinion has not been left to political scientists and social historians; Herbst (1993) has complained that it has been. Our approach to this contingent phenomenon is to connect history with logic. With his habilitation thesis, Habermas (1962) blazed a trail in this field. However, this approach needs to become considerably broader so that it transcends culture. We still lack thorough and comprehensive analyses of home-grown equivalents to modern European public opinion in other cultural spaces and historical epochs. The 'anthropology' of power relations – that is, how Islamic, African, and Oriental cultures organize the legitimization of their power relations and processes, both logically and in terms of role distributions – has still to be investigated thoroughly (but see (Bratton 2003; Cherribi 2006; Gibreel 2001; Grant and Tessler 2002; Koker 2004; Mujani and Liddle 2004; Salvatore and Levine 2005; Voigt 2005).

Time and again, as we have seen, public opinion has been linked with rhetoric (Daniel 2002). In the Occidental cultural space, there are strong historical indications of this: all higher Roman magistrates were required to have studied rhetoric (the word 'academy' has its root in Plato's school in the Akademeia grove outside Athens, where the the 'mathematically impaired' were enjoined by a sign over the entrance: Ἀγεωμέτρητος μηδεὶς εἰσίτω; for 600 years this was the cradle of all modern universities). Now, rhetoric does not mean 'figures' (as per Quintilian's treatise); primarily, it is a determinate practice. As a practice, it focuses on the distribution of power, not its legitimization. Since power was distributed by rhetorical rather than forcible means, it became the dominion of a unique legitimation logic. The absolute monarchs heaped all power upon themselves in order to legitimate it. Yet they still required an ideological apparatus, be it divinity (of Roman Emperors), investiture, divine right, or a constitution. The display of monarchic power and might can be described as permanent rhetoric. For instance, the rhetoric of the Imperial, Royal, or Pontifical' court ceremonial guarantees that power will always be concentrated in a monarchic fashion. Modernity, though, cannot content itself with rhetoric. It has instituted an extension to the power rhetoric in the form of permanent tribunals. For rhetoric, ultimately, a single opponent can suffice – especially for the eristic dialectic, where the whole point is to be right *per fas et nefas*. With the tribunal, however, over and above opposition accedes a third instance of judging and sanctioning. Even though teleology serves both rhetoric and tribunal, the resulting cultural and historical forms developed in different directions.

Every culture possesses ancient rites for distributing power (and these rites encompass tribunals, and also those before whom power must legitimate itself). In European antiquity, tribunals became increasingly (though not totally) differentiated from parliaments (the modern term for βουλή council, *consulta*, etc., even though the *comitia tribunalia* were just the other wing of the Roman judicial–parliamentary system, alongside the *Senatus*). This differentiation, however, was never quite clean; for instance, the patrician Roman Senate retained its jurisdiction over patricians. There are older models even for the tribune, whose competence it was to adjudicate legal affairs for his *tribus*, which later, in the course of Roman republican history, occurred in the first forms of positively codified law. In the context of the Roman cultural sphere, these models included the very ancient practice of divine ordeal, for whose various forms there existed particular types of priesthood (e.g., *haruspex*, *augur*) with somewhat obscure ritual bases.

Theatre was among the most ancient tribunal rites in the Athenian cultural sphere. Its origins seem to have been connected with a certain type of blood justice (*ius gladii*, *Blutgericht*) in the name of the god Dionysus. Theatre developed its form within the framework of the religious festival, which created precise distributions of roles, spaces, and temporal rhythms. It thus amalgamated teleological meaning with historical cultural contingency. For the production of meaning, this amalgam was a cultural basic technology. This production of meaning did not always exhaust the entire breadth. Theatre could also serve as mere entertainment, especially in the comedy form. Most important, theatre as an institution severed its link to the Dionysia. Aristotle collected to his *Poetics* the breadth of variability of theatrical meaning as it was prevalent or customary in his day, but nothing could prevent cultural development from continuing along the path of abstraction. Public opinion represents one fascinating but highly abstract variant among others. In modernity, contributing to the development of publicity in particular was a quite novel constellation of power relations.

As we have seen, public meaning is graspable teleologically in the form of pragmatic rules of action. The question then arises: Which sign processes are involved in order to bring forth publicity and public opinion? Seen in historical–cultural perspective, the domain of public opinion is the control of power – but in a particular way, not formally as in jurisdiction and legislation. Public opinion does not simply designate what everybody opines;[18] as we have seen, it is precisely *not* what representative opinion polls hypostasize into a collective subject.[19] Public opinion enacts its power in the form of an opinion that all share. Since this opinion is never that of all, the one who has it has to become 'all' without *being* all or even having the hope of *becoming* all.

Peirce's method of authority provides a valid pragmatic and logical model, but how is that model to be enacted as a practice? Today, practice usually means mass media practice (though other spectacular media are imaginable). In the sense of a rule of conduct, the relationships among established roles can describe an established practice quite well. This then constitutes the specification of public opinion within the general model 'publicity.' Public opinion exists as a meaning effect by means of quite determinate role relations.

How public opinion functions as a specific text and constructs meaning can be explained through the historical conditions of its possibility. At least this is the easiest way.[20] At which moment in history, and by what means, did public opinion originate? It originated under two precise conditions: when in the public sphere[21] (a) the power bearers (or dominators) and the dominated were set apart; and (b) a need arose for legitimization before those from whom the power of the power bearers emanated. This model of non-formal legitimization can be extended to any other social domain where analogues of power are identified.[22] For semiotic, as analysed earlier, the basic principle of formal and non-formal legitimization is the same. Building on this common basis, semiotic theorizes their difference as a 'constructive sign' in an additional sign relation or interpretation. Formal legitimization produced institutions (e.g., divine right, General Estates, parliaments, plebiscites), and this removed the onus on the powerful for them to justify their decisions as they came under dispute.

Let us address, then, this practical question: If public opinion must operate without the effects of formalism, how is it nevertheless technically possible to be legitimated? How can it establish and sanction rules justifying the contraposition of two (in principle) different types of actors? Those two being 'weighty' actors; and emphatic non-actors, in whose name the former are legitimated to act. This amorphous mass is the public.[23]

3.4 Public Opinion as Theatre

The asymmetry among actors finds a prominent cultural model in the theatre. The orchestra pit marks a difference in essence between active actors and spectating actors and at the same time establishes a relationship of the one side to the other side. The active act (or *speak*, as the term λογεῖον demands) in order to be looked at; the spectating (οἱ θεαταί) look in order to judge. This is the theory-θέατρον or the praxis-drama of the stage or λογεῖον; in short, action as *spectaculum*.

Once theatre is an established social practice, the arsenal of meaning needed for understanding the others' action is literally 'expressed' in this procedure. The other acts in a way optimized for *theoria*. For this reason, Aristotle's *Poetics* uses the tragic theatre as the model for all narrative representation, down to simple storytelling. Its focus is on narration's logical processes. One can project these processes equally well onto pragmatic roles that are spatially and architectonically distributed (Bieber 1961; Pickard-Cambridge 1953). This makes it possible to visualize in space who contributes, and how, to the single action – in logical as well as operative regards. Action develops from its own unity – here in radical contrast to acts performed in the real world. This applies first of all to temporal unity. It applies as well to the unfolding of the one action into partial, intermediate actions. In the theatre, the only real unity of action is in the mind of the god (Dionysos). In the theatre architecture, this logical function corresponds to the logically transcendent locus of meaning called θεολογεῖον,[24] that spot above the scene (*proskenion*) from which the 'gods speak' and interfere in the action. Here below and immanently, this place is taken by an altar to the god Dionysos (θυμέλη, which was situated in the centre of the orchestra). Those who do not directly act, but who are closely linked to the action as a whole, are called the chorus, which owes its name to the circumstance (quite literally) that they stand around (around = χορός > χορέω) the altar, dancing in place. In the most ancient times, these were all participants; later they ceased to dance in the orchestra round and were limited to 'theory' (i.e., to looking on). This completed the distribution of the wholeness into diversified roles.

In what did the holiness of the *trag-odia* consist? The term combined 'song' (from ἀείδω to sing > ἀοιδή, contracted into ᾠδή) with 'billy goat' (τράγος), because the god of ebriety, wine and ecstasis, so beloved by Nietzsche, had goat feet, as he had originally been the 'foreign god' of farmers. This is not the place to expand on the cultural antecedents of the various Athenian Dionysia, or on the enrichment of the Dionysos cult by orgiastic elements. These were considered foreign to Greek culture, so that Dionysos always seemed to be a foreign god, importing earth and fertility rites. That said, some of the cults outside the Great

Dionysia (τά Διονύσια τά μεγάλα) in the countryside (e.g. Agrionia) also contained a whiff of death and human sacrifice, which in Athens was limited to the sacrifice of a black billy goat and to the human sacrifice on scene of Agamemnon's daughter Iphigenia (or Iphianassa). Our immediate concern is only public opinion, and we will limit historical considerations to what is relevant to that. This relevance is established in the competitive representations of three tragedies and three comedies during the Great Dionysia in classical Athens.

Action in Dionysian theatre always took place in a sacred context, which applied *a fortiori* to the Dionysian and Bacchantic orgies.[25] In this way the spectators were contextualized as participants in a rite (the chorus of bacchantic dancers and those assisting were originally not separated, either spatially or in their pragmatic roles), who had to perform *rite* (rightly) that which lay beyond all of them. This mandate was realized in different ways once the roles became differentiated. The actors on stage were not free; they were answerable. The spectators, on the other hand, had to judge the action. Applied to publicity, this means that those who act receive their mandate and that those who look (better: contemplate) must judge 'in the name of …' Except for that, spectators in Dionysian theatre were unorganized in the sense that they were the 'all' who participated in the rite. Of greater interest in this differentiation of roles was the 'third place.' Historically, around the altar of Dionysos, the chorus represented the legitimating and sanctioning presence of the god. Public opinion, respectively their leaders (κορυφαῖοι), had the same function as an in-between. Thus it was not the opinion of the public (as surveys pretend to be[26]); rather, it acted as the mediator (of the god). On the one hand, it interpreted the actions of the heroes to the public; on the other, it interpreted the will (expectation, reaction) of the public to the heroes.

For journalism operating in the context of today's public opinion, this modelling of meaning brings a considerable gain. The advantage is that the authoritative competency of its role is founded on the pretence of possessing the opinion of 'all.' That all, however, can never mean a numerical or statistical all. How could journalism possibly bring together the opinions of all individual persons under a single opinion and – even if such a single opinion existed – gain access to it? Where does the capacity come from, and where is the opportunity for that? Neither can journalism, nor can statistics, provide this comprehensiveness through a mere 'head count' of individual opinions, actions, and so on. The result of such measurement is merely an aggregate, which cannot render a single opinion of a single individual person; aggregates like these never allow any retro-operative inference in the elements of a population. Thus the possession of authority, or participation in it, becomes the decisive factor in journalism. One would not want to maintain explicitly that journalistic authority today goes back to a privileged access to the divine knowledge of the whole; that said, knowing-about-the-whole is, even without the gods, almost godly. It is at least equally mysterious in its genesis; but for all its mysteriousness it is still an operation in need of a stylistic scaffolding that constructs by narrative means a journalistic role of authority (Zelizer 1990, 387f).

Action in this mode is spectacular, or a spectacle – that is, something to be legitimized. In this process, the two roles are posited as those who, in principle, look; and those who, in principle, represent themselves. For the Greeks, spectacular action was never limited to the great Dionysian festivals. From the stage it was easily transferable: first, to power holders, passing through 'all' (the powerful, together with the highest priests, always had the best seats in the theatre); second, to 'all,' when they sat in judgment (a public process, originally in the βουλή of the citizen of Athens, excluding the *paroikoi* and foreigners); and finally, to the high society of 'all' (proverbially *le tout Paris*, which punishes through ridicule and honours through reverence).[27]

Regarding public opinion, in the narrow sense of an industrial practice, what does it mean today to have a public opinion? Chesterton answers this question perfectly: 'Every man speaks of public opinion, and means by public opinion, public opinion minus his opinion.' We have already seen (§3.1) that the public opinion of mass media starts with the appropriation of an object. This is enacted in the manner of a drama by means of the explanatory monopoly of a strong teleology comprehending every single event and aspect. Landowski's idea, mentioned earlier, of applying the institution of the theatre to public opinion, acquires even greater explanatory potential once it is comprehended in the full Dionysiac context. Instead of interpreting it as a peculiar formation of the general enunciation, the Dionysiac evidences a particular case of teleology. The result is action under predetermined teleological rules. This is obvious enough in religious ritituality, in which the one unified action vanishes as a result of being differentiated into roles. Carey brought public opinion into a ritual context (1975), though his insight did not follow through to the ultimate consequences. Ettema wanted to go further into a Turner-type 'processual ritituality' (1990, 310f), which is germane to the transformations brought about by our ancient theatrical rite. Those who consider the link too far-fetched find a 'secular' equivalent in the social sciences. Goffman's idea of 'Framing'[28] is not simply the collection of subjective points of view. Frame analysis – more generally, the 'dramaturgical action' – is modelled on theatre logic, albeit without the historical connotations. Public opinion constitutes precisely these sorts of interlocking relationships among different frames. Nevertheless, in framing, the drama itself remains absent – it is merely a diversity of dramaturgical modes of action.

Compared to the Dionysiac drama, public opinion cannot claim a full unity of action. To admit this would amount to claiming divine knowledge for one of the actors. Those who own this knowledge, however, are not acting – they are merely judging. The roles are here simply rules of behaviour that remain constant through a number of variations: the chorus (χόρος) and the chorus leader (κορυφαῖος, *coryphaeus*, or πρωτόχορος); in the Greek theatre the face-to-face of the spectator (mostly called a 'point of view' = θέα, Latin *cavea*[29]); and the stage (λογεῖον) with its actors (ὑποκριταί). The chorus and its leader have their place at the altar to Dionysos (from which the orchestra later originated), as non-actors and non-spectators as it were on a vertical axis to the audience and the actors-*hypocrites*. To the former, they explain (what is really taking place); to the latter, they interpret (what they are about to do in good or evil actions with which the destiny of the god has them entangled).

The mass media today, as an industry practice, distinguish commentary from news. In light of the theatre model, this distinction is a marketing instrument.[30] This separation contradicts the logic of the spectacle of actions as it has developed in our culture from the Dionysiac theatre; it is also unethical in the true sense of that term, for the purpose of representation through teleology consists exclusively in grafting an *ethos* onto the simple doing (see §3.1 above). This fact has been reflected on theoretically at least since Aristotle's *Poetics*, but it has yet to bear all its fruit in the broad consciousness of an entire professional group. In 'media ethics,' for example, one still encounters – and not just occasionally – claims to an ethical duty of truth. The plethora of ethics codes, which are enforced variously by editorial departments – sometimes voluntarily, sometimes through the complaints committees of professional organizations – bear witness to the strength of this deliberate misunderstanding. In the journalism departments of universities, the fundamentally and irremediably narrative character of the product is well known and taken into account (cf. Roeh 1989); even so, the fiction in professional discourse continues unabated. More often, empty debates are staged as to how correct a story is, even though it is precisely this question that is undecidable: purposes of actions, as we know, are never real (*facta*) but always future (*facienda*; cf. §8.6).

An unintended illustration of this misguided discourse is provided by an episode that took place during the Second Gulf War. It started with a true story in *Newsweek* in May 2005 about a number of desecrations of the Koran at Guantánamo Bay – events that dated back to 2002–3. This story spread through the world like a wildfire, resulting in a number of deaths. The bone of contention (albeit secondary) was whether it could be proven as a fact that a copy of the Koran had been flushed down a toilet. The Pentagon's first response was that a prisoner had only claimed as much and that he could not prove it. Clearly, this ignores the fact that teleology – and not the fact – is at the core of every narrative representation of an action. It could never be known whether the purpose of this humiliation (or any other) was (1) desecration and defilement; (2) 'softening up' or wearing down; (3) another Christian crusade against Islam; (4) self-defence against terrorism; (5) a sacrilege; (6) ham-fistedness or *maladresse*; (7) something else; or (8) no reason whatsoever or whatever other purpose or aim of any amount of over-intention or under-intention: All of this by necessity has to remain undecidable. Only a θέατρον makes judgment necessary, and this judgment must be present in order for an action to be understandable.

Public opinion, then, is the miracle of action-with-predetermined-rules, and from these rules an ideal unity of action results. It is impossible to claim this for real social life, where we encounter so many actors, who dwell in this space with all their diverse goals and action purposes, and whose coordination is highly complex. That is hardly a unity, and as we have seen, it is difficult to grasp theoretically as 'society.' For a divine instance, or for personifications as public opinion, it is much easier. In the first place, this generates its teleology as the creation of unity; it can then by these means sanction in the name of 'all.' 'All' are in the immanence, in the absence of gods, in the place where norms and the instance in-the-stead-of-divine knowledge reside. However, public opinion is no longer allowed – in Dionysiac fashion as the chorus and central instance of commentary – to dance around the altar. Also, a deritualization has taken place in the theatre institution; for the more 'realistic' theatrical practice becomes, the more all commentaries slip into the actor's role – which expresses itself on the stage itself, if one can say so, as *oratio obliqua* in the guise of *oratio recta*. Even without religious ritual, we keep as a constant the division, the mutual conditioning, and the construction of the roles of spectators and the role of mime or actor as player – together with a conspicuously neutral in-between.

In Greek theatre, the opinion of the chorus and its leader was public. By contrast the modern media have adopted, with undeniable logical consistency, public opinion-of-the-orchestra-pit with regard to events on the world stage – the *theatrum mundi* – as a model for their own role. Historically around 1750, this began as literary prose in para-parliamentary pamphlet literature (Baker 1990). The ideal of objectivity contributed to the decision among the quality press that they would not appear as their own destinators but instead would dissimulate themselves behind the 'reality itself' (cf. Schudson 1978). However, it is certainly not wrong, as the national economy approach does, to consider news as primarily a commodity (and one with a very short shelf life, as R. Augstein, founder of the German weekly *Der Spiegel*, used to say). In fact, the news offers itself to the consumer–reader both economically and as meaning; and in the latter case, it does so in the guise of a destinator, or instance of enunciation, equipped with the corresponding competences. In the *simulacrum* of their own role representation, however, the actual relationships are reversed: the customer–reader becomes the destinator, the seller the one destinated to fulfil the need.

Downstream, public opinion as θέατρον also emcompasses the spectacular as entertainment, aptly conceptualized by the term 'infotainment.' This word is not meant to denigrate '(spectacular) politics' as shallow. Entertainment must be taken in a theatrical sense – as the cause of purification, as Aristotle's catharsis through pity and fear.[31] This entertainment is, if not ritual, at least profoundly moral, and it has the capacity to grasp profound emotions.[32]

3.5 Public Opinion Operates by Constructing the Role of Enunciation Instance

Let us now return from the cultural-historical form to logical construction. To explain public opinion historically by means of the θέατρον apparatus is impossible unless the *modus operandi* of theatrical meaning is logically understandable. We concluded earlier that the strong teleology carries its quite determinate meaning into action. This opens up a field of opportunities. We will next show how this logic makes public opinion a determinate *vis-à-vis* power and the objects of that power, determinate social roles, and a limited number of determinate programs of action for those roles.[33]

How does semiotic determine meaning? How must the sign process look? What is semiotically determined? Which relations in the sign help generate public opinion? That the meaning of public opinion does not fall under aesthetic feeling should be obvious; nor does it constitute the peremptory constraint of a fact. In the first place, then, the Third Correlate in the sign correlation must be determined more closely, because as a strong teleology, it is absolutely dominant. Without knowledge of purpose and goal, public opinion would no longer be an opinion with a potential for sanction. We will see in our further discussions that the first two types of meaning contribute to public opinion as well. The dominant contribution to meaning, however, is in the enunciation. Enunciating, before any enunciated, has already accomplished the explicit purpose of public opinion. This is a quite specific use of the sign. We will soon turn our undivided attention to this dominant sign of 'purpose.'

Knowing the goal or purpose, knowing what is to be done, is of course not everything in public opinion. The sign relation is always triadic. This means that it also always must integrate two correlates that are of a different nature. After the pragmatic goal, and now under its aegis, the Second Correlate in the sign is always the Object, and this by necessity implies its opposite, the Subject. Simplifying, one can say that this is all about the possibility that 'I'/'we' can say 'this here!' This has the double effect just mentioned, for public opinion is also a matter of (bivalent) truth, facticity and an oppositional identity. However, this can only happen in the mode as specified by the Third Correlate, and not 'because the world is such as it is.' For this reason, factual truths must appear in a triadic sign relation, designated by terms such as 'objectivity.' As sign, facts mean the resistance of the real placing itself in op-position to cognition and to the cognizing subject. The resistant real then en-counters me in the form of the living genuine doubt – in practical terms, when a subject surprised by an unexpected real then ought to make something meaningful out of this surprise. Furthermore, by subjecting different realities to doubt it is possible to produce different identities. This has a simple expression in the syntax of persons (i.e., of most Indo-European languages): 'I–thou,' various (inclusive, exclusive) 'we's – various 'you's,' 'it.' For instance, an object is different if it is *my* object or simply *it*. Later we will apply all of this in our analysis of how public opinion makes use of this identity, the polar opposite of the Object, for a rather subtle form of meaning. Under the heading of 'metatext' – which is a macro-organization of meaning – we will be able to describe this form as a determinate industrial practice.

Peirce calls the First Correlate (or the Category Firstness) very generally, quiddity (*quidditas*) – that is, in the OED's definition, 'that which makes a thing what it is.' In public opinion, this is about what one entertains as an opinion. It is a type of narrative universe as soon as a teleology constitutes it. That step excludes many options. Excluded, for instance, is public opinion about timeless being (nature, pure theory), or non–goal-oriented time (music), unless it is 'framed' by a story. We mention the First Correlate therefore not just for completeness's sake but also for its indispensable contribution to the dominant meaning. However, this is so general and self-evident that we can let this matter rest in this context. This is not the place to expound a general narratology.[34]

Without entering into the subtle possibilities of the sign relation in general, we will nevertheless make use of that potential in order to analyse media scandals. The complex possibilities of sign constructivity and degenerativity will enable – albeit only in their details – subtle meaning processes. Here it is merely of importance to note that types of interpretation can be traced on the basis of industrial practices and habits of consumption. Later we can return to these types.

Finally we come to the highest sign correlate, which is so constitutive of public opinion. How does teleology see the light of day as the publicly opined? The primordial event for that purpose is an enunciation. It is therefore not enough to understand the sign; we must also understand its use. Immediately this introduces an enunciation instance as the construct producing purpose and meaning, showing, demonstrating, representing, and serving as the ultimate point of reference for narration. Even though this is a necessary construct that constitutes the text, it can assume diverse styles and degrees of conspicuousness.[35] Public opinion – especially in the sense of rhetoric – can count as the most visible and most explicit instance of enunciation. The changes in the visibility of the theatrical function of chorus have already been discussed. The most invisible instance of enunciation is in the classical–modern practice of historiography, where it hides almost completely behind 'the things themselves'; a middle position is taken by the (style of) reporting in the quality press. All of these are variations in the role of an enunciator who represents to a receiver.

The concept of enunciation is prone to being misread, in light of the linguistic use of the term. Comprehending the idea of sign as an artefact merely made use of (as if signs were 'as things are') is a fundamental though avoidable mistake, one that throws us back to the separation of pragmatic and semantic (dating back to Morris), or to linguistic pragmatic (as we have seen in Habermas's borrowing from speech act philosophy). Both 'pragmatics' miss the point of Peirce's Pragmatic Maxim. There is not the sign on the one hand and its use on the other. Unity of 'conception-controlled behaviour' is of primary importance, for this stands for nothing less than realism in semiotic. Neither is semiotic reducible to a classification of signs (such as semiology has them as a sort of Linnaean taxonomy), for signs are not static. They are not 'vehicles of sense,' but relations. This nominalist sense of signhood may be freeing itself from the molesting real, but it does not result in a cognitive grasp of the world. The triad of semiosic relation comprises the dyadic relation to factual reality. The sign process, therefore, cannot be fixed and immobilized as one state. Doing so is a purely theoretical logical operation of classifying all possible relations, which is the whole point of Speculative Grammar. In fact, sign as a real process cannot be reified, nor can it be grasped, because it is intrinsically open in all three directions. First, 'downwards,' because abutting on the First Correlate, as sign material, are all preceding interpretations, onto which this correlate builds new interpretations. Second, 'outwards,' for the concrete meaning of this interpretation is determined by the common universe of discourse of the speaker and receiver in their respective reality constraints. Third, 'upwards,' as a new interpretation achieves a new level of generality without being terminal. Enunciation, then, means attaining a new relation based on a precedent relation. Enunciating is interpreting.

Enunciation being a simple upshot of the sense of sign as a process – that is, an interpretation – it is not coextensive with purpose or text. It is merely the unconditional presupposition for textual goal construction. How does teleology become text? How does text become teleological? Not every sign is already teleological, but every sign is always general.[36] The reason is to be found in the logic of representation, for necessarily something is a case of something. We see a 'the,' for example, but we understand 'the-ness' or the general idea of 'definite article.' Pragmatically, this constitutes a rule on how to behave (always) in this case. Calling this a relationship of destination, like Greimas, confines it perhaps too narrowly to generality of the teleological kind, as *quête*, quest, the goal one must pursue. The rule, then, no longer connects with the reality of a factual world, as Pragmaticism tries so hard to posit. It connects only to an arbitrary will of an enunciation instance, in a nominalist fashion, which then concludes the circuit of interpretation.[37] In order for generality to become the ideation of a general goal, a logical operation is needed that is more complex than a mere destinatary volition. It needs the connection of at least two events of the same, of which one is the first, the other the second; and their alteration is interpreted by means of final causality.[38] Volition is merely a paradigm of finality. Once this logical effect (as originary sign, as it were) is in place, the instance causing this logic can conceal itself gradually: in adjectives, camera angles, tenses, *consecutio temporum*, verbal modes, focal lengths, types of montage, sentence conjunctives, and so on, there exist a plethora of style variations of its visibility. The only important factor is that it always be present.

How is the instance that is enunciating public opinion present? Its mode is typical, for news stories, programs performed on the world stage, need framing programs. The latter provide from outside to the former their justification and purpose, the quasi-divine 'whole' of the action, as discussed earlier. Public opining on narratives refers back to these 'roles above the action,' which enact a meta-action that commissions and sanctions the dependent single action. As in ancient tragedy, the actors act under the god's mandate. Since they fatefully[39] misunderstand it, they fall to tragic perdition. Actors on the world stage 'must' act similarly. To them, too, this meaning effect, the mandate, is given from outside (for some: from above).

Somehow, enunciation must become attached to the drama or text. Inclusion of the destination instance, however, seems to contradict its exclusion from the place of the action. There is, though, an excellent way to penetrate the text: by expressing judgments. Doing so, this instance can realize its specific role, from which it must never depart – that is, it must never become an actor itself, but must limit itself to destination and sanction. With the ownership of the wholeness of action in the form of the pragmatic purpose, this instance is also the ultimate court of appeal for all actors, in the name of 'all' (but no longer the gods). It is absolutely constitutive of authority to blur the difference between 'all' and the role of public opinion. Otherwise, how could one justify the logically impossible – that is, knowledge of the general pragmatic purpose? Only when 'all' entertains public opinion can the power of sanction become totally self-evident. In the Pragmaticist context, this reminds us of settling doubt in (what Peirce called) the 'method of authority' (cf. *supra*). This role construction, though, is as old as the chorus and its κορυφαῖος in ancient Greek theatre in the *vis-à-vis* of the θέα/κοῖλον and the λογεῖον with its ὑποκριταί. Its pattern of meaning is re-enacted as an industrial media practice. In particular, the quality press ideal of objectivity reflects this pattern. Otherwise, there would be no logical or rhetorical reason not to appear openly as one's own mandator but rather to dissimulate oneself behind 'reality itself.'[40]

The meaning potential in enunciation is considerable, and it will become evident how journalists' professionalism could develop from it. This profession's proper task is logic – that is, the production of teleology. Normally, however, this must remain obscured, since the attention goes mostly to the product, where journalistic teleology has congealed into a narrative universe. Only in the decisive initial spark of a scandal does the constructive work of teleology appear. What is inherent in the act of storytelling itself, as a profession, is subject to cultural conditions of production. These conditions mediate among the constraints of the logical operation and industrialization of the product within a society. This cultural level must therefore be abstracted separately. We will take account of this layer by describing, upstream of the text level, another level of metatext where the logical labour occurs before the product. Public opinion actually does not exist as visibly as – because it is not distributed over places as much as – the spatial distribution of roles in the theatre. Instead of a configuration of space, journalism operates with personal agencies, which, notwithstanding the divine role, are its normal human performers. The performers must display these operations in the type of their enunciation. The only exceptions to this otherwise closed universe are certain metadiscourses, which impose themselves when the teleological universe is in crisis. Then another object discourse describes the role that journalists ought to enact. These metadiscourses can only be repair mechanisms if the metatext fails to produce its evidence. Normally, however, one should be able to discover in the product itself what has often been described as the interest of the media to present themselves as the Fourth Estate. This is indeed the enunciation role integrated fully into the text itself.

4 Publicity in Media Theory

Is the public sphere 'something,' or is it 'just' meaning? In terms of society's viewpoint, is media publicity different from – and more than – the simple negation of social privacy? We have seen how the meaning reality of publicity is construed as sign by means of teleology and how it is realized in cultural-historical models. Let us next address a no less central determinant of meaning – mediality, and how it is constituted in media. The meaning of publicity as such is constituted teleologically, but that meaning varies in terms of whether it arises from a citizen's meeting, a caucus, village gossip, or the media. The first three of these are not a merely 'miniatures' of the last, of mass media. So it is crucial for media scandal research to understand mediality and to obtain an adequate concept of medium.

A medium has always been viewed in connection with society; the two concepts seem somehow to depend on each other. Thus medium can be viewed as a sort of cement for society, and society provides the concrete the logic holding it together. Even the media industry views itself as quite unlike other industries: as a social practice for a social purpose.

This chapter will begin by critically examining one of the most prominent media theories qualifying as a theory of society: Niklas Luhmann's system theoretical approach. While the concept of medium is central to functionalist theories of society, such as Parsons's, in both Luhmann and Habermas it keeps its explanatory power, albeit in different ways. It also plays a central role in both men's approaches to mass media, and – interesting to note – for both, medium 'swaps in' agency and the logic of human action as *explanans* of society.

Pragmaticism cannot be deprived of action, a concept that anchors it in factual reality. In the subsequent section we will see why a semiotic Pragmaticism need not follow the path of Habermasian *Fundamentalpragmatismus* seeking a functionalist complement for a too narrow concept of action.

The third section brings us to a Peircean understanding of society – one that is based on action controlled by signs. This is a more complete concept of action – indeed, it is the anchor of meaning in totality, embracing more even than the whole of society. Sign is the concrete, next cognition, but as such it is a logical operation that transcends its present workings towards an ideal of truth. Without question, it encompasses the meaning of publicity as a mass-mediated social practice, one that imitates (falsely) the attainment of cognitive truth.

What is society operating as a sign? The fourth section sounds out the glue of sociality, as a triadic sign relation of meaning that is not simply the usual society-as-rule concept. The two lower correlates make an important contribution to the full meaning of society, also as action-guiding pragmatic principles. All of these correlates in the triadic sign relation of society have a direct impact on the meaning produced by mass media.

We reconnect in the fifth section with standard current debates in communication sciences. Here, our findings from semiotic position us to weigh the merits of media theories based on technological determinism, various media aesthetics, and other efforts to determine the 'nature' of different media. As a first benchmark for the semiotic comprehension of media, we use the complex media phenomenon of televangelism.

4.1 Media – Functional or Semiotic?

In some theories of society, media are almost magical in terms of how they connect form with society. In particular, functionalist social theories use media to 'solve' the multitudinous levels in the system's organization. Here, neither a naive realism nor a simple nominalism is at work. A simple, pure precognitive reality standing opposite us as the absolute other is thinkable. Semiotic and the functional-structural systems theory of Luhmann agree on this point. However, the two theories dissolve the simplicity of reality in radically different ways. Semiotic allows space for a modal being;[1] systems theory allows space for a mere reflex of the complexity of the system itself.

For both theories, sociological nominalism is too facile a solution. As an alternative, objectivation of meaning (of whatever kind) arises as a possibility so that meaning is more than mere subjective agreement. Thus the next radical alternative now arises: sign or medium?

Being-in-a-medium is a quality that sociologists from Parsons to Luhmann have connected to functions of society, be it in a structural-functionalist or a functional-structural way.[2] Only because it is a symbolically generalized medium is public opinion positioned so that it can work as the central function of legitimization for other functionally differentiated social systems within society as a whole. Luhmann's (1997) theory of the communication medium operates on two levels or sides: one of loose elements ('Medium') and one of strictly coupled elements ('Form'). This succeeds in integrating a semiological idea that is strongly reminiscent of André Martinet's double articulation. Luhmann repeatedly traces his inspiration to Fritz Heider's gestalt psychology of perception laws (Heider 2005); but as well, his own interpretation of Heider's medium/form (i.e., loosely coupled elements / the same elements strictly coupled) relates these to Saussure's *signifiant/signifié* (Luhmann 1997, 208f). Both his interpretations fit the complementary terms into system and environment differentiation, albeit in a unique way. The explanatory *charme* of a perception gestalt is that it is a law of perception as such; it is therefore independent of any underlying perceived matter. 'Form' in Luhmann's hands turns into a tool of systemic autopoietic self-organization; thus it becomes a means of system differentiation and emergence in the evolution of media-form: each new form can become the medium of an emergent form merely by drawing a new difference between loose and strict coupling.

Functional media theories are much more than roughly congruent explanations of the products of the mass media industry. They invariably assume an architectonic importance. Media theory also plays a crucial role in Luhmann's understanding of meaning. Is meaning a system on its own, with its own self-referentiality and auto-reproduction, or are there only instances of two meaning systems: psyche and action? In the former, thought is the medium, whereas the latter functions with communication as medium. This is Luhmann's profound ambiguity – and it has consequences. If meaning *in se* were an autarkic system, it would require a proper selection criterion in order to maintain its boundary with its environment; this difference constitutes an otherness as 'world,' the other of meaning. But what would be the proper medium of the system 'meaning'? It is not through the elements and operations of thought, nor is it through communication, that meaning becomes a system, because these are the selection criteria of the two systems using meaning (already presupposed). Why, then, is something treated as meaningful? For systems theory this cannot be because the world object is in itself meaningful. Since Luhmann framed his entire theory as a theory of differentiation, that something cannot be marked and unmarked space at the same time once the distinction is drawn – in the sense of Spencer-Brown's Law of Form (1973). Before it is drawn, there is a state of indistinction of system and environment, which Luhmann calls 'the world.' Meaning, therefore, is also a perfectly closed system, recursively self-reproductive, self-referential through system re-entry (in other words, the system is not justifiable from outside, but only through itself; *v. infra*, in this chapter): it must use only internal structural elements and conditional operations to represent the system-relative world or environment. While this almost constitutes radical constructivism, Luhmann is somewhat ambiguous when it comes to the status of a 'real world.'

Let us suppose that the formal description of meaning can be accomplished even without a clearly identified proper medium. Then the difference medium–form is applied to the two sides of meaning *in se:* the actual meaning (which is the form), and the potential meaning (which is the medium).

This is a very common way of conceiving meaning, with no reference except to itself. Even though Luhmann framed it in a later stage as medium, its core philosophical insight is still in the earlier phenomenological description of meaning that used to be termed appresentation. This is a decidedly Husserlian concept, which we will be exploring it in more detail below.

Regarding the medium concept itself, the medium establishes an emergent system that can be understood as a new universe. Used operatively for the purpose of observation, it thus becomes the reality tailored for this system. With such a configuration of internal operations and elements, this system observes its external environment and obtains information from it. If this entire process takes place based on a medium, for those operations it carries the advantage of being irreversible, no longer negotiable. Disappearing as merely one of many alternatives of selection, this medium becomes the normal operation of this system. Media can thus behave as if they were rules, even though they do not owe this power to a logical constraint but merely to the emergence of this system.

In semiotic, relations are fundamentally different from those of media. That there is regularity at all is not based on acting behaviour. It is in behaviour, certainly, but this regularity is not limited to action. Though Peirce acquired his major reputation as a Pragmaticist, this does not mean that his proofs rely on acting. Action, rather, is itself subject to justification. That we can act regularly or according to rules needs to be justified by the categorical analysis of reality. As it is encountered by us (and not the *Ding an sich* – which is not experienceable), reality must itself be rule. However, reality can be encountered as fact *or* as quality. Peirce's phaneroscopy or phenomenology is only the laborious analysis of this modal nature of reality (this is not the place to do justice to it, though[3]). Everything that is, is not simply, but either is-necessary, or is-existent, or is-possible. Based on these categories, the sign relation establishes its own specific relations to the real, which resurface in their modal ways of being in the sign. This version of realism is starkly at variance with Luhmann's constructivism, in which two meaning systems create their own reality. Through the recursive operations of thought or communication, a basis of correlative world is created, which is then specified as the three dimensions of object, time, and sociality: all there is has whatness, occurs in time, and is attributable to me or not-me. The pattern of this correlativity of a system-relative world replicates itself in a medium-specific manner, where it also creates a specific world. To summarize, these presuppositions demonstrate that sign and medium must be of two different natures, even though their descriptions sound similar in some respects.

The practical purpose of media in Luhmann's theory design is connected to a constatation – that complex social systems can be coordinated by means of language. Only media can accomplish this; such highly complex systems could not otherwise survive their own complexity.[4] Of what does a medium consist, then? In the most immediate sense, as we saw, it is a two-level mechanism: the lower, loosely coupled and called medium; and the higher, strictly coupled and called form. Each couples the same elements (Luhmann 1997, §2.1). Semiology uses a cognate device, the purest paradigm of which is the phonemic/phonetic differentiation, where the two levels of coupling the same elements are most easily understood. Systems theory, however, views the higher level as an emerging system and not as an arbitrary system of compositional values, as in semiology. So the question arises: How can systems emerge when an evolutionary teleology is not supposed to be in operation (something that systems theory must flatly deny)? This translates into the question of how systems can evolve that are not governed by meaning, because meaning can only be the result of such evolution. The most general principle of systems' behaviour is differentiation; indeed, this is the fundamental operation in systems theory. This functions only after postulating that 'there are systems' (Luhmann 1984b). Systems mean that the system and its environment in their differentiation also 'are.' In the wake of the most recent paradigm change in systems theory, systems are referred to as self-referential – which amounts to a substitution for the dichotomy of open and closed systems (cf. Luhmann 1984b, 25). The guiding difference ('*Leitdifferenz*,' i.e., the determination that produces information) is 'the difference of identity and difference' (Luhmann 1984b, 26). In the last characteristic, Luhmann is connecting with, and into, the logic of Spencer-Brown (Spencer-Brown 1973).

Why does Luhmann adopt from Spencer-Brown the difference of system and environment, of the form and its other? He can substitute completely those figures of thought in the philosophical tradition that distinguish a cognizing subject from its cognitive objects, the world. But one should not expect any sort of realism from systems theory, especially not a dualistic sort. What, however, connects a system with its environment? This question remains unanswered, since systems theory rejects all forms of realism – and not just the naive realism that prevails in the naively understood practice of natural sciences, especially in the form of a general mechanics of causality. Contrary to this view, Willke repeatedly emphasized the fact (!) that no causality can conform to the many causal leaps and exceptions in nature. The solution to this question involves differentiating between internal complexity and a completely independent external complexity. The former then serves as the 'problem solution' of the latter by relating to it through a reduction in complexity. This reduction constitutes the system boundary. The most fundamental determination is thus the boundary between an identity and its environment. Boundaries behave as auto-selectivity in the relational achievements of the system and maintain a drop in the level of complexity. A system is only a system when its internal mechanisms, elements, and operations reduce the complexity of the environment to which it relates. Internal system differentiation repeats the system–environment difference within the system itself.

The traditionally understood problem of cognition is in this way completely subverted, for a systems theoretical approach is no longer oriented either towards a world or towards a cognizing subject. Consequently, all problems are redundant that ponder synthesis achieved in a thinking I, the forms of this synthesis formerly known as categories, and the presence mode of the sensual world. Now all of this is the perfectly auto-referential system, which is no longer thinkable as a centre of convergence in a cognizing I, since every system is a centre, and this precludes there being an absolutely stable and unchangeable centre of identity. Not even in the very special case where a system is 'self-conscious' – that is, autoreflexive – does this principle change; for in that case, those systems have merely formed mechanisms of reflexive self-referentiality.

Only those complexities are systems which can also produce the unity of the manifold. This differentiation indicates that it is the system's own internal operation, and not the environment's complexity, that adjusts the complexity of the system. Internal complexity forces a system to adopt selectivity by posing a guiding difference ('*Leitdifferenz*'). It is no longer permissible to associate self-reference with consciousness and the subject (self-reference used to be self-organization in general systems theory; only through Maturana did it develop into autopoiesis). Now, it is abstractly 'die Einheit, die ein Element, ein Prozeß, ein System für sich selber ist' (the unity, that an element, a process, or a system is for itself; (Luhmann 1984b, 58)). If a self, however, has itself as point of reference, this must be redundant – or better, tautological or paradoxical. This situation will be auto-destructive, if what Luhmann calls 'system re-entry' cannot solve this. A system must take additional measures to reacquire its determinability, and this enables it to become connectible again. Self-reference, in a 'virtuous circularity,' is thus destined to be unfolded.

How is causality conceivable (our original question)? It is not the effective causality of the system on the environment. For Luhmann, it is a production that places, '*einige, aber nicht alle*' (some, but not all; 1984a, 40) causes of a determinate effect into the system and in this way selects associated causes in the environment. Determinant for the systems' identity and information processing, however, is again a difference: The elements as different from relations among elements and their unity, and then the further difference from these relations subject to conditions. Reflexive self-referential systems have emerged as systems capable of observing their own operations through their own operations. As its most radical consequence, the internal organization of a system does not depend in any way on the environment reproduced by these internal operations. When systems are self-reflexive they form their own structure, which can react adaptively to the environment only *in toto*. However, a system perishes if it cannot adapt (we will come back to this later in this chapter).

Complex systems have differentiated an ultra-large number of elements that are impossible to connect with one another. This in turn implies a constraint on selection, therefore contingency, therefore risk. The manifold is in principle a problem for any epistemology centred on sensory impressions. Kant came to terms with this empiricist inheritance by means of his transcendental concepts; Peirce's semiotic approach had no use for these and flatly rejected them. Luhmann (1984b, 51), too, maintains against Kant that the systems theoretical approach, in its attempt to bring the manifold to unity, does not need any auxiliary concepts such as 'transcendental subject,' '*Ding an sich*,' and apriorism. What is postulated here as a solution, though, on closer examination consists merely of effacing the last remnants of realism. Those who abolish a 'raw reality' (however that is conceptualized) need not worry about bringing it into a relation with cognition. If both reality effect and cognition originate within the system, then any possible corrective for cognition outside the system itself is abandoned. As we have seen, Peirce did not resort to this facile solution with regard to reality, though he, too, had shed Kantian apriorism. He, however, succeeded with a theory that was not tautological and that therefore stayed within the framework of a critical theory of cognition.

Reality's function of otherness is not simply abandoned; rather, systems theory imitates it internally. Every system constructs two poles – identity and diversity – when determining itself. If that system also functions selectively towards its own selecting, then it has become doubly contingent. Only then does it possess a reflexivity of its own selectivity, which Luhmann calls meaning, which is defined strictly as '*auch anders möglich sein*' (being possible also in a different way). By this definition, meaning *in se* is symmetrical and the selection of elements and their relation by the system is reversible. As soon as the time dimension is specified, the system becomes asymmetrical and takes its course in one direction only. In the time dimension, the elements must be connectible; otherwise, the system breaks down and comes to a halt. One form of complexity reduction for meaning-based systems is action. When action is communicative action, at least two autopoietic systems act together in such a way that the other appears in one's own environment. Each system is then subject to irritation by the other, which, through communication, has become part of the environment and can force adaptation. In this process, everything is asymmetrical action; thus, communication is doubly contingent: it can break down at any moment when no continuation of action is taking place, and furthermore, environment reactions force various adaptations upon it. Up to this point, action systems coordinate themselves through private codes. As soon as a medium emerges, however, the doubly contingent communicative action as an emergent system becomes selective and forecloses many possibilities of meaning construction. Media embrace everything from gestures to mass media, and in increasing their media density (a higher leans on a lower medium), they become more selective in their connection possibilities. Even if (in theory) two communicating systems of action can adapt to each other by whatever means – including entirely private meaning – a medium predetermines any public meaning. That latter meaning might be the 'episteme' of a society, or truth, the medium of the subsystem science.

Luhmann's derivation of meaning from the principle of differentiation – which is not the same as difference in semiology – is supposed to constitute a radical break from what he polemically calls the 'old European' epistemology. Actually, though a closer scrutiny beyond the terminological barrier reveals how much Luhmann's concept of meaning is indebted to Husserl's egology, which Habermas interprets as a subjectivist philosophy of consciousness (cf. Habermas 1985). In Husserl's theory of meaning, objectivity is not somehow inherent to meaning but can be reduced to an intentional act as its act-correlate (Luhmann 1996). In Luhmann's interpretation, that is but a small step from differentiation.

Meaning as 'appresentation' follows Husserl's thought closely ('be possible also in a different way') – though owing to the double selectivity, it is also doubly aimless. The concern of the concept of medium is to grapple with the aimless ateleology of meaning. Each emerging medium allows communication to ascend one level higher in meaning. With each higher selectivity, meaning becomes more complex. Luhmann is not rewriting Hegel's history of the spirit; nevertheless, it is quite clear that the complexity of meaning, the form of communication, has a direct impact on the evolution of society. It is not desirable to describe this development in terms of a philosophy of history. Nonetheless, the underlying active principle is meaning alone, either as evolution or at least as levels. Luhmann explicitly and systematically excludes from his meaning concept any association with logic, or rationality, or Hegelian spirit. It is, therefore, precluded that the rules of thought apply to the development of meaning, to which he admits only system differentiation.

Peirce's antitranscendentalism, noted as superficially resembling

Luhmann, is devoid of knowing purpose and end of the spirit, or history, or even of the evolution of social rationality. The method of Pragmaticism – that is, the method 'of science' – for settling doubts is merely a hope. At this point, any resemblance ends. Peirce abandoned epistemology in the sense of a program for critically comparing cognition with an incognizable and not cognized reality; nevertheless, he established a relation to raw reality in a strictly non-dualist way. This is lacking completely in Luhmann, except perhaps in terms of the altogether unspecific adaptation pressure (of a chaotic environment on a system) called 'selection risk.' From risk, however, it is impossible to derive a teleology except in a primitively vitalistic sense. But how can a theory be justified without any corrective, either in reality or in a *telos* of evolution? This deprives it of all the reasons to recommend it on grounds of truth (existential relations) or – more complicated – of the future of finalistic relations.

Systems theory views itself as a supertheory with a universalistic claim (cf. Luhmann 1984b, 19) – though this cannot ultimately be justified, contrary to transcendentalism. A functional equivalent to ultimate justification must be quite different from traditional universalistic theories, metaphysic, theory of science, and transcendentalism. Systems theory is designed antimetaphysically. For its own ultimate justification, it has a formal requirement in place – the capacity to treat itself theoretically by reflecting its own tautology. It seeks distance from 'old European' thought by refraining from arguments centred on the subject. Instead, its justification is 'fruitfully circular.' Since this cannot qualify as ultimate justification, Habermas turned it into an accusation of circularity (cf. Welker 1985, 77ff). His tone is resigned, however – he sees no possibility for discourse with meaning explained without language (Habermas 1985, 442f).

It is utterly clear, then, that Luhmann's systems theory treats only on the basis of its own foundations and methods, which justify themselves in an avowedly circular way. As we will show, if this justification fails, systems theory comes out as a less than universal thought gesture. Welker attempted this in the form of immanent criticism, based on a handful of foundational assumptions in systems theory. A central assumption relates to how the behaviour of every system, including the ultimate 'world society,' is regulated: the interest in self-preservation and identity, enabled by the drop in complexity level between system and environment. Identity and survival belong to the definition of systems and are therefore quasi-transcendentally certain – if there *are* systems.

Before we continue, this question arises: Why only *immanent* criticism? Why is systems theory impervious to justification from the real? Moreover, asking in the most general sense, what question is answered, what problem is solved, by systems theory? Its immediate concern is not a solution to the communication of significance between meaning-using subjects as actors. This is just one special case. As originary premise of sorts, Luhmann must postulate instead that there *are* systems to begin with and that they do not constitute merely analytical schemata. The fundamental fact, therefore, is the existence of infinitely complex states and *'daß es Systeme gibt'* (that there are systems; (Luhmann 1984b, 30). The problem here lies in the fact that these complexities must be controlled or steered in some way. This used to be the domain of natural laws; but these now appear to be exceptions, part of middle-level theory at best. Indeed, nature is seen to be a collection of contradictions – that is, chance, non-linearity, from nuclear physics to evolution. In the theory-of-science field, this reminds us of Kuhn's speaking similarly of 'mopping up operations' (Kuhn 1970, 24 and passim) in 'normal science.' Here, the task becomes to 'accommodate' theories so far as to also have them covering irregular data, which otherwise would amount to 'anomalies.' This practice of science, however, treats laws as if they were the (possibly total) collection of all facts, and not a cognitive type *sui generis*. Willke, as a systems theoretician, concludes from this that there is no meaningful way to formulate laws because they will always fail to govern such complexity. Analogously, law-based cognition becomes a mere illusion. Systems theory sees itself as positioned to offer a better and more general solution than conformity to natural laws by proposing a complex multiplicity of systems that react to other systems by means of control. The first principle of control must be found in the reduction of complexity, where a controlling system reduces the complexity of the controlled one. It is thus a clear vision of chaotic reality as a fact that invalidates the real from becoming a corrective for theory.

Only with this extension can one say that systems theory answers the same problems as classical epistemology. The solution, however, is at such great variance that cognition and experience would be reduced to merely particular forms of complexity reduction. What this means, as an 'epistemological' consequence, was eventually spelled out in radical constructivism. For the social sciences, the consequences are no less radical: when systems theory starts to address a classical problem such as division of labour (Smith, Simmel, Durkheim) in terms of the dissolution of segmented societies, the result becomes functional differentiation (cf. Willke 1989, 19–23).

Systems theory must also be subject to a philosophical critique, from outside. In view of its claims to universalismty, the following question can no longer be dodged: How can the system be justified in the last resort, even before a 'system re-entry'? Regarding this question, the reflexive structure of the science system serves, in keeping with systems theoretical premises, as the functional substitute for Kant's transcendentalism. When one system of action observes another system of action, the former has the latter only as its environment. Thus for ego, the internal complexity of alter ego (as a psychic system) has no relevance. Ego, with its own complexity, can make its own internal model of alter ego, which – in the sense of double contingency – can make its own action reflexively dependent on the contingency of alter ego's action.

The task now is to come to a different, double reflexivity, in connection with an ultimate justification of the system of science. Albeit a partial system, it nevertheless is one of the three systems that cover the totality of everything meaningful. In it, society itself reflects itself in its entirety, reflexively ascertaining the total society in its mode of functioning. This functional analysis procedure approaches another system, cognition, no longer as environment but rather as a system. In short, this constitutes the cognition of cognition, which can only be cognition of the functionality of the system. However, this can no longer take place in the form of an auto-observation closed in on itself, because then the determination of the system would no longer come from its environment; it would merely be empty determination in pure arbitrary, tautological circularity. In this way, the science system must enter into a double reflection of the tripolarity in which another system is no longer environment but must remain system. However, a system becomes system only by means of its identity, which it maintains against the environment. How, then, can the science system maintain its own identity as an observer? Clearly, it must assume the identity of the observed system in order to analyse it functionally and not to reflect it, according to its own internal complexity, through environmental selection.

In its attempt to distance itself from 'old European' figures of thought, systems theory is nevertheless making some more or less open assumptions. Foremost, but almost latently, is the assumption that time-based systems must evolve. Were it not for the permanent adaptation pressure, which compels systems to change themselves, theory would have almost nothing to pronounce on systems. If systems theory were not insisting on naming this unfolding process a mere evolvement of the system, one would be inclined to look at it from the end, as a pursuit of an end,[5] and then name it teleology. This would inevitably raise the question of how to determine the end. Evolution also involves the temporality of the system evolvement – not just that certain asymmetrical systems exist that contain temporality (and thus are mostly unidirectional). In this context, Luhmann speaks of the evolutionary qualities of systems – for instance, when they introduce boundaries (cf. Luhmann 1984b, 53), but also with increasing complexity and the ensuing concomitant need for selectivity and therefore an increase in risk. If system is explainable only tautologically as system and non-system, identity and difference, then within such tautology time is only graspable as a systemic asymmetry. From the system idea itself, however, a need for temporality at its base does not result.

Another presupposition of systems theoretical subjectless nature relates to system behaviour's close imitation of consciousness – as contradictory as this might sound. The clearest instance of this is when meaning is introduced into temporal systems (v. *supra*) following the model of Husserl's appresentation (Bednarz 1984, 60–5; Green 1982, 23f). Luhmann's systems theory explicitly intends to succeed the philosophy of consciousness and subject philosophy (Luhmann 1984b). Habermas criticizes that 'Die Selbstbezüglichkeit des Systems ist der des Subjekts nachgebildet' (auto-reference imitated the subject; Habermas 1985, 427), but in reality it replaces the subject completely. But is Luhmann justified in cutting the Gordian knot of subjectivity in what he calls 'old European' thought? Habermas counters that Luhmann not only substituted reflection philosophy, but also inherited all its inherent problems. It was already difficult for subject philosophy to think of itself in its Self, without being ensnared in reified self-reference or falling into the circularity of positing a finite mental ability as absolute. In a similar way, systems theory encounters an analogous difficulty of providing a rational identity to society in a manner comparable to absolute knowledge as the self-knowledge of the totality.

Only then does it become a problem for systems theory that it has rejected subjectivity when it reflects itself. A 'system re-entry' allows merely for an application of systems theory to itself, and the reflecting observation system science is merely a single particular one among other systems. One such reflection relates to the treatment of meaning through meaning – where, however, the perspective of the observer need not coincide with the internal perspective of the observed system.

What guarantees that the observer sees the observed system as it is: For whom? For itself? For other observers? For *all* other observers? This question does not come from nowhere but is the direct result of the universalistic claim to comprehend everything – comprehension included – as system. Systems, being autopoietic, are their own reference; they organize themselves according to their proper criteria of selectivity and internal organization. What a system 'is,' then, only the system itself can know. Other systems may be observing it, but they must employ their own system-immanent difference, which selects and constitutes its elements quite differently than the observed system does for itself. Cognition of the outside reality is in principle an illusion, since it is merely a reality effect that is required for the system as the difference from itself. In this situation, only one question is reasonably asked: Is the system consciousness (cognition or science) capable of being affected by the object of observation, and if so, how? Luhmann is ambiguous on this point (Scheibmayr 2004); he apparently felt that he had to break up the total isolation that would otherwise have resulted from his theory. That, at least, is what the 'interpenetration of systems' amounts to, which for systems theory substitutes epistemology, truth theory, and theory of science. While seductions of naive realism can be safely excluded, a certain form of idealism[6] cannot be ruled out – at least for the system of cognition, which is the only one available to human beings.

Despite all its attractiveness for social sciences, Luhmann's systems theory has been sharply criticized from various directions. While he managed to keep the bulwark of defensible assumptions high enough to ward off the classical epistemological criticisms, he remains vulnerable on two fronts: in terms of the axiomatic hidden in the basic description of system, but also in terms of the internal contradictions generated when he tries to fit systems into the traditional role of cognition.

If one dissolves even the possibility of something like 'truth,' then it should at least be clear from which point it might be possible to criticize a cognitive act in the systems theoretical sense of the term. One could not attribute this act to something like 'nature,' or an 'innate idea,' or a Platonizing 'idea,' but it clearly constitutes a cognitive claim. It must be legitimate in the systems theoretical context to ask for an ultimate justification of the system perspective as such. Luhmann uses complexity reduction as a functional equivalent of 'meaningful experience,' but he fails to indicate a third point of critical comparison. With system re-entry there are actually only two.[7] This led Raden to unmask the resulting relativism and to highlight the subterfuge of Luhmann's use of the God-Chiffre. For Luhmann's systems theory, relativity is so 'holy' that it must hide its triviality.[8] That reproach is not trivial, for it strongly suggests why systems theory is in systemic need of religion. It must assign a place to religion in the total system called world society (*Weltgesellschaft*); otherwise the entire system would collapse.

The problem is that God must be communicated in order to become relevant for world society. Then question is: How can God be communicated at all? The communication of God (gen. subjectivus) is *sui generis* and unlike any other communication situation. Succinctly put: God communicates but cannot be communicated. For Luhmann's sociology of religion this is both the problem and the solution in a nutshell (Luhmann 1977). A brief summary shows the immanent need for religion in his systems theory:

1. There are no proper speech forms though which to designate God.
2. Conversely, 'God' in speech designates everything and is not a discriminatory term. (This is universal. It does not just feature in animistic religion or in the religious philosophies of the *deus sive natura* kind; it also corresponds to the biblical prohibition against the use of the name 'God.')
3. Even though, in a system operating with meaning, it is not possible to observe 'God' (i.e., to differentiate one part of the system-produced reality as 'God,' and the remainder as 'not-God'), the system itself can behave as if observed by God. The communication of God (gen. obj.) is thus based on the communication of God (gen. sub.).
4. In such a meaning system, observation by God is a 'difference that makes a difference' – that is, creates information for the system.
5. Only a difference that produces such a difference that it transcends immanence (everything that is 'real' to that system) can produce as well an immanent 'placeholder' for this transcendence.
6. The 'Chiffre' holds the place of the transcendent in the immanent. It can stand for any (immanent) meaning but has itself no meaning.
7. The God-Chiffre is a placeholder of global meaning, so the risk of the founding selectivity for meaning systems becomes treatable. Systems select, thereby reducing the complexity of their environment, but they cannot 'see' what is excluded (that which is negatively selected, i.e., not attributed to its Self but to its Other). The invisible (not the meaning-less, as this negation would be treated

again through the means of meaning) remains present as a risk and as an ungraspable threat (i.e., that the meaningfully selected might have excluded something vital for its survival). Meaning is exclusive (in the double sense), and its reflexive Other is risk.
8. The 'Chiffre' translates threatening risk into treatable risk, but the price for this function beyond selection is that it has no information value; it literally transcends that which is selected as meaning.
9. Systems can behave as if the Cipher were a meaning, by assigning to it a differentiating function: What makes meaning itself meaningful (and discards as 'nothing' what does not make meaning)? The paradox of the origin of the meaning-creating differentiation cannot be observed with meaning, as systems see only meaning as a result of this differentiation. They can only be observed by a transcendent God. Then the effect is a positive/negative difference in the immanent world.
10. There is, however, an instance where the unity of the distinction of meaning and its other is mirrored in the (auto-referential) experience of the soul and the (allo-referential) experience of God. The unique place of this paradox is the language of the mystics. This is the paramount case of religious communication in its purest form, but (or *because*) its meaning is never clear. The (auto-referential) soul understands herself as immanence – that desires, however, to observe God as her transcendence because she sees herself observed by Him. What is communicated by the mystical soul? Is it its own psychology? Is it God, the Other? This example relates to the selection risk of the psychic system. The social system also establishes a religious subsystem that straddles the same boundary of meaning itself. Analogically, therefore, the Church as Mystical Body always remains a paradox – or it ceases to exist.
11. Because mysticism as 'transcendental experience' (*contradictio in adjecto*) is difficult to sustain and even more to transform into societal institution, the transcendent can also become the sacred and produce an innerworldly difference, the profane, or the morally good and bad, and so on. Such an immanent transcendence, however, cannot sustain its risk-treating function.

The circularity of the foundation of systems theory could not have been resolved more elegantly. It is certainly not a theological statement, but as a foundation of communication it concerns the foundation of society *in se*. As its latent selection paradox, God has no information value for any communication. Without information value, God has no usefulness in practical interactions, and not even the attribution of secondary values (as used in soap operas) can 'sell' God in a propagandistic manner (i.e., through a discourse of appraisal). The communication of God (gen. obj.), a meaning system that observes its observer, can occur where the selection risk of meaning as such is felt. The psychic system, one of the two meaning systems, depends on interiority, where the risk can become angst – a still unnameable risk.

Now, how can one communicate that which by definition has no meaning? Furthermore, what are the technical consequences for mediated communication? A technically viable solution for the mass media communication of God is His transformation into Self-display. When we blend Luhmann's media theory with his sociology of religion, the society-founding God has the potential to turn not just into news but (even more) into entertainment. The differentiating code in the system of mass communication is not truth, but novelty: the media produce actuality through their system operation. This means, therefore, the rejection of everything that is as unchanging as truth (which is a function of the scientific social system) on the basis of simple credibility (facts of actuality are credible inasmuch as they are probable and predictable). Such selection criteria reject the non-actual non-events, which somehow must remain co-present (i.e., 'appresented' v. *supra*) as the other side of the stream of novelty. In Luhmann's theory of mass media (2000), the selection risk of an unquestioned credibility of the news is compensated for by a questionable credibility of the advertisement component of mass media and the stereotyped freedom of selection for the entertained subject. It is therefore in this locus of the mass media landscape that the communication of God becomes a possibility: God must become a matter of subjectivity in order to become communicable. Conversely, the 'God' of mass media is a selection neither of actuality (positive code) nor of 'beautiful appearance' (as negative code of the actual). However, 'God' is linked with the very selectivity of mass media.

'God' must not escape the boundaries of entertainment lest it be destructive of the paradox of the system-founding selection itself. Launching unmitigated mystical language in the mass media should have a similar exorcising effect as Orson Welles's radio experiment with Martian landings. The Middle Ages and the beginning of modernity had their own mystical mass phenomena: Luther's adversary Thomas Kreuzer, the Anabaptist Republic of Münster, Giacomo da Fiore, Tommaso Campanella, los Alumbrados, Loudon, the Hussites, and so on. Announcing the end of the universe is absolute news, certainly, but not a news item. As a news item it would at once destroy the credibility of the news system's selectivity. This sort of destruction is wrapped as entertainment when it becomes 'demoniac possession' in movies such as *The Preacher* and *Guyana Tragedy: The Story of Jim Jones*.

A mystic's language shares, with the mass media, the conditions of the communication of God only insofar as it must be relegated to subjectivity. On this common ground, however, we encounter the potential for producing the discriminate public meaning 'God,' both as publicity and as entertainment. In the orderly world of entertainment, subjectivity is the display of one's Self and its interpretation by another Self (see below). This possibility is realized in the mass media system, first, through the reduction of the communication of God to the display of the two selves of enunciation, and second, in narrative techniques of displaying selves. If interiority is the locus, one must display it externally as interiority. In this passage a crucial change takes place:[9] interiority ceases to be I-experience and is transformed into Me-display. For mediated religious communication this means, first, a public self-identity that displays its religious experience, and second, another Me (requiring a social identity to receive the display).

Since self-reflection of the total society can never obliterate the system-founding latency, except in the God-Chiffre, it still must ascertain communication. The contribution to society *in se* of the mass media system is at the same time irritation (novelty) and a stable latency. This comprises communicating God as society's transcendent solution to its paradox, and therefore mere intersystemic viable representations, as public relations are conceptualized, are not up to that ultimate task (Hoffjann 2001).

In the scientific self-reflection of the total society, of which science is merely a single (albeit quite special) partial system, this question immediately arises: What exerts the ultimate pressure to solve the problem of which the system is the solution (selectivity pressure, risk)? This question concedes that subjectivity is not the standard measure of systems theory (Welker 1985) – a strong temptation, especially when the comparison is between cognition and the science system. Quite the contrary, the problem of ultimate justification arises from within functional systems theory itself, for it is embedded in the very definition of systems that there be a drop in the level of complexity. A relatively more complex environment exercises a pressure on a system to solve the problem of complexity by reducing it. The higher the environmental complexity, the higher the internal system complexity must be; but in any case, it needs to be lower than the complexity of the environment. Despite its evolutionary openness to ever-expanding systems (Luhmann 1977, 165), there needs to be an outer boundary; otherwise, the ultimate system would collapse. Traditionally, the boundary of the cognizable was constituted by the *a priori* determinable cognitive capacity of the subject. This boundary now comprises another totality, 'world society.' The pressure for adaptation comes *per definitionem* from outside; this applies also to every partial system determined by functional differentiation in its relevant system environment.[10]

The place assigned to religion within 'world society' calls for a critique of two ambiguous or unsolvable problems: the world horizon, and the reflexivity of knowledge. The world is the quasi-environment of the world society and thus constitutes the ultimate total complexity equal to the *tohu-bohu* of total chaos. However, the environment is always the environment of one system, whose environmental selection achievement determines the relevant objects to which it is capable of relating in order to solve them as its problem. Environment and system determine each other, since every system has its proper environment. With the highest and ultimate system, however, that can no longer be the case. If there existed another possibility for differentiating what is system from what is environment, there would have to exist a further system, from the perspective of which this differentiation would have to be enacted. It follows that the ultimate system can have no opposite except in an environment determined by that system. However, a system without its proper environment cannot be. So this is where God provides to everything immanent a last difference in His transcendence – or at the appearance of it.

The original promise of the medium idea for functionalist theories was for a bridge over the otherwise deep abyss between the real and the concept, the chaotic environment and the organized system. Setting aside the inherent ambiguity in Luhmann's account, the solution involves assuming a drop of the outside level, when the central organizing power resides in the inner system. That still does not give the independent real access to the rule making, whereas it gives total control to the system. All realist – and *a fortiori* all empirical – theories demand a corrective function for a brute force outside the idea upon the idea. Without such corrective influence, the gap persists unilaterally.

4.2 Is There a Need for a Separate Semiotic Media Theory?

The medium concept was intended to fill central lacunae in systems theory. Because Habermas is taking his cue from Parsons's functionalism, that concept plays a similar role in his fundamental pragmatism. Without the medium and the relative fixation on an emergent system that it provides, the increasing complexity of system differentiation would no longer be practicable. On this basis alone can a new system emerge. Media become the building blocks of a completely formal conception of system evolution, which is thus thinkable without thinking consciousness or a progress in cognition. The systemic place of the medium in systems theory, then, is quite different from that of the sign in semiotic. It might be tempting, nevertheless, not merely to compare but even to amalgamate the two ideas.

No one seems to claim seriously that Peirce's semiotic and Luhmann's systems theory are one and the same, on principle. Though from a certain level of idea development upward, at least in some places, it should not prove too difficult to show some sort of similarity. On the other hand, there have been repeated attempts to show that these two fundamental ideas can conveniently complement each other and thus counterbalance their respective 'weaknesses.' This has happened mostly in cybersemiotics. Yet the path to such a goal inevitably leads to some quite forced interpretations, and the part being adjusted is usually Peirce's semiotic. Even though a general openness towards thinking in systems could probably be realized through semiotic means, there is no real basis for an ontology of sorts in systems theory of the Luhmann type. Attempts in this direction (Jahraus and Ort 2001) are instructive, because they can only prove by their failings the radical diversity of the two approaches. After Brier had attempted this with von Foerster (Brier 2003, 2005), Scheibmayr (2004) in a similar fashion – with Luhmann – tried to remedy the resultant shortcomings. In particular, Luhmann's ambiguities and vacillations are in his inadequate awareness of signs. Borrowings from a Peirce-ish semiotic therefore are suggestive. However, not even here do we see a genuine reconciliation or mediation of the two architectonic systems of thought – at best, we might view this as one borrowing from the other.

Moreover, there is no natural vantage point from which one can compare Peirce's semiotic with Luhmann's systems theory. If at all, one might see possible agreement on an at first sight surprisingly deep logical level. This possibility, however, relies on the historical fact that

Spencer-Brown – whom Varela and (at a later stage) Luhmann applied to their system theories – understood himself as an interpreter and follower of certain Peircean approaches in the (alpha part of the) existential graphs. This corresponds to the logic of entitative graphs preceding the existential ones (Peirce, CP 3.468ff The Logic of Relatives 1897 cf.4.434 Logical Tracts, No. 2 c.903). Luhmann, however, interprets Spencer-Brown from the beginning in a direction where he identifies boundary logic as system boundary.

How Luhmann managed to make Spencer-Brown's 'calculus of indications' bear fruit for his systems theory has been described in various degrees of detail (Clam 2000; Schiltz 2007). But this should not obscure the fact that the introduction of this calculus took place at a relatively late stage in theory development (Clam 2000), and even then outside the strictly logical context of the origin. Luhmann merely makes use of this protologic, which some judge as an elegant (albeit surrounded by an aura of strangeness) logical semantic of Boolean predicate logic. For the 'calculus of indications,' however, this strictly logical context is decisive. Kauffman (2001, 80): 'In essence what Spencer-Brown adds to the existential graphs, is the use of the unmarked state. That is, he allows the use of empty space in place of a complex of Signs. This makes a profound difference and reveals a beautiful and simple calculus of indications underlying the existential graphs. Indeed Spencer-Brown's true contribution is that he added Nothing to the Peirce theory!'

As a reception of Laws of Form, Luhmann's approach has been the object of controversial appraisals. The reason is that, in view of the 'creative' reception of Spencer-Brown, Luhmann often is no longer compatible with the original. By imposing the logic of the 'calculus of indications' on the properties of the system already previously established, he disperses effectively the whole logical stringency of the calculus. This especially applies to Spencer-Brown's 'distinction' when it is reflected directly onto the drop in the level of complexity between system and environment. Henning criticizes this from a logical point of view, for in the 'calculus of indications' exist only the two states 'marked' and 'unmarked.' There is no possibility of a higher complexity ('$<_x$') existing in the unmarked space than in the marked one. In Luhmann's theory, by contrast, this is constitutive of the system, the very definition of its boundary. Hennig (2000, 167): 'Der Differenzbegriff der Laws of Form weicht aber von dem hier geforderten $<_x$ ab. Er ist nicht symmetrisch (in dem hier geforderten Sinn) und nicht transitiv. Vielmehr findet man, wenn man' B = $\overline{A|}$ als, A $<_x$ B' liest: A $\neq_x$ B

⇒ A <$_x$ B und B <$_x$ A. [...] Ein Spencer-Brownscher Operator kann nur die bloße Verschiedenheit oder Nichtverschiedenheit (Identität) zweier Objekte ausdrücken.'

Spencer-Brown's difference is strictly a contradictory one and can only be expressed as a total negation (which is precisely the meaning of the corner-like operator specific to the syntax of Laws of Form); whereas in Luhmann the difference is not only relative ('higher than') but also only a contrary one (which merely negates parts of the affirmed). However, this is difficult to state in an unambiguous manner, given Luhmann's sometimes rather imprecise terminology (Scheibmayr 2004). Now, such a marked space is constitutive of the system – for example, the guiding difference (*Leitdifferenz*) or contrary difference (e.g., between lawful/unlawful that constitutes the law system). If, in this case, law constitutes the marked space, that does not mean necessarily in Luhmann that as difference there will always be an unlawful as appresentation (borrowed from Husserl, cf. §4.1). Luhmann is capable of replacing Spencer-Brown's unmarked space with another antipole as well. It makes his systems even more malleable that this can be done even *a posteriori*, contributing to an impression of arbitrariness. Then there exists on the one side positive law; on the side of the unmarked space one can substitute for instance any non-positive religious justice (e.g., 'justice' or righteousness in the biblical sense). All of that would be (literally) unthinkable in a 'calculus of indications,' as Hennig has shown.

This form of differentiation reminds us more of positional differences in Saussure than of Spencer-Brown's distinction (Hennig 2000, 176–8). However, in Luhmann it is never exactly clear whether the form concept is owed to Spencer-Brown's form or is taken from the gestalt psychologist Fritz Heider's distinction between medium and form. Since he named and used both sources, supposedly Luhmann believes that he can identify one with the other. But at least for Spencer-Brown, this destroys the logic. It is safe to say for Luhmann that the form analysis in Spencer-Brown's sense was not the original expression of systems theory; but in view of the contradictory interpretations, it was not a congenial one. It is clear that the system idea was cast into the form concept later on, but in such a way that Spencer-Brown's form had to be bent and adjusted considerably.

If we applied this form concept to systems theory, and not systems theory to a concept of form, we might arrive at results different from Luhmann's. Then we might well conceive a cybersemiotic, especially if the origin of that form in Peirce's existential graphs were acknowledged

(Kauffman 2001). The alpha part of the existential graphs, as much as Spencer-Brown's Laws of Form, originates in a treatise on the logic of implication. The unusual notation of the 'corner' over the right side of a variable owes its origin to Peirce's 'sign of illation,' in *The Logical Algebra of Boole* (Peirce 1976, NEM IV, 106–15). Originally this involved an attractive idea of combining negation (for which the stroke above the letter stands) with the plus sign (Kauffman 2001, 81–3). The reason for this was the insight that implication, A implying B, is logically equivalent to the expression 'not (A and not B)'. The negation was graphically notated in the existential graphs as a circling, or with an oval. In algebraic notation, however, the same matter became the sign of illation.

If we follow Kauffman's argumentation (2001, 100-9), Peirce's mathematics even contained, as 'sign of itself' (CP 2.230-2), what corresponded to Spencer-Brown's later 're-entry.' We are referring here to an interesting occurrence of self-reference, where a sign explains itself even though in normal circumstances it needs an object as its other. As an instance of this self-reference, Peirce used the example of the map that must itself appear on the terrain it represents, at one determinate point, and then has to interpret itself. This is applicable also to language, as it always must be used when language itself is being investigated. This does not lead to a collapse – or as Luhmann used to say, a tautology – respectively a paradox (e.g., the paradox of the Cretan asserting that all Cretans are liars). For Peirce, this leads to a completely different solution. His mathematics and philosophy know of infinitesimals, the real continuity of the unlimited, and 'self-reference is infinity in finite guise' (Kauffman 2001, 105). Peirce proves his point with the example of time. 'It is difficult to explain the fact of memory and our apparently perceiving the flow of time, unless we suppose immediate consciousness to extend beyond a single instant. Yet if we make such a supposition we fall into grave difficulties unless we suppose the time of which we are immediately conscious to be strictly infinitesimal' (Peirce, NEM III, 124 'The Question of Infinitesimals'). If the present were an instant, we should experience an infinite succession of instants; what we really experience, however, is a flux of time in which there exist no distinct, infinitely short instants. This is why only because of distinct instants can Achilles never overtake the tortoise. Modern mathematics with Bolzano, Cauchy, and Weierstraß learned to operate with limits and attained a mathematically precise grasp of this philosophical insight. However, we would be going well beyond the limits of our inquiry by attempting to reconstruct the metaphysical consequences arising from

Peirce's logic and his presuppositions. Peirce himself expanded on this in his late philosophy, calling the comprehensive philosophical reflection of continuity synechism.

In Luhmann there is no connection left to all this. He sees his systems theory confronted with the identical problems of the tautology of the selection, but he is incapable of going beyond a 'fruitful circularity,' which with Spencer-Brown he terms, rather quaintly, 're-entry.' Actually, he is no longer capable of treating his systems theory with its own means (Scheibmayr 2004), except by referring to his peculiar Spencer-Brown interpretation. The theory of form and medium is incompatible with the Laws of Form (Hennig 2000; Scheibmayr 2004) and ultimately only makes patent the ontology of radical constructivism. On this level there is no possible bridge to Peirce's very idea of the sign.

If there is ever a need for a serious discussion with semiotic (and from Luhmann's constructivist side, there is no reason at all), this debate will have to take place at a deeper level. One will have to acknowledge that systems theory wants to take its central principles from a sort of protologic, which has its architectonic equivalent in the fundamental level of categories in semiotic (Brier 1996). That will peg us firmly to Luhmann's Spencer-Brown interpretation. It remains highly doubtful, though, whether the logic of Spencer-Brown is indeed as central to the architecture of systems theory as Luhmann claims (i.e., that it is more than an auxiliary *a posteriori* justification of system differentiation). At the same time, a serious debate of Spencer-Brown's logic is beyond our scope here, though it deserves to be taken up elsewhere. For Luhmann, the practical advantage consisted in the first place in justifying the selectivity of the system with the proto-principle 'draw a distinction!' in Laws of Form. In his interpretation, though, the very reason for making the difference, the choice of the side in 'crossing the line,' is no longer capable of being reflected, for if one could indicate a purpose for a goal of selection, one would be beyond the difference with an identity. Whether it would still be apposite to speak of evolutionary thought, then, is questionable.

4.3 Signs of Society

Of greater immediate importance is this practical question: Is a semiotic pragmatism in need of a medium, and if so, why? Why would it (or not) need to turn into a media theory providing the glue to social functioning, and, besides, a social explication of the media industry?

Conversely, why does Luhmann need the form–media difference? The keystone of Luhmann's approach for a theory of society was to overcome any theory based on the concept of action. That concept seemed to him a vestige of foregone ages, of metaphysical thought, and, with regard to society, of a hierarchical concept of governance. The *system* was thus meant to replace the subject, its action, and the objective world of its action. What became an architectonic necessity in Luhmann – that is, to enable evolutionary levels of emergences of systems – need have no correspondence in Peirce. Otherwise, should Luhmann have discovered a rule relevant to any evolutionary thought, including Peirce's? Would the infinity of interpretations in the sign process be well served if interpretative levels could be formed, if relational constructivity and degeneration could be limited? Peirce, for his part, was no sociologist *avant la lettre* and did not directly apply semiotic to society (it is probable that he did not even have a particular interest in sociology, except for economy). Outside critical commonsensism, Peirce exerted no further explanatory pressure, and, here, his scope was limited to the sociohistorical conditions of cognition, its advancement (or the absence of it) through cycles of doubt and belief. Perhaps there exists a nucleus of Peircean sociology or proto-sociology, when he takes up topics of historiography and economics. For functionalists such as Parsons and his successor Luhmann, the global explanation of society *in se* – and the universalistic explanation of all in terms of society – was the original problem and approach.

For Luhmann's sociological proto-premise against action-based theory, it would constitute at least an indirect challenge to consider the original intuition of pragmatism. It is more than a historical coincidence that precisely this pragmatism generated, in the Chicago School from Dewey to Mead, a sociology oriented decidedly towards a concept of action. It is puzzling (and continues to be so) that in the first formulation of pragmatism, in Peirce's *Popular Science Monthly* series, any allusion to semiotic is wanting, though Peirce even by then had a solid grasp of it (Hookway 2000). In his many expositions of pragmatism – which by then, for better precision, he called Pragmaticism – the later Peirce had to wage a constant struggle against it being misinterpreted as a 'practical science' of useful ('vitally important') matters in the sense of William James. In the original version, then, there is no trace of an equivalent to Luhmann's medium (except perhaps in the method of authority), not even in the guise of signs: no trace of solidified rules of observation (if that is what a medium stands for), and not even a Habermasian 'linguistic liquidification.' In its origin, all is centred on the problem of cognitive certainty (i.e., truth), which further constrains behaviour to the practical consequences of a cognition. Even then, Peirce in this article series conspicuously does not deny that there are other types of behaviour or action that are not under the control of pure cognition, but rather (for instance) under the control of tenacity, authority, and the metaphysically pleasing. All those other, non-scientific methods are lacking in their sustainability, which implies that ultimately they fall under the control of experience with reality.

Precisely in light of the abyss between Peirce's own pragmatism as a theory of truth and that which made pragmatism so famous in later social sciences (down to symbolic interactionism), this question arises: How far can society be a cognitive matter of science, if at all? If it cannot be scientific, must it be abandoned as a cognitive object altogether? Could it be that society consists merely of an illusionary feeling (possibly comparable to a gigantic 'symbolically generalized medium' in Luhmann's sense)? These suspicions are kindled even more by Peirce's disparaging remarks on 'vitally important topics.'[11] This has the effect of placing all social domains firmly outside strict behavioural control by experience, which in turn imposes on a scientist the need to be 'detached.' As a consequence, in acting socially one would have to abandon oneself to tenacity as a method (which is easily encountered in ideology, partisanship, and the like), or act with methods of authority (which, since the age of enlightened despotism, appears almost to be a normal state of public affairs, down to such minor contemporary forms as technocracy). This – which Peirce called the *logica utens* – would stand a good chance of functioning quite well for a certain time. Ultimately, though, for social action, a method that learns from experience must also exist. This alone is the practical meaning of being a method of science. For society to be scientific, it would have to be capable of learning through experience and of changing as a consequence of new experiences. Nothing seems to be more resistant to change, though, than social rules and regulations.

This is not so much the question of whether something like 'society' exists at all. That question is derived more from the questions generated by sociological methods, which have very good reasons to doubt the validity of a methodological construct called 'society.' One might speculate, though, whether behind this (not so absurd) question lies the *real* one: Can the methods of objective sciences grasp society? For society certainly does not exist in the sense of bivalent physical objects (see above). The real question then becomes: As what does society become a datum? This question is nonsense for all those who reduce reality to the physically existent and who would then turn it into 'protocol sentences' in order to make at least symbolic, onto-semantic manipulations possible. But if reality is more than the merely existent, there must be more than one single cognitive behaviour that appropriates reality. That there is indeed more than one single mode of reality can only be ascertained when we actually change our cognitive behaviour – that is, when we behave differently when experiencing non-physical reality. World appropriation and appropriation of social reality are two different types of behaviour from which a metaphysician might deduce different modes of reality. Since this is behaviour that is controlled by these types' respective rules in the real or imaginary world, this is also a case of a triadic relation between a rule and a case (which in turn consists of 'whatness' and 'hereness,' quality and event, quiddity and haecceity). Every controlled behaviour is therefore immediately a sign relation, which means that it can be interpreted.

In social behaviour, our actual object is a duty – how we ought to behave. Society means the regulation of what can be acted legitimately, not the action itself: 'society,' then, resembles a second intention by being something *in* something else. 'Oughts' differ essentially from 'musts'; the latter express necessities derived from the rule-like constraints of reality, whereas the former cannot be cast directly as cognitive rules. From an actor's perspective, society represents ethical behaviour, which is present only as a feeling for the 'right thing to do.' Not even the sum total of experiences of the past constitute an equivalent for the right thing, because that lies, by definition, in the future and can never consist in a repetition of a past thing. Legal hermeneutics, for instance, is a practice not of *applying* a law but of *interpreting* a situation – at hand or in pure imagination – in such a way that it is seen as a class of past experiences, which can then be generalized as a general normative rule.

In a quite radical departure from Kant, Peirce's pragmatism rejected the triplification of critique of cognition, ethic, and aesthetic. There is no reason to exclude ethic from the realm of cognition, as if it consisted merely of individual interests, which can be generalized only in an abstract way. Here, too, common sense comes to bear, if the attitude is in the first place a conservatively 'holding fast to what one had held on in the past.' Peirce (CP 1.573): 'Ethics is not practics [i.e., Antethics]; first, because ethics involves more than the theory of such conformity [i.e., of action to an ideal]; namely, it involves the theory of the ideal itself, the nature of the summum bonum; and secondly, because, in so far as ethics studies the conformity of conduct to an ideal, it is limited to a particular ideal, which, whatever the professions of moralists may be, is in fact nothing but a sort of composite photograph of the conscience of the members of the community. In short, it is nothing but a traditional standard, accepted, very wisely, without radical criticism, but with a silly pretence of critical examination. The science of morality, virtuous conduct, right-living, can hardly claim a place among the heuretic sciences.' In this work, one of the many versions of the *Basis of Pragmaticism in the Normative Sciences* (1905–6), Peirce attempts to lay the ground for his philosophy as a whole in normativity. He concerns himself with an ethic (respectively, with 'antethics' or 'practics') as science, not simply with a practical science that describes or prescribes the conformity of practices with existing ideals. This ethic is, properly, behaviour towards an ideal. The 'silly pretence of critical examination' refers to particular ideals that, because of their contingency, are not investigable under the regard of general principles.

For the same reasons, society *in se* is not deducible from descriptions of concrete societies. The question then arises: Are we capable of ever striving for such an absolute concept of society *in se*? Do we not always deal only with *concrete* societies? In this problem context, the place of normative sciences in Peirce's architecture becomes crucially relevant. These three normativities effectively constitute – as a direct and necessary result of the pragmatic approach itself – the critical basis for a metaphysic, which applies principles of logic to reality (cf. Peirce, Houser, and Kloesel 1992, II:376).[12] This, however, is not the real situation of scientific research, which has no concerns for metaphysics. Research cannot lean upon an abstract 'final opinion'; it can thrive only by being constantly corrected (*pace* Thomas Kuhn). In real-world cognitive behaviour, one must learn from experience – and one is fallible. But the cognitive value of science is not the only behaviour control.

For behaviour enacted under the control of ethical values, in a similar way one can assume a control mechanism typical of this behaviour. This control, too, must come from experience, but not in the same mode as scientific cognitive behaviour. Is ethic not cognitive, then? There is no need to go so far as to postulate an entirely different mode of cognition. Owing to the ordinality of Peircean Categories, expressed in their relational versions as Firstness, Secondness, and Thirdness, the scientific research process comprises a component based on instinct. In terms of argumentation theory, this process is called *abduction*. Peirce coined this concept as an intermediate link between *induction* and *deduction*, while insisting on the independence of this mode of inference. Instinct in research consists in doing mental-imaginary experimentation with a problem and then in suddenly finding a fitting solution. If this solution is valid, it is applied deductively as a second step to any number of cases; from that point on, it is confirmed repeatedly – albeit never finally. The mental or real experiment is merely inductive inference, which could never achieve any result without abduction.

Instinct has the same abductive function in ethically determined behaviour as it has in scientific cognition. Ethic is also concerned, like all commonsense situations (but not metaphysic), with 'ideas and beliefs that man's situation absolutely forces upon him' (Peirce, CP 1.129). At any rate, this is already more than pure imagination, or pure '*Spieltrieb*' as Peirce says, for this is the nature of the Firstness of aesthetics. Abductive instinct adds a shock of experience with outside reality – comprising imagination, of course – by reason of the ordinality of categorial relations.

What, though, does ethic lack that cognition has? Certainly, an important difference relates to the uncertain, non-physical object, which never allows arriving at the same habitual certainty in cognition. This cognitive certainty obtains with the so-called 'laws' of nature (even though these are not more than particularly stable cognitive habits of behaviour). Furthermore, there is a lack in possibilities of deduction because this would require laws of ethic. The only law of ethic that Peirce envisages as a normative science that 'distinguishes what ought to be from what ought not to be' (Peirce, CP 1.186) is the pragmatic value of bivalent truth (which assumes only two values: true or false). The implication of this is the ethical duty to let oneself be affected by the real.[13] The learning capacity of ethical behaviour depends on acting becoming behaviour – that is, deliberating and oriented towards all future acting. Peirce (CP 1.574): 'It has been a great, but frequent, error of writers on ethics to confound an ideal of conduct with a motive to action. The truth is that these two objects belong to different categories. Every action has a motive; but an ideal only belongs to a line [of] conduct which is deliberate. To say that conduct is deliberate implies that each action, or each important action, is reviewed by the actor and that his judgment is passed upon it, as to whether he wishes his future conduct to be like that or not. His ideal is the kind of conduct which attracts him upon review.'

The ideal originates in normative aesthetics and is then integrated into the triadic sign relation, whereas learning concerns the recognition of consequences and foresight. Peirce (NEM IV:142): 'To learn is to acquire a habit. What makes men learn? Not merely the sight of what they are accustomed to, but perpetual new experiences which throws them into a habit of tossing aside old ideas and forming new ones.' In a certain sense, this is already a generality to which feeling can enter into a relation. Peirce (CP 1.574):

> His self-criticism, followed by a more or less conscious resolution that in its turn excites a determination of his habit, will, with the aid of the sequelæ, modify a future action; but it will not generally be a moving cause to action. It is an almost purely passive liking for a way of doing whatever he may be moved to do. Although it affects his own conduct, and nobody else s, yet the quality of feeling (for it is merely a quality of feeling) is just the same, whether his own conduct or that of another person, real or imaginary, is the object of the feeling; or whether it be connected with the thought of any action or not. If conduct is to be thoroughly deliberate, the ideal must be a habit of feeling which has grown up under the influence of a course of self-criticisms and of hetero-criticisms; and the theory of the deliberate formation of such habits of feeling is what ought to be meant by esthetics.

The generality of deliberate conduct is not immediately what is today usually called 'society.' So far, this is clear. It is still necessary that – albeit bound to a subject – the feeling deliberate one's own conduct critically as much as that of other persons regarding future consequences (*sequelae*). To this corresponds the *summum bonum*, quoted above from the *Minute Logic* (CP 1.575).

Any Pragmaticist vision of the social in principle holds a concomitant ethical definition of society – but this is not to imply a moral definition. Ethic in Peirce's sense is part of reality, inasmuch as it is part of common sense. In this treasure of past experience, everyone believes and holds on to those beliefs until unexpected experiences force themselves onto these believers. This ethical common sense is absolutely binding as long as no living doubt proves it inadequate or false. Since all reality is the triadic relation instantiated in conduct, but also in the sign relation, ethic is a necessary part of all reality. This applies as well to cognition, which is a conduct – not a conceptual grasp of sensory data, and not consciousness that seeks its other by means of intention.

Ethic introduces an element of uncertainty into the cognition of reality. This becomes evident in the ethical instinct, which, though it forces itself upon us as absolutely binding, nevertheless does not require us to hold on to it permanently. Hyperbolically, one might call it a 'firm contingency,' provisionally absolutely binding. This is the consequence of the Pragmaticist approach as such, which does not consist of mere rules of conduct. Similarly, one would be doing away with a theory of society if society were merely deduced from rules, which is the approach generally taken by the so-called agency theories. Next to rules, instinct forms part of society. The 'inventive,' the self-confident customs, those cultural contingencies that in a given situation instinctively find solutions to which they hold on – all of these constitute ethical correlates in triadic relation to society. A Pragmaticist understanding of society could easily be taken for an institutional theory, if there were not real and living doubt besides, if there were not a certain playfulness in that theory. This means that any theory pretending to be both pragmatic and semiotic must provide for both: a place for instinct, and a place for rules.

This inclusion of ethic into a theory of society need not stop us from concerning ourselves with what might be called a 'metaphysic of society.' The interest here is in spelling out the consequences for reality as such, which result from a Pragmaticist approach to the social.[14] This last reality as such, however, is quite different from the common sense of social reality, within which our concrete behaviour takes place. Clifford Geertz seems to concur, with his reservation that not much interesting stuff can be cognized thither of 'thick descriptions,' which are loaded with concreteness. The rest is very general observations on very general, anthropologically constant human solutions to problems. Metaphysics results in a kind of cognition 'from the end' – that is, from an ideal state of perfect cognition. This is a position that nobody can ever take in – except, of course, if this is done in a philosophy that draws the most general consequences from the logical form of concrete behaviour in its entirety. The only analogy to this social metaphysic is the philosophy of nature, which Peirce calls 'material metaphysic.'

In Peirce's well-known 'Fixation of Belief' section, where he describes the four methods to 'free ourselves from doubt and pass into a state of belief' (cf., CP 5.372), we find a quite pertinent illustration of commonsense conduct. The 'method of tenacity' is nothing other than making feelings an absolute point of reference. It is impossible to deny an absolutely binding character to feeling – as long as we have one. Similarly, one must recognize that feeling's function in cognitive behaviour is irreplaceable. Furthermore, the 'method of authority' is not confined to 'organized faiths' (CP 5.380). On the contrary, it is normal scientific practice – a point that Kuhn makes quite famously:

> Mopping-up operations are what engage most scientists throughout their careers. They constitute what I am here calling normal science. Closely examined, whether historically or in the contemporary laboratory, that enterprise seems an attempt to force nature into the preformed and relatively inflexible box that the paradigm supplies. No part of the aim of normal science is to call forth new sorts of phenomena; indeed those that will not fit the box are often not seen at all. Nor do scientists normally aim to invent new theories, and they are often intolerant of those invented by others. Instead, normal-scientific research is directed to the articulation of those phenomena and theories that the paradigm already supplies. (1970, 24)

The conservative resistance against innovations is justified because the 'living doubt' must be ponderous enough to produce a genuinely new belief. If one wanted to live knowing that all knowing is preliminary, this could never be a practical solution but at best metaphysical knowledge – a metaphysic derived from Descartes's methodical doubt. On closer inspection, the 'method of science' is a step backwards even before the metaphysical '*a priori* method,' for the latter 'knows' too much, or too permanently. There is no place for fallible truth, which not only is in an opposite position to doubt, but also must integrate doubt into truth.

A semiotic theory of society stands in the same situation: that of choosing between society as an 'eternal' institution consisting of its rules, and society conceived as ethical conduct. Media scandals evince the practical meaning of this difference. The 'eternal' type of society is modelled in the θέατρον, as we saw in our discussion, where 'eternal' divine knowledge shapes and rules proper action on the world stage. Public opinion as teleological culture is entirely fixated on rules. Whereas in the ethical conduct model, while still holding fast to what is firmly believed, one cannot close oneself to unexpected experiences. This model would otherwise yield to 'authority' – a method that, while still instinctive, is nevertheless no longer ethical. Here, too, the production of scandals in mass media shows how teleological knowledge cohabits with coercion, particularly with sanctions. Thus a scandal in the media, in its essential characteristics, differs from ethical indignation. The latter has the capacity to change our basis of right conduct; for ethic, while a feeling, still partakes in surprises. It therefore shares the hope for progress in knowledge. That, however, cannot be understood in the sense of an effective causality, as an accumulation of true knowledge, but only in a Pragmaticist-fallible sense and therefore as subject to correction – at least in the long run. Ethical instinct in most circumstances acts rightly on the basis of a treasure of experience. When a scandal shakes that instinct, it can adjust and correct the basis of its feeling. In a media scandal, by contrast, the instinct is teleologically predetermined. It can strengthen this predetermination of knowing the rightness of action only in a conservative pattern. Its basis is not experience but the predetermination of a goal.

Unfortunately, a too narrow exegesis of Peirce's *Popular Science Monthly* series tends to treat pragmatism in a way that obfuscates the semiotic aspect. As a relational process, semiotic is nothing less than a determinate abstraction of cognitive behaviour. At the time those articles were written (1877–8), Peirce was reconceptualizing semiotic as a relation. He had succeeded in this task by 1882, but only around the turn of the century did semiotic assume its definitive form. In Peirce's middle creative phase, accordingly, there is an almost total lack of intensive interest and work on semiotic, in favour of natural science, logic (the *Grand Logic* is from 1893), and metaphysics (1891–3). This perhaps explains the silence in the semiotic treatment of pragmatism; it also indicates the direction it took after the turn of the century: never again did Peirce miss an occasion to emphasize it in his presentations of Pragmaticism.

What constitutes the appropriation of the real in society? How is social cognitive conduct possible? How does it take place? Peirce's answers evince the crucial extension that he introduced with semiotic into his later version of pragmatism, now called Pragmaticism. Instead of pursuing the somewhat sterile metaphysical question as to how the perfect cognition can ever be attained, in the long run, through the self-correcting 'scientific method,' we concern ourselves with the concrete next cognition. This interest is not occasioned by our object scandal, but is owed to the systemic organization of Peirce's thought. For the goal of Pragmaticism is not to speculate about a perfect *adaequatio intellectus et rei* – that is, to imagine an absolutely true cognition. Nor is it really of interest to sound out an Adamic state of cognition – that is, to approach cognition as if the object of inquiry were the 'first cognition.' What is relevant, rather, is an inquiry into the comparative truer or better of a truer or better cognition, without an ideal origin or an ideal end. *This* is the concrete, practical concern of what Peirce calls interpretation.

Without question, not all define the problem in this way. In many climes, the debate is still over whether a 'proposition corresponds to a fact' (even though the discussion in the later Vienna Circle led to the acknowledgment that there are no pure data without theory). This attitude continues to thrive under the rubric of media objectivity, or the facticity criterion, as well as in the popular self-conception of empirical social research. Hookway rightly emphasizes the fundamental difference between a philosophy based on usual truth conditions and Peirce's philosophy, which is based on the sign relation. The former is interested in the relation between a name and its bearer, proposition and referent. This relation also subsists in the sign relation; Peirce, however, recognized that this relation between proposition and referent is effective solely if it is interpreted as standing for this object. The interpretation is a decisive moment and cannot be presupposed tacitly, or suppressed, as in the first approach. Hookway tells us that 'according to Peirce, by contrast, the fundamental semantic relation is triadic. A name denotes an object only by being interpreted as denoting the object; a sentence expresses a proposition only by being understood or interpreted expressing it' (2000, 141).

If the purview is no longer monopolized by the relation of the sign to an outside reality, but includes interpretation, does the matrix of relations quickly become complex? Outside reality continues to dominate the conventional comprehension of sign. As a bivalent (true or false) placeholder of a state of affairs, the relation is a simple one, because it is no more than dyadic. The attractive insight of Peirce's semiotic consists precisely in understanding the relation as a genuinely triadic one, and not as a transitively triadic one that turns back into a dyadic placeholdership after being successfully interpreted.

Triadic relations are not unordered tuples of three elements. If that were so, any arbitrarily chosen element could be inserted at any arbitrary position. Whereas in a triad each element has its own nature, which is deducible from its position in the ordered series. Simplifying, one might say that in the first place must be a What (*qualitas*). At this stage, though, it is premature to speak of characteristics, as this would involve the thought of an object. This undefinedness evinces that 'what' can be anything – that is, *can* be, possibility. Such a relation obtains only to itself and is therefore monadic. Only in a further element is the mere possibility confined by existence. Only then does a relation exist between a *vis-à-vis* (*haecceitas*) and its what-ness (*ali-quid*). This relation is already more defined than merely possible, since it too must be either true or false (here the principle of the excluded middle applies). That the relation, a dyad, exists between two elements does not mean that these elements can be equal. Only here does the order of the elements in the relation come into play. As the semantic of First, Second, Third (and not one, two, three) suggests, the third element implies a second and first, but not the inverse, an upwards open scale. Quality comes first, in ordinal order, to existence, *haecceitas* before *hicceitas*. Much less exists than is possible. Existence therefore is less numerous than possibility. This fact is also seen in predication – for instance, 'the stove is black' contains a subject and a predicate. The predicate *is black* is much less determined than the subject *stove*, because everything that is possible can have the quality 'blackness.'

In expanding our example sentence to 'the stove is black through remnants of imperfect oxidation,' we enter the realm of triadic relations. This sentence conveys a general law of chemical oxidation of carbon, which adds to the simple joining of black and stove a new aspect of a different nature: law, or necessity. In our example we use a sentence, but a single term can also convey law. Then 'oxidation' is a triadic term, whereas 'blackness' is merely a monadic one. Though in the outside reality in both cases something becomes black, if that happens as oxidation, then we observe a law being enacted. Such connections of law are again much less numerous than existences or possibilities, but they contain the lower-order lower-adic relations.

In summary, every concrete cognition is in the sign, and signs are a triadic, ordered relation among three correlates, each of a different nature. It would be a big mistake to reduce signs to material indication-things, as is current in ordinary language. Sign means nothing less than this: that the entire cognitive world appropriation is specific relational processes.

As always, one can also represent the sign process as action – more precisely, as behaviour. Peirce himself, in the Pragmatic Maxim, did that. Most important aspects of the sign process, though, are also graspable in psychological terms. Yet in taking this route, one should never become oblivious of the foundation in the semiosis, from which psychic states are derived. Every correlate contributes always and unconditionally to every cognitive – that is, to controlled behaviour. The first correlate (Firstness, quality) answers the what-question of behaviour: What is to do? The second correlate (Secondness) answers the truth-question: Is it true or false, there or not there? Only the third correlate (Thirdness) addresses the general, the goal: For which purpose, what for? This simple determination of behaviour is not exhaustive, however, for the logical nature of each correlate is broader than this example of a simple action. Especially in social behaviour, the determination through the correlates turns out quite differently from, for instance, cognitive behaviour.

As it is never a mere material thing but always a relational process, a sign never 'is' simply. It is not only triple, but also in an ordinal ordered series in such a way that the first correlate (called the null correlate or 'medad') presupposes only itself, the second the first, and the third the second and first. A pragmatic illustration: a general goal of conduct always presupposes that it takes place or not, and the result must always be 'something.' If the behaviour is predominantly determined by the first correlate, it can remain a mere ideation of something. In more precise terms, the relation is degenerative and constructive, and thus a triad can degenerate into one determined by Firstness or Secondness. Granted, it is semantically rather generous to extend the term 'behaviour' or conduct to such a degree that it also accommodates 'possible behaviour' controlled by such a degenerate sign – still calling it behaviour. In practical life, daydreaming and fantasizing would correspond to this kind of behaviour. There exist hardly any social rules for this, except for psychotherapeutic 'diagnoses.' So it is impossible to reconstruct a concrete daydream from the designation. Yet even this sign and the first correlate have an indispensable role to play in social behaviour, as we will see later.

A Pragmaticist theory of society is clearly built on behaviour or action. The idea of action here is radically different from phenomenological theories (going back to Schütz) as well as from 'agency' theories. What phenomenological subjectivity of action – Schütz's 'subjective meaning' – is concerned about, however, is addressed by behaviour determined by Firstness (as we discuss below, as the First sign correlate). Furthermore, Pragmaticism also stands for realism. Social behaviour is quite literally unthinkable without a corrective in the real world. Regarding ethical behaviour, we have already discussed this as the capacity to learn – even as instinct. This alone is a foundation for any behavioural corrective by reality, even if it is strictly only an individual feeling.

Realism means, in fact, nothing short of postulating a way to bridge the hiatus between interiority and the outside world. Even today, many theories start from such a hiatus – for instance, when Habermas construes for this purpose a distinct validity claim, authenticity, which refers to the interior psychic world and to a dramaturgy of the same subject's external, social representation. Such a validity would be superfluous for Peirce; worse, it would be the telltale sign of a fundamental misunderstanding, which he fought in the subjectivism of William James (whom he criticized for mistaking thoughts for qualities of feeling). How could Peirce avoid resorting to a completely private world with 'privileged access' (as in Habermas, modelled after Popper's Three Worlds cosmology)? What allowed him to reject the arch-Cartesian dualism of interiority closed in on itself, on the one hand, and a mindless material world, on the other? The first position corresponds, among others, to James's psychology (cf. Peirce, CP 8.81); the latter can be seen as a merely unavowed consequence of the former. Both entail radical dualism. Under debate is a philosophical position of radical interiority, as distinct from privacy. As a subject matter, privacy is constructed by publicity as the negation of the public in the public role of 'private citizen' (Petrilli 2004, 72ff). Radical interiority not being self-evident, Peirce's first counterargument is factual evidence, not metaphysical reflection. Evidence of general experience, in principle, is encountered by everyone at all times – not just in special sciences through special methods. By contrast, psychology as a special science depends on these general conditions of cognition, which are logic; and not logic on psychology, as John Stuart Mill claimed (Eberlein 1994). Peirce fought this tendency in a logician contemporary of his, Christoph von Sigwart, in various places, especially in the *Minute Logic* (CP 2.19): 'This feeling is made the sole evidence of logicality, underlying every other, it is, to all intents and purposes, made the essence of logicality.'

Crucially important for the argument favouring a common world, and against the solipsism of interiority, is the experience of one's own body (Colapietro 1989). Ultimately, the cognitive necessity for signs is deducible from body experience. This conclusion can be drawn from Peirce's early work – in particular, *Questions Concerning Certain Faculties Claimed for Man* (1868, Peirce, CP 5.213–63), in which he negates intuitive self-consciousness. To be conscious of myself I need my other. We owe it in the first place to ontogenetic reasons that we experience our body as a quite special object. It is through their own bodies that infants begin to experience their world. In the beginning, our body is the world, in which we have absolute confidence. From the start, then, the world has become an interpreted one, since we interpret the world in our body. We are not interpreting our body *per se*, but our body in reference to an object that is beyond the body. In the course of their later development, however, do infants experience their body as an error, if it stands in contradiction to the signs of authorities – for example, parents? By then, infants have already acquired openness to the testimony of language from their environment. Language becomes so authoritative that it even succeeds in denying what originally was our absolute authority: our instinct. Our corporality, then, makes us relate to the world through signs. Because the body is the original link, Peirce very early (in *The Logic of Science and Induction* lectures at the Lowell Institute, 1866–7) spoke of man as a symbol, in analogy to the word: 'Every state of consciousness [is] an inference; so that life is but a sequence of inferences or a train of thought. At any instant then man is a thought, and as thought is a species of symbol, the general answer to the question what is man? is that he is a symbol. To find a more specific answer we should compare man with some other symbol' (Peirce, CP 7.583). The human being as body is always a sign. Later, other types of sign join in; but all of these signs, not only our bodies, we interpret with reference to an object.

In conclusion, corporality and the sign nature of cognition render untenable every form of dualism, from Descartes to James. For social reality, this would include individualism. All of these dualisms are reductive forms of an original connection or continuity – which for Peirce is a characteristic of the mind. Peirce, in a cosmological context, has formulated this as synechism. Logically this appears as continuity (Peirce, CP 7.570f). 'Ideas spread,' and based on this insight, society must be a continuum. In a temporal sense, ideas spread in society further and further; in a 'topological' sense, ideas cannot be prevented from jumping over cultural boundaries. Thus society can be conceived as a temporal entity. As temporal, it is never complete and a whole.

The dualist, reductive counterposition, however, tends to treat the human being as a consciousness adhering to a body. The latter is reduced to an accident, and the substance of communication takes place from consciousness to consciousness. In Peirce, the fundamental idea – which includes the human being – is clearly antidualist. Human beings are bodily dialogists, not consciousnesses with bodies. Humans in themselves are conversation, and thought is by essence an inner dialogue – that is, thought interprets thought. Since the body, as feeling, is also a thought, it stands on the same continuum. Through the body, feeling-thought extends into the objective world, cognizable only because capable of being cognized – that is, in some way suited for the mind and cognitive behaviour. Corporality and the sign, however, mean for consciousness that it is embodied in a medium. The body is this medium (Peirce, CP 7.591). It is perhaps difficult to conceive of a larger all-connecting reality such as society, if the starting point must be consciousness in the emphatic singular. Simmel is evidence of this in his intentionally nominalistic theory of society. Yet consciousness in every single one of its acts is already outside itself, because it consists in interpreting signs. It can be taken therefore as a compelling reason and place in which to find an approach to connection and continuity. This does not mean that one must deny the individual, the discontinuous; for we have seen that the categories are ordinal and that relations of higher adicity include lower-adic ones.

This allows us to approach the problem from both sides: How is it possible that the feeling of individuality arises, if everything stands in a relation of continuity? Or conversely: How does the concrete event of an individual behaviour generate the connection in a general, larger continuum? These questions usually arise in the context of social philosophy as the insoluble contradiction between the individual and society. In semiotic, however, this contradiction dissolves.

Peirce's late work *Issues of Pragmatism* (Peirce, Houser, and Kloesel 1992, II:346ff) contains a semiotic version of the Pragmatic Maxim; it is also an almost poetic account of the proper life of symbols: '*symbols grow.*' As society can also be seen as a 'living symbol,' it is possible that Pragmaticism harbours an explanatory potential *sans pareil*, greater than functionalist theories. It can include an actor's perspective into sociology, since the sign an individual interprets is also symbol. In that interpretation – that is, interpreted as a symbolic-triadic relation – meaning grows beyond the individual and capacitates for the social and for society. The symbol is not simply the sterile logical unit built into sentences. Rather, every symbol by its very nature is characterized as possessing a history of its own, since by necessity it affects other signs in the process of its interpretation, which is accomplished by the individual as much as by society.

The term 'society' is usually not associated with the growth of meaning; this frame might stretch the limits of its commonly accepted usage, where it stands for rules in the most general sense. Pragmaticism frames 'society' cognitively, however, as one interpretation affected by another, and again another, without end. This is much more than a given set of 'social rules' by which everyone abides (one hopes). Meaning affecting meaning and spreading wherever it wants is not only not static, but also living. The whole of this continuous process is present in every single interpretation *en miniature*, but never *in toto*, as knowledge. While the continuum of interpretation of symbols is scaffolded by general rules, this applies to all kinds of behaviour (which, in contrast to simple action, is always controlled rationally). Behaviour as such is social, then. Most action, indeed, is not even felt to be regulated, because it is controlled by the invisible hand of meaning. If we become aware of rules, this indicates, on the contrary, that they are imposed on us contrary to meaning. That is the case with public opinion. Imposition brings up a fascinating semiotic situation. How functions predetermination, the meaning of which somehow must be integrated into the continuum of interpretations? If imposed meaning functions effectively, the theoretically unlimited continuum of symbol affecting other symbols occurs only in the endless future. This first consequence from the fact of public opinion (tantamount to Peirce's 'common sense') tempers the theoretical nature of the continuum by qualifying it as a state of affairs that can and will never concretely be reached, but that is present in every interpretation as a guideline or hope. We are in an always unstable situation of a contingent common sense; but critical commonsensism stands for the possibility that we will be able forever to continue interpreting.

Is the individual dissolving into an unlimited sequence of interpretations and an endless network of symbolic relations? In contrast to such an impression, on their side nominalistic theories seem to have the appearance that the individual as a real carrier of actions exists, and that all 'collective actors' are merely metaphoric subjects of sorts. When acting as 'social beings,' we would really be acting as individuals with private interests, which happen to be oriented towards cooperation. There is no need to refute this type of individuality, for it is not in contradiction to a Peircean continuum. On the contrary, it is precisely situated in the act of will. In absolutizing the will in itself, by necessity one must come to the view of a purely numerical collection of individual subjects of will. As in Gabriel Tarde (1989) or Simmel, once the problem is defined in this manner, we have no other option but to solve it nominalistically with an external, formal unity, as a form of socialization (*Vergesellschaftungsform*), or worse, as a mass psychology of imitation. Semiotic can counter that by emphasizing that there is no such thing as pure will. This point was made clear in Peirce's Harvard lectures on pragmatism from 1903 in a famous ironic illustration involving a notary attempting to perform a pure will act, without any content. Peirce (CP 5.30): 'Here a man goes before a notary or magistrate and takes such action that if what he says is not true, evil consequences will be visited upon him, and this he does

Publicity in Media Theory 143

with a view to thus causing other men to be affected just as they would be if the proposition sworn to had presented itself to them as a perceptual fact.' This act of assertion is absolutely meaningless, even though it might well be the perfect expression of an individual will.

That there exist selfish individuals is undeniable, of course. For Peirce, selfish individuals are merely the negation of full individuals. By nature, they are designed in such a way that they reach beyond themselves and through meaning grow beyond themselves. Except that they are capable, if they choose, of negating this relationship in the act of will. Semiotically, this can be realized as a simply degenerate, Secondness-dominated sign relation. Ethical behaviour (in the Peircean sense of the term), too, is guided by instinct and therefore is not yet under the full behaviour control of symbols. In this sense, the absolutely binding decision to follow the ethical instinct is a perfect paradigm of an act of will, even though precisely this act need not be felt as a free one. With regard to sign interpretation, this domain of human behaviour is an interesting case of an Energetic Interpretant ('will always involve an effort'; CP 5.475). A Logical Interpretant, by contrast, becomes efficient only when the behaviour is being performed as controlled in a general, genuinely social way.[15]

Up to this point we have represented the nature of the social as something general in individual behaviour. This must leave the impression that 'society,' as an independent reality, does not exist. From within a Pragmaticist framework, a reference to the pragmatically derived metaphysic invalidates this suspicion. The general here is one of three modes of being. The nominalistic negation, nevertheless, implies this question strongly. Regarding the question of human individuality, the problem returns in a sociological context. For the definition of an individual identity, the initial assumption is that only manifold single reactions are individual ones. There is at least corporeal continuity in these reactions; the single reactions thus have a natural unity in the temporal and spatial continuity of the body. This, however, cannot apply in the same way to society. Which single reactions in social behaviour are held together by a continuum? This question calls for explicit reflection.

The problem starts with the difficulty of imagining for a sheer collectivity its reactive contact with the world, and this includes Energetic Interpretants as meaning. Can it be said, in more than a purely metaphorical way, that societies have a reaction to the objective world? Would this not imply another kind of 'embodiment,' as with the man-symbol? Even the word-symbol has a physical presence in the Representamen. Where would that locus for society be, where would it be embodied? Yet 'body' need not be taken in the sense of a biological or physical unity. What it means is its function – in this context, as being a precondition for an 'effort,' or resistance. Now, society does not react because it constitutes a physical continuity (then it would be a 'tangible' subject, as it were). Society must be seen more in analogy to the word-symbol. The word exists, too, in many sentences, in expressions, in the concrete multiple usage, in all sorts of pronunciations or graphemic graphies. Nevertheless, one and the same word is used. This continuity can conventionally fixate itself as a phonetic or graphic rule; this functions for unicorns and snarks or similar non-existing objects as well as for my (certainly existing) head. This kind of rule corresponds to human corporeal identity; as such, it needs to be differentiated from the rule of interpretation.

Peirce differentiated between types of rules by relating them to 'two worlds,' the 'inner' and the 'outer.' As a consequence, there are also two different types of behaviour, depending on which world is being referred to. In these terms, we will succeed better by freeing this illustration from too much of a semblance to consciousness – which Peirce would certainly have liked. Society can then exhibit an 'inwards' behaviour, provided that 'feeling' is not taken as a psychological entity. Peirce (CP 4.157): 'Habits are either habits about ideas of feelings or habits about acts of reaction. The ensemble of all habits about ideas of feeling constitutes one great habit which is a World; and the ensemble of all habits about acts of reaction constitutes a second great habit, which is another World. The former is the Inner World, the world of Plato's forms. The other is the Outer World, or universe of existence. The mind of man is adapted to the reality of being.'

Social 'habits of feeling' are the equivalent of the word-symbol and do not concern the outside world of reactions. Peirce (ibid.):

> There are two modes of association of ideas: inner association, based on the habits of the inner world, and outer association, based on the habits of the universe. The former is commonly called association by resemblance; but in my opinion, it is not the resemblance which causes the association, but the association which constitutes the resemblance. An idea of a feeling is such as it is within itself, without any elements or relations. One shade of red does not in itself resemble another shade of red. Indeed, when we speak of a shade of red, it is already not the idea of the feeling of which we are speaking but of a cluster of such ideas. It is their clustering together

in the Inner World that constitutes what we apprehend and name as their resemblance. Our minds, being considerably adapted to the inner world, the ideas of feelings attract one another in our minds, and, in the course of our experience of the inner world, develop general concepts. What we call sensible qualities are such clusters.

This inner association of similarity, comparable to cognitive behaviour when comparing shades of red, functions in a similar way in social behaviour. Rules of courtesy, gendered behaviour,[16] and so on – in short, everything that a society recognizes as belonging to the same type of behaviour – refer to a social inner life. Consequently, such rules are strongly dependent on culture and epoch and still have nothing to do with the handling of a social outer world. For the latter, a reaction is needed. Peirce (ibid.):

> Associations of our thoughts based on the habits of acts of reaction are called associations by contiguity, an expression with which I will not quarrel, since nothing can be contiguous but acts of reaction. For to be contiguous means to be near in space at one time; and nothing can crowd a place for itself but an act of reaction. The mind, by its instinctive adaptation to the Outer World, represents things as being in space, which is its intuitive representation of the clustering of reactions. What we call a Thing is a cluster or habit of reactions, or, to use a more familiar phrase, is a centre of forces.

That society defines 'things' is certainly one of its sustainable and decisive *raisons d'être*. Individual subjects would be hopelessly overburdened by such a task. Such social definitions exist at least in the form of language, hidden in the semantic wealth of words, or as explicit instructions for behaviour, such as laws, theories, and the like. Peirce (CP 4.157): 'In consequence, of this double mode of association of ideas, when man comes to form a language, he makes words of two classes, words which denominate things, which things he identifies by the clustering of their reactions, and such words are proper names, and words which signify, or mean, qualities, which are composite photographs of ideas of feelings, and such words are verbs or portions of verbs, such as are adjectives, common nouns, etc.'

A semiotic pragmatic permits us to leave behind the contrast between individual and collectivity, which was once considered fundamental and beyond debate. 'We' are both a corporeal and a symbolic continuum – one, moreover, with the capacity to become individualized in both cases. The unity of the body is liable to be destroyed by the dominance of one sense and the suppression of the other – at least up to the threshold of pain, where the body reclaims its rights. The social body, the symbolic continuum, is undermined by selfish behaviour. In selfishness, one's own immediate purpose ranges before the broader, longer-term, and more general goal of behaviour. However, both individualizations – of the human and the social body – must remain borderline cases; behaviour – normally – is regulated by real general rules, not selfishness. Behavioural rules include determinations by the raw reality of the outside world. Pragmaticism, clearly, entails not a *nominalistic* but a *realist* theory of society. Owing to this potential, the Pragmaticist theory of society need not reduce the quintessence of social nature to structure or to pure rules. Much as in Schütz, this allows a new perspective on actions not subjectable to any rule; but quite unlike Schütz, this is not conceived as a contradiction to rule – rather, it is integrated constructively (and degeneratively) into the rule itself. With this insight, we need not sacrifice, in the 'objective sense,' communicability to a 'subjective sense,' as Schütz does.

Mass media, too, assume in this theory a position quite different from that of any other nominalistic two-world theory (see Tejera 1996). There is no need for a bridge between interiority and the objective world, or between the three worlds, as in Habermas. Media, contrary to the approach taken by systems theory, are no longer the (system-immanent) equivalent of the (external, environmental) universe, which is thereby reduced to sheer chaotic entropy. On the contrary, in an emphatic sense everything is already sign – that is, medium – from the body up to the symbol.

To summarize, drawing consequences from a Pragmaticist theory of society for semiotic, such theory could not have been a sign theory closed in itself, reposing in itself, and autarkic. Such was Saussure's idea of semiology; small wonder that it figures prominently in Foucault's view of the social as power relating visibility to episteme (cf. Ehrat 2005a, 518f). Sign processes presuppose both certain modal reality and certain behaviour, where reality is connected with behaviour, because the former determines the latter. The key to all, then, is the real being in its modes of being. Phaneroscopy can demonstrate this in a general way, albeit only an *actual* way (meaning that everyone at any time can make that general observation without resorting to special instruments or sciences). Furthermore, the modality of being cannot be proven, otherwise it would be an '*a priori* method.' Ultimately, the nature of the real is revealed in our ability to behave in different ways:

- *qualitatively* – as feeling, because the real pre-existentially is a possibility, and then it is neither individual, nor continuous, but purely virtual,
- *reactively* – because the real exists resistantly as event and individually, *and*
- *cognitively* – because the real itself assumes habits and is a continuum.

Semiotic concerns itself with the *abstract* form of relations, which, owing to the different modes of the real, are necessary and possible. Ultimately, semiotic owes itself to the corporality of the cognizing subject and is, therefore, itself a token of the continuity of the real and the spiritual.

4.4 Functions of the Three Correlates in the Media Sign

After describing both the human being and society at large as a sign, we now focus on this sign itself. In keeping with the results of our discussion of signhood in man and in society, the term 'the media' will not ensnare us into treating media empirically, as if they were things, for society itself is sign relation. Mass media, as social media, can only be specifications of the sign society, not objective things, and even less a *vis-à-vis* to society. This by no means excludes the mass media as an industry, which exhibits a quite determinate form of behaviour. This industry does not produce printed paper or electromagnetic waves, but meaning. It is best to grasp this meaning abstractly – that is, in terms of an abstract form of control of behaviour – and not objectively.

The First Correlate. The sign – the triadic sign relation – is always specified by means of correlates and their nature. In the sign relation the First Correlate determines cognition qualitatively, as the material sign or Representamen. In his early work *Questions Concerning Certain Faculties Claimed for Man*, Peirce connected cognition with the body, with the consequence that there is no cognition without an interpretation of a previous interpretation. Everything in advance of an interpretation is a sign. Signs present the '*Quale,*' the 'What,' which an interpretation links to a new generality. In this way it produces new meaning. For an interpretation, it is of determining importance which nature possesses its quality, its 'What.' Often that nature is skipped over. A mental experiment with this neglect, though, would soon show how quality affects interpretation. To grasp the extension of one's house, for instance, one can calculate it through an algebraic formula or one can gauge it with a pictorial sketch. Even though the problem at hand is the same, the interpretation, meaning, will typically be different.

Sign-quality of mass media is of great importance, and one should not follow the custom of rejecting the meaning configuration potential of the First Correlate. At one's own peril, one would mistake media as being only of the abstract-logical kind owing to their massive unequivocal diffusion – as Legisigns in the first trichotomy of the sign classification (as if, for example, letter fonts were a reason why newspapers convey only abstract ideas). Pop music, for example, would then fall through the mesh and could not be grasped as a mass medium. Music, as such, is already a sign relation – one that despite styles, rules of harmony, and so on aims directly at feeling. In order to attain that meaning, the qualitative First Correlate has to be taken in such a way that its regularity is upwards limited; in this way it is accessible to feeling.[17] What, however, changes at the moment that music becomes a mass medium? One might start by asking what possible weight one can assign to 'countless reproducibility' when it becomes the quality-nature of the sign. Massiveness is concomitant with an enormous reduction of 'Whatness' (quality). The resulting mass meaning is distinguished from other, traditional practice of musical performance. This is so clearly the case that sheer massiveness could generate a number of social practices such as fandom, comprising fan sites, fan articles, and so on (Hills 2002), as well as music as an industry and even listening and consumption practices.

The mass media characteristic has an impact not just on things so especially Firstness-determined as music; signs of language, too, produce different meanings, if an important part of their sign-quality consists in the massive distribution. At one time, grand rhetorical performance counted as massiveness in its highest degree; nowadays, the peak is probably a carefully staged television appearance (e.g., of Barack Obama). In the strictly pictorial realm, the sign-quality also changes under conditions of mass communication. It is banal to note that a nature magazine, or a nature documentary film, cannot convey the sensory richness of nature itself. In a social context there must be space for imagination. This requirement is more important for the quality question of the mass sign, where less room for sensory finesse is to be expected in the sign. As semiotic process, a monadically degenerate generality (Thirdness) is enacted. Even specialty channels, such as the Discovery Channel, must frame nature into a story, based on which they can then wax lyrical or contemplative as they choose. All of this is part and parcel of a complex industry product: the massively produced 'sound,' encompassing celebrities, fans, marketing, and a USP (unique selling proposition) – also, the narratively teleological temporality, which is produced in many mass media products, even in nature features. Though the narrative goal is logically a generality, the temporal order with its 'planned surprise' leaves enough room for imagination even in a strict teleology.

As a mass media sign quality or Firstness, narrative imagination is especially conspicuous. The importance of this most frequent characteristic is particularly obvious in the realm of scandals. Here, the imagination (along with the teleology) is as central as the teleological goal of dramatic action. Of particular importance here is the role played by the imagination – How could things have been differently? – which is not properly predictable. This generates alternative universes, which have been constructed through pragmatic imagination from normative goals of action. Since this concerns mere imagination, there is no need to reach an agreement on a norm. The free play of imagination only requires the open horizon of alternatives. Only in a second step will these alternatives be evaluated into better and worse ones, and this is the contribution of the Second Correlate.

The phenomena of entertainment and other social fantasies need to be recognized in their necessity. This is important for a Pragmaticist understanding of mass media – and, in general, for any social sign. Possibility, in logical terms, is condition for necessity – the reality of the imagination of the possible is the precondition for the reality of the rule. Every social theory is thus confronted with the problem of integrating the width of individual and collective utopias. Even before it becomes a will, and is thus directed towards an object, human action is undoubtedly a fantasizing experimental acting – and probably in the great majority of cases, it is left at that. (It is irrelevant for these reflections whether social fantasy is treated as the First Correlate, in the sense of a Percept, or directly as a monadically degenerate sign relation.)

The importance of the role of Firstness in mass media is clear if we contrast all of this with Luhmann's functional-structural treatment of mass media systems (Luhmann 1995). Luhmann's work brings, rather elegantly, a traversal connection among the three media modes: actuality in news, beautiful appearance in advertisements, and apparent freedom of choice in entertainment. The latter could perhaps count as the functional version of the First Correlate in the mass media sign. These three together operate in the same way (i.e., through the selectivity of this autopoietic system); they are distinguished only functionally. Moreover – on the level of its medium – the doubly contingent communication is the object of this system's meaning-based operation, and not of human action. The treatment of imagination is evident as well in the *limits* of functional-structural systems theory. Here the width of the logically possible does not influence change in the selection achievement of the autopoietic system, because this is already precisely determined through its selection criterion. The system, then, is incapable of learning; it can only be replaced by a new system that is better adapted.

Abduction is the inferential logic of this semiotically conceived imagination behaviour. It is by no means illogical or uncontrolled, as we saw in our discussion of ethical behaviour. If one always *expects* only a rule, one will always *see* only a rule and exclude everything else. Discoveries, in contrast, are always unexpected. Does the unexpected allow us to act? Acting is not yet possible, because in order for something to be unexpected, everything must be already (bivalent) true event; only then is the negative finding the object of attention. This corresponds to the logic of laboratory experiments. Before the experiment, however, stands the fortuitous chance surprise. This need not be event at all; it can also consist in a mental flash when musings show a possibility hitherto unimagined and not covered by any rule. Only then can one test in an event experiment whether what was seen mentally as a possibility exists in reality. This is the best scientific practice, which reflects also a research economy. In normal social behaviour, however, we find all types of settling opinions. These include abductional behaviour equivalent to scientific practice, which we might call 'problem awareness.' Problems do not exist, they are discovered.

Let us return briefly to Luhmann. His functional structuralism is only true to itself when a system observes what it is capable of observing and no more. There is thus no need to theorize about how systems learn, because that would entail their own restructuring induced from outside. The system behaviour is *in toto* arbitrary – that is, self-referential. Should adaptation to the environment be inadequate, only a non-survival risk corresponds to the selection risk. Therefore, there is no way to 'discover a problem,' because here the system would have to pass beyond its selection tautology into a third position.

From a pragmatic perspective, the discovery of a problem is problematic, since from the point of view of a rule a problem should not exist. If the world exists only as a law, then there is only a nominalistic way of escaping that dilemma: this is the position of structuralism. But if there are indeed problems, then there exists more than just deduction; there is also the reality of the possible, being-possible as mode of being, reflecting the First Correlate of a sign.

How, then, is problem awareness to be transferred into behaviour and communication? Action without goal does not have an object either. Action would thus have to stop before its realization. Playful action, and experimental action (of which Peirce gives an amusing description, of an anticipating deflection of danger as performed by his brother Herbert[18]), are very difficult to communicate, and when either of these is, it is as a doubly degenerative sign.

The Second Correlate. Secondness, too, is indispensable. Neither controlling sign nor controlled behaviour can be thought without it. Secondness, moreover, is the kernel of the philosophical realism of both Peirce and the Pragmatic Maxim. The basic idea is extremely simple – a bivalent relation of sign and object, which common parlance calls 'real.' The real object is either true or false; it can only accept two values. However, by the fact that it is followed by a Third into which it is integrated, Secondness escapes the snare of shallow realism (as might have been inspired by the onto-semanticism of the Vienna Circle, which later informed Carnap and Charles Morris). In the social realm, a naive realism is completely out of place – except perhaps in some conceptions of social engineering. Regarding its contribution to social meaning, the closest Secondness can get, here, is through reality constraint on the coordination of actions. Without some type of link to an objective reality, a society loses its capacity to learn. This constraint cannot determine any common pragmatic goal for society, because such a goal is essentially the contribution of Thirdness. It prevents the arbitrariness of conventions, though. No theory of society that accounts for this pressure can content itself with the explanatory power of conventionalism. Despite being always largely embedded in conventions according to the doubt–belief schema (and *per extensionem* commonsensism), conventions can become unstable. Instability is a consequence of outside pressure – a point made by Peirce in the famous 'diamond in cotton wool' example (CP 5.403) directly after the Pragmatic Maxim in '*How to Make Our Ideas Clear.*' Even more, however, the next better convention must rely on this corrective; otherwise it would not be a better but rather an arbitrarily exchangeable one.

Is exposure to the unexpected, to the raw real, unconditionally necessary in order for cognition to function? Obviously, ideas are not clarifiable solely by the 'method of science' – that is, by ways which are corrected by experience. In 'How to Make our Ideas Clear' (CP 5.384), Peirce describes the other three methods and acknowledges them explicitly as workable. That they are not *sustainable* – each for its own reasons – is the only restriction he adds. In the last resort, then, there remains only experience, to which all must be exposed together if progress towards more adequate regulation is to be hoped for. Adequate rules for behaviour can indeed become *more* adequate. That comparative assumes that experience with the real has a corrective effect on interpersonal behaviour. Cognitive behaviour is the highest form of adequation to the real; that said, contact with reality is not lacking in instinct-guided ethical behaviour. Here, Peirce's laboratory illustrations and examples must not confuse us; for in principle, interpersonal behaviour as a controlled (i.e., not arbitrary) behaviour is also possible solely due to rules subject to falsification (i.e., due to a capacity to learn). Social convention *qua* convention implies arbitrariness. Yet instead of convention, the coordination of human action passes in reality through a common world object. Some might want to call this world view; it suffices, though, that the one segment of the real exists to which a dyadic sign process relates at this very moment of its signhood.[19]

The reality constraint on social behaviour, as ethic, has a clear and direct impact on behaviour itself. This is a case of instinctive constraint. As this constraint, ethic cannot turn into cognition, and it will always remain a habit determinable by instinct only. In practical terms, an 'odd feeling concomitant to my acting' is all that remains; though cognitively a philosophical discourse can take that up as ethics. Only the *reflection* of behaviour is cognitive, not the ethical in the behaviour itself. Earlier, we worked out in more detail how society *in se* constitutes this ethicality. It can be formulated as rules, one may grant; but in the matter itself, society is an instinctive relation to reality (yet indeed a reality relation).

This statement might sound odd for a theoretical discourse about social behaviour. Is society not theory, as we analysed above, if considered through the Second Correlate of the 'sign of society'? Would it not be damaging for such theory if its object were not the object itself, which instead is reached by the sign? Doubts such as these have moved Luhmann to write about the society of society (1997), in this way explicitly including sociologizing as a social practice. Here, Peirce's solution is radically different. For him, society is not transported into a transcendent form; rather, reflecting its earthly nature, it remains an ethical behaviour, 'vitally important matter.' Society is never dissolved completely as a scientific cognitive object; there remains an overhang of Secondness, a non-cognitive 'remainder' that is instinctive behaviour. When this is turned into a scientific object – that is, in the sense of semiotic constructivity of a further interpretation – it is still the same object, albeit no longer the same behaviour that we feel as 'society' (i.e., as instinct).

There is a practical consequence to this: Even if we wanted, we could never regulate ethical-social behaviour to perfection. This perfect state would be no more than an exceedingly general rule: 'Do the good!' A rule of this sort is banal because no one can want to do the bad. This is already the analytical consequence of the concept of action, since action presupposes a goal. Beneath this banality, of course, the actually desired goal is merely a search – not a rule, and not a sentence valid once and for all, but a search. And search behaviour is genuinely ethical because it remains permanently abductive: one must keep inventing rules by abiding instinctively by a feeling.

Peirce proposes seriously that ethical behaviour stay as conservative as possible – that it abide by past experiences as long as viable. Such advice can easily be turned (formally, at least) into general rules (examples: country lore, Baltasar Gracián's *Oráculo manual y arte de prudencia*, Confucius' *Lun Yu*). Yet treasures of the past (tradition, language) are only of limited help, mainly because they are not generalizable in a scientific way. What is the 'teaching' of tradition, of history? Even as past, the treasure remains a collection of events that – in hindsight – correspond to ethical behaviour and are respectively reinterpreted in that sense.

Society as society, not as theory, is a permanently dyadically degenerate triadic sign, so that it remains a 'vitally important matter.' Turning it into science might bestow an 'administrative' touch for the 'disguised' purposes of political or educative intervention. But this touch cannot suppress the type of behaviour itself, or the class of sign that controls it.

One would surmise that an ethical context is part and parcel of scandal. As we have seen, this is how some authors see it. There is indeed a Secondness in scandal – but that is quite different from what has been claimed for it in this debate. In particular, the quality press has an almost ritual urge to establish a connection to 'proof.' Only the way in which this relation is established turns 'something' into an oppositional correlate of the fact, which can then be true or false. This does not mean that the proof sought in the media resembles 'laboratory' proof: the event occurring unexpectedly. Therefore, this cannot be mistaken as impulse for a new doubt–belief cycle, where something is integrated as a Second Correlate into a medial sign process. On the contrary, there is an absolute preponderance of teleology in the scandal. When a singular event is made to stand out from within this logic, it is only for the purpose of demonstrating the general in the concrete singular. No negative proof or answer can invalidate such a strong generality. On the contrary, the charm of teleology consists in the fact that there are no all-quantifiers; thus the opponent cannot come up with a single example of the contrary in order to falsify the proponent's law. Instead, this generality works in reverse: the proponent again presents a new proof to the opponent, so that the logic of the goal is supported by a series leading up to it. The series of facts is more than all of the facts taken singly. The series is law, and facts are merely single instances of that law. What is false is merely not part of the series; it is not a proof to the contrary. In a scandal, teleology has reached such great heights that it is not actually falsifiable; it can only be substituted by another series. Judgment of behaviours is not control of behaviour. In the former case, one need only *suppose* a motivation in order to judge its value; in the latter, one must find a concept that is capable of regulating 'all conceivable consequent' behaviour, as the Pragmatic Maxim says. Much as with tribunals, one attempts to bring events into a series that shows lawfulness or unlawfulness; the one or the other is immediately supposed, then. With behaviour, by contrast, the encounter with something unexpected leads to a stand-off, since one cannot keep acting when there is no rule for the unexpected situation. This compels a prospective actor to search anew for a rule that can then be applied consciously. Only then can the impression be preserved that one knows what one is doing, that one is in control over one's own behaviour.

The Third Correlate. Thirdness, in every sign process, means rule or law. A rule is no longer true or false, but more or less general. If an existential relation, a dyadic fact, contradicts a rule, this means merely that it cannot be integrated into the rule. Consequently, the rule must be expanded or refined. However, many rules have to 'come to an arrangement' with exceptions over time, when facts are no longer (or not yet) explainable by the rule. Then impressions of 'covering theories' arise, as if hypotheses could be formulated as restricted to certain sectors of a reality. For instance, 'explanations' for telepathy can also fall under 'covering theories.' All we require for that is that someone observe, as an entirely unexpected and unexpectable event, what are apparently (at least) identical thoughts with another person. If the premise is an entirely individual inner world – this is, as we discussed, not justified – then it is *per definitionem* impossible for two individuals to exhibit an identical interior world constellation. This begs an explanation, and 'telepathy' is the magical-parapsychological, albeit content-empty, formula of an explanation. At any rate, such a theory is merely insular and is not connectible with the remainder of the world comprehension. Telepathy thereby proves only a semiotic pressure towards Thirdness. If there remains an impression of unexplainable exception, it maintains a pressure to find a common general rule for the explained and unexplained exceptions. The reason for this is deeply pragmatic – it is impossible to possess a behaviour towards exceptions. Behaviour needs rules in order to be controlled.

Durkheim's classical *fait social*[20] is precisely not a fact, in a strictly logical sense. His sociology understood society as rule, here even as external, extra-mental rules in the form of sanctions. For Pragmaticism, rule-based behaviour is grasped more precisely as controlled action. So we need not follow Durkheim's opposition to defining the social through individual states of consciousness. The concern behind this opposition is well addressed in Thirdness. The general definition of controlled behaviour, though, is too broad for social sciences, for it includes any form of knowledge as a determination of cognitive behaviour. Sociology's cognitive interest focuses more on the control itself. This amounts to, at the same time, setting oneself a nominalistic trap, so typical of traditional sociology – as if control existed independently of behaviour in the real world (as Pragmaticism argues against nominalism). The two worlds theory manifests itself not only as a separation of interior and exterior world, but also in the not less annoying split between the individual and the continuum of the 'unlimited community' (Peirce, CP 2.654); it merely expands on these two worlds to engender a third, a social one. This trap is only avoided when the (triadic) control is in a relation with (dyadic) reality and (monadic) quality. This makes semiotic especially interesting for the social sciences and their basic methodological problem. It could, however, also constitute an invitation to apply the entire breadth of the sign process. As a side effect, this would also eliminate the ugly abyss between empirical and theoretical sociology.

Comprehending controlled behaviour in a semiotic key also means surrendering behaviour to the single Interpretant. In Durkheim's eyes, probably, this would miss the social object. In fact, a semiotic interpretation could bring sociology into the neighbourhood of symbolic interactionism with its vilified situation dependency of sociological cognition. This cost the latter its capacity for grand social theory (for which stand the likes of functionalism, Habermas's fundamental pragmatism, etc.). However, semiotic is not reducible to symbolic interactionism, since semiotic interpretation connects precisely with the continuum of generality. Besides, semiotic reaches further in both directions, including in the direction of an absolutely individual (albeit not private) meaning construction. In the sign process always occurs an interpretation of an oppositional quality (this what) towards a relatively more general. This *what*, though, need not be an individual concrete object. As an object, it can of course also be a complex reality. Take the sign 'debt,' for instance. As part of the complex text 'economy,' a quite different behaviour would entail than in the text 'morals.'[21] As a social behaviour, 'debt' thus becomes part of extended texts with their coherent logic.

Semiotic's particular solution to the legitimization problem is what makes it interesting for sociology. No one claims that sociology has an interest in *any* human act – to do so would invade the domains of kinesiology, psychology, and so on. Social acts are acts that have been legitimated or that other interactants react to deliberately with their response-acts. The legitimization of even a single action, if behaviour is understood as behaviour under the control of meaning and sign, is occurring *ipso facto;* because it is comprehensible behaviour, one can always act according to this rule, and everyone who understands the rule can as well. This we have to distinguish from a valuation of behaviour of that type. One can understand murder as a legitimate behaviour in this sense, even while appraising it as abominable.

Thirdness in scandal also consists in the production of behavioural legitimization and especially in reprobation, in negative judgment. Every time a sign, which controls behaviour, interprets something as law, this places the behaviour under a rule. This must be understood in an exclusively cognitive sense. It simply implies that everyone can comprehend a behaviour by interpreting it as corresponding to a determinate rule. Whether or not this corresponds to positive law or to social mores is another question altogether. Yet this is what the semantic differentiation between legal and legitimate signifies.

The most important result of semiotic Pragmaticism, with regard to social sciences, is the necessary co-presence of all three correlates in the sign process. The (controlled) action in social behaviour also, therefore, can be realized only when all three contributions are in place. Compare this to the systems theoretical media theory, which does not reach beyond differentiation, and wherein media, as it were, represent the other as the identical (e.g., in public relations).

If society is indeed sign, and this in all its three modes (as outlined above), then a leap to social media is no longer far-fetched. There is a rich potential for society to be not only conceivable from an actor's perspective, but also and at the same time already a sign. Now that we have opened semiotic to the social, a caveat is called for: a sign in the sense of semiotic is not a linguistic sign, but rather a determinate relation, one that can also be realized as language but need not be so. In the same way, the reality of media in society is a relation that can – but need not – be realized in the mass media industry. There exist other social media in the broader sense of the term, on which inquiries have been made – for instance, rites (Gennep 1909; Turner 1969, 1974, 1979). No claim is therefore being made here that society is coextensive with mass media. On the contrary, we will see that the richness of the semiotic perspective will always try to break out of the rigid confinements of industrial meaning production.

Semiotic offers the entire spectrum of a society living 'in' its media; the sublunary reality of a media industry is considerably narrower. Industrialized meaning, while practically deafening, has a very narrow spectrum. From its fringes, art keeps open a certain space for manoeuvre; art, however, is in constant danger of being engulfed by its commercial evaluation. So it is not surprising that the following question has great currency today: Are media, in their essence, constraining social life? This in effect posits that media determine social reality by their very form. In its extreme variants, this stance has been attacked often and sharply as media essentialism. Yet it also encapsulates a larger question concerning the formal nature of social media, as industrial practice as much as aesthetic form.[22]

4.5 Technological Determination or Sign Process: The Case of Televangelism

Media as technology: the Toronto School has given memorably prominent – indeed, sometimes quasi-cultic – expression to this theme. Since *The Gutenberg Galaxy* (McLuhan 1962), it has become customary to talk about the logic of technology, if not about technology of mind.[23] Technologies produce epochal changes; moreover, every technology is ultimately a media technology because it impinges not just on culture and economy but even more on the senses. As much as, for example, the introduction of microphones rendered absurd and obsolete the architecture of cathedrals, so 'televisioning' could not not but leave its traces in religion. (For the Toronto School a phenomenon such as televangelism might have been of interest, had it existed then, inasmuch as it concerns radical changes to religion as they relate to the technology of television.) Evocative of McLuhanite discourses, all of this also calls to mind the similar theories of Walter Ong. An inquiry in the spirit of McLuhan, though, is not intended here; in this kind of logic-of-technology discourse, arguments are dubious and difficult to reconstruct, however replete they are with original insights. Not surprisingly, outside the 'camp' this has stirred up reflexes of rejection. Technological determinism has been the charge leading what nowadays calls itself 'television studies' (a discipline that views itself as analogous to film theory) to reject such a position. For that domain, it is more customary to use a different metaphor: 'encoding/decoding,' or the social space network (Hay 2001). This, however, makes it extraordinarily difficult to speak of 'the' medium if it were merely described in codes. These codes would first have to be shown to be specific, and then that they describe a medium comprehensively.

Obtaining a 'critical' purchase by reducing media to codes is the real intent of media theory. Analysing technology 'critically' is a laudable enterprise, but one that requires a more extensive consideration of logic. Proceeding in the manner of critical theory would seem a natural choice. Yet Habermas's total reliance on the language form presupposes, for his media theory, that language is the most complete medium – indeed, the most rational one. His sign theory is so unduly restricted to language that compared to Peirce's semiotic it represents a considerable regress (cf. Ehrat 2007). His basic idea of sign-controlled – and therefore rational – behaviour is inspired by a pragmatic model, however. With regard to the television medium in particular, which is controlled not just by language – the logical control of behaviour is much more complex than 'propositional' sentences and their linguistic pragmatic. Despite this, defining the problem as logical predetermination, or as meaning determination by a technology, is neither redundant nor deviant. On the contrary, it promises a path for connecting media technology with meaning and not just with the senses.

Toronto School, television studies, critical theory – all offer a sublunary model of mass media, mass meaning production. It is now time to show how semiotic is more than a grand theoretical edifice of meaning *in se*, but an analytic tool as well – and that it still has its specific approach in the sublunary practices of meaning production.

Logic – in a semiotic Pragmaticist approach – is the key to understanding a technology defined by a certain practice of meaning production. In that practice, it unavoidably enters into conflict with other meaning practices. One of the deepest conflict situations exists with religion. This would not be disturbing were it not for the totalizing claim of each meaning – a claim also of the mass media, however. Now, mass media try to avoid as far as possible getting embroiled in all-out battles with other domains of meaning, of which there are a number of candidates. One is science that is, scienti-fic practice, which literally 'makes know' all; and knowing excludes opinions, which are the truth of media if shared by 'all.' Its strategy is mostly different – more a sort of *envoûtement* of the victim. Two meaning practices of a different nature must cohabit in one architectonic structure. Religion reflects back on media meaning production, its form, its technology; it is also a certain threat that the media must somehow counter.

Religion and the public sphere have been viewed as entering a conflict of rationalities. 'Televangelism' is interesting because it comes close to a self-contradiction (cf. Newman 1996). Two logics collide in this mass media phenomenon, either by cancelling each other's effects or by forcing one into a compromise under false pretences about itself.

This statement is not self-evident, for in the field of mass media and how they manifest themselves, Feyerabend's catchphrase 'anything goes' seems to apply. Media are in the habit of sucking in whatever they can borrow from existent forms of expression, but cross-fertilization can occur in both directions. In order to see a collision despite this manifest media irenism, we need two theoretically informed comprehensions: first, of technological determination, and second, of self-representation of religion *in se* (as far as it is relevant for communication). Over and above this understanding of religion at large, the specifics of single religions are pivotal (e.g., religions of revelation compared against religions based on interiority). Not appearance but theory alone achieves comparability, and this is a presupposition for observing incompatibilities between television practices that are but options of the same. The choice of theory, however, is decisive. Media technology theory, which claims to have a grasp of everything that is relevant to culture, is one such theory. Its purchase on religion and the media is based on locating both in a history of culture and history of technology. It is doubtful, though, how far this collocation constitutes an explanation. A pragmatic theory must call this in question. The question raised by technology is too interesting, though, to be dismissed by mere accusations of essentialism. To comprehend media as signs in the full sense, we must distance ourselves from the 'extension of the senses' metaphor, though Pragmaticist semiotic integrates feelings, including feelings as percepts. In a sign framework, neither can we brush aside considerations of technology as determination, especially if we take technology as a cultural practice, as preinterpreted signs. Technology appears then as nothing less than a pragmatic rule of behaviour.

A purchase on religion is considerably more difficult because religion is clearly more than a cognitive behaviour. Peirce dedicated to this problem his famously enigmatic 'Neglected Argument for the Reality of God' (CP 6.462–85). Within the limits of our context we will not be able to do justice to this work (Anderson 1990, 1995; Behrens 1995; Canteñs 2002, 2004; Caspar 1980; Roth 1965; Sullivan 1979). Fortunately for our purposes, there is no need for a complete semiotic comprehension of religion: our subject matter limits us to religion as a product of public opinion. In this sphere of culturally determined behaviour, we can observe the appearance of a player pretending to have her behaviour controlled by completely different rules. This same cultural practice has hitherto placed under the pseudo-rule of privacy whatever it has chosen to exclude. According to this rule, everything that publicity does not succeed in construing as a reality, is private. The kind of behaviour from which this excluded reality constitutes itself in the private sphere, however, is only negatively determined as 'the other behaviour.' Public evangelism should not possess a right of residence, according to the logic of the media of public opinion. When it does, it violates the objectivity rule as much as do other time-honoured practices, even genre conventions of the television medium. That it exists, nevertheless, is an anomaly for television practitioners, one that demands an explanation for why its existence is possible.

There is probably no imaginable form of religiosity more public than televangelism. For some it broaches, even oversteps, the boundary of the scandalous. Here, faith has given itself a social form that is almost diametrically opposed to the bourgeois banishment into privacy. Does this pervert modernity? Contrary to Weber's sociohistorical analysis, has the postmodern world view regained its premodern substantial unity? According to Weber, the unified substantial world image has disintegrated into rationalities, bringing the rationality of publicity into counterposition to the rationality proper of social religion.

It does not follow from this that religious matters cannot become the content of the media of public opinion – albeit as the Other (just like other Others). Where media take the stage with valid enunciations (assuming accountability for what they are stating as valid), normally they are prevented from presenting themselves as religious and public at the same time – that is, if Weber was right with his disintegrated world image. But leaving aside his historical speculative analyses, we had better focus on the semiotic content. Signs used as public are found in each of their cultural determinations as teleology construed into media technology in a practical way. This has been outlined in the θέατρον. If, semioticly, publicity is largely determined, the next issue to address is the semiotic determination of religion, and after that the problem of the conflict between the two sign processes.

In Habermas's diversification of validity claims, the incompatibility between the logic of publicity and that of religion could also be expressed as a difference in the type of validity. There have been attempts to apply the validity approach to media genres: Ekström (2000, 466) has treated information ('bulletin board'), entertaining narration ('bedtime story'), and attraction ('circus performance') as differently valid. Likewise, religion would probably fall under the claim of interior-authenticity validity (if for argument's sake this factual claim stands). Only the subject has privileged access to this validity, expressed as reconstructable by others. This would apply to religion as much as to any other feeling. While all there is in this field is authenticity, its representation is quite problematic. Though narratological insights[24] could supplement Habermas, there is still the basic limitation of how meaning as such is conceptualized by measuring it as rationality in 'propositional' language.

Televangelism offers a paradigmatic solution to how publicity opposes itself, as a validity, to religious validity. It also tells us under which conditions one validity subordinates itself to the other. Were we to take Habermas's validity claims as a basis, in televangelism the impossible would actually occur (otherwise, it would not be at all what it pretends to be: religion). In its country of origin in the present day, the phenomenon of televangelist shows may be at its nadir (albeit after a spectacular rise); yet at the same time we see exuberant manifestations of it in many African and Latin American cities. As a representation genre, it is older than television itself, but it still is an interesting borderline of the communicable in the public sphere.

Is the medium of television a constraint for communication? Outside the Toronto School, television has been accused – especially by so-called 'critical' theories – of being a medium with meaning constraints (in a negative formulation), or of being technologically determined (expressed positively).

Prominent in Habermas's *Theory of Communicative Action* is his attack on Luhmann's media theory in general, and, on that basis, on mass media in particular. We might object that the media system constraint, as feared by Habermas, is no longer pertinent as soon as we break out of the straightjacket of ordinary-language analytical philosophy (in *Fundamentalpragmatik*). Otherwise, political economy approaches in communication science would perhaps hypothesize mass media's 'coloniation of the life-world' (cf. Habermas 1981, II:489–547), present in rudiments already in Adorno, Lukács and Benjamin (Couldry 2004). Despite his critique of media theory, Habermas's lopsided language orientation tends more towards a systematic media obliviousness. But this is not yet a compelling reason to adhere to symbolic generalization, in a functionalist sense, outside a systems theoretical systematic (for the reasons for this dismissal, cf. §4.1 above). In Habermas's attempt to comprehend television as a form of communicative action, it appears as success-oriented and therefore as strategic action constraining life-worldly agreement. This limit amounts to the equivalent of the otherwise paradigmatic medium money, inasmuch as television procures the legitimization of bureaucratic power. Television communication is, thus, far from the ideal speech situation, the necessary point of reference for any communicative act.

But does this kind of analysis really do justice to the medium? And before this: How did Habermas succeed in integrating two approaches as different as functionalist media theory (taken from Parsons) and validity analysis of speech acts? He derived the human communication ideal not from a macroscopic simple meaning system (such as binary or quaternary difference in semiology, respectively semionarratology), but rather from microacts of pragmatic linguistics. He relates mass communication to the dialogic ideal as a sort of extension, as *ceteris paribus* communication, without a difference of essence,[25] except for the systems constraints. The measure he uses for mass media remains the one of the validity of speech acts between dialogists. This approach, in our context, has the weakness of being utterly dependent on spoken and written language. This prevents a grasp of important sign classes such as iconic signs, whose crucial contribution to the ethic part we saw in social communication. This is compounded by the loss of the pragmatic potential of roles differentiated by these sign classes,[26] because validities are not anchored to their roles in speech acts. What counts ultimately is, on the contrary, the object ('what') of speech acts, and this object consists, for Habermas, in three types or even worlds. Despite all linguistic pragmatic, there seems to be an option for realism (interpreted positively) such that these three worlds can stand as placeholders for a modal ontology.

'Technological determinism' – as its critics call it – is a quite different approach. This term usually groups together the Toronto School (Marshall McLuhan, Harold Innis) and Walter Ong, though it is not clear at all what exactly its theoretical foundations are. Is it a kind of history writing, comparable to Fernand Braudel's *historiographie non-événementielle?* Grossberg, Wartella, and Whitney presuppose this when they see in communication technology a causal agent of historical change of the *longue durée*. 'Printing altered the very structure of human consciousness and thought,' they write. 'According to McLuhan, the physical relationship between the reader's eyes and the text comes to define a linear mode of thinking. Just as eyes move across the page, line after line, in a rigorous and necessary way, so too does one begin to think in similarly rigorously linear fashion, one idea logically connected to the next' (1998, 33f). From this linearity, they are capable of deducing direct consequences for the two (transcendental aesthetic) modes of apperception, time and space. 'It is in the age of printing,' they later continue, 'that European powers explored and colonized the world, spreading their culture, their politics, and their religions across the globe. Time becomes a linear vector moving toward an indefinite future defined as progress. The belief in progress reinforced the drive for knowledge and discovery that printing had opened up. What followed was the age of scientific discovery' (ibid., 43f). Though Curran criticizes this analysis because it 'makes no reference – even in passing – to any conventional historical study of the media' (2002, 3), this precisely would have been the point of writing history in Braudel's manner, and would also have missed the point of a historical causality construed beyond events. Instead of relapsing into an event-determined historical causality, only extremely long temporal spaces evince a possible existence of causal agents, such as fundamental communication technologies and their slow changes. Was this indeed the cognitive interest of Ong and the Toronto School? McLuhan is notoriously difficult to grasp, and even though his work is used generously as a quarry for quite alien interpretations; it is obvious that his claims reach far beyond mere historiography.

The first decisive frontal attack against technological determinism came from Williams (1974). He, too, supposes a certain understanding of historical causality, which he uses against the technological determinists. For example, quite in opposition to Braudel's point, Williams posits intentions of human agents and their institutions.[27] These have desires and needs, and they invent and use technology to fulfil them. This subjectivization is supposed to settle the problem of media essentialism within technological determinism.

The Toronto School and Ong, though, could also be interpreted more sympathetically, without having to brand them as technological determinists. An interpretation as aesthetic form, deploying its effect as social form, becomes a principle that could liberate us from the narrow horizon of the historical causality problem. In film theory, arguments of this type have had a right of residence at least since Bazin (1985) claimed that realism is the essence of the film form. Since Simmel, at the latest, and then the Frankfurt School of Adorno, Marcuse, and Benjamin, the connection between the two forms has been firmly established (where the aesthetic form has its home in Kant's philosophy of the Transcendental Aesthetic as *a priori* form of apperception). McLuhan, in his capacity as literature scholar, borrowed (cf. Cavell 2003, 7f) from the formalist Frank (1991) the categories of space and time, which were so central to his thought.

In the television studies domain, Altheide (2004; 1979) and Real (1989) connect to this aesthetic tradition, thought not in McLuhan's or even Simmel's strict sense. But these scholars at least share the claim that television as logic, or as form, is in principle capable of predetermining meaning and sociality. To represent this ordination as the logic of a technology is only meaningful either in a metaphorical sense or in terms of aesthetic form (reminding us of Kant). The cultural studies group then thought that it had to extend this determination to further ('cultural') code systems, which could then be encoded and decoded. This is not the only imaginable shaping of media meaning, though; political economy (of the property and production conditions) can also determine media meaning, in substitution of technology.

Television studies – in particular, television criticism – continued to refer to the television form as more of an intermediary between aesthetic form and social form.[28] The former stems from literary theory and the genre debate; some have associated the latter with Simmel's social form. For Simmel, this form was also aesthetically relevant. Through this link, television studies established a bridge between audience (spectatorship) and conditions of production.

The basic intuition that television determines meaning is probably as easy to comprehend as it is difficult to prove. Since this form is an industrial product of meaning, the potential factors contributing to its meaning are more numerous than with the paradigm of a lonely individual author's work of art (and of the paradigmatic *auteurs* in cinema art). The speech-act validity approach can address aesthetic with little more than authenticity, the validity for interiority. Clearly, this is a limitation when it comes to an aesthetic socialization form. Similarly, Simmel's approach – which for its aesthetic and social form borrows rather explicitly from Kant – suffers from the limitations of its presuppositions. The *proton pseudos* is, on the contrary, interiority *in se* as the aesthetic locus. From there (inside), the aesthetic must be expressed of which only an extraordinary genius is capable. Aesthetic degenerated into the 'geniality' of the artist and the corresponding good taste of consumers.[29] External auxiliary constructions, and not inaccessible forms of interiority, therefore, can alone construe the principle of meaning determined by television. Such determination, as social, is more than individually interior; as an aesthetic, it is also cognitively dependent on feeling.

The idea of semiotic, in its novelty, thus also proves helpful when we turn to the question of social aesthetic form. The idea of sign makes all dualisms (such as language) forms of apperception or social rules, and thus redundant for mediating cognition with its other, the real world. Instead, mediation itself is a relational process among three essentially different correlates. As we know (cf. *supra*), the First Correlate is always a sign for its interpretation (and a preceding thought can also be a sign). According to the logical qualities of this sign, it can only be interpreted in a certain sense. Without falling into technological determinism, it can indeed be said that the sign quality of television also determines the meaning of the Interpretant. These qualities cannot be simple, of course, in such a heterogeneous medium – but neither can they be arbitrary. Instead of supposing a determination of technology, sign classification clearly offers much more flexibility. Furthermore, to each sign class there corresponds a habit of behaviour, and thus a sign is immediately relevant for social action. If media technologies are endowed with logic, this trait expresses itself directly in the conduct required by the sign. Technological determinists are right only in the sense that the

First Correlate decisively determines every sign interpretation. How this functions for the signs of public opinion was shown in §4.3 above. If there is a unique specificity for audiovisual media, it is in the one-to-one relation of their production, which, as it were, subscribes to them 'truth' (as long as one knows about the apparatus of recording, and it is not animation film).[30] Yet even here, a sign can become a degenerate or constructive relation, which reminds us that this relation is guided by enunciation, by sign usage.

With regard to the quality of the media sign, it is possible to consider letters as drawings (i.e., calligraphy). As much as letters can be interpreted as drawings, 'television' does not coincide tout court with reportage, sports transmissions, talk shows, etc. While semiotic is interested mainly in the logically highest-adic type of relation, it is evident from the constructive/degenerative nature of semiosis that sign use can always fall back on a lower or higher determination than in a previous interpretation. Good examples of this are the interpretations of cultural theory itself. When they see the operations of ideology on television – which *per definitionem* should stay latent – the cognitive object is certainly no longer the immediately received televisual sign (i.e., what is perceived by the 'audience'). Cultural theory clearly interprets far beyond the living room. This does not imply, though, that these interpretations are illegitimate. The decoded codes merely originate from a much more general sign than the moving image of television – which, however, remains in both cases the (Dynamic) Object of the sign.

Desperation with the substantial difficulties of grasping the sign qualities of television is perhaps what has driven so many in communication sciences into the arms of 'active audience' theories. The 'solution' here is to simply leave the interpretation to 'the' spectators. This fits the notion that the 'activeness' of their role can be taken for granted. It has become a ritual (what else?) to refer time and again to rather outlandish concepts such as Lazarsfeld's 'hypodermic needle,'[31] 'two-step flow' (Katz, Lazarsfeld, and Columbia University. Bureau of Applied Social Research 1964), and so on, which originated from postwar propaganda research. This 'activeness' is explained in diverse ways that contradict one another – for example, we have Hall's encoding/decoding theorem, and vague borrowings from hermeneutics, and even a simple extension of Katz's uses and gratifications. All of these obtain their revolutionary aura through such *epitheta ornantia* as 'resistance,' 'subversion,' audience 'empowerment,'[32] and the like. Without entering into a debate with these increasingly woolly concepts, there is a solid reasoning behind the idea of 'active' interpretation. That idea, however, is much better served in a fully developed semiotic; because rule, understood as behaviour, is there already in the hands of agents regulating and controlling themselves. This theory can survive perfectly well without psychology and therefore does not need to hypostasize evil or good motivations of powerful, powerless, or empowered agents. Though thereby deprived of its revolutionary charm, it stands to gain, in exchange, in explanatory power of the prime object, which is the medium itself, which in cultural studies tends to become reduced to a mere occasion for various decoding exercises.

A critical perspective should be capable, in all aspects of its practice, of a precise awareness of the semiotic qualities of television. It is not enough to leave all of that awareness to spectator interpretation; nor should the price for a critical vantage point be a semiotic narrowed down to the cognitive dimension of meaning production through language. Over and above the above-mentioned problem of a too-narrow sign concept, Habermas's restriction to propositional sentences has another drawback: it prevents awareness of larger linguistic units, such as texts. Texts are no *ceteris paribus* extensions of sentences; just in themselves, they are meaning organizations. For instance, without a handle on texts, narrativity – so important in the news genre – would fall below the radar of the treatable. In a similar vein, mere feelings, in many ways of crucial importance in mass media – from music to television – are present only insofar as self-representation (in Goffman's sense) constitutes a validity.

Validity is an abstraction based on goals of speech acts. It requires communicative action to be effective. Habermas's fundamental-pragmatic models this effect on a Mead-inspired coordination of actions for object manipulation. With mass media, however, this coordination does not occur in the same way, for no one in particular is being addressed. To avoid this involvement at all times, there exist the genre characteristics of diverse program forms signalling objectivity. Where the enunciation instance, television, chooses to manifest itself, the involvement prohibition is the principle of operation; this applies analogically to 'fictional' types. In the latter types, this avoidance is necessary for a purely narrative reason – to put into effect the 'temporary displacement' of narrative illusion. This is part of the narrative contract. It is put into effect by the uncoupling of the narration universe from the narrative universe. In the former types, though, there is no coupling of the two universes either, of the text and of spectators, but only the illusion thereof.

This requisite for text construction allowed Greimas to speak of the two illusions: reference and enunciation (Greimas and Courtés 1979, s.v. 'énonciation'). The first causes a reality effect; the second effectuates credibility of the enunciation. To conceal the lack of a true illocution, a complex apparatus of media conventions and their associated forms is necessary; these simulate illocutionary acts. Most of these textual strategies insinuate a locutionary universe: everything that is said is not 'said' but 'is' (according to the speech act pattern 'is p,' = predicate). In terms of logic of predicates, propositions of this type are meaningless unless in the indicative mood of the present or past tense. This strategy reflects Greimas's referential illusion. The television apparatus accommodates and prefers this practice through the presentic nature of its imagery, which is incapable of producing tenses for a lack of morphemes (the 'second articulation'). Complex strategies merely achieve pseudo-morphemes.[33]

Habermas's orientation towards 'agreement' is also defeated in mass media texts by the fact that they habitually conceal their enunciation instance. Speech acts beyond pure locutions must assume an identifiable speaker instance, so there is no meaningful performative or illocutionary enunciation without the identity of the speaker. In audiovisual programs this instance is always neutralized (as much as in the scientific *genus litterarum*), but supplanted by its imitation. Because news anchors, or news readers, cannot behave in the manner of a physics journal, their 'objectivity' must be simulated. This media practice is graspable through Habermas's Ideal Speech Situation only negatively, as violation of those ideals, their claims, and their discursive production.

The medium itself, as such and in principle, limits the communication situation; narrative genres then add to this imposition further constraints on communicative roles. The narrative illusion is not only in the 'fictional' content but also in the uncoupling communication, which produces a separate narrative universe in the first place. News stories in particular try to treat narrations as cases of illocution (i.e., everything that 'is,' becomes an 'is said') with validity claims of reality assertion. Certainly, the narrative universe must be taken as real in the sense of a *narratio probabilis*. But what is special in this case is that this reality must be guaranteed by one single role that can be noticed in the text itself: Ricoeur calls this *vox narrativa*. Reception aesthetics uses the coupled terms 'implied author' and 'ideal reader' (*énonciateur/énonciataire* in Greimas). Just as with speech acts, narrative uncoupling has purely logical roles whose sole function is to establish communication with a text – under the correct conditions of comprehension and power. This frame role, like intratextual roles, is an illusion; it belongs not to a experiential 'real world' communication, but to a represented one.[34]

Television derives from the uncoupling logic two communication attitude principles, which Weinrich (2001) has called 'commenting' and 'narrating.' In practical terms, this distinguishes in the text not mutually exclusive but rather co-present attitudes. Returning to the genre paradigm of scientific papers, here the authorial presence of comment is hidden to the maximum. In a narration, on the contrary, obfuscation is painstaking. Thus, television either manifests its (authorial) enunciation instance through public opinion genres, or conceals it behind the enunciated, as in entertainment genres. When it is concealed, no one can make television responsible; whereas in public opinion, this instance must first prove its credibility. These parameters also allow a 'discourse analytical' differentiation of program types – for example, in cinema or in feature films, fictional subjects signal their being staged playfully; whereas those subjects are 'earnest' when someone assumes responsibility to the spectator for the represented universe.

To conclude, we have discussed three variants of attributing to the medium a predetermination of meaning. Each theory's idiosyncratic attributions have been debated in the communication sciences. A genuinely semiotic solution that closely analyses the medium as sign has not been attempted. So far, the argument that religion contradicts the illuminated rationality of public opinion media hinges on Weber's parameters; whereas technological determinism is too broad in scope to apply to contingent media practices. Semiotic, being much more complex, cannot offer neat contrasts; even so, in practical terms it is relevant for conflict constellations that involve public opinion and religion. In semiotic analyses of this conflict, technological or media essence is not a useful construct. Nevertheless, we can state that the medium, television, is not neutral. Furthermore, it is much less interesting what meaning potential the sign material *in se* could determine than what it determines practically. No one can prevent television from being used as video art (in museums); that said, industrial practice has restricted the medium's potential. Industry, in the main, needed a narrative medium in order to construct public opinion and determine the main operation logic of that medium through narration. Moreover, the same narrating can be used for entertainment in drama format. In the age of infotainment, separation is no longer so strict as in quality newspapers, where the 'press' has succeeded in differentiating itself from 'literature' – albeit with substantial, industrially relevant grey areas.

Now that an industry has snatched narrativity from literature's sanctuary, this question arises (as for religion): How has public opinion's narrative dominance been reflected back onto dramatic narration? Film adaptations of literature have reduced their sources to entertainment. The influence of television aesthetics on film aesthetics has resulted in the Hollywoodization of cinema. This has brought about a strong emphasis on narration or (conversely) on the reduction of aesthetic film elements to strong narrative causality. This is a consequence not of television technology (which in industrial practice has moved much closer to the product 'film'), but of the dominant vicinity of public opinion. Television aesthetic amounts to the hypotaxization of film aesthetic.

As indicated by the most extreme examples of televangelism, religion finds itself in the same predicament of hypotaxis under public opinion. Linguistically, hypotaxis is achieved by 'shifters' (Jakobson) or *'débrayeurs'*[35] (Greimas). Often, dependence is hardly noticeable: stories seem to tell themselves, or realities just 'are' (i.e., rather than being reported by someone). Modern narratology has capitalized on this effect under rubrics such as 'marks of enunciation'/enunciated (Benveniste), discourse/narration (Genette), and commenting/telling (Weinrich). These linguistic vagaries have not hindered Casetti from applying this effect to pictorial media by identifying audiovisual equivalents to the linguistic shifters of tense, mood, and person. One part of meaning subordinates the other part, and this is analogous to hypotactical sentence order modalizing the subordinate clause in its meaning. Enunciation presents something as being true (possible, necessary, dubious) or not. For media-dependent religion, it is merely a matter of judgment whether one sees in this an alteration or a constraint; it depends on whether one is prepared to think of televangelism as genuine religiosity.

Under what conditions, then, does religion find itself under public opinion? Typically, it has become public opinion practice to represent religion as *feeling*.

4.6 Godcasting: Meaning Apparatuses of Religious Self-Display

A privileged hypotaxis mode of religion as public is its display as feeling. Technically, this must be realized as display of feeling subjectivities, of public personae who feel religiously – which is not as trivial as it may sound. This first step involves transforming the subject of religious experience ('the mystic' in Luhmann's sense, cf. §4.1) into a visibly religious subject. The process almost never stops here, but calls up a second transformation into a higher text format, be it narration or the drama of public opinion. These two logics cohabit in entertainment, which offers a second stereotype for self-display and self-reception, to be used also by religious communication.

In a first step, religious experience (which in Luhmann's sociology of religion is the ambivalent mystical meaning without meaning, cf. §4.1) turns into a visible, distinguishable, and publicly communicable meaning, when a displayer-subject makes its Self visible to a spectator-subject. The subject's skill consists in displaying its religious experience as a subjective quality, which is diverse. As quality of a pragmatic subject, it can now be handled in the usual way of acquiring pragmatic competence. This is the difference between preachers and mystics: the latter lack the subject quality that would enable them to act a determinate pragmatic *telos*. We can, in formal reconstruction, analyse this meaning effect – designated as 'preacher' (subject quality as display of religious experience) – in a normal sequence of the three Greimasian tests («*épreuve qualifiante, décisive, glorifiante*»).

Test 1. The preparatory stage of the first, 'qualifying' test transforms the mystical (in Luhmann's sense) religious subject: 'I show my Me to God (and God observes me)' becomes now a religious identity: 'I show my Me as a transformed one (i.e., presupposing the first).' Practically, religious experience acquires its communicable visibility only as conversion (in the broadest sense of the term), and religious identities are qualified as converted identities. Public religious personalities such as televangelists, therefore, imply always two personalities: one visible after the conversion, a religious Self, and an implicit one that existed before. This transformation is accomplished in the next two tests of the Self's realization (before- into after-subject). While the task of religious Self-realization is a classic *topos* in legends (ascetic Self-perfection: '*vince te ipsum!*' or St Anthony's temptations), this is rarely an explicit topic in mass media religious programming, where one usually finds fully realized subjects. However, every public religious communication, from confessions to liturgical interactions, must make use of religious visibility of some sort. Visibility's dowry to invisible conversion is action constraint, which brings a new logic, teleology, to bear. 'I let my Self be converted' in a teleological (narrative) frame needs the implied cause: 'God has transformed me.' This means, in Luhmann's context, dissolving transcendental ambiguity, the God-Chiffre of religious language, where it remains undecided whether something comes from God or from the human psyche. In teleological speech it is now no longer God of whom we speak, but: 'I am transformed and there is a destination instance for this.' This is equivalent to saying: 'God is my destinator' ... 'the meaning of my acting was given to me.' God is thus only comprehensible as the invisible destinator of a visible course of action.

Test 2. The convert, the now visible religious subject, changes into a preaching subject: 'I show my Self to your Self so that it may also be converted.' Here we are clearly in the realm of enunciation but not yet in that of mass media enunciation. The first subject becomes enunciator, the second enunciate, and both are equally involved in the enunciation of religious meaning. Therefore, religious proclamation needs to be analysed as (a) enunciation (b) with two roles of two Selves each, and thus two teleologies, and this is (c) stereotyped through entertainment (cf. Test 3). Enunciation as such contributes the hypotaxis relation of subordination to meaning. Enunciators not only subject the enunciated to their modes (which must be made to appear, as necessary, possible, certain, obliged) but also condition their counterparts, the enunciates, who have to interpret.

Test 3. The third transformation turns mystics, then religious subjects, into entertainment stereotypes. With the action logic teleology in place, the communication of religious Self-display becomes a specification of a type of action. Whatever action specifies me as a religious Self, it must also adhere to the constraints of action representation in the entertainment media. Identities in mass media are publicity-created roles, not psychological states. Coming back to Luhmann, in his theory mass media are an autopoietic system, which has its own proper selection operation and medium. Media select according to the criterion actuality, and the positive information code is the 'new'; however, this selection risks that the actual will have no certainty as to its reliability. Internally, it deals with its own selection risk, unreliability, by instituting an opposite as the negative code of the system selectivity, the reliably unreliable advertisement section with its world of beautiful but knowingly untrue appearance. Functionally, it repairs the selection constraints of actuality in the news section, which is further safeguarded through a plurality of news sources (which does not, however, make the actual more reliable), established news criteria, news sections ('desks') with proper journalistic routines, and so forth. The result is not truth with its own systemic resistance against its own operation ('critique'), but rather a mere notoriety of a world as it is known to all, a reality effect that no one questions but that allows everyone to entertain a free and different opinion.

News can cover anything as long as it is actual, but it cannot 'cover' God (who is without information value, in Luhmann's sociology of religion). That said, conversion can be covered through subject identities. I have attempted to demonstrate the semiotic construction of cinematic identities elsewhere (Ehrat 2005b). The collective identity 'all' is not a real identity, but a sort of 'One' ('one believes that'). This constraint is handled functionally by entertainment. In the mass media system, noticeable subjectivity as a proper system operation fulfils a compensation function. Imposing an unquestionable world of actual events constrains a great deal for which free opinion cannot fully compensate. While one has no choice but to believe these events, still one desires to regain some control over the selection operation. Advertising dictates taste without freedom of selection except for choosing among limited alternatives, yet it is incumbent on entertainment to provide freedom of selection. Only here can a subject shed its own reality constraints by assuming vicarious experiences of other identities, personal histories, personal universes, and times. That these identities are again stereotyped and modelled (on stars and on genres) is not so important, just as long as they lead to an operation of selection and identity. Religious communication meshing with drama – which is the domain of selection freedom – is, therefore, a viable alternative – even an escape route – to hypotaxis from publicity. Technically, outside the public sphere, it turns into entertainment, which is the only place in the fixed common universe of the mass media system where identities and universes can change. Each test displays a different self:

- (Test 1), the 'convert self,' comprises four virtual elements: If 'I' is a transformed 'Self,' it must show the following: Self *statu quo ante*, Self *statu quo post*, its transformation, and its 'destinator.'
- The enunciated Self (Test 2) contributes 'I' as a represented is 'I-for-you' plus the reflexivity of this: 'I know that you see Me' (not 'I' but 'Me' in Mead's sense of the terms).
- (Test 3) For mass-mediated preaching, the reflexive 'you' becomes meaning determinating. Meaning at this stage is only enunciator/ enunciatee or speaker/audience.

All of this translates textually into a religiously (receptive, hostile, not-receptive, indifferent) audience that must interpret the meaning, and for the display of this meaning an enunciator (showing, not showing, hiding, demonstrative). The 'communicative interests' of these two partners can be arranged in relations of the different negation positions: identity, contradictory, contrary, subcontrary negation, each for each partner and one relation for the alignment of interests.[36] Greimas's semionarratology found in these differences of negation a basic leitmotiv, called *carré sémiotique* (Greimas 1970a, 67–91 'Pour une théorie des modalités'). The problem with his *carré* is that it claims a certain generative automatism, paradigmatic and syntagmatic *articulation logique* (Greimas and Courtés 1979: s.v. 'carré sémiotique'), along the negation (op-)positions. However, it is evident that only the contradictory opposition is perfect and logically stable in both directions, whereas the contrary is only a partial negation and therefore always arbitrary. 'White' may be the contrary of 'black,' but so is 'red.' From 'red' there is no certain relation back to 'black,' as it relates contrarily also to 'cool' and so on. The articulation of a 'semantic category' in its isotopies is therefore rather 'ad hoc' in the *carré sémiotique*. In predication logic since Aristotle's Περί ἑρμενείας, Boetius, and St Anselm of Canterbury/Aosta, these negations are well known: contrary, subcontrary, subaltern, and contradictory negation. Contrary propositions can both be false but cannot both be true; subcontrary propositions can both be true but cannot both be false; subaltern (logical or = *vel*) are true if one is true, false if both are false. St Anselm developed the modes of not-being as a reflection of the logical square, as being brought into opposing relations: *non facere essere* is not-(p & q), which is logically equivalent with not-p or not-q. Not-p & not-q, equivalent with not-(p or q), is *facere non essere*. Whereas p or q (equivalent with not-[not-p & not-q]) is *non facere non essere*, which is implied by *facere essere* ([p & q] > [p or q]). In a further step of formalization, Greimas went on to modalize doing through being (competence before performance), enriching his modalization theory with 2×2 modalizing relations. However, this could only be done in not recognizing the primacy of being before doing, as was clearly seen by Anselm and the medieval logicians (Beuchot 1997).

The general positions of the 'communication interests' of two subjects on display to each other can be outlined in the Skopic Apparatus (see Diagram A) as a simple combination of the interest of an active subject and those of a passive one.

Applying this to a televangelist show, let us consider the active enun-

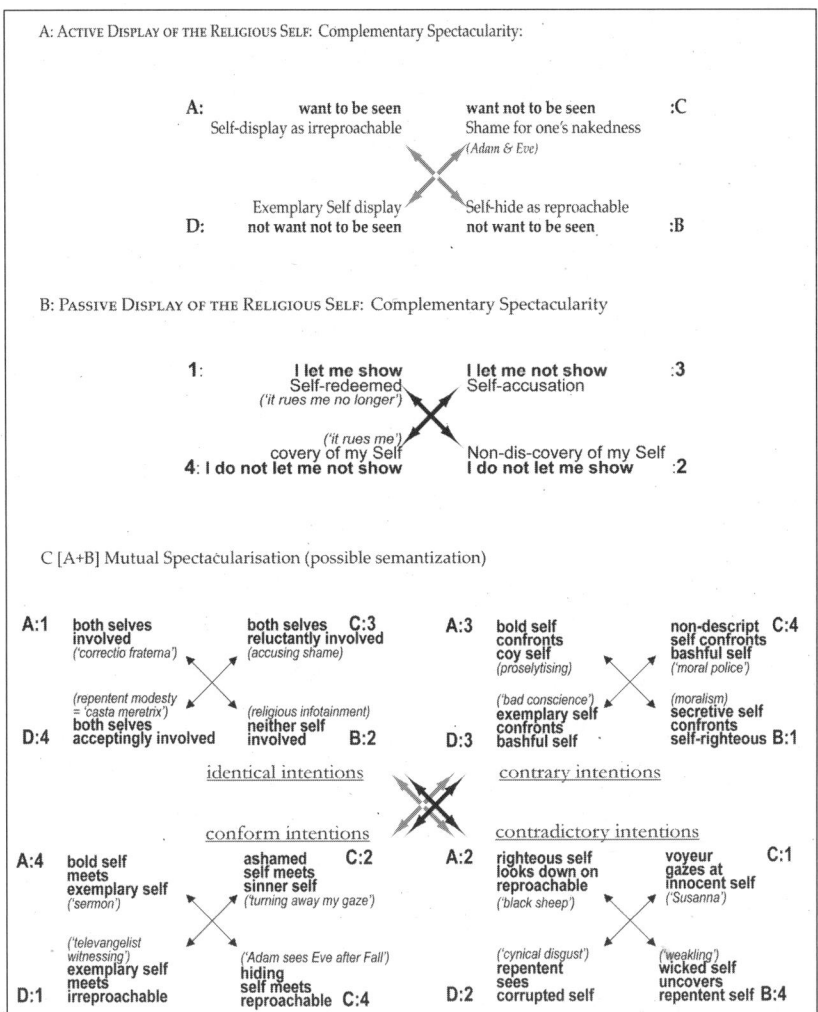

Diagram A: Formalism of the Skopic Apparatus

ciator Self in itself (suspending the passive spectator) in some standard situations of religious communication and media programming. Considered formally, Jimmy Bakker's *Praise the Lord*, for instance, is foremost a display of religious Selves in a programmatic sequence. These shows focus on some sort of transformation. That transformation displays or implies three kinds of religious subjects in a precise order: (1) The one who is perfectly 'blessed' – usually the host – and whose state is beyond conversion, an 'irreproachable state,' as the logical *origo* and termination of the converting transformation. Were this subject to exist alone, there would be no narrative of transformation. (2) Thus, the next in order, and the starting point of the conversion narrative proper, is its contradictory opposite: a Self who 'not-can show its Self' – that is, a reproachable Self. In a televangelist show, this is the big Absent One who is exorcised in the sermon as the Evil One. As soon as the narrative passes to its implied negation, its non-substitutable function is clear. (3) Next, the rueful sinner. In televangelist shows, this is one of the most prominent roles. In the revivalist liturgical tradition, this prominence was given to the part called 'witnessing.' While the reproachable subject has its contradictory opposite in the irreproachable, it implies merely a (no-longer or) non-reproached. This subject 'can not-show its Self'; and its opposite is again a subject who 'not-can not-show its Self,' which then is (4) redeemed sinners. These must show their converted Self – that is, PTL or 'Praise The Lord.' As a liturgical function, this is incumbent on the choirs and singers, but first of all on the subjects responding to the 'Call Forward.' They quite literally present their Selves as morally converted, cleansed personalities. By implication one returns from this meaning position to case (1), which exists now as a reconfirmed subject of 'exemplarity.' This rendering of the televangelist show only represents one-half of the meaning, though, as it does not yet include the passive spectator Self. Yet it is clear that these shows imply certain kinds of spectator subject. An audience research, as an investigation of the meaning experiences of spectators, can in principle only discover these formal positions; the formalism should even induce the investigation of *all* positions, not just the desirable ones.

Of course, there is more to religious communication than just televangelism. This formal Skopic Apparatus can be applied to further instances as well. In particular, it applies to communication subjects under public opinion, as soon as asymmetrical roles are involved. As media programming, this is fairly standard. In all moralistic discourses that church leaders have a habit of falling into, this type of meaning is used with great success. The same display form is used in anticlerical variants ('look how unredeemed, quarrelsome, scandalous, fanatic they are'). 'Moralism' is incomprehensible unless spectators form part of the meaning, because the basic idea of this Self-display is that I (the enunciator subject) do not show my Self as sinner (reproachable), but rather the other Self (the receiver subject) as a negative exemplary subject. Thus, to produce this particular meaning, the syntactic starting point is position (2) for the receiver and (A) for the enunciator (cf. Diagram A:A).

Applicability of this Skopic Apparatus in mass media reaches its culmination in narration and drama. As religious meaning production, this should be called a pseudo- (or even anti-) 'hagiographical' genre. 'Modern saints,' old legends of edification, portray exemplary subjects, and of course the corresponding villains. The central operation here differs from 'witnessing,' and not simply because it adheres much more closely to the rule in Aristotle's *Poetics* (48a2f). The difference is also in the positioning of the edified spectator, whose conforming or identical communication intentions are supposed in the narrative contract.

These meaning formalisms hardly exhaust the complexity, for we have deliberately abstracted from the spectator Self display. Unfortunately for the study of religious communication, the role of the spectator has often been deferred to 'audience studies,' even though audience is already part of the meaning itself. Thus, for the meaning of a religious spectator, the passive religious subject taken in itself, possible positions are summarized in Diagram A:B. The general presupposition of religious proclamation from the side of the spectator is that the enunciator does not encounter meaning position 2 in the spectator square: spectators must have at least some willingness to let themselves become involved into a process of conversion of their Selves. I will illustrate this with a biblical story, the David and Uriah story (2 Samuel 11.2–12.13, rather than with a media situation. The story is a passage through all four positions. It starts with position 2: David does not want to know. He believes that everything is well concealed. However, as soon as he agrees to listen to Nathan's parable (2 Samuel 12.1), David becomes a religious subject 3 (who wants not to let himself show his crime). Nathan's parable is, of course, a complete narrative trajectory in itself, beginning with 1. David's aporia of 3 is broken when he is told: 'Thou [art] the man' (2 Samuel 12.7), which brings him effectively into 4 as the reluctant acceptance of his own Self as sinner. When he repents ('I have sinned against the Lord') and is saved by the Lord's grace, he is finally, in 1, a newborn Self: 'thou shalt not die.' The same trajectory, but with three separate subjects, could also be shown in the parable of the Good Samaritan and in many other parabolic texts.

Taken in themselves, the passive and active subjects of the formal diagram cannot render the whole meaning, as concrete texts would have to produce it. As one meaning only, they are the display, of which one cannot assume that there are complementary or conforming interests. In our Diagram A:C, the simplest case is B:2, where enunciators do not-want-to display their Selves and spectators do not-want-to let themselves become involved. This situation is abortive and immediately terminates the narrative meaning production. Such is the case with religion as pure information, as is common in newspaper practice, where the style demands that this mutual disinterest in each other's Self's spectacularization be the basis of the story (Silk 1995). As a perfect, irreproachable enunciator-Self encounters a spectator-Self that wants-to let itself show because it does not need its transformation, the positive case A:1 is not very interesting. This is tantamount to two subjects mutually confirming their probity, which is a standard talk-show situation: 'saint meets holy,' where no one is challenged and everyone saves face. C:3 and D:4 are still in the Square of identical interest. D:4 is only a subtle variant of A:1 since it refers via implication as double negation to A:1. The semantics of 'ir-reproachable' indicate this, much like 'certainly,' which is richer than a simple 'yes.' At this meaning position, the transformation trajectory is implied: the Self is redeemed. The result is a feast of sinners, shown, for instance, in the final sequence of *Babette's Feast*. In C:3 this process of Selves-transformation is still fully under way.

Since publicity, as it is realized in the news genre or in journalistic activity, has sacrificed on the altar of the objectivity convention and style all sorts of subjective involvement, it is evident that the imaginary freedom of public identity is greater in narration and drama. Diagram B contains some illustrations of the meaning positions of Diagram A:C, mostly in narrative films about religious subjects.

The films mentioned in Diagram B are: C:3 *Journal d'un curé de campagne* (Bresson 1950); A:1 *The Apostle* (Duvall 1997); D:4 *La leggenda del santo bevitore* (Olmi 1988). This last (The Legend of the Holy Drinker [1988] / La légende du saint buveur [1988]) is based on Joseph Roth's autobiographical novel, *Die Legende vom heiligen Trinker*. There is no single scene in it that illustrates this meaning position, but in the trajectory of the narration – which tells the story of an alcoholic who must pay back his debt of honour to Thérèse of Lisieux in the Ste-Marie-des-Batignolles chapel, but who loses out to his addiction – the final sequences of the delirious dying alcoholic in the arms of a stranger named Thérèse asking for forgiveness become significant in this sense: 'Gebe Gott uns allen, uns Trinkern, einen so leichten und schönen Tod'

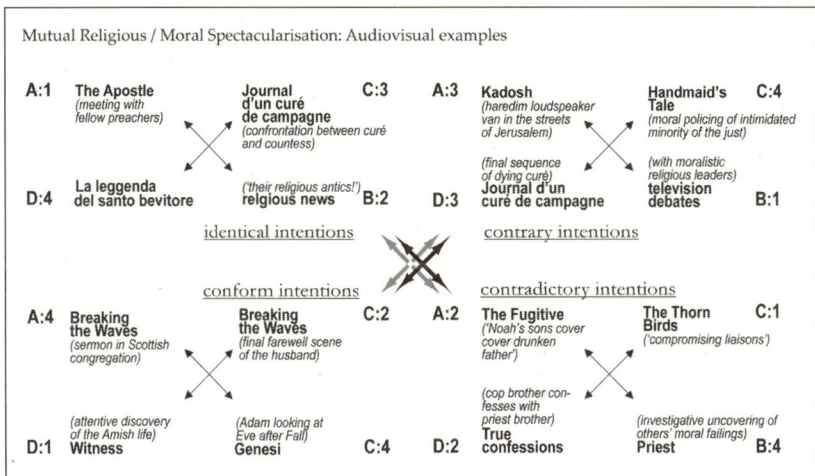

Diagram B: Audiovisual Illustrations of Diagram A:C

(word by word translation: 'Give God us all, us drinkers, a so light and sheen,' archaic for beautiful, 'death'), the haloed failure. *Genesi: La creazione e il diluvio*; *Kadosh* (Gitai 1999); *The Handmaid's Tale* (Schlöndorff and Atwood 1990); Schlöndorff's film uses Harold Pinter's screenplay of Margaret Eleanor Atwood's homonymous novel, the cover of which summarizes the storyline in these words: 'She must lie on her back once a month and pray that the Commander makes her pregnant, because in an age of declining births, Offred and the other Handmaids are only valued if their ovaries are viable.' *Breaking the Waves* (Trier 1996); *Witness* (Weir 1985); *The Fugitive* (Ford 1947) which uses the storyline of Graham Greene's novel 'The power and the glory'-; *True Confessions* (Grosbard 1981); *Priest* (Bird 1994); *Daryl Duke, The Thorn Birds* (Duke 1983).

5 From Jubilation to Scandal

Media of publicity have their own ideology built in (be it conceptualized as rationality, meaning constraint, technological or aesthetic determination, or teleology). Their logical claim is all-encompassing of things public, relegating to the private what they choose to ignore. Religion could have been private for the public discourse, but between the two are a number of conflict areas in matters of morals and customs. One way of avoiding this constraint is the public self-display, a public identity carried into a drama that is freer than the θέατρον of public opinion. As entertainment, the imaginary play with identities in this drama is still part of mass media, but not of publicity. Since publicity is logical construct, which through the logic of mass media becomes a determinant of society *tout court*, it cannot coexist with a logic that also claims social determination – that is, religion. From this clash between two logics much can be learned about the operations of publicity, which is our interest. Whereas, on the other hand, a sociology of religion such as Luhmann's (1977, 1984a; Luhmann and Kieserling 2002b) argued with a certain cogency that religious transcendence under the impact of social function turned into moral discourse. The public opinion operation, especially as scandalization of religion, reveals much about its meaning premises in its treatment of religion.

The first section of this chapter concerns itself with a basic social expression of religion in itself, not upstream but outside the public sphere – that is, even before becoming a private matter. In the section after that, before we approach semiotic analysis, we connect briefly with current debates in the communications literature, especially television studies and certain media aesthetic discourses.

A closer study of self-publication of private religion – a reversal of the private sphere – in the phenomenon of televangelism leads us to a first semiotic analysis of some of its central form elements. What it means to be construed through media manifests itself in the first place as construction of time and space, regardless of the represented object. When religious performances become those representations, they undergo the same construal as everything else, only here the difference in meaning is more evident. In a second moment, in the analysis of the dramaturgic pivot of televangelist shows, the 'call forward,' we notice and observe how much this sort of religious dramaturgy owes to the media form. Together with the third strong moment, when exemplary persons give witness of their successes to an astonished audience (this is the literal meaning of *miraculum*), we can analyse here an instance of one ('of self-realization') of the two metatexts of media of public opinion (as we will describe them in chapter 6). Metatexts are, in short, the stories behind stories, which are so much the basis of the functioning of this meaning of publicity that they can simply be presupposed without needing to be told over and over. The fourth pivotal feature of televangelist shows, the display and construal of (the host's, preacher's, evangelist's, healer's) authority, instantiates the other metatext ('of power legitimization'). Both metatexts originate from the medium, not from religious meaning *in se*.

In the final section of this chapter, we conclude from our media analysis, in a generalizing reflection, the principles of how public opinion media relate to public religion. In the commencement of an antagonist relationship, religion becomes public opinion's primordial scandal: two exclusive moral institutions in conflict.

5.1 Religious Meaning outside of Public Opinion

The hybridization of religion in the public opinion media produced, among other things, televangelism. Our aim is to inquire into the 'religion of media' as one of public opinion's most astounding feats, ranging from show to scandal. Before that, however, it is important for us to ascertain the *status quo ante* in order to grasp its transformation by public opinion. More than any other 'social object,' religion is subtle, evanescent, and difficult to grasp.[1] The transforming process by the media can be analysed directly not as a conflict of two incompatible logics or sign classes, apostrophized as rationality, but as the interpretation of a sign.

How media transform religion is especially interesting because of the complexity of both the meaning constellations involved. There is no way to predict how a mutual interpretation can take place and what can come out of it. The privatization of religion suggests that there are no overlaps between public affairs and private beliefs. Difficulties begin with these questions: Is there indeed a common cognitive object? Do signs interpreting religiously and those interpreting publicly intend the same things at all? If they intend things of a different nature, there can be no conflict, but perfect parallel universes coexist irenically. Yet our Θέατρον model of public opinion has found a pattern of theo-logic. This obtains not only for the ancient paradigm, but also when everyone – including a monarch – must respond indiscriminately to the absoluteness of the judgment instance, modern epigones of the instance of gods. There are, then, solid factual grounds to assume that religion and publicity are vying for the same judgment.

A magnetic field applies a polarizing force on publicity as well as on religion. With regard to religion, this field influences a reality that exists independently outside this field, and that did so long before it came under the purview of publicity. The same cannot be said of the publicity itself, though, because there is no point in publicity existing independently. Only when they are free of polarization can religious actors determine their own pragmatic goals. Religion, as this original practice, creates its own publicity, a public outside the religious fold – and here the word 'audience' truly applies (cf. Ehrat 2005c). There are many ways in which religion reaches beyond its internal sphere towards 'the other'; one of them is κήρυγμα (a herald's proclamation, which is how St Paul referred to his preaching of the gospel). Inquiring into the rhetoric of preaching uncovers an anti-eristic principle. Once it comes before an instance intent on determining everyone's goal (including the preacher's), however, one notices immediately how rhetoric shifts into one of justifying one's own pragmatic teleology. This was the core of the historical experience of Pentecostalist assemblies, who used to see themselves as mandated by the Holy Ghost. The transformation from 'evangelical assembly' into televangelism was accompanied by this traumatic experience of evangelists turning into celebrities and becoming involved in scandals, raising doubts about their pretended pragmatic goals (Hadden 1993). Interestingly, a converse insinuation of pragmatic purpose occurs when 'obsessive missionaries' (as the anti-'neocon' press portrays them[2]) are publicly 'discovered' as surprisingly normal, friendly fellow citizens with political orientations more differentiated than could have been assumed (Shapiro 2004).

The difference in teleological predetermination before and after subjection to the magnetic field of publicity manifests itself as clear meaning. This takes the form of an interpretative either–or. Indeed, this either–or has developed robust genres with hardly any ambivalences in the ways texts must be taken. Thus, the preaching genre is a very clear meaning. It is perfectly comprehensible on the basis of a teleological pragmatic determination, but it occurs in a very subtle way (subtler than in public opinion). The mandate for a chosen one is truly a vocation, not visible and by necessity inaccessible to someone without this calling. Public opinion, by contrast, almost demands that all actors respond to 'all,' thereby recognizing the mandate of 'all.' If those who are called are preaching, they must simultaneously proclaim their vocation. Otherwise, the determination of the pragmatic goal falls back to the level of self-interest, or something similar. The meaning genre of preaching is not very narrow, though. If the divine (as in the Dionysos cult) is directly represented, then the preaching text type could include 'magic' genres in the broadest sense. Conventionally, this happens in the crude form of numinous awe (in the sense of Aristotle's *Poetics'* fear). Nowadays, however, God is not granted the privilege of being on television shows. That sort of direct divine appearance can occur only on Indian television, which has produced a purely divine drama, the *Ramayana* (Sagar 1986). This television series was so successful that it has generated imitations and sequels. In practice, such things can today be conveyed only in narrative wrapping. God's agents populate horror films *en masse*. They are also the mainstay of diverse exorcism films, of sect and Satanic films such as the *Guyana Tragedy* (Graham 1980), of dystopian films (*A Handmaid's Tale* [Schlöndorff and Atwood 1990]), and of ethnographic films (*Yeelen* [Cissé 1987]).

Preaching rhetoric in the real-world social life outside the realm of media can be packaged a multitude of ways. It is, however, always also a representation of 'something,' not simply roles. Something in the rhetorical sense of a *narratio probabilis* manifests itself, and the content of this 'something' is meaning, not a discourse on meaning. Theology and proclamation are radically different: the former talks about meaning; the latter represents it and makes it subject to experience, either directly or by means of narrative identification.[3] Churches' preaching also must represent narratively, and there are a number of forms for this. The classic example here is St Augustine's *Confessiones*, which has had many sequels up to the present day. Any kind of confession can be such a form, the most important strategy of which involves a transformation of the subject. Automatically, this produces a before and an after.

Televangelist shows, however, are structured to exhibit traces of their mediatization. But all of these have to change while being transformed into a mass medium: the preacher role must be fitted into the horizon of roles populated by public opinion, and the proclamation content, its representation of meaning, must become integrated with the predetermined rhetoric of the medium. No other form of religious representation has become so much part of the mass media universe as televangelism, which in some cases has no substantial existence outside the television studios and various address and donation databases. Equally ambivalent, it seems, is the mode of participation: Does watching a show constitute media consumption, or is it a religious service where an audience participates in the show? For the most part, televangelist preachers personally instruct their audience in the sense of a service. Some, for instance, solicit their viewers to kneel in front of the television set, to touch it, and to bow for prayer with the virtual community (Villaseñor 2001, 145f) – which suggests faint echoes of McLuhan. Most of these shows are merely well-made television. This effect is reflected as well in the historical fact that televangelism is evolving into an ideological and political vehicle (Timmerman and Smith 1994; Villaseñor 2001; Wilcox 1989). In the medium of public opinion, this reality effect is a consequence of the format itself.

Televangelist shows, as television products, know how to impress through elaborate choreography, the construction and organization of space and program time, witnessing, music, and the central place of the sermon. The faith healings with their characteristic triangular structure of phatic-appellative interaction among studio audience, preacher, and spectator are especially compelling. This format expertise did not come out of nowhere, though; in particular, it was not copycatted from other television formats. On the contrary, existing 'liturgical' forms have been transposed onto the television medium. Even (at first sight banal) elements of the *PTL* show have an age-old pedigree. This is evident from Weber's historical-sociological comparison of Protestant sects – historical as well as modern ones – in his sociological investigations of religion (Weber 1920b). Especially interesting in this comparison is the diversity of solutions to the same task. The task of liturgy, in the most general terms, is to give a representation to faith. By its very nature, this is not representing *ad extra*, nor is it representing horizontally towards a congregation; rather, it is representing vertically, transcendentally, towards God.

But as soon as faith has turned into a public display, the addressee of the representation has changed. To what degree this change has its remote origins in certain practices of Quaker congregations is an interesting question in the history of liturgy – or, as in Weber, of sociology of religion. In our present framework, however, our emphasis will be on communicative behaviour.

5.2 Television Studies and Aesthetic Form

Television formats are the concern of television studies. Unfortunately, that discipline has shown scant recent interest in the properly aesthetical form of television. Neither methods nor theories are homogeneous; generally, they are shared over the entire domain. Nevertheless, some areas of interest and research methods can be identified. Television genre theory, for instance, concerns itself mainly with questions of reception,[4] understood as 'cultural practices' and explicitly exclusive of 'issues that may seem outdated to some media scholars, whether they be the formal and aesthetic mechanics of texts or structuralist theories of generic meanings that seem incompatible with contemporary methods. The central questions motivating many media scholars today – how do television programs fit into historically specific systems of cultural power and politics – appear distant from those that typify genre theory' (Mittell 2000, 25). In this way, the narrative audiovisual form degenerates into an instruction sheet and preinterpretation, similar to the decay of rhetoric in antiquity. This results in mere questions of the *genus litterarum*, whereby the *rhetor* must pull out the correct stops, such as language style and level, address to public, tropes, the right common places, and so on. This has definitively broken the organic connection between the aesthetic and logical forms; rhetoric has degenerated into an empty 'pure rhetoric.'

The same criticism applies to theories of 'pure aesthetic' – and there are a number of variants of this sort of 'formalism.' To speak of television rituals is rarely more than a rather vague parlance, one that tries to suggest how round-about atavistic effects operate in religious societies. Such parlance comes easily to mind for televangelism. But it hardly explains anything, except the explicit intention to negate 'functionalist' transmission communication.[5] At any rate, this approach has no purchase at all on the aesthetic qualities of the audiovisual sign.

Among the four types of television theories listed by Corner, none pays particular attention to that medium's aesthetic and formal characteristics. To the small extent that they do, they are turned immediately into an aesthetic of political representation. Corner: 'Such an approach [mass communication research] inevitably resulted in a radically foreshortened view of television's character as a whole new system of socialized aesthetics, one in which quite unprecedented interconnections between "the real" and "the imaginary," between depiction and social subjectivity, were being established and in which the visual image was quickly becoming of momentous political and cultural importance.'

We often see attempts to classify audiovisual theories on a *tour d'horizon*, such as Corner's list of 'core[s] for theoretical accounts' (1997, 249): theories of representation, of the medium, of the institution, and of the process. An earlier attempt is Bordwell's (1985), which distinguishes mimetic from diegetic theories. Carroll's overview books (1988a, 1988b) also work with classifications, which are completely different from Bordwell's. Not that these classification attempts would tar everything with the same brush; they do, though, somehow turn out to be such that it is convenient and profitable to distance one particular type from the rest, or they declare theory construction in this field as generally unsatisfactory. This is when the moment comes for 'middle level' theories, respectively the 'piecemeal theorizing' after the demise of 'systematic theories' (Carroll 1996, 2, II–IV), or 'grand theories' (Bordwell and Carroll 1996).

This demise does not solve the problem of audiovisual theory construction, for (1) it may be impossible to escape the requirement of theoretical coherence, (2) neither may we have escaped the lure of an all-explanatory theory construction. Regarding (1), nothing perhaps is easier than making short shrift of various unsatisfactory pastiche theories in the cultural theory tradition, concocted as they are from diverse Marxisms, structuralism and semiology, and psychoanalysis. These theory conglomerates begin to unravel at the lightest touch, which suggests just how arbitrary they are in terms of their analytical applications ('empirical research'). With regard to (2), there are plenty of examples of cinematic ontologies that are so all-comprehensive that any analysis would confirm them. Except for Deleuze's, all of them are listed in Bordwell's caustic animadversion (1989). But when we reject them in principle as a type of theory construction, does this free us from the dilemmas they pose?

Yet we should not lose sight of the nature of the object, which is always a product of meaning. This has consequences for theory construction, which can no longer be simply true or false (as is possible with factual objects). Meaning can only be interpreted by other meaning. It is possible to reify meaning methodologically – for instance, as empirical behaviour that is investigated as if it were factual. If we were to forget here that behaviour is also meaning, we would arrive at completely false certainties. Conversely, if we treated meaning as if it were immune from experience, as if it were a functionally autonomous, autarkic system, we would be dealing with what Peirce called the 'metaphysical method' of making ideas clear. This kind of theory can only be exchanged, *ad libitum*. Carroll might well be correct when he criticizes this kind of theory as 'media essentialism' (i.e., all the grand classical film theories of the Russian Formalists, of Bazin, Arnheim, and the like), which then manifests itself in 'media specificity' and media aesthetics. However, *abusus non tollit usum* … It would be enough to find a theory of meaning that is capable of dealing with the qualitative characteristics of the object.

It cannot, moreover, be denied that television, both practically and in fact, means television usage (which applies also to radio, literature, newspaper, film – in short, to all mass media that do not fix their usage). Tackling usage of meaning artefacts is a theoretical endeavour almost diametrically opposed to form aesthetics, especially in the form of ethnomethodology. There is, however, scant need for ethnography to imagine how family relations play out, sediment, and change in living rooms (see *Sex, Lies, and Videotape* (Soderbergh 1989)); even meals could be investigated ethnographically for the same effects. That the telecommand has changed television usage has become a banal insight; it might well also be banally short-lived to investigate changes arising from television usage in computer windows during work, with fluid limits towards other Web content. The possible 'usages' of television consumption – the many, mostly unforeseeable possibilities of 'spectator activity' (to use the catchword of cultural theory) – are as variegated as life itself. It is very probable that the producers did not foresee all of these,[6] which would imply that they were not produced as meaning.

To propose a semiotic method is not to imply that all of these meaning determinants are rejected (as Saussure decided to do); on the contrary, it is quite easy to integrate them into the chain of interpretations in the sign process. Nevertheless, it is quite reasonable to stay as close as possible to the 'preferred reading' in an analysis, because arbitrariness and unforeseeability increase with each additional interpretation. Semiotically said, the relation to the Dynamic Object remains the same, but the Interpretant can change (constructively as well as degeneratively) more freely the more regularity there is in the First Correlate, the Sign-in-itself.

This is not much of a surprise in the context of Continental Philosophy (the continent being Europe). All methods going back to phenomenology and hermeneutics have always taken into account that meaning is interminable. What semiotic *adds* to this is a particular attention to the sign quality. This would never allow the isolation of the sign quality from the triadic relation (except as pure abstraction), and then derive 'media effects' from that. A medium never brings about its effects in isolation; it does so only in the (ordinally ordered, iterative, triadic) relation between a Sign, an Object, and an Interpretant.[7]

5.3 Media Construction of Religious Space and Time

For televisual religiosity in televangelism, a limited number of parameters are meaning determinant. Since these are vehicles for meaning in other liturgical contexts as well, a comparison is especially instructive and affords an understanding of the change in liturgical meaning production. Neither space nor time simply exists, either in liturgy or in television. On the contrary, both must be constructed carefully and actively, especially in television. In anticipation of possible objections, this preliminary remark is called for: constructions of space and time are rather vague signs (i.e., double degenerate, Firstness) owing to the nature of the First Correlate. Because of that fact, such signs can be interpreted in almost any direction of general meaning. To prevent wild interpretations, the rest of the context must be strongly taken in account. Nevertheless, it is remarkable how strong a contribution such vague signs make to the meaning construct of televangelism.

Formed space, architecture, has always been action pragmatically solidified as conduct, a form of socialization as much as any other pragmatic space whose structures have been locked one way or another. Foucault's thesis about the ideological form of the central perspective is well known. It is not only the prison apparatus of total observation that is owed to that form, but also modern theatre architecture. Everything is oriented towards the loge of the sovereign, the ideal point of view of the subject *par excellence*. Only from that vantage point do illusionist *coulisse* and wing constructions acquire meaning, since this is the point of the omniscient observing eye.

From their agonistic origins, stadiums have a different orientation than theatre buildings. The central perspective, however, is built into the television camera. Stadiums are precisely where the principal form of the tent revival was transformed into mass dramaturgy (at Billy Graham's hand). Together, television camera and stadium have the effect of a very specific placement of spectators in a spectacular space. The guiding idea is that of 'sacral space,' in delimitation from the *profanum*.[8] Spectators are placed as a *vis-à-vis* to the *sacrum*, potentially as before (in the double sense of the word ante) the *sacrum*.

Technically, this is realized in television by three elements: altar, distance range, and control of illumination. The rich cultural context of the first elements need not be emphasized. The quintessence of such a place was the Roman Capitol, where today an *Altare della Patria* obstructs the view to the *arx* and the *capitolium*. On the *arx* was situated the temple of Juno Moneta – that is, the goddess of femininity as 'she-who-warns' – which explains the *fascinosum* of the inexhaustible 'money.'[9] On the other side of the *asylum* was the guarantor of Roman power, the *imperium*, Jupiter Optimus Maximus. Power has always needed a sacral *mise-en-scène*. This staging could be achieved when necessary by the reinterpretation and recycling of religion,[10] and 'altar' is and was a point of focalization in this process. Here the marriage could be celebrated between transcendental omnipotence and the principal power below, which acted as the efficient, valid, and necessary sacerdotal mediator. All others were reactive-passive assistants, *per definitionem* and *per altar* architecture. This form idea has been determinant in televangelist shows from Billy Graham's first crusades to Schuller's Crystal Cathedral (and other megachurches); the oratorial *vis-à-vis* of an audience, instead, as a form idea was not so influential (which would have been too similar to how political mega-events are staged).

With the help of lighting contrasts, the 'consensus of perception' of all on the object of attention can be construed: the lighted significant contrasts brightly with the dark non-space. The mass-communicative staging of the televangelist show demonstrates this impressively. However, it would be too much to deduce special characteristics solely from such a widely used technique. Only in connection with formal borrowings from the staging of sacred power is the especially televangelical feeling of space clearly evident. In the context of all other elements, it is manifest that power is bound to a sort of *pharmakos* personality, whose redeeming emanation expresses itself as the power of conscience for moral conversion, the power of knowledge for prophecies, the power of healing and exorcism. Wielders of political power may have similarly total power. A comparison, though, shows how the destinations of these two power investments are different. This difference relates in part to the formal element of space construal. Politicians receive their power from the people (or from the nation, or history, or sometimes even God Himself, albeit mediated through the people, as shown by Leni Riefenstahl's *Triumph des Willens*[11]). This dependence on bestowal makes necessary the symbolic presence of a destinator. As a consequence, the asymmetrical space vector of destination must be expressed correctly: vertically and concentrically as 'We mandate You!' Sacral power originates from above, which implies an asymmetrical vector in a different spatial orientation. The difference between a party convention and a televangelist show with its empowerment of God's proxy lies in how space is orchestrated.[12] Space construal needs support from the representing medium of television, in particular through temporal choreography. Where this cannot be achieved, the impression of great physical space is cancelled by the medium.

Which spatial experience is brought about by the televangelist form of television? This spatiality lends itself to comparison with various other refined sacral architectures – for instance, the strong contrast between Jesuit and Calvinist Baroque churches. Yet television has no aptitude for showing huge spaces; the small, blurred screen format works against this. Attempts to represent big spaces nevertheless must obtain the effect of a screen overpopulated with confusingly small forms. Freed from cinematic requirements, television found its own visual 'grammar' without wide-screen images and extended depth of field. Specifically, it found its own sort of power by relying on clean, simple compositions. Its lack of depth, which in practical terms meant almost two-dimensional representation, was thereby compensated. For deep space, Television compositions rely heavily on complex positional order on the depth axis, as well as overlaps, camera movements (zooms, pans, dolly shots), striking camera angles, and framing. Television is, much more than cinema, a medium of metonymy: the fragmentation of the space by quicker editing rhythms, and close-ups of decisive objects (which enable a clearer presence of the instance of enunciation), have helped simplify television images and thereby disambiguate the dramaturgy.

Televangelist shows are employing the television medium effectively for their space feeling when the camera movements emphasize asymmetrical vectorization. In Billy Graham's shows, the camera swept down the aisles of the stadium to the rhythm of the music, always towards the centre, extensively in the beginning and then later when it mattered most: during the Call Forward. Conversely, the camera was strongly concentrated on the preacher when space did not matter at all: during the sermon. Similarly, today's televised preachers are allowed to act freely and use their own wide space for their expressions, thus construing their own pragmatic space. This contrasts with certain other representations that glue preachers to their pulpit. Through 'reaction shots,' the pragmatic space of the preacher is extended even farther by the space of the congregation's or audience's reactions. Furthermore, the imaginary closeness of the verbal address is directly translated into image closeness, when close-ups of the preacher are cut into close-ups of a single spectator (this is the image equivalent of the Pentecostalist evocation 'Hallelujah! Praise the Lord!').

Space aesthetic is a highly refined construal in televangelist shows – one that has an obvious effect on the form of communication and thus on the interpersonal subjectivity of a clearly determined form of public religiosity. The model for this spectacularized religion, before Billy Graham's crusades in sports stadiums, was the Wild West tent revival. These tents were arranged spatially in such a way that revivals could culminate in a massive stream forward on the 'sawdust trail.' Thus the built-in vector was one of concentric conversion towards a moral model, the Bible, the evangelist-preacher.

Is this original liturgical model still practised today? And was it in the 1990s, the peak decade for televangelism? One could object, for instance, that the *PTL* shows of Tammy and Jimmy Baker were so contaminated by the generic format of the talk show that they no longer exemplified the televangelist aesthetic. But this would be deceptive: the show's guests chatted with Tammy and Jimmy on a plush sofa, but this was not yet part and parcel of the shallow auto-exhibitionism genre. *PTL* was not in the business of celebrities-for-the-people. That particular form allows celebrities to disclose certain salacious details from their glamorous lives (carefully selected by their PR agency or 'celebrity handlers') to the receptive host, and in this way celebrate their celebrity status. What Tammy and Jimmy's guests disclosed was closer to what was typical for tent revivals and evangelism: confessions and blessings. The high recognition value of this show, as a televangelist one, was also supported by formal elements, not simply in terms of rhetoric and discourse but also in terms of a recognizable temporal course and the dynamic of *PTL*'s dramaturgy. Aided by the logic of the course of events, all the well-known formal elements appeared – in particular, the focus on the preacher and the spectator reactions, which could be interpreted as conversions.

Construction of temporality is the next parameter. As much as space, time is not simply there – it has to be represented. Televangelist shows require a precise measure of time (cf. Altheide 1979, 201; Real 1977, 171–80) in two dimensions: the time of inner feeling and the temporality of the course of events. A consistent rhythmization is especially typical for the initial and final sequences. Though this is also found in professional television shows, televangelism had no need to borrow from television professionalism at large – revival services existed long before television saw the light of day. The musicality of those services (hymns, gospels, jazz) found its way into the entertainment industry and became a generic American cultural good, finding its way even into sports spectacles. In televangelism, music and its accompanying temporal forms have always served the expression of religious feeling. There is no need to expand here on the warmth and security, the peace and enthusiasm, that music's rhythms can bring.

Over and above the temporality of its course, the televangelist show displays a temporality of feeling, or dramaturgical dynamic, that is vectorized towards conversion: the 'giving over to the Lord.' Up to this point, the program builds an arc of tension; only in the tears of relief at the moment of surrender does this tension yield to distension. This is typically quite different from the dynamic of liturgical services outside the Evangelical tradition. The exteriority of this dynamic is especially different from sacramental liturgies. The perceptible culmination of the feeling of redemption – ideally at the moment of surrender – is contrary, for example, to the otherwise similar going up to the altar to receive the sacrament of Communion, despite some theological similarities. Moreover, the sermon culminates in the Call Forward to redemption, which is visible in the trail forward. Owing to this concentrated structure, temporality can only be an *accelerando* or even a *sforzando*.

The temporality of television at large amounts to the framework within which the religious temporality of televangelist shows must be achieved. How is this done? The temporality of the *spectaculum* – from the theatre, to cinema, to television – has changed no less radically than the spatiality. The reason for this change was in the first place the conditions of television production, which, like radio, offered a presentation format based on regularity. The aim of television was to provide reliable entertainment at all times. This in itself changed the nature of the object: news stories instead of history, formation of opinion instead of transmission of knowledge (cf. Goddard, Corner, and Richardson 2001). The most important representation formats had to adapt their production to this new requirement for periodicity. Television – which did not invent periodicity – had somehow to distance itself from radio and newspaper formats. In its early years, television newscasts amounted to nothing more than radio news with photographs sometimes inserted. Yet even here, a tiny change was noticeable: those photographs acquired a new rhetorical function – to prove the truth. To this point, the determinant feature of news had been the mainly nominal style of speech (exemplified the news-speak avoidance of historical conjectural conjunctions suggesting too much causality, such as 'therefore' and 'consequently') in combination with certain narrative tenses (avoiding the historical tense, though). All of these factors served to dissipate doubts about the objectivity of the narrative causality as presented. With television, however, came the new objectivity and truth guarantee of the image. Television has since come to guarantee almost total authenticity. Even when the fictional character of the content is obvious, the program format of Reality TV (which is not called that by chance) takes on the character of a 'realer real,' despite the clarification, and against one's explicit knowledge. Periodicity has become an emphatic *now* of immediacy; the tense of television is, therefore, the present.[13]

The definition of television as a narrative medium acquires another, quite different potential once the narrative or historical past tense was eliminated. In the old media, textual construction was regulated by a 'sense of an ending,' as the title of Frank Kermode's monograph goes. It gave a text a structure and let it become a unity – that of the story. Television now, however, is perfectly a narrative medium, but it no longer has a 'natural' ending (except perhaps a background feeling of an apocalyptic ending – but that is another subject).

This formal view does not constitute technological essentialism. It does, though, tell us what the serialization of the narrative form produces as a consequence of such a formal redefinition. Instead of a narrative *telos* orientation, television now has perennial duration, the lasting search for something unattainable or some unknown. It is impossible to know what is really happening in a television series, since there are only events without goal or ending. Yet it is not 'as in real life,' because the serial narration must continue. While technically realized as the plaiting of narrative strands, its deeper motivation is rooted in an ominous quest. Thematically, for instance, the unending fight against crime realizes such a quest. Similarly, in pure 'persecution' series, one must sacrifice one's identity in order to survive as a mere I, and one is permanently engaged in seeking one's happiness without ever finding it. As narrative technique, the unnameable ominous is serialized in fixed role constellations, with the occasional guest (villain) who only confirms the inescapability of the rigid role constellation and thereby solidifies it. This, of course, excludes any character development, since that would give away hints of goal, character maturation, an ending of the *Bildungsroman* type. Narrative reversals (μεταβολαί) can never occur; there can only be disturbances from the outside, which can be cleared up in the next episode.

It has often been shown how serial narration in television has a social impact on behaviour and identity. In particular, this has been shown for *telenovelas* (Hagen and Wasko 2000; Tufte 2000). What does it mean for us that sociality can no longer be narrated as a 'configuration of actions' (as Ricoeur translates his mimesis II, the narrative act proper)? This configuration consists in subjecting all elements to the logic of a narrative goal, which, however, is endlessly delayed in serials. Apparently, the narrative medium of television functions well, as well as sociality derived from it. Narrative closure, therefore, must somehow have been achieved as meaning. Nevertheless, if the narrative as act of communication continues, then closure and configuration do not occur on the narrative surface at all, but in a metatext that is never narrated. This metatext could very well be the one of the medium itself, in the sense discussed above.

Perhaps it is more reasonable, though, to draw the context even further towards an aesthetic form of the individuality of modernity. It would then correspond to the awareness of individual life that is under a permanent obligation to realize itself, without ever attaining its goal. This obligation is being burdened with a (life-)task, without ever escaping the restlessness of also having to search for the goal of that search, and being unable to come to an end in it, as in the search itself. This precisely is, as described above, the metatext II of self-realization and identity.

The televangelist shows have adapted to these temporal constants of the television format. This has been an interpretative achievement, in the sense that they have been able to import the publicity of the metatext of the unending quest into the visibility of a problem solution. The quest has been explicitly turned into subject matter. This amounts to an enormous facilitation of the recognizability of problems in need of salvation if they are to be expressed as standard drama problems. In this vein, it is no surprise when televangelist shows promise solutions to money problems, marriage break-ups, alcohol problems, and the like;

in short, we see resurface the entire arsenal of serials and soaps, *Dallas*, *Dynasty*, and their children and grandchildren. This 'visibilization' also determines temporal cadencing, which as a rule prescribes that together with the problem one must also show the solution. Counter-inserts – for example, of incoming phone calls, money pledges, numbers of conversions, Bible sales ... All of this with the *accelerando* of suspense heightened by live cameras, enthusiastic dances of joy by the show's hosts if the number goals are reached, all greeted with Praise the Lord! ... All of this is a time form of visible, audible events taking place. Televangelist shows, in this sense, share the depth temporality of their televisual environment, the various television show formats and their temporal structure.

5.4 The Call Forward

The Call, or Call Forward, is the heart of televangelist shows. There exist many variants of it, but it is always, unfailingly *there:* it is the 'phatic' element that cannot be ignored and that is inescapably obvious to everyone. It is also where the effect of a form tradition manifests itself. A certain type of religious sociality that is in need of publicity determines the interactions of individuals in possession of probity. By the same token, a coupling to interactions in television communication is becoming possible, which is at the root of televangelism being a phenomenon of a society with a public morality.

The Call has its roots in what a biography of Billy Graham has termed 'hitting the sawdust trail toward the anxious seat' (cf. Real 1977, 177ff). Tent revival missionaries in Western frontier towns probably thought that a rather drastic instrument was required to give a moral uplift to the 'fallen' populace. Notwithstanding this immediate instrumentalization, the revival tools were rooted in the mainstream of American religious practice, and *only* there. Weber made various Protestant sects – Quakers, Methodists, Baptists, and others – research objects for his sociology of religion. In his view, the development of 'capitalism from the spirit of the Protestant work ethic' was born in 'spiritual virtuosoship.' That virtuosoship, as a form of communication, rests in the determinate social and religious identity of particularized individuals, on a merciless 'particularism of Grace' or *unbarmherziger Gnadenpartikularismus* (Weber 1920a, 124) unfortunately, Parsons does not translate that term in his rather imprecise English translation (Weber, Parsons, and Giddens 1992). This merciless Grace is a consequence of uncertainty about one's own salvation and the desperate search for assurance and certainty. This form explains for Weber the ethicization of religion: only after succeeding in proving their probity would Methodists be admitted to baptism. In this regard, belonging to a Methodist congregation practically meant having unlimited credit (in all senses of the term). None of these practices concerned the depths of the soul, into which only God could have insight. For our context, this fact is of crucial importance. On the contrary, the individual had to prove everything before a congregation capable of observing, attesting, and certifying visible probity. Everyone, at all times, was under observation by everyone else, especially in terms of economic behaviour. Probity was earned through a time of probation, analogous to a noviciate, which was often crowned (e.g., among the Anabaptists) with baptism (cf. Weber 1920b). The theological justification for this community behaviour was, responsibility before the Lord for keeping the table of the Lord pure from sinners. It follows that the testimonials and accreditations were composed as certificates for itinerant brethren, so that they could participate at the table of the Lord in foreign congregations.

There were two consequences of this responsibility: external visibility, and the moralism of behavioural correctness. The former was a practical requirement if a congregation were to be able to judge. Two unfailing tokens of predestination were admitted: the perfection of moral conduct, and stirrings of emotion. Conduct was visible in the realms of business, family, and civility; stirrings were confined to religious service proper. Famous in this regard are the spiritual awakenings in Quaker congregations in the form of shaking. But in other sects as well, lay preachers could receive their credentials only through some clear sign. Before one was allowed to take the word, one had to be attested by signs of the Spirit, and this had to be confirmed by the *Amen!* response of the congregation. The two testimonies of chosen predestination are intimately linked; what together they ultimately bring to light is purity, freedom from sin and evil deeds. The darker the knowledge of God's true salvific will of election, the more important the congregation as the ultimate form of the assurance or cert(ain/i)-fication of faith.

These two elements are present as both content and form in televangelist shows. In the Call Forward they merge. Ultimately, it is not Billy Graham who calls, but The Call that calls. Furthermore, this is only the *visible* conversion, which later can be told in a narrative before-and-after form, 'sinful to moral (returned to being).' Visibility also leads to show-ability and to that impressively telegenic mass conversion after the sermon and the Call. From the dark depths of the stadium, the abject subjects rise into the bright light of the altar at the centre, where they are welcomed by the congregation of the elect. It does not change the principle when today this congregation consists of so-called counsellors, and when the document of attestation has become a database entry in an evangelist enterprise. A formal equivalence is still established even when some shows merely cover the ringing telephones and the counsellor call centre with their cameras. Supposedly, these counsellors are praying with someone personally while also taking orders for books and literature. The conversion is, in any case, a public one, motivated by emotions, and has a moral quality. That quality especially impressed an early sponsor of televangelism, the press baron William Randolph Hearst, who observed how morally abject persons publicly renounced their former criminal, immoral, unproductive lives during a stadium revival in Los Angeles. Indeed, some Angeleño underworld celebrities were among the converted. Show-ability as proof of election (of those intrinsically uncertain about their salvation), applies as well to the other 'blessings' of the handing over to Jesus. Mainstays of certain shows (e.g., the Calvinist Pastor Schuller's *The Hour of Power*) include topics such as earthly riches, age, health, happy marriage, and success in business.

    The manner of conversion in televangelist shows takes the form of a sudden experience of emotional decision. This form, called 'Decision for Christ' or similar, has its historical model in the Calvinists' onus of proof on the elect, who could never be certain about their election. As a sign of their election, they had to stand out from the less fervent. This attitude was found among the Pietists, Methodists, and cognate sects,[14] but also in the Baptist and Anabaptist traditions. Yet the interior nature of religious conversion is such that telegenic qualities are lacking in a decisional breakthrough, even if it occurs suddenly. This raises problems for a television show – somehow, that conversion must be transformed in its form and substance into a culminating moment, and this must happen towards the end of the show. The sawdust trails of the first tent revivals provided the key to the solution here, even though these revivals were, of course, not limited to thirty or sixty minutes, including credits and self-promotion. The visibility and massivity could now stand out. The conversion itself, the 'handing over,' remained private, but it was connected to the rest of the congregational element in the form of 'counsellors.' The essential was thus hidden to the television cameras; what remained was a shell of visibility.

The timing in a one-hour televangelist show calls for a climax between the fifty-third and fifty-seventh minutes. In early Quaker congregations, it could be an hour before someone was shaken. However, as Weber observed of the Quakers, that speaking-moved-by-the-Spirit came in an unusually well-crafted formulation and was very erudite, and the congregation had usually predicted in advance through their seating arrangements who would be moved. This need not imply a lack of authenticity; the point is that the timing seems to have been viewed as an organizational problem that had to be reconciled with the Quaker tradition of suddenness and immediacy.

The transformation of visible, emotion-based conversions into television form meant an enormous change in religiosity's form. If, in the tradition, the aim was that one obtained certainty of belonging to the congregation of the elect, and if the congregation was regulated in such a way as to sustain one's certainty of being elected, then this form of salvation certainty could no longer be wrought in televangelist shows. This left only a telegenic remainder of the original salvation assurance practice. It was to be expected that in a televangelist show there would be momentous shifts in the function and accoutrement of election itself. It could now be excluded that it was the congregation who were elected, and who would have to sustain their election-certain diversity through internal ascetic regulation. Such certainty could now manifest itself only in a concentrated form in the televangelists themselves – and sometimes the televangelist's entire family.[15] In the sectarian tradition, the downside of one's own election, which could be made certain by the assembly, was always a certain amount of disdain for the undecided, the tepid, the state churches. Now, however, it is the televangelist in person who is allowed to hand out the verdict to the world, especially against its moral, visible abjectness. The tirades of a Jimmy Swaggart against the pornographers of this world and their lackeys in courthouses and parliaments can be fully understood against this background. Only when one's own probity has been established, and therefore one's own election is a certainty, is it reasonable to speak in this way. Another question, however: How is one to re-establish one's probity rhetorically after a fall from public grace (Legg 2009)?

The concentration of pragmatic competence on one side entails a weakened competence on the other side. Instead of living accepted in the assembly of the elect, the newly elect have ended up as database entries, 'accepted' by a counsellor, and facing no further obligations except to pledge money (i.e., to support the continuation of this global, colossal ministry). This is indeed a far cry from those ascetic, sober, industrious Quaker and Reformed congregations, who were constantly certifying the authenticity of their election. In its place, the 'Decision for Christ' has become a more or less inconsequential albeit telegenic feeling. Television can only simulate an assembly; it can never sustain one. Ideally, the newly converted believers should have been passed on to local church assemblies. In the early Billy Graham crusades, this still occurred, and as a rule, in the days following conversions, home visits were made. When crusades became shows, those who experienced their conversions before the television set were still asked to send a postcard to the organization. 'Electronic Church' at that point was merely a suggestive metaphor. Such churches have been criticized for their phantom nature and for siphoning members and donations from local congregations (cf. Horsfield 1984, 138–51). Databases are incapable of producing more than personalized letters, at most. Incoming petitions for prayers and counselling are categorized according to problems and then answered 'personally' in the name of the televangelist by computers through suitable text pieces, professionally formulated. Furthermore, one can become a 'member' by investing money in, for example, theme parks owned by the organization (as was the case with PTL, which founded a sort of religious Disneyland mixed with elements of Club Med).

The Call Forward remains the pillar of every televangelist show, though there are many variants of it, which do not always demonstrate their liturgical heritage. The unmistakable feature of urging this life-changing decision is what distinguishes televangelism from advertising and campaigning. Upstream, there is also a distinction from its origin both as liturgical form and as spirituality in its decisionist type of religiosity, so characteristic of some Reformed sects. Weber linked this spiritual and economic conduct to the Protestant theology of predestination. This constitutes a good pragmatic as well as a semiotic explanation as meaning, invariant over many variants, and one that differentiates it from signs with formal and aesthetic similarities, such as advertising.

5.5 Witnessing

Witnessing, testimonies, and the like are the second pillar in a televangelist show. In the realm of television, however, witnessing has proved to be as much a chameleon as the Call. What on the one hand has its deepest reasons in a certain pious conduct is, on the other, interpretable as a purely voyeuristic television genre.[16] Moreover, this camouflage is supported and enhanced by its execution. In keeping with what is supposed to be proven, it is mostly famous personalities – even celebrities – who go onstage, and they are introduced as such. This brings to mind how the mass media handle celebrities and the star system as a whole (Dyer 1986; Gamson 1994; Hills 2002; Rindova, Pollock, and Hayward 2006; Timmerman and Smith 1994; Turner 2004; Weiskel 2005), as a faint recollection of witnessing. This deliberate churning together of celebrities and time-honoured media formats serves the purposes of televangelism, for the exemplarity of witnessing can in this way become a double-purpose characteristic, when, properly speaking, two stories are being told at the same time: the explicit one of televangelism, which is about conversion; and the one about the personality's success – which is a well-known television genre. We know why the mass media generate stars and celebrities, but why would televangelism need such models? In both cases, the logic of representation makes the same presupposition: that it is highly uncertain – indeed, highly improbable – that one can master one's most important life task successfully. Stars are different from the masses because by achieving fame, they have vanquished the insignificance that is the fate of others. These 'blessed ones' have gained God's blessings by making a decision for Christ and have thereby escaped the general punishment for sinners. In televangelist shows, however, only the latter punishment is being told explicitly, while the mundane success story is merely implied, self-represented in the notoriety of this guest's personality.

The stories are structured around the simple principle of before (struggle) and after (success), with a decisive moment as the pivot. The 'before' follows the familar formula of starting from an 'aporetic fate' (out of which success – the 'after' – is achieved). At the pivot point, this *status ante* manifests itself in prayers of such insistence, taking God 'by His word' and then present to Him His own will in such a way that He has only the one option of acting in accordance with what is forced upon Him as His own will. The decision for Christ takes the form of a sudden, unexpected event, object, illumination. Often, this is at the same time the after, if the object is the one for which the intercession has been made. The audience/chorus often interrupts the narrative with chorus-typical interjections like 'Praise the Lord!' 'Hallelujah!' or similar. In the televangelist productions, this 'planned surprise' conversion is heavily ritualized and arrives as the first culmination of the show.

This ritual form contrasts with the banal content, as for instance 'enormous business success from difficult beginnings.'

Since the deuterocanonical tradition of Hellenistic late antiquity, flowery miracle stories have been common currency; that said, whatever their formal similarities, these miracle narratives have acquired new dimensions. For example, when the Heritage USA Christian theme park received its construction permit, Jimmy Bakker did not hesitate to call it a miracle. In the biblical tradition, one witnesses preceding events as reliable messengers (ἄγγελος); in televangelist shows, in contrast, depraved souls and rotten morals are witnessed as the preconditions of the moment of conversion, which places the election of the subject itself, and success as the proof of it, as the centre of interest. This has turned the purpose completely upside down. A rather good explanation for this revolution comes from the ideal tradition from which this form of pious conduct representation derives. Since televangelism is no *creatio ex nihilo*, it has had to lean on mediate and immediate predecessors in the spiritual control of behaviour. This behaviour is quite complex, but it is still identifiable and distinguishable, not only in the realm of liturgical service, but also in terms of morality.

From what, then, does the stylized form of televangelical witnessing derive? The 'testimonial letter' genre of the congregation of brethren is probably not the direct formal model for witnessing in televangelist shows, but it constitutes precisely the environment where one must express one's probity before the assembly judges. At any rate, the conduct must be observable so as to allow an ever invisible election to be made provable, and only this kind of conduct can be testified. Above all, such conduct is represented as success. This is the deeper reason why business success 'counts' in televangelist shows, for it is a means to praise God for His grace. This also explains why, in the same environment, advice is offered on *how* to achieve business success. These are the exact opposite of the ascetic exhortations to monks: both are intended for the attainment of perfection, but the interpretations of perfection are wildly divergent.

If we place in parentheses for a moment that the Reformed tradition limits probity to the visible, there is another model beyond that observed by Weber, and here too we encounter a significant breach with tradition. With that breach, the form of conduct and the semiotic of the conversion narrative change. The primordial form of all confessions is St Augustine's *Confessiones* (cf. Jauß 1977, 200ff), which over the centuries has become the matrix for all imitators. One of the most significant offshoots was the *Confessions* of Jean-Jacques Rousseau. After Jauß, the rupture of form came in the context of Calvinism: «L'idée d'un Œil omniscient et juste est inséparable du ciel de Genève» (Jauß 1977, 209). If Weber is correct with his thesis on the genesis of modernity and the role of Protestantism in that genesis, then the autonomous I (Rousseau: «se suffire à soi-même») constitutes itself by appropriating certain divine qualities. This appropriation comprehends first and foremost 'knowing good from evil,' which means being one's own judge. Thus Rousseau could open his *Confessions* with: «Que la trompette du jugement dernier sonne quand elle voudra; je viendrai ce livre à la main me présenter devant le souverain juge. Je dirai hautement : voilà ce que j'ai fait, ce que j'ai pensé, ce que je fus. J'ai dit le bien et le mal avec la même franchise à j'ai dévoilé mon intérieur tel que tu l'as vu toi-même» (cit. in Jauß 1977, 209; Rousseau 1782). The rupture with tradition consisted mainly in the exchange of roles between the subject and God, who in St Augustine is the sole scrutineer of the soul's depths. But this darkness is not very practical for the public version of probity. Only if I myself do not know my true motives and intentions will the predestinating will of God have an effect on me. In that case, however, I am no longer morally fully responsible for myself, neither before God (who alone always knows everything) nor before a religious assembly.

But the genesis of the I, or identity, takes place not reflexively within oneself but rather in front of a third instance. In religious terms, it is the merciful eye of God resting on me. In secular terms, I must see in the other ego a mirror of my own. In view of the modern individual's uncertainty of salvation, Rousseau can direct his appeal to humanity for a judgment only on the construed self of the author (or his literary doppelgänger). The judging other, be it the assembly or the appeal to assembled reasonable humanity (in Rousseau's case), must in any case be so immensely greater that it can grant certainty. Through this grandeur I make certain for myself my own feelings about myself ('conscience'), if it prevails before the generality of humanity. All others, too, will have this within themselves as an idea. This heritage comes from the rationality of the Enlightenment, and the result is the complete solitude of the individual.[17]

Rousseau's thorough restructuring of the original Augustinian vision of the self with the eyes of God indicates, as a literary genre, some striking similarities with the political genre of public opinion. Both are constructed as tribunals with a transcendent, larger-than-life instance of sanction. If, now, televangelism implicates religious practice, this too will have to stand before a tribunal, except that this tribunal is no longer the God of St Augustine but the quasi-transcendent 'all.' How deep this rupture is becomes evident as a form of conduct when we compare, say, the secrecy of the confessional with the 'testimony' (that is, before the assembly and now before the public); clearly, the latter is much more modern. The television form, as a global metatext, organizes itself around the indiscretion of exemplarity, and this is true of would-be celebrities (which also entails a celebrating ritual) or merely of those who owe it to the instantaneous focalization of television that they exchange their 'anyone' status against a focalized exemplarity.

Witnessing, in this form, can no longer be what it was for St Augustine: the new man's *confessio peccati et laudis* looking back on the old one with the eyes of the merciful God. The I of televangelist shows belongs entirely to modernity. It is, thus, an individual who constitutes himself only by separating himself from the whole of a society, while permanently referring to this background. The form of individualization may have another trajectory than the one originating from the division of labour in the material reproduction of society. Here it is the particularity of one of the elect, who does not owe his election to God, because this is shrouded in uncertainty. On the contrary, the election is an act of the assembly on the basis of visible proofs of probity, and only this can confer the greatest possible certainty, which amounts to actual election by God. From a purely logical perspective, this places an enormous burden of proof on the assembly itself. The Donatist-Calvinist theological *topos* of 'keeping the purity of the table of the Lord,'[18] which forces the ejection of unworthy elements from the assembly, merely renders this *onus probandi* in theological terms. The lack of *certitudo salutis* is only numerically reduced, proportionally to the number of elect, but not in principle. From there, it is no great leap to reduce the number of the elect to 144,000, leading to various Armageddon-mysticisms. Since it is a certainty now that there will be only this number of elect until the day of Reckoning and ultimate certainty, one must fight for every single one of these exclusive places. At the end of the course of grace particular to modern Protestantism, according to Weber's known thesis, it is through ethic that we reach multiple rationalities. Weber also showed the economic consequences, including division of labour, rational optimization, and quantitative increase in production.

There is almost nothing new in connecting the logic of divine grace (*more Protestanti*) with economic logic, since this nexus has its common ground in the same particularization. Thus the demonstrative aspect of witnessing in televangelist shows has deep roots and logical coherence. Here we see an expression of a life feeling – better, a life anguish – that is utterly modern at its core. If we are not to embark on historical speculation, this meaning needs to be evidenced by concrete sign usage. Those signs do indeed exist, but only as metatexts (in the sense discussed earlier), because they operate at the level of predetermination of meaning. Downstream, in every actually used sign, this predetermination can be found in the First Correlate, in analogy to the 'knowledge' being deposited in the treasury of language. The two metatexts of public opinion discussed earlier must therefore be conjugable under determinate circumstances with the religious predetermination of meaning. In the case of televangelism, this conjugation is feasible based on grace particularism. This brought not only an individualization as principle, but also the need for everyone to realize himself and to control (the other's) power, for individuals have particular interests. This must also apply to sovereigns, who can no longer be trusted as guarantors of truth and justice (as Montesquieu opined) and who also have their own particular interests.

Metatexts evince fundamental constants of public, visibly coordinated life, in a plethora of mass media forms of communication. In this regard, consider the television series format and its metatextual precondition, as we demonstrated in the constitutive logic of television temporality. The representational object itself, however, shows constants of meaning. These can be condensed into aesthetic and dramaturgical program formats. Once they are established, any number of programs can imitate and vary them, time and again. Our question has been this: Why do all these forms of public confession resemble one another, to the point of the aesthetic-dramaturgic form? That question could not be answered if there were no stable forms of meaning predetermination. It is much less complicated to demonstrate this meaning semiotically than to show it in a superficial description of industrial practices or professional conventions.

5.6 PrayTV Yields to PreyTV: Acts of Televangelist Authority

If it were not for the differences in role competence, sermon and testimony could cross each other formally and with regard to content. The sermon has an important function in the structure of the televangelist show insofar as it builds up the fullness of power that makes the Call possible. So when there is no direct sermon, a functional equivalent must substitute for it. It is quite surprising how peremptory televangelist sermons can sound. Without any doubts being admitted, massive condemnations are proffered (sometimes giving the impression that almost the entire rest of the world is condemned as evil). In a grand style, and to an astonishing extent, direct demands confront the audience and spectators. So it is not surprising that Schmidt and Kess (1986) inquire into the linguistic similarities between advertising pitches and televangelists' 'appellative speech acts.' However, one would misjudge the speech authority of televangelists if one were to attribute the vehemence of their demands for donations (and similar duties) only to the speaker's personal interest (Howley 2001). While the external forms might be comparable, the earnestness of televangelist sermons derives from a quasi-divine authority. The certainty of election needs to be implied; conversely, the advertisers' pursuit of profit is blatant. Visibility and feeling certify the televangelist's authority; or at least it is assumed that such a pragmatic form presupposes this kind of certification. Next to the authority for the Call, the televangelist also has the power of prophecy and sometimes also of miraculous healing.

This global suprahuman speech authority has two effects: it places the audience in principle in the role of the non-elect or not yet elect; and it makes the televangelist extremely vulnerable to scandals.

Televangelists have become notorious for their susceptibility to scandals (Abelman 1988; Fan, Wyatt, and Keltner 2001; Frankl 1987; Johnson 1997; Smith 1992). This has led to the demise of entire televangelist enterprises, such as PTL (Brown 1991). Weber's merciless particularism of grace has proven accurate, but in ways previously unimaginable. Today it is no longer the Protestant ethic that is the backdrop of condemnation, but public opinion as a replacement for religion. As in Rousseau, it has taken over God's position – and struck back. Before this merciless tribunal, no televangelist can prevail for long, especially if he assumes a pragmatic exemplarity at the expense of all others, the non-elect, the tepid ones. The certainty that ethical ideals are unattainable is almost as great as the uncertainty of Calvinist salvation. As election becomes visible, so does non-election as it finds its televangelist expression in condemnations of the evil world.

The simple reason for this backlash is the polarization of roles that arises from the televangelist's role. Believing Christians enter into the role of sinners through their faith. This brings them into the role of the freely redeemed sinner. A look into the past (i.e., the *confessio peccati et laudis*) equates unredeemed bondage with sin; and sin is always rescinded when it turns into our new identity with our original dignity restored. When it comes to accusation, however, things are quite different. Here the roles are indisputable and almost no appeal is possible; such accused people can only accept the consequences and take the seat reserved for them, the 'anxious seat.' In the text structure, the pragmatic competence of the one is proportionally reciprocal to the competence of the opposite other (i.e., the televangelist's exemplary power encounters the condemned's destitution); also, the object transfer is initially absolutely asymmetrical. The sinner can, however, 'repay' this transfer with commensurate contributions as the sermon demands them – hence the peremptory tone of sermons. At the formal level, the media metatext finds in all this a congenial field of operations. The role construction is tailor-made, as it were, for the metatext of power legitimization, which the media of public opinion like to attribute to themselves. The merciless moralizing of some variants of public opinion – for example, the notorious attacks of the British tabloid *The Sun* – allows even the most extreme televangelists to appear in a positive light of mercy. At the same time, the producers of public opinion are better protected than politicians and televangelists; after all, there is no third vantage point from which one can judge the judges.

Regarding the contents of the sermon, only general remarks are possible. Real (1977) with his analogy of televangelist sermon and ancient tragedy is correct only insofar as his comparison's *princeps analogatum* is merely the general representing of human action (corresponding to the configuration of action, mimesis II, in Ricoeur's narratology). Otherwise, it is precisely *not* the tragic pity and fear, ἐλεός καὶ φοβός, not ὕβρις (even less so in the modern, quite different sense of the term), but the guilt (ἁμαρτία to which ὕβρις can also belong). Tragedy would mistake the thoroughly ethicizing character of televangelism. Identifying televangelism's formal model with the splashy effects of variety shows (Altheide 1979, 208ff) may also play down the model's nature. In Altheide's perspective, it may be impractical to derive a show's choral music from the rituals of ancient theatricality and its sacred origins in *caeremonia* (literally: religious awe and fear). For a regular, ordinary show, such convergences with religion may seem far-fetched – in particular, if there are closer similarities. For a televangelist show, they are the key.

Prophecies – another mainstay of televangelist authority – have made some televangelists just as notorious. But instead of explaining this as part of the usual rhetorical media exaggeration, one would better strive to see the logical coherence and consistency of prophesizing; for as soon as the televangelist has visibly empowered himself, his pragmatic competence can become effective in a corresponding performance. This is so when his word has wrought what it said. If that word deals with relatively imprecise predictions of success in the form of 'if–then,' then it is doomsday prophecy (this is relatively rare and apparently has no place in televangelist shows, in contrast to chiliastic discourses). A general form, though, is very widespread, and this gives televangelist shows a strong aura of certainty. In this way they distinguish themselves clearly from almost all other forms of prediction in public discourse. In 1987 the televangelist Oral Roberts created a furore with a prophecy. He was on a fundraising drive – for which he received instruction directly from Christ – that apparently was not meeting his expectations. So he declared that God had spoken to him thus: 'I want you to use the Oral Roberts University medical school to put my medical presence in the earth. I want you to get this going in one year or I will call you home. It will cost $8 million and I want you to believe you can raise it.' Then, in tears, he prophesized that God would 'call him home' if he did not get at least that amount by March for his ministry. On 1 April of that year, he announced that he had received $9.1 million, with rumours that an understanding millionaire had fulfilled his wish in order to ensure that the prophecy did not come true (i.e., the ultimatum passed).

Healings – again an element of a televangelist's higher authority – are seldom seen on televangelist shows. That said, spiritual healings – and raising the dead, in the case of Oral Roberts – are among the 'hottest' events in this venue. When they *are* shown in front of the camera, they rank at the top of the 'blacklist' of the media of public opinion (Ostling 1987). In fairness, we must emphasize denominational differences in this regard, notwithstanding the professed non- or supra-denominational self-portrait of televangelists. Even though healings are a common and fixed element in the tradition of Pentecostalism and in the Assemblies of God, fundamentalist Protestantism is clearly not admitting them to their shows. Sometimes, though, fundamentalists concede so much, having counsellors pray for healing for those spectators who follow the rolling text on the screen and call them up.

Healings do, however, occur as a crucial liturgical element. We will leave aside here the more notorious practitioners of faith healing and resurrection of the Oral Roberts type. That leaves us with lesser figures. For instance, an evangelist stadium crusade at the Montreal Forum in

1988 dominated Canadian media headlines for days. But the evangelists did not control this publicity on their own terms, for it took the form of 'objective' reporting, which includes detached style. Healings are difficult to integrate with the media and impossible to adapt to the media universe. They affront our commonsense *doxa* so strongly that Quebec's medical association planned court proceedings against the evangelist Lacroix[19] on the grounds of public contempt. Remember, though, that even in the Western cultural sphere there existed equivalents of shamanism until the scientific episteme overwhelmed all other forms of Aesculapian – that is, medical – practice, including that of all Cagliostros and quacks (called 'empiricists' in those times). Note as well that long before the spectacle of televangelism, there existed a spiritual charisma of healing in early Christian communities, which continued in the Sacrament of Unction and the Exorcism. Indeed, spiritual healings have long been part of Western narratives – for example, see Dreyer's film *Ordet* (cf. Ehrat 2005b).

In public opinion, healings are 'borderline' religion. Nowhere is the incongruence of meaning more obvious than where the corporal being of humanity becomes social: The publicly prevailing image of the body is formed by ideals of producible beauty, with the body itself an accessory *for* expressing mass individuality, comparable to some fashion article. This alienation of the human body is not conducive to Christian sociality. Conversely, there is also an ascetic instrumentalizing of the body, especially in monastic societies, but there it is supposed to lead to a more natural corporality because it is closer to perfection. To idealize monasticism as an extreme rationalization of parsimonious, efficient forms of production – as the ideologists of early capitalism thought – is to profoundly misunderstand. *Ascesis* derives from 'adorning exercise,' after all, and should in the monastic context not be used as a term for the rationalized exploitation of the body. In the televangelist form of representation, both forms of body meaning must coexist, and this is possible only through mimicry. For a metatextual reading, healing is most acceptable if it appears as a spectacular version of the human pursuit of happiness in medical victories (spectacularly successful operations, miracle drugs, etc.). From this perspective, televangelists' faith healings become part of other miraculous healings that surface regularly in mass media: reports of Philippine miracle *curanderos*, Russian magic healers, organ transplantations, and so on.

On the other hand, there is a reading from the perspective of Christian holistic corporality, which sees no advantage in the materialist separation of body and soul. Here, no spectacularization is needed – indeed, it is rather a hindrance. On the contrary, body and soul are only together integral to the holistic faith experience itself, which is capable of abandoning itself heart and body to God. Yet that experience does not need the unfailing proof of the power of 'God's servant.' In televangelist shows the authority to heal is always directly proven by the healing's success. Unfailingly, cameras catch these culminating moments live, as a proof for the antecedent claim – this is, for instance, a pivotal point in Oral Roberts's rhetoric. The proof of God's mercy thus turns directly into an exhibit usable in the court of public opinion. Only in this way can the miracle be cashed in; in Parsons's sense, it becomes a medium of truth that can be transferred to any other context. Mainly, it increases the power of the televangelist (as fundraiser, but also as politician and presidential candidate).

Nowhere is the price higher that the telegenic spectacularization of faith must pay to the media metatext. The rule of mimicry requires ambivalence – that is, it is capable of being understood correctly in one context even while being misunderstood in another. Nowhere is this inherent requirement as scandalizing if misunderstood. Nowhere is such a compelling and unavoidable alternative choice to be made between two meanings, which harmonize only on the mimicry surface but are otherwise deeply mutually exclusive, including as pragmatic conducts.

This brings us to the more general, technical production question: How does television produce or dismantle authority? How are auctorial authority and speaker visibility produced, together with their corresponding spectator attitudes? This is of particular importance for televangelists, for on the one hand, they have full control over the logic of the camera as they produce their own programs, whereas on the other, they expose themselves mercilessly in the public sphere to hostile camera logic. What in Gadamer's hermeneutic is called *auctoritas* – defined literally as augmenting meaning in its double hermeneutical and theological sense – here becomes a textual strategy in the narrower sense. This means that through the audiovisual text, the speakers must be qualified in a role that permits them to demand to be heard on 'their' subject. Prophecies and healings would never function without such auctorial qualification. For these 'authorizations' by the enunciation instance, television, external authority is intrinsically irrelevant unless enunciation decides to pick up what is offered by authority. In effect, church organizations possess a strict regime of speaker authorization that reflects complex criteria and gradations. For example, since the time of St Paul, bearing witness to faith has been vested with less authority than the magisterial authority (which was necessary to weed out a certain rank growth in the Hellenistic community). All of that, however, need not be of any interest to an enunciation instance.

Television can enhance beyond measure the speaker authority of believers professing their faith, extolling them as absolute stars or heroes. This power is equalled only by the authority of 'reality itself' when it is made to speak by the enunciation instance, television. Many elements contribute to this effect. One of them is the camera focus that is specific to certain genres. Close-ups and medium close-ups, for instance, cancel the impression of space, especially when there is no more background or it is out of focus. This also cancels the impression of distance. The spectators, as it were, are placed immediately in the interiority of a person, whose face they can easily read (quite contrary to social standards of politeness). However, this moment of television witnessing is very delicate, because the camera has the reverse power to erect a screen before the interiority of speakers by turning them into liars. In this case, then, the camera itself penetrates interiority by its own authority (which can be justified by whatever obligation it has for truth[20]).

What all of this shows is the following: the speaker authority of the camera is always there but is not always shown. By receding into invisibility, the camera grants, or leases out, a speaker authority to a witnessing subject. It alone vests the subject with authenticity, by offering spectators access to the subject's interiority worthy of spectators' trust. Sometimes the examination and authorization of the subject by the camera instance can be reconstructed visually. This purpose is served by a strategy of feeling its way to a subject in certain ways, such as (editorial) presentation of a subject qualified by an adequate role, or framing, or the camera angle. In principle, the camera is empowered to grant verisimilitude to everything *except* itself. It alone is emphatically true, as an instance of demonstration. The only exception it makes is when it conceals itself by granting some the privilege of conveying their reality directly. For example, a vested Church authority, such as a bishop, happens to be (judged as) veracious and is (in his own mind) true. Only if the camera instance dismantled the bishop by its own means would the incongruity of both speaker authorities become evident.

5.7 Primordial Scandal Religion

It seems that absolute speaker authority equates with openness to scandal. Authority and scandal then arise from one and the same action. The downfall of renowned televangelists, megachurch preachers, and bishops illustrates this in a quasi-Nietzschean circularity of the eternal return of the same. Once they reach their apogee of public fame, they come under siege with regard to probable misdemeanours. It seems that in the universe of public opinion in a constellation of principle, religious roles are prevented from becoming 'normal' and are cast as either heroic or scandalous. Why such extremism, which seems to exclude any middle ground?

Public opinion keeps permanently close tabs on other social institutions, but these do not have to reckon with the principle of scandal as a basis. Pujas (2002, 150) has identified four preconditions for an eruption of a scandal in the political realm. Of these, one usually applies to religious institutions as well: 'tensions between social and political values and eventually the breakdown of some social norms in a new social context' (here, replace 'political' with 'religious'). Churches have a reputation for defending values considered reactionary, non-modern, and oppressive, especially when those values are expressed as moralist critiques of prevailing lifestyles.

A Pragmaticist equivalent to social functions in lieu of sociological functionalism, was described earlier; so was the role of public opinion. In this constellation, religion seems to lack a real social function. Public opinion, which is the guardian of all social legitimacy, is saddled with the unenviable task of fitting in religion – albeit hypotactically, subordinate to its own authority. Public opinion has a tense relationship with the Church, because the two collide in their respective claims. Thus, for the Boston Archdiocese, it must have been a hard learning experience that there was no way to 'sell' the Church by the public relations playbook. One cannot do normal, run-of-the-mill PR for the Church. In an analogous way, religious scandals are almost too easy to foment, and this is not the case with other social institutions. The reason for this is found in the peculiar constellation of mass media institution and the social institution Church.

What is so unique to religious scandals? Is there any possible way to integrate religious with public conduct on conditions acceptable to both sides? Religious actors have a quite peculiar teleological predetermination. This is demonstrated clearly in Jesus' famous reply to Pontius Pilate, which characterises Jesus' own action with the determination of this goal: 'My kingdom is not of this world' (John 18.36); whereas he characterizes Pilate's action: 'Thou couldst have no power at all against me, except it were given thee from above' (John 19.11). The point of concern here is a pragmatic-teleological universal, before which actors must answer for their actions – that is, the problem is both the source of both destination and of sanction, and these two goals cannot be reconciled or harmonized. The two actions cannot yield a common text; to stay within the theatrical image, they cannot come together in one drama, one overall plan (i.e., of the god Dionysos). Two dramas are playing on two stages, as it were; furthermore, one drama is going on in the θέατρον, whereas the other is in a transcendent space without a chorus.[21]

Religious actors claim that the source of their pragmatic destination or mandate is fundamentally different from any other, and moreover, that action mandated in this way is 'above' any outside judgment. This inevitably leads to a conflict with other modern instances claiming for themselves to mandate or destine every public action (in the logic of the classical θέατρον model described in §3.4). The primordial scandal, therefore, is an actor's attempt to evade public accountability.

In practice, though, this occurs only on a selective basis, for religiously destined actors ('God's messengers') love making use of public opinion, if the sanction happens to be a positive one. For them it would be tempting to influence media through PR or social marketing as instrument of propagandistic[22] discourse. The most striking example of this schizophrenia is, again, televangelism, which thrives on the explicitly visible and publicized exemplarity of its protagonists. But this sharply exposes them to the negative sanctions of such exemplarity by means of media scandals. The same – *mutatis mutandis* – applies to the Roman Pontiff, who is likewise under permanent pressure to justify his exemplary position and discursivity. Thus there have been repeated attempts to drag Popes into scandal. The most successful attempt so far has been the German playwright Hochhuth's accusation against Pius XII in his play *The Deputy, a Christian Tragedy* that he did not do enough to help the persecuted Jews. Despite compelling evidence – including libel proceedings launched by the Pacelli family – it is still possible to spread this *topos* safely today (e.g., not too long ago the film *Amen* (Costa-Gavras 2002) was luridly advertised with swastika posters). Furthermore, Paul VI's pontificate suffered from a scandal targeting his encyclical *Humanae Vitae*, which was diametrically counterpoised to the prevailing metatext of self-realization.

Roles that are the direct result of the faith act leave their distinguishing traces also in the text itself, as a contrast to genuinely public roles.

The religious teleology creates a sort of meta-action and with it the goal and the role of an elect. Election means that God alone is responsible for destination and sanction (1 Corinthians 4.4: 'ὁ δὲ ἀνακρίνων με κύριός ἐστιν / but he that judgeth me is the Lord'), and human beings can be instruments of His destination, at most. Social publicity admits such roles only as exceptions.[23] This actually demonstrates the rule, for in normal circumstances, public opinion cannot admit something like divine election. On the contrary, it would react to it as a challenge, as it would with other 'dictatorial' breakdowns. Crises in the public destination or mandate relation always arise when power bearers take a position against their power-granting destinators. Such is the case when politicians claim a higher mandate against public opinion (in this way enhancing their pragmatic competence while increasing their power). In this claim they act in the name of the nation, or under the dictates of economical reason or history or national security, or by *Dei gratia* in the name of the Almighty (cf. Landowski 1989). Today, such opposition to public opinion can no longer be a permanent confrontation. It will be softened by assuming the destination of the 'public opinion of the future,' of a 'better informed' public opinion, or of similar contraptions.

In the public opinion of modernity – in contrast to ancient tragedy (e.g., Oedipus) – the destination is a representation without mythical support. At best, this makes it functionally equivalent to divine knowledge or not-yet-knowledge. Representation of destination functions by present-ifying as '*praesens*-ation' (i.e., 'being-set-before'). By asking for a mandate from public opinion (the legendary voters' mandate), power bearers place public opinion in a position to serve as their sanction and destination instance. They themselves are, however, *de facto* the destination instance (vote!) – which instance *de jure* they cannot assume, nor can they the spectacular role. In such a case, they would be shown as manipulators, demagogues, or (worse) dictators with a personality cult. In agreement with its theatrical representation, publicity (cf. n1) is supposed to know all, to have the right intention, to personify wisdom. But because public opinion only has the faculty to react to problems defined by others (or suggested by the wishes of others), it cannot really manifest itself in this kind of power attribution through the right to act. It does, however, achieve a thorough teleological determination of values (of the desirable) – that is, 'what is to be done?' and 'what do "all" want?' From this will of 'all' originates the power of sanction, as in the θέατρον. In public opinion's conception, holders of religious office probably should be subject to the same candidacy for public destination. The fact that they do not live up to this expectation leads them to be suspected of using power without control. There is no place for other types of destination.

Let us assume the point of view of the other side. What is the situation of a public sanction when the communication is not public, but religious – that is, based in an existence of faith, acting where God determines the pragmatic goal? Translated into a type of text, representations of legitimizing destination are not effective here, nor can any public verdict 'derail' the righteous. If we thus leave aside this purely religious teleology, pragmatic destination and sanction, election and condemnation, we still go no further than the mixing of two dramas. From the point of view of one, it is not quite clear what is being played on the stage of the other drama.

Public opinion can dismiss 'election' only as imposture or pretension, as a clever attempt to escape public accountability. Conversely, those who view themselves as called by God can interpret an assent to 'human recognition' and punishment only as a temptation, which they must resist for sake of their vocation's purity. In this critical interpretation, public opinion and public scandal become mere usurpations of false divine attributes, or they are sheer force. In this situation, one misunderstanding encounters the other (from their respective perspectives). In the case of confrontations, this is at least unmistakably clear; situations suggesting that the two have identical interests are more devastating. Religion then exploits public opinion to make propaganda; or public opinion uses religion for purposes of moralizing. One can investigate these misunderstandings as the mimicry of the one in the logic of the other.[24] A typology of religious media scandals can be derived from this mutual disguise, since scandal encloses us firmly in a space of confrontation. From these basic constellations of two teleologies one can deduce all further scandalous matter with religious specificity. In negative sanction, this becomes scandal. In positive sanction, the text type is heroicization – seen from the perspective of public opinion. One source of scandal or heroicization is the predetermination of the pragmatic goal for religiously motivated action; another is the qualification of its actors (see §6.4). Before this, however, we must gain a better understanding of the logical scaffolding of scandal.

6 Judgment: Bringing into a Scandal-Position

The next three chapters relate to one another, in logical sequence, as program, performance, effect. In handier words: script, action, result. Together they describe the whole of media scandal. This chapter discusses meaning in terms of its institution, space and positions, time, and allowable sequences. The script's enactment becomes performance and thus temporal sequencing, which is discussed in chapter 7. Chapter 8 then discusses how the performance results in the concrete effect upon social reality.

Scandal as script, or program, is one possible instantiation of public opinion meaning and thus an especially eloquent replica of the dramaturgical god instance. The cultural history of this meaning apparatus commences in the Dionysian θέατρον and continues through an array of meaning practices, all the way down to industrial practices of public meaning production. The meanings defined by these cornerstones can produce public media scandals through a number of operations. In the first place, a destination instance must prevail over attempts to elude the judgment. For endeavours to scandalize religion, they need to prevail over the view that a life of faith is 'above any human judgment.' This is accomplished by means of a determinate sign logic that makes one part of text dependent on a higher one. In the next section, this is applied to the industrial practice of investigative reporting. In the section after that, we address the deep logical structure of the industrial practices of public opinion in the two metatexts. Investigative reporting presupposes its own right to legitimize and delegitimize the actions it reports. Since it would be too bothersome to justify this privilege each time it is invoked, it saves energy to have already in place meaning apparatuses that are capable of subordinating the meaning of the represented object. For investigative journalism, that apparatus corresponds to the 'fourth estate' ideology, which technically speaking is a metatext of power legitimization. Both metatexts derive from the same logic of publicity. As a consequence of these meaning apparatuses, in the final section, we show how it is possible to classify scandals in terms of the logical roles that are the object of scandalization.

6.1 Scandal Technique

How does one succeed in dragging someone before a tribunal that the other does not recognize? How does an institution impose itself on other institutions as a sanctioning suprainstitution? This question relates no longer to the historical development of public opinion as a truth equivalent, but rather to the technical aspects of the operations that make this truth effective. In public opinion, these operations do not constitute a science with criticizable truth claims. They merely pursue the purpose of making one opinion win over another – but they have to do so without logical constraints. The opinion at the centre of our interest here is the one that claims it can cognize the 'whole,' not particular facts. Since it cannot rely on a victory of the truth (or of the better argument), it brings itself into the winning position through its 'decisive moment.' The effect, at any rate, must assume the power of a quasi-logical constraint; otherwise, sanctions could not function without the cooperation of coercive force from an established authority.

This first hurdle is critical and consists of a number of mutually interlocked constructions. The practices of industrial media production must presuppose these as a condition of their possibility. In this way, the justification of an industrial meaning practice is transferred to a position *ante quam* and no longer interlopes with its concrete, day-to-day usage. The justificatory upstream of public opinion practice, is not easy to grasp, however, for it bars as a basis of explanation all strong theories of society. A functionalist (structural-functionalist) theory would have no problem dealing with this question, since it 'knows' beforehand the function of the system. The public opinion system's special function is to establish legitimacy between systems. For modern societies, which can no longer be 'centrally managed,' this special system in effect conditions all other systems. In semiotic Pragmaticism, that sort of theoretical grip would preclude any role for experience. As we have seen, when truth is the control mechanism, it is harder to justify a theory than would be the case if the mechanism were based in pure difference. In terms of semiotic, this leads us to consider the triad of correlates and modes of being. If public opinion were indeed a 'method of science' (Peirce, CP 5.384) made dependent on truth (cf. §3.1), then its operations would also have to be reflected with regard to its presuppositions. This reflection is the task of the normative sciences and phaneroscopy. Peirce does not reflect on the individual action of a subject (as Schütz does); rather, he is concerned with all action *in se,* classified according to the diversity of possible conduct.

Public opinion, however, is merely a truth equivalent with unique teleological knowledge functions. Bringing it into a working position is no longer the task of the teleology itself. Here it is an antecedent knowledge, which in a historical context might be identified with the bourgeois ideology, for the teleological 'whole' reveals itself as having certain presuppositions. Moreover, it continues in its need for further and further reasons: Why is this sanctioning opposite necessary at all? Why is one not permitted to simply act? Why is the power of the powerful in need of control? Clearly, this last is the open question behind the bourgeois idealization of a rational politic not already torn apart by irreconcilable conflicts among vested interests. Furthermore, why is the sanctioned subject subjected to success and to becoming a better self? Then, regarding the identity of the pragmatic public subject, why does it not simply exist? Why must it instead be created and then justify itself before an instance (cf.§6.3.2)?

Yet none of these questions are posed – rather, they are presupposed in public opinion as being already answered. These answers are the metatexts (see below), because in public opinion they do not exist as texts but can be deduced from its texts. Actually, they are not obscure theoretical constructs; rather, they exist explicitly. They exist as justification labels on industrial practices, such as when 'investigative journalism' epitomizes the 'serious' press, or 'lifestyle' justifies the yellow, gossip, or scandal press.

There exist two interconnected metatexts, or practice specifications. Each implicates religion in public opinion in its own way. This is demonstrable with negative sanctions in particular, by which religion becomes a scandal. Legitimization of power means that religion must first be enabled; only then can it act. Between acting and empowerment to act, then, an instance is inserted in the logical form of the knowledge about the goal of action – if the operation succeeds. Once this instance exists, it can decide for itself which action it empowers or enables, and which other irrelevant actions can occur (i.e., 'private,' autarkic, and without empowerment). For a long time, religion was excluded from public discourse and was considered a private act. But this does not mean that religion was irrelevant to public opinion, for religious acting brings into question the legitimization of public opinion itself. Small wonder, then, that from a historical perspective, the public sphere repeatedly assaulted the supposedly private sphere of religion. But note that in this regard, Certeau offered plenty of examples of how religion developed for its own survival subversive strategies that allowed it to retreat into the private sphere – while still maintaining the appearance of being adjusted to public opinion's pressure (Certeau 1980).

It does not matter whether religion subjects itself voluntarily to public opinion for the sake of a PR advantage, or whether it gets entangled. Meaning conditioning always takes place under the dictates of both metatexts. This starts at the lower threshold of religious witnessing. Here testimony factors in 'success' – that is, in the persuasion effect on the object being targeted. It ends where churches as moralistic monopolists in public opinion compete directly with public opinion itself.

The bourgeois dichotomy of private and public is relatively recent; likewise recent is public religion as distinct from private interiority. This does not mean that religion had been private before now – only that the distinction did not exist. Liturgy – quite literally, the 'work of the people' – has always been a devotion practiced in common. Even the sacrament of penitence was an act before a congregation. When we examine liturgical expression form from a historical perspective, we find that the first step towards making religious privacy public was a contingent historical event. At that event, the (irremediably interior) subjectivity of faith was made visible probity for exhibition purposes. The original idea of liturgy included no demonstrative acts proving something to someone. Even other external expressions of faith (such as processions, Beguines, ecclesiastic Estates, regulated life regimes with visibly distinguishable garb in religious orders … not even *autodafés*) were not at their heart demonstrative acts. The religious revolution, together with history of ideas, had been kicked off by the principle of doubt in divine election, in the spirit of Protestantism (in Weber's sense, cf. *supra*). The requirement for reliable, visible signs made a virtuous life in probity a sign of salvation. This now occurs in the form of performance signs of pious subjects and in the form of sign interpretations by other subjects – that is, not by God. The righteous must find grace in the eyes of the assembly that is vouching for them and granting testimonial letters.

As per Weber, the beginning of modernity – and especially the beginning of the bourgeoisie – coincided with this liturgical revolution. With the rise of the bourgeoisie, society was no longer stratified in terms of social ontology and Estates; instead there developed a sociality of competition and mobility. These felicitous conditions made it possible for the bourgeois press to take root in a foundational myth of conflict-free public opinion prevailing through reason. This myth, which was in effect an ideal abstraction of bourgeois society, merely had to revisit the Θέατρον idea of spectacularity. In the same way as 'all' can never be at fault, and as much as they can even judge in the name of the god, so the bourgeois, as particularized subjects of opinion, became 'all' again by doing one thing in common: judging.

This power of representation is expressed in technical steps. It becomes text in the form of hypotaxis. Public opinion predetermines the pragmatic goal. In our case, this means prevailing first over the religious teleology. After that, in order to make scandal function, it can proceed to construct the theatrical stage. From a logical perspective, this model of meaning, this creating of public opinion industrially in mass media, inevitably produces and imposes its own teleology. This logic construes a certain type of sign in which a Third Correlate of a determinate nature dominates (see §3 above). Technically, this sign process is realized through the text's construing of a double feature:

(1) *Parti-fication.* Texts have sentence parts just as sentences do, but it is not possible to transfer sentential parts (such as subject and predicate) directly in texts. One must, therefore, sever the ties to grammar by taking a semiotic[1] approach. Semiotic recognizes in the sentence subject the delimiting ('oven') and in the predicate the more general part ('is black'), which is existentially determined by the possession or non-possession of a quality. In the case of triadic sentences, however, inferences take place[2] in which a rule is always placed somewhere (and the exact position of that rule constitutes the difference between the three modes of inference). If texts are argumentations or are similar to conclusions, then we find a division into parts where parts are determined according to their logically different nature: The (a) rule in texts is different from the factual (b) case and from the (c) qualitative characteristic. Only in this (logical) syntactical order can text parts be subordinated to one another (in a hypotaxis).

(2) *Order.* Parts are logically related to one another. In this context, the sentence models of hypo- and hypertaxis can be generalized. Logical rules, indeed, stand behind the particles combining sentences in natu-

ral languages ('because,' 'in order to,'[3] 'which,' etc., along with corresponding negations); these rules also apply to texts. One can give these text dependencies an anthropomorphic description as dependencies of narration and of commentary (enunciation instance). This is only a particular determination of a general representation, which is always an interpretation of 'this as something,' and here specifically the interpretation of event-leading-towards-a-goal, be it (teleo)logical or temporal, or both.[4]

So far, teleological determination applies to all texts. One can also say that their argumentation structure or rhetoric originates there. A news story, though, is distinct from other texts – even from narratives – by its peculiar dependence on the goal. That goal reaches far beyond the narrative proper. Such goals are no longer explained by the narrative, yet they carry into the narrative a goal determination. This meaning overhang is clearly recognizable and is largely sufficient for differentiating the news genre from other narrative forms. Above, we described the overarching goal, within the θέατρον framework, as divine knowledge of the 'whole'; but that goal found its literary form in the news story structure.[5] The formation principle of 'inverted pyramid' reaches upstream beyond the story itself. Logically anterior to the headline and first paragraph of news texts stands the metatext. It is effective exclusively as 'opinion on' the whole – not as opining, having-an-opinion-on, statements of others on the represented reality. Every single news story is, therefore, an episode of the 'Whole.'

The number of possible news stories is limited; the number of metatexts is even more limited. News happens only in categories or 'slots' such as these: 'politics,' 'economy,' 'international affairs,' 'science,' *curiosa* (gossip, *'faits divers,' 'cronaca nera,'* 'human interest,' etc.), op.-ed. ('page 7' in some broadsheets), *feuilleton*, and so forth. Within the framework of each category or slot, there exist certain established narrative patterns (war, compromise or coalition, crisis, debate, success or failure, etc.); the rest is mere variation. The logic of this has found its expression in journalistic routines. 'News value' research attempts to inquire empirically into what merely is empiricism of industrial practices. The news industry, in fact, bears no relation to the 'objective world,' which the various stories try to represent in their respective ways. 'News value' research can be framed as a false alternative between objective and 'journalist-derived.': 'What is the epistemological nature of news values? For instance, are news values objectivations of journalists' self-deriving meanings? Or are they premised upon an objective ontological basis? These evidently crucial questions have never been raised before, resulting in news values being potentially seen as arbitrary features of journalism' (Lau 2004, 696).

Research into news value is largely an effort to explain why one factual statement becomes a news item and the overwhelming majority of facts do not. Disregarding the primary effort of narrative meaning (which, beyond the story itself, is meaning organized coherently by an institution that depends on other institutions as sources), events (i.e., news report appearances, or silence) are treated as if they had a normally distributed chance of existing or not. 'News value,' however, does not relate to chance events (though this is the Gaussian normal distribution presupposition of empiricist probability that something is, or is not); rather, it is at best a planned surprise (which is how Ricoeur translates the *Poetics'* metabolè, as *coup de théâtre*). In this context, 'planned' encompasses the widest possible meaning framework, including dominant ideologies – that is, historically contingent models of meaning. Beyond narrative customs (from θέατρον to genres) are social mythical texts, which we try to grasp as metatexts. News value, as an existential (reported or not) or interpretational (spin, advocacy) selection criterion (cf. Liebes 2000), is deducible from the metatextual organization of meaning (as tragedies, comedies, etc., are deducible from the Dionysian action or drama). The gods know what is worth telling (and so does the chorus with its *koryphaios*, i.e., 'all').

Metatexts became the basis of the industrialization of meaning in the form of genre and brand recognition. The mentioned theatrical god, of course, might be substitutable also by a functionalist-structural insight of society – though one can avoid the looming debate over societal ontology by simply acknowledging the industrialization of meaning. This is the idea of metatexts, which exist only as goals upstream of the goals in 'factual' narratives, and these are general stories of 'all.' In our Pragmaticist context, this has been described as pragmatic rules determined by the method of authority.

Metatexts make self-evident what normally would require an argumentative justification: the subordination (hypotaxis) of represented action, along with the investment of the actor with qualities of competency, where subordination is a precondition of the competency. Only a theory of society *in se* could hope to justify this claim – for example, as having a social function. As we conceive the problem, however, we need only demonstrate that those texts of tacit presupposition – which in analogy to metaphysics we call metatexts – are indeed posited before all actual texts. But if such metatexts are and remain unwritten, how can they be proven? They are never spelled out; thus we find their traces only as the presupposed-without-justification in actually produced texts. While presupposing itself as justified, such an actual text posits its represented object as one that must be justified or that is likely to be vindicated. The legitimizing is itself not legitimized; instead it presupposes, in its sign usage, that everything publicly acted needs a good reason to be acted. Since the legitimizing text lacks proper legitimization, it knows that it cannot insist on being legitimate; it thus passes its own justification on to a sovereign legitimization instance: 'all,' an emphatically inclusive We, in whose name and on whose orders the text is representing.

'Metatexts' as a concept describes a product of meaning, usually approached in communication sciences from an industrially immanent angle. The specific in this meaning's construction is equally graspable as practice, as professional ethos, as the 'code of ethics' in the self-regulation of a branch of industry, or even, simply, as the unwritten rules of 'this is how we do that here.' Tuchman's organizational observation of news production (1978) covers certain aspects of the metatext idea. Owing to her phenomenological method, however, as 'participant observer' she describes more the subjective meaning construction of newsrooms. A newsroom perspective pure and simple, from an absolutely immanent point of view, reflects the objectivity ideal. Strangely, some research agendas assume the same immanence. This topic is then conceptualized as a journalistic purchase on the real. Regrettably, this is often accompanied by a disregard for the meaning-formative or configurative contribution of the journalist's text. True reality is often the quintessence of the endeavour of 'investigative journalism': 'When journalists (or news organizations) have not only developed an issue, but originated it, sometimes against stiff opposition' (Aldridge 1998, 115). This Holy Grail of journalism constitutes the paradigmatic pure form of one of the two metatexts.

6.2 Investigative Journalism and Objectivity

When a not-to-be-legitimatized instance (cf. Curran and Seaton 1981) represents the meaning of power as to-be-legitimatized, we will call it 'metatext I'; and this is the exact program inscribed on the term 'investigative journalism' – only with a negative sign. A police inquiry is called an 'investigation' (literally: 'following traces'). When journalists play police, they call themselves 'investigative.' Their methods of inquiry and the instruments they bring into action are almost identical to those of law enforcement (or at least those of private detectives). This operative imitation, as the semantic suggests, amounts to hitching journalistic operations to the state's judicial authority, thus to share epiphytically in that legitimacy. Modernity normally presupposes the state as a last-resort remedy against anarchy and the law of the jungle. For public opinion to place itself in parallel to a genuine state function, however, would necessitate proper, formal legitimization. Public opinion in its operations and prerogatives is implicitly and conventionally assumed to be the opinion of 'all' individuals. As individual opinion, it is sacrosanct (and accordingly is enshrined as the constitutional and human right of freedom of opinion); and as the opinion of 'all,' it constitutes an equivalent to truth for everything that no longer has a truth in itself but can merely be considered an opinion.[6]

Investigative journalism has harnessed itself tightly to the basic ideology of public opinion. Chalaby (1996) saw this form of journalism as an Anglo-American invention, though – of course – similar exists and has existed in other places. The quality press's embrace of methods and styles once encountered only as the vilified characteristics of the 'scandal press' is indeed noteworthy. In the New York microcosm of the 1920s, this clash played out as acrimonious competition between the *New York Times* (which itself started as a penny paper) and the Hearst and the Pulitzer newspapers.[7] The former viewed the latter as garish. Strong efforts at legitimization have been required to elevate muckraking methods – which have not changed at all – into the realm and service of a higher purpose. This aspiration has been able to mutate into a kind of parallel state purpose; evidence of this mutation is manifest in diverse formulations. For example, interested parties speak of a 'higher loyalty' when the critical press – and *a fortiori* its investigative sibling – operate against the government. This is allowable only when it is labelled 'social responsibility,' which is thereby manoeuvred into the position of highest loyalty.

Our present purpose is neither to describe the details nor to challenge underlying ideological assumptions, but rather to comprehend the complex meaning processes that constitute investigative journalism: What must be taking place when some call themselves investigative journalists? What is the uppermost meaning decision, which then conditions all subsequent practical decisions? We should not be deceived if, in this context, invoked here is a 'Fourth Estate' (Clem and Paul 1999,

45; De Albuquerque 2005), or the 'watchdog' function (Rosenbaum and Duncan 2001; Zhou 2000),[8] or the claim that press freedom is a necessary precondition for democracy.[9] For one thing, this does not explain how the press became what it has become (i.e., for the time being, and in these present circumstances, and not as elsewhere, or as it was in the past). Furthermore, civil society is still well equipped with the instruments necessary to combat power abuse – for instance, system-immanent 'parliamentary' and external electoral control – provided there is a will. That, however, no longer makes use of the hypostasis of a 'public opinion,' which has been monopolized by the mass media.[10]

'Objectivity' is the banner under which a journalistic attitude seeks to maintain (equi)distance from sublunary worldly matters over which people can come into conflict. For its meaning effect – and the corresponding self-comprehension of its practitioners – it is irrelevant that crude reality is quite different. 'Being objective' merely means extricating oneself credibly from involvement in the matter as represented in the first person singular, as 'self.' As a mere social fiction, objectivity simply serves the practical purposes of a generally 'viable'[11] (Hoffjann 2001) world view. This objectivity relates not to physical 'states of affairs' – to data without mediation artefacts, with which certain scientistic philosophical programs are concerned. Journalistic objectivity is the world of 'all,' and therefore no longer my subjective world. It is an ideal that means no less than considering a disputed something from an elevated perspective. The most widely used journalism textbooks have operationalized 'objectivity' (for the American press) as five professional attitudes: 'detachment,'[12] 'nonpartisanship,' 'inverted pyramid,' 'facticity,' and 'balance' (Mindich 1998, 8f). All of these translate directly into textual styles that manifest themselves in stories. In this way, they also translate into narrative logic. 'Detachment,' for instance, as a literary, narrative technique, translates mainly as third-person-singular narrative with minimal insight into the subjective logic of the actors. Foisting motivation onto actors (though knowing a literary actor's interiority presupposes a novelist's omniscience) violates this professional code, notwithstanding that this often happens and is easy to do.

With the professional attitude of 'objectivity,' the die is cast. Thereafter, the *auctoritas* of the speaker can be latent and borrow authority from 'full reality.' That latency in turn obfuscates the speaker's reasons for representing reality – and note here that truth and reality do not represent themselves. There is no automatism for the purpose-free contemplation of the gentle reader; moreover, representation starts with an oppositional attitude. For good reason, Gitlin points out with sadness in his discussion of the decline of present-day journalism: 'What's at stake here is a reluctance to be an opposition press. Why one should have thought that the press might feel a certain spur to be oppositional is an interesting question in itself.' (2006, 5) 'Objective' reality comes to stand against the 'others' (of 'all') – that is, the power holders. Officially, this is justified somewhat inevitably in terms of 'social responsibility,' the steward, loyal responsibility towards the generality, as whose watchdog or advocate the journalist poses.[13]

(Would-be) 'watchdogs' love to claim historical models for their role. Thus the historical role of the *tribunus plebis*,[14] or of the *censor*, takes a privileged position in the self-legitimization of investigative journalism. In ancient Rome, the *censor* (of the Patricians or the Optimate Party) or the *tribunus plebis* (the common people) could merely forbid (*intercessio*) with his '*veto!*' (i.e., neither had any *imperium*) what the Senate of the Patricians (in imperial times the Senate also had plebeian members) decided to enact. For that reason, they were sacrosanct (vested with *potestas sacrosancta*) and protected against any political or judicial prosecution. Similarly, investigative journalists claim their supra- or paralegal privileges.

These privileges include the protection of sources. The unflattering label 'access journalism' (Gitlin) describes the resulting practice. This was obvious, for example, in the unmasking of CIA covert agent Valerie Plame. Here, *New York Times* journalist Judith Miller became entangled in the 2005 stratagems of the Bush administration, which have since come to light in their wider 'information warfare' scope. The 'sources'[15] turned out to be anonymous administration officials with straightforward strategic intentions. Miller's resistance against revealing her sources was finally broken by coercive detention (Abrams 2004; Friedman 2006; Gup 2004; Lehmann 2005; Mermin 2004).

Throughout this process of legitimization, however, the real audience or readership is not taken into account; it is still the mythical 'all' of public opinion. And this does not mean a real-life television audience (on a given channel at a given time) in search of entertainment (who, thus qualified, are being marketed to advertising clients). Even so, the 'all' procure the right to be allowed or even obliged to know something. To these 'all,' the journalists provide their knowledge, which they extract from those who would connive to hide it from 'all.'

The crude reality behind that shroud is always a little different, of course. Facts *in se* are never for or against someone. For that purpose, one needs a further configuration of social and political conflicts; for 'we all' owe, to the enemy of the enemy, that reality turn itself 'against' the 'other.' In this way, 'we' become – *per implicationem* – friends of the opponent's opponents, who (selflessly, of course) as sources provide us with the reality to wield against their opponents. This 'birth defect' then displays itself in the product form itself, where it can be analysed (cf. Ettema and Glasser 1988). As a professional skill, this has evolved into the high art of spin doctoring and the precisely aimed calculated indiscretion. In journalistic practice this has led to the further problem of 'anonymous sources,' which are used in 21 per cent of news stories (Clayman 1990; Martin-Kratzer and Thorson 2007). It is difficult if not impossible to burden them with the responsibility for what has been stated (this is Gadamer's concept of *auctoritas*). Thus, every statement falls back onto the journalist. This has resulted in practical fundamental problems regarding source treatment. A consequence of the 'objectivity' principle has led the *New York Times*, for example, to declare strict rules for the treatment of anonymous sources. These have been made explicit in various versions of the *'New York Times Ethical Journalism Guidebook'* and *'Confidential News Sources'*(*New York Times* 2004a, 2004b, §13), which the 'public editor' of that newspaper has expanded on with further comments (Calame 2005).

From crimes – a second important type of 'hidden reality' – 'reality itself' must be snatched somewhat differently. Here the journalist brings reality to light against the criminal 'in the name of justice' (and no longer for the sake of the enemy's enemy). A different source for objectivity must be postulated for uncovering evil. This type of unmasking is not disinterested, but it is not a source authority (e.g., the police) that is doing the shrouding. To justify thus this sort of 'unmasking,' a single element is necessary: a clear goal. Objectivity against the powerful in political scandal is justified by 'us' (i.e., the powerless); with criminality, 'we' turn into the righteous who must contemplate objective facts about evildoers. Only a sense of justice shared by 'all' justifies this second type of unmasking – which is, note well, without legal consequence. This corresponds again to the θέατρον, which separates spectators from the stage not only spatially but also logically.

Investigative journalism can be described as a ritual extending of the θέατρον (or even as a 'strategic ritual,' as Tuchman (1972) defines objectivity). Θέατρον spectacularizes public opinion as a model of meaning. What functionally amounts to divine knowledge (θέατρον) in the self-comprehension of investigative journalism is 'social responsibility.'

This meaning device touches on more than simply 'higher loyalty'; it is a reference to the mythical 'all.' Only when investigative journalism succeeds in assuming this 'deputy' role can mass media attain a power capable of rivalling political power.

The invention of objectivity in the penny press at the end of the nineteenth century was not simply a gradual historical progress towards democratic control over governments, nor did it merely involve a minor change of format. The party press in this respect was more truthful *because of* – and not *in spite of* – its partisanship. Such one-sidedness could not even pretend that there was 'the' equally clearly objective reality for all. It is noteworthy that Edwin M. Stanton, the U.S. Secretary of War during the American Civil War, singlehandedly invented the inverted pyramid, one of the five central components of objectivity.[16] The pyramid indicates how, historically, information flows became controllable through 'objectivity,' for by the same token this hierarchical format can foist on objectivity a hierarchical thematic as a logic. In present-day political newspeak, this would come out as spin. Evidently, any identical set of objective facts can be hierarchized in many different ways and thereby insinuate a multitude of logical dependencies.

When it comes to religious scandals, this text-transcendental, fundamental determination articulates itself in the professional self-estimation of journalists and as industrial practice. This will become clear in our analysis of the *Boston Globe*. An investigative hero snatching 'objective facts' from obfuscating forces was clearly part of the meaning construction in this scandal, but that was not the substance of the story. In the text itself, we see this only in the framing. That this is practised so easily as a meaning apparatus is a consequence of its being 'offshore' as metatext, and not within the text itself. In the case of scandals, passionless 'detachment' quickly gives way to a passionate 'attached journalism' of indignation (cf. *supra* n176), which slips easily into the advocacy role of the *tribuni plebis*.

Investigative reporting can also profit from being analysed as a literary genre. Once we leave the standard objectivity problem behind, a literary perspective offers characteristics that allow us to distinguish news narratives from satire and 'one man' scandals. Not all news stories are 'straight,' however; some strive to mix themselves with satire, irony, sarcasm, or similar (cf. *supra*). When Schudson was accused of demoting objectivity-ritualistic journalism to a sort of fictional literature, he defended himself convincingly: 'We didn't say journalists fake the news, we said journalists make the news' (Schudson 1989, 263). Indeed, demonstrating that objectivity is a ritual (Schudson 2001; Tuchman 1972) as well as a token of journalistic professionalism says nothing about facts. The reality relation between a news story and whatever preceding material (most often already in narrative form) is an entirely different question.

Rearguard skirmishes with 'just the facts!' ideologies are a pointless exercise. Avoiding such bunfights may be desirable; that said, a certain type of news offers a closer relationship to reality. Molotch and Lester try to show this in their inquiries into the Santa Barbara oil catastrophe (Molotch 1999; Molotch and Lester 1974, 1975, 1999). They argue that scandals and catastrophic accidents evidence a different type of reality than the usual one. Ethnologists will certainly be quite familiar with this constructivism (Molotch and Lester 1974). It is the idea that a given event can be construed in terms of more than one reality, depending on the position from which it is seen – that is, from above (the point of view of elites, power holders, and the rich) or from below. While the information industry usually renders the reality from above, this coherent world view evidently has fissures when viewed through scandals. It seems, though, that Molotoch and Lester are too optimistic in their treatment of scandals and accidents (as well as other chance events), which they see as worldly states of affairs not graspable as typified reality. It may well be that they are merely different types – that is, 'from below' types that, when compared with those 'from above,' give an impression of a 'realer' reality. This conclusion suggests itself especially when we see it from the perspective of Schütz's phenomenology of meaning and reality construction: every 'objective' sense or meaning is typified (see §1.7; Ruggerone 1999).

At any rate, in connection with semiotic and Pragmaticism, such a debate on objectivity and interpretation is redundant. A type-like teleology (θέατρον) models the industrial practice. The whole point of this typing is to interpret interpreting – that is, sanctioning verdicts can indeed interpret in various ways with different outcomes when narrative teleology is an invariable type. Conversely, something transformed into narrative cannot revert to prenarrative reality, for this would dissolve the 'matter' itself. Indeed, public opinion consists in opining on something, which is a story, not a fact. What is styled factually (Fishman 1980) is actually nothing more than an authoritative story (e.g., coming from an administration in administrative possession of information oriented towards administrating).

The only possibility for resisting this logical constraint is not a 'just the facts!' myth, but narrating another, different story in an equally compellingly styled way. Only then reality is 'realities' – a territory of conflict. Yet even conflicting stories still require a common ideology of 'all'-hood, without which there can be no sanction (or conflict). It is not the facts that justify sanction, but that 'all' opine something publicly. Ultimately, this differentiates news from rumours (for instance, a blog breaking the Clinton–Lewinsky scandal). Rumours, individual opinions, and outsider views might very well be factually true, but they will not cause scandals because they all lack the sanctioning potential. Carey (2007, 10): '[Historically], the public was, in Robert Park's happy phrase, a group of people who gathered to discuss the news.' For that purpose, it needs the authority of a viable reality construction, which merely means that all relevant players must consider it plausible.

Satire is merely a playful renunciation of the sanctioning potential of 'all.' The price that satire pays for its play is that it lacks any authority for its reality construction, which it shares with the most extreme forms of tabloidization. In their methods, though, investigative journalism and satire are at least comparable if not identical. *Le Canard enchaîné*, for example, is France's foremost satirical publication, but it also engages in investigative journalism – indeed, it must be credited with pioneering that form in France. The same style combination existed in German organs such as *Pardon* and *konkret*, and has existed since 1841 in England in *Punch*, which itself imitated the French satirical paper *Charivari*). The rest of the media world, however, largely ignored these periodical. Nevertheless, as a rule they could not be accused that their facts were wrong (libel litigation would have made this too costly, because these facts would normally stand up in court). The difference consisted really of disrespect towards public and economic institutions. Against their orthodox story writing, satire was afforded the sole option of writing paradoxical stories. The genre rules of satire, moreover, required that there be no exceptions to disrespectfulness, which could in principle target all parties, companies, ideologies, and any sort of belief.

Only by raising moral claims can other products of investigative journalism, such as political magazines, escape the strictures of the satirical genre. But however such claims are raised, their aim can only be the deviant's moral sanction by 'all.' While satirical magazines intend mere ridicule, and glossy magazines mere embarrassment (of stars, celebrities, scandal magnets), investigative journalism seriously claims an obligation (not just permission) to pass moral judgment on others.

This competency must be derived from somewhere; it is neither automatic nor self-evident. Upholding generally recognized values and norms provides exactly the needed justification.

As the extreme moral (but not formal) opposite of satire, the extreme exaggerations of investigative journalism turn into exposure journalism, in the hands of a persecution instance outside the judiciary framework. It would be difficult to discern who should bear the palm for the most extreme form of public inquisition. In Cold War Germany, at least, a contender was Günter Wallraff[17] with his dogged exposures. The reverence in which his admirers held him approached cult status. Yet according to his detractors, he published what amounted to no more than partisan distortions of reality. This kind of journalism no longer pretends to be opinion journalism; instead, its self-declared goal is to snatch the facts from its victims against their will. Usually, only criminal investigation officers have this concession for the sole purpose of averting dangers to society.

Mere sensationalism continues to thrive in the domain framed by satire on the one hand and investigative journalism on the other. Tabloids continue to proliferate, their circulation in the millions; and on television, the genre of Reality TV has grown some astonishingly bizarre blossoms. But rather than covering actual scandals, the scandal-mongering press merely blows inconsequential facts out of proportion, then justifies them with utterly overblown moral judgments. These entertainment industry exaggerations, despite their numerical mass, take nothing away from (nor, though, do they contribute to) the (self-)-justifications of investigative journalism. Their exaggerations merely cannibalize investigative journalism, which from its own perspective grows from the hardest kernel, the very essence of journalism bound by objectivity.

What, then, justifies investigative journalism? As a child of the history of ideas, public opinion is equipped with quasi-divine nature, with the right of 'all' to know the whole and to sanction the acts of the powerful. This rhetoric and dramaturgy has helped the bourgeoisie fashion its political model. In light of this logic, it is no surprise that journalists enact sanctions just as much as the judiciary. Though just another industry, it has succeeded in latching itself to the logic of power and the operations of its legitimization.

In practice, investigative journalism has crossed boundaries that it shouldn't. What right do journalists actually have to obtain information by any method, including police methods (Goddard 2006)? Relative to private investigators (such as Kroll Inc., once a branch of the world's biggest insurance company), journalists have little to envy in terms of tools of the trade. How much of what they do is legal depends on the laws in their jurisdiction (see for details de Burgh 2000, 126–55; Waisbord 2002); that said, Ian Fleming would have envied their present capacity. From spies and private detectives, journalists have borrowed means and methods such as (and these are the known ones) hidden and mini-cameras, extreme telelenses, and acoustic surveillance.

Besides these, journalists have at their disposal more important methods for obtaining information. For example, they have their anonymous but 'well-informed' sources. Collaboration between journalists and these sources results in the dissemination of 'proofs,' which can be paraphrased where it is illegal to publish them word for word. The semantic for these sources varies greatly. News items, rather neutrally, often apostrophize them as 'reliable sources.' From the perspective of victims, though, these sources are 'moles,' 'informers,' 'spies,' 'undercover agents.' Wallraff, for instance, earned his epithet 'IM' (*'informeller Mitarbeiter'* of the Communist secret police, the Stasi; indeed, traces of Wallraff's collaboration have been found in archives) through his now classic methods of 'role reporting.' This *Rollenreportage* entailed joining an organization under a false identity in order to report on it. Against the Springer press, Wallraff obtained a court injunction prohibiting them from applying this epithet to him. These practices, at any rate, raise serious questions relating to the constant and onerous pressure to legitimize them as acts of a people's tribune (Clayman 2002).

Other questionable practices relate to whistle-blowing. Most often, whistle-blowers are employees – in companies, political organizations, or administrations – who provide to the sanctioning instance of public opinion information damaging to their organization. Since the Enron Scandal in the United States, whistle-blowers have been extended comprehensive protection under the 2002 Sarbanes-Oxley Act;[18] in internal administrative prosecutions of irregularities, this can work against the efforts of 'competing prosecutor'-journalists. Sometimes state organs themselves act as whistle-blowers. That is, they take their matter (political agendas, aims of criminal prosecution) to the press in the hope of facilitating their (legitimate) goals with the support of sanctioning public opinion. In some countries and political cultures, personal data collected by the police, betraying investigative secrets, routinely come to light in this way, even when the matter is *sub judice*. Similar incidents took place at the beginning of the Boston CSA scandals, in 2003, where lawyers succeeded by these means in influencing the judiciary process.

'Realist' theories of journalism strongly object when journalism is described as guided by interests. 'Antirealist constructivisms' (Fishman 1980; Molotch and Lester 1974; Schudson 1989, 2001, 2006; Tuchman 1972, 1978) are criticized for philosophical reasons. These critics declare journalistic objectivity to be possible and, moreover, ethically obligatory (Gauthier 1993, 2005). If it is not perfect objectivity, at least it is the natural kind (Lau 2004). In this regard, Gautier treats news as factual statements, applying Searle's theory of intentional speech acts.[19] From a semiotic perspective, of course, any attempt at realism is welcome, and because of the Second Correlate in the sign, this realism is not to be contradicted. Does this assertion grasp the essence of news? Does the news assert facts, or does it indicate *goals* by using a series of facts?[20] News is, in logical terms, precisely *not* a sentence with a subject that existentially determines a predicate but where a general rule determines (cf. *supra*). Furthermore, this rule is indeed a goal. Goals are not reducible *salva veritate* to dyadic existential relations (Gauthier alludes to Searle's 'brute facts,' and thus uses a Peircean concept). Logically, this reduction amounts to reducing a triadic relation (e.g., of 'gift') to two consecutive dyads ('object transfers'). However, the transfer of X from A to B will never make it a 'gift.' For the logical nature of news, this means that news cannot be reduced to facts. On the contrary, the goal of organizing some facts into a single series and then explaining it under a rule must be found and explained in itself, independently of its organized facts. The main adversary of these 'realists' is the phenomenological method. In their attack on Berger and Luckmann, Lau and Gauthier ignore the systemic purpose of the phenomenological *epoché*. For Husserl, this was a conscious suspension of the natural cognitive attitude as a means of ascertaining painstakingly immediate consciousness contents and operations. We can object to this post-Kantian method, but we should not overlook that there are two essentially different levels (v. *supra*). Constructivity is related to the *epoché* level and is not the natural attitude (something Husserl not only did not deny, but even gave a reflexive expression in the life world, *Lebenswelt*).

For news, the question of goals is the truly interesting one. Much more relevant for teleology is the investigation of the narrative form of news and of its social context. Highly indicative is how television news developed as a form, and here, Baym (2004) offers an interesting investigation. Especially for (what he calls) the 'news package,'[21] he shows how the narrative predetermination of a goal became more closely connected with facticity. In television, furthermore, the factual is endowed with specific reality indices. The journalistic predetermination of a goal became increasingly manifest in this development; at the same time, new television formats turned professional storytellers into news anchors – stars with a 'news identity,' personified news, as it were. Yet this qualification leans on a professional ideology (Deuze 2005a, 2005b), which we describe as a metatext.

Finally, investigative journalism gives scandal its form. It is important to understand this journalism as determined by a clear goal that defines its form. This goal is more than a simple predetermination of 'objective information,' called bias.[22] This journalism fits so well into the meaning processes of public opinion *in se* that it is negatively goal determined as 'adversarial reporting' (Tumber and Waisbord 2004b, 1144) as a result of its antagonism towards power holders. Also positively, however, it implies the construal of an ideal, modelled after the spectacularized θέατρον logic. Antagonistic, partisan (telling the story of the adversary), sanctioning: its intended product is not representation but effect, not reality but transformation – 'effectual reality,' as it were. Its effect can have different loci: by distinguishing good from evil and condemning evil, it is effectual from within a moral discourse; from within a political discourse, it weighs power through legitimization. The former is topical for scandals, the latter gives form to struggles of all kinds. These effects presuppose, however, that investigative journalism is conducted seriously and not as a frivolous exercise in the style of what some have called 'bonk journalism' (Esser 1999; McNair 2003). Undeniably, since the 1990s the instruments of investigative journalists have been used increasingly by voyeurs (Tumber and Waisbord 2004b, 1148f), which has generated a blooming industry branch through tabloidization. It cannot be assumed that this form of journalism is still intent on having serious effects, except to increase circulation.

There are many varieties of journalism, but they all follow one basic pattern. It looks more like marketing rhetoric than substance when the 'committed' press flaunts its 'advocacy journalism,' the 'serious' press its 'investigative journalism,' and the citizen-oriented 'service' press its 'public journalism.' All share in the same fundamental ideal, adapted for different markets, in a variety of styles. This ideal generates scandals, its negative form, as public opinion, but it also boosts some reputations. The positive form is the realm of a separate epiphytical industry, public relations; in the case of celebrities, a *genus mixtum*, positive and negative coverage can be difficult to tell apart.

Our chief interest is in the form. This description of investigative journalism has deliberately omitted the bulk of anecdotal wisdom, its heroes and their feats, the history of its triumphs and its spectacular failures. The form, however, of this zenith of a practice turned industry is more than just a literary convention: it forms meaning, creates sense after its own shape. All attempts to reduce journalism to scribeship, transcribing facts onto sentences, amanuensing slavishly in the production of objectivity, do not reflect its creative contribution. Meaning is created, not found, and journalism is a form of creation. It has its own rules, making more probable certain effects, impossible others. Effect in this context means reality, the world, pragmatic universe as outcome of a story.

Some might consider this a traversal approach. Instead of starting from what is 'out there' and then proceeding to its textual equivalent, we began with the configuration form and ended with a meaningful reality. The alternative would have been a naive realism, which is philosophically not at all 'critical realism,' as some have claimed. If it is true that there is 'no cognition but in signs,' then semiotic is aware not only of the 'brute facts,' but also of the rule ('law') of meaning. In this sense of journalism, it follows almost inevitably that scandal owes all to its form. It might be a difficult approach, seemingly counterintuitive, to deduce scandal from journalism itself and not from its social effects. From this deduction, scandal inherits the focus on the meaning-creating form and its use of facts. The standard treatment of scandals, however, is tempted to put the question this way: Is the 'objectivity' of a scandal a human behaviour ('fact' in the literal sense) or is it a text product without causal connection to behaviour, *'journalists' self-deriving meanings'* (Lau 2004, 694 and passim)? Obviously, this only complicates the general issue of journalistic objectivity. Nevertheless, it is a false alternative.

There can be no doubt that media scandals have objective effects. (We will address this in a separate chapter.) Scandals force human behaviour to change. But questions about *how* require us to find causes, not describe consequences. In other words, they call on us to look upstream from the scandal.

Likewise, it is beyond doubt that it is not only the media who produce scandals, but also the social dynamics at play in human aggregations. In social groups, scandals are real as behaviour, be they planned or unintentional. If what René Girard termed the 'mimetic conflict' effectively and historically exists, scandal is even a pale imitation of an ultimately lethal hate/love. Waisbord represented press scandals as 'violations of trust' (1994, 21), but his choice of words turns political power into precisely this Girardian object of hate/love. Whether it is wise to apply 'trust' to public opinion is another question, but one that resonates in the textual stylization of its actors (can we trust, in the real sense of the word, someone we have never met?). Being a post-structuralist myth theorist, Girard even applied his theory to the Dionysian principle, making it the transparent mythological foil for human behaviour. Since it also serves prominently as mythology of the Θέατρον, the mimetic conflict has here its foremost textual representation. For our present purposes, this framework is far too wide, and therefore unwieldy; it also leaves open our question of how mythological texts relate to behaviour – or behaviour to text.

Briefly put, the mimetic reality of society, which includes its scandals, does not explain public opinion and some of its outstanding phenomena. There is much more to gain from representing the logic of scandal first as a text, and then see to its effect. This does not mean that the question of causation is being dodged. It merely places it in a new form in the semiotic-pragmatic context. Based on our previous analyses, this asks more exactly: What causes an interpretation of a sign, when it first becomes teleological – and does so in a quite determinate way? What is being invented here is not the facts (or even Gauthier's 'brute facts'), but the goal. The pure facts supposedly are, by and large, correct in commercial media products. Not least, under the pressure of company lawyers and the legal advisers of editors and television stations, factual assertions are usually formulated so vaguely that they are longer justiciable. The problem is not the petty burglary into a Washington condominium, or the soiled dress of a White House intern, or the close contact of homosexual youths with a priest. He who asks here 'What happened?' wants to know, as a rule, the purpose in a higher-order action, or even the deeper intention of an actor. These are no longer facts. A purpose is a new proper interpretation and becomes a new sign (with the fact-sign in its First Correlate).

There remain the effects of sanctions or media scandals in the real world, if one rejects the notion of scandal *in se* as a real-world fact. This aspect, too, will be considered in greater detail later on.

6.3 Metatexts: Simplifying Sanctions in Public Opinion Texts

Metatexts stand for the industrialization of the θέατρον meaning manifest in genres (e.g., investigative journalism). Metatexts, as it were, are the logical apparatus of the theatre structure, not the play's performance. This idea is not unique. Communication science has a comfortable term for this, borrowed from the cognition science metaphor 'frame theory,' and probably also inspired by Goffman's classical 'frame analysis.' Entman offers this description of it: 'Framing essentially involves selection and salience. To frame is to select some aspects of a perceived reality and make them more salient in a communicating text, in such a way as to promote a particular problem definition, causal interpretation, moral evaluation, and/or treatment recommendation for the item described' (1993, 52). This 'fractured paradigm' admits to being a rather vague and imprecise explanation (1993, 51). It is not by chance that such a program evokes memories of the classical Aristotelian Poetic (perhaps indeed its 'core knowledge'), for in reality it consists of textual or narrative causality. In other words, framing consists of the teleological causality of a pragmatic task ('problem definition'); a positively or negatively pragmatic goal represented as value ('moral evaluation'); and a sanctioning distance ('treatment recommendation') of public opinion (θέατρον).[23] Thus the inquiry-guiding metaphor contains both the frame and the framed.[24]

In a semiotic context there are good reasons to disconnect frame from framed and substitute a relation of interpretation and interpreted. Metatext, thence, refers only to outer part of the framing, for the frame adds a decisively important interpretation. The latter must remain latent within the framed itself; it must not take place there. The universes of discourse of the two must remain separated – for instance, in the θέατρον logic of publicity. Here both parts constitute in themselves (narrative) discourses. This characteristic explains why we call only some interpretations metatexts. Whereas any sign interprets other signs, the interpretation in metatexts is conventionally fixed, socially practised, and automatically recognizable. In short, as an effortless interpretation it is self-evident to the point of being unconsciously presupposed. Many social practices need this presumption – be it called frame, symbolic generalization, or something else – but our focus wil be on the two metatexts we encountered in publicity as presently practised in our culture.

In a wider humanistic, poetic context, the idea of metatexts is nothing new. Reception aesthetics (better known in communication science as 'reader response theory') for some time now has concerned itself with the problem how reading and understanding processes function by constructing an ideal (Beetles and Harris 2005; Elliott and Elliott 2005; Ettema 2005; Iser 1972, 1976; Knight 1999; Scott 1994). Hermeneutic literary theory, the origin of this aesthetic, was interested in the strange constellation of the *vis comica* in comedies and autobiographies, for instance. Earlier we saw Jauß's impressive descriptions of the third instance of judgment for Rousseau's *Confessions*. It is always operant when we laugh about characters on stage – something that enables us to laugh about ourselves (Jauß 1977). In ancient theatre this third instance was akin to controlling tragically ignorant actors in their power to act on stage.

Framing – investigating how the communicator's presentation of an event (news story or problem) influences the recipient's opinion – ultimately is simply a sort of media effects agenda. Put simply, the θέατρον, as modelled in the semiotic-pragmatic framework allows us to see more. Metatexts interpret texts. Regarding their special mode of interpretation, semiotic is handy to us because it uses a range of sign relations. As textual order, the hypotactic dependency relation becomes an interpretation of an interpretation – that is, under a new rule. For publicity, the foremost interpretation, as noted earlier, is narrative teleology. In addition, there are other interpretations of hypotaxis – precisely for scandals. The reality effects of 'objective' news, for instance, are unrenounceable. The metatext thus conveys also a sign relation determined by Secondness, of facticity, for otherwise news would be novels, mere stories. The interpretative effect of metatexts is not limited to purpose and fact, though. Signs of emotional qualities, determined by Firstness, can also become relevant for metatextual interpretation of stories, turning them into news stories of a particular kind. We see this mainly in 'human interest stories,' but certainly also in scandals. We will have to see how all of these signs emanate from coherent metatexts that create through their specific interpretation the 'newsness' in news stories.

Metatexts, consequently, are a quite determinate part of canonical narration along with reality effect and emotional overtones, and not merely 'selections and saliences,' as with frames. They are, precisely as frames, relatively fixed conventions that not only have become genre conventions but also are part of the scaffolding of the industry of mass media meaning production. Since they predetermine this meaning even before any text is generated, they must have their reason in the self-comprehension of that particular meaning production as such. The quintessence of metatext I, as interpretation of an interpretation, is most evident in investigative news stories. Here journalism is at its best, according to a consensus patently shared by industry practitioners and consumers. Metatext II, for its part, as an industrial meaning practice, describes more 'soft news' or even 'lifestyle news' as found in glossy magazines. It is clear, however, that neither of these two basic models of press or mass media exists in this pure form; each is always *genus mixtum*, infotainment, 'human interest story,' and so forth.

Metatexts are derived as much from the publicity idea as from textual hypotaxis or enunciation – they are historical-cultural-social constellations in text form. Metatexts are concrete, enshrined in practices. They are instrumental in claiming topics as political agenda, issue framing (Gamson and Modigliani 1989; Jacoby 2000), prime definers (Ferguson 1990), spin doctoring, and so on. Framing, both as putting into, and as covering with, a frame, is exercised for a purpose that transcends the frame. What Joshua Gamson calls 'Institutional Morality Tales' (2001) is the relatively fixed relationship between value-sanctioning publics and powerful actors. This relationship often manifests itself not directly, though, but as crisis of a societal institution, which is that intermediate normative 'thing' postulated by public opinion: 'What is revealed in sex scandal discourse is not simply societal norms – sexual or other, institution-specific, or not – but also the institutional operations and relations of news media' (Gamson 2001, 187).

The regulation work of norms is best treated as a separate text, because its interpreted dependent text is not regulating explicitly. Upstream of any text, the logical construction of metatexts is concerned with explicit or implicit justification. If a scientific article, for example, were not questing for truth, it would not exist as such. This duty-of-truth quest does more than inform it intrinsically: that quest is set antecedent to any research activity or redacting, for 'text' in this context is not a composition of sentences but any pragmatically meaningful practice. A novel, by contrast, is logically founded on the author's fantasy. Only mass media texts express public opinion as coming 'from a higher place.' Such texts' self-legitimization is passed down from above, with the same right to subject the represented to the hypotaxis of its judgment. Both are one compact meaning formation condensed as metatext I of publicity ('legitimization of power').

Publicity discursive universe relates to pragmatic universe of the represented in that the former modifies meaning in the latter. Metatext modifies text. It is, however, not arbitrary or chance how the subordinate meaning is subject to a mode. Indeed, this is so characteristic that anyone participating in such communication must recognize 'public opinion' as a specific meaning. Part of this specificity entails not exhausting the entire spectrum of theoretical possibilities. It limits itself instead to two types of appropriating foreign meaning through hypotaxis. 'Public metatexts' mean exactly these two specifically modalized dependency relations. That publicity consists only of these two metatexts is a cultural contingency, or ideology (which we can only describe, cf. § 3.3), but these two complement each other logically.

First, metatext I ('power control') is formally defined by legitimizing the power, or the grant-to-act, of the actors by means of a truth equivalent, the opinion of 'all.' Second, again in a formal definition, the actor as subject is brought into relation with the sanctioning instance. This metatext II is called 'self-realization,' but it could also be termed the 'hedonistic metatext.'

The two metatexts' specific difference, and complementarity, is no chance. On the contrary, it results logically from the rule that public opinion is not itself a pragmatic subject. Metatexts constitute different kinds of control with the two logically separated areas of public opinion: with the mandated, established in teleology, on the one hand; and with the action's execution or performance on the other. The competence of the pragmatic subject is controlled by the power-metatext (I), while the identity-metatext (II) controls its performance. These two aspects, regardless of their terms and semantic trappings, are formally present in every text that produces public opinion. As metatexts, they merely need to be developed into an accordingly modalized narrative program. If a narrative considers action in itself, it defines a pragmatic subject by the goal, the object for which it is striving. If such a narrative's concern, however, is judging this action, then it has the quality of the pragmatic subject in sight, and only incidentally the achievement, the success. If, therefore, through sanction and destination public opinion is to determine action without acting itself, its central and only purchase is pragmatic competence and the performance[25] of the action. From a subject's perspective, acting is conditional on being-able-to-act and being-actor.

To summarize, these two formal goals of public opinion are realized by metatext I: the intention to control the permission to act ('can-act') must subject that act to a legitimization; and by metatext II: the intention to judge the pragmatic subject itself must tie the subject self's realization to the sanctioning instance's predeterminations. Direct interference in the acting is completely different: the only option for public opinion to act itself would be to enhance or diminish the power of the pragmatic subject. Yet acting as helper or opponent is clearly not the meaning of public opinion in media.

6.3.1 Metatext I: The Permission to Act

What is performance? Clearly, it has much to do with the will and its result. It therefore consists in a volitive act, which in turn consists of a subject bound through will to its other, where it materially realizes its will. Object, the most general term, renders the resistance aspect, but it is comprehensive of everything that can be object of the will of a subject (persons or physical matter). A will binds in various ways. If performance is a transformative relation of a subject with an object, the subject attains or obtains 'something.' If this 'something' to which volitive action relates is a person, then a different meaning results than through material acquisition. The pragmatic subject's performance is not a simple 'yes or no' result, but varies in its meaning.

In the volitive relation, the scale can reach from the robot-like being at the service of the object to the father-like relations of a loving model. The mode of conjunction in the former is 'possession' or 'loss' – that is, the mechanical subject 'has' when it owns or loses an object. When a pragmatic subject relates to another subject as its volitive object, in the latter, it 'is,' which constitutes 'love' or 'hate' (i.e., one does not 'have' another person). A material object contributes little to the possessing subject's quality; a loving or hating subject undergoes interior change. Though the oppositional *vis-à-vis* of subject and object obtains, material possession is much more dyadic than love. With possession, the Third Correlate is exhausted with the legal idea of property; whereas love is not reducible to a static legal rule – its triadic meaning is richer and includes mutuality and a rich time dimension. Both cases are ordered triadic relations representing the interpretation of opposition. Yet it is much less complex to interpret unity in the case of possession than in the case of love. Here the subject becomes 'father' and the object 'son,' so abstracting the unity of both as 'love' is not very informative.

When material possession substitutes for a human relation, this very subtly reinterprets performance. Here it is not only a machine but also the state, the economy, or nature that can 'will.' Lexicalizations such as 'official church,' '*magisterium*,' and so on produce this kind of meaning. Thus, 'officialdom' can only 'have' subjects. Despite its current language usage, such volitive materializations were originally personal lexicalizations: thus church (κυριακὴ) means the Lord's (i.e., assembly), and ecclesial (ἐκκλησία, *ecclesia*, *église*, etc.) means the chosen (i.e., literally called out by God).

Since human sociality is the topic of most media, the mode of relation should normally be more relevant to meaning than the mode of possession. The usage of these performance modes can therefore be a strategy of meaning. 'The economy' – a paradigm of the possession mode – can hardly be sanctioned. Instead, failures among managers, politicians, and the like are sanctioned. Choosing the respective alternative is therefore meaning determinant: the known personalization tendency in the media is conducive to sanctioning. Where there are answerable persons, no anonymous state apparatus with unwavering functional operations 'does' this or that; it is highly placed politicians who do this or that. Through this meaning trick, action becomes personally attributable. The result (which alone counts) is that possession of an apparatus becomes part of a person's relational mode. Institutional activity is of the 'object possesses object' type; the personalization trick disguises this truth. Booming economies, bull markets, are objectively difficult to bring into a positively sanctioning interpretation, but their public performance is based on that presupposition. This also applies *a fortiori* to the ecclesial subject. Bishops thus have had to take personal responsibility for the social secularization process (as certain surveys suggest[26]). Glorifications operate in a similar way, in that light figures of the good appear in the Church (e.g., televangelists, popes) and are attributed great moral authority.[27]

Metatext I is lexicalized as 'power legitimization' because power derives from *potere* (to be able to act), which concerns performance. The special regard whereby personifying media are interested in all sorts of acting is the ability to control as a destination and sanctioning instance. Sanction and destination, however, are interested more in the development of subjects according to their being, and not so much in the becoming of a subject-apparatus by means of accumulated objects. This allows the observation of a kind of fixed idea in the media, the ritual of legitimization of can-do and do-do. Legitimization is brought up as an issue only because it allows in the first place the narration of the relation to the sanction. This meaning presupposes logically that one can attribute something to a pragmatic subject through a pragmatic object, that a subject is transformed (changes, grows, becomes more) through its relationship to an object. Subjects who simply are, and do achieve nothing, are not narratable and thus not sanctionable. The army of the grey masses is uninteresting because in their being-subject nothing changes, even should they change whole countrysides to the point of unrecognizability. Only for personalities who stand out from that mass does acting become self-generation or self-realization (through the objects attributed to them).

This process is especially manifest in narrative programs of power holder sanctions. What the powerful have attained in influence, force, wealth, glory, popularity, and so on must be justified to someone. Usually this need arises in view of resistance. In religious discourses, for example, it arises when the hierarchy is challenged by lay movements for bishops' accountability (e.g., see Henningsen 2004; National Young Adult Reporter 1977). This places bishops under a constraint (generated by this effect): they must justify their acquired hierarchical authority. So much has this become a commonplace that catchphrases have been coined such as 'the last absolute monarchy' (implying a sanction program for the Pope), 'hierarchy' and 'lay movement' (as contenders for the scarce resource power), and 'lay people referendum' (as a narrative program this amounts to a *fronde*). It is important for us that power holding is not so much a possession but a being-powerful, which is attributed to a subject after its transformation.

6.3.2 Metatext II: The Scale of Self-Realization

Metatext II, the second formal meaning procedure in metatexts, targets competence. It implies subjects as developing, the transformation of one subject-state into another. In a teleological narrative program, only changing subjects can become roles. G.H. Mead constituted a subject in transforming an 'I' to a 'Self,' generalizing the ego as alter ego. However, he reconstructed this increase in generality in psychological terms. The still to be realized I becomes the happy and recognised Me, very similar to the 'recognition of the hero,' a Self, in Propp's fairy tale functions. It is the underlying gold foil of 'successful life' stories, heroization of exemplary people. The real problem relates to a logical transformation in the pragmatic of conduct. Subjects who in acting are only concerned with themselves – that is, who syntonize their wills only with their own feelings – are a different kind of subjects than those who have in their will a general goal.

While not convinced by psychological arguments, Peirce could still construe his first version of a pragmatic truth theory from the subject perspective. A pragmatic subject is neither simply in possession of the truth nor completely deluded.[28] Because Pragmaticism burdened itself with reality as a corrective to cognition, the subject cannot be self-sufficient but can only be an inquirer – that is, someone who doubts or believes (in a doubt–belief cycle). The subject is never totally with the general truth, nor totally with its mere own singular feelings. The different methods of 'how to make our ideas clear' are thus different performances of the pragmatic subject. These methods for clarifying doubts describe also a subject-transforming cognitive behaviour and learning. The same logic, more mundanely, enables public opinion to predetermine the subject's purpose 'in realizing itself,' in changing in accordance with the public model. What it can mean to achieve success and 'lead a successful life' is predetermined or prescribed in ideals, stars, and celebrities, and respectively in scandalous monsters or failures – beyond the private sphere. In many fields, such abstract models become concrete 'careers,' from sex[29] to profession.

The old ego alters into the alter ego within a range of variability. The two extremes of the range from pure transitivity to pure resistance are quite easy to grasp. If a resistant subject behaves as a reflex of its own I – in other words, if it mirrors only itself and learns nothing – it can hardly itself open to a model for its alterity, its otherness. At the other extreme is pure transitivity, which occurs when the exemplary model alone has an effect on subjectivity. When a transitivity subject starkly resembles its goal or alter ego, when it looks like a copy of it, then it can be judged to be developing, learning, or growing. Novels of personal development (*Entwicklungsromane*) operate according to this pattern when young persons – usually in the hands of seasoned experts – are shaped. Public opinion, though it does not direct like a 'governess,' defines public roles and predetermines lifestyle ideals for the personal development of subjects. With already fixed roles – for example, of politicians – it is presupposed that pragmatic competence corresponds to the ideal throughout. Here it is more indeterminacy that is negatively sanctioned (some U.S. presidential candidates apparently have paid a price for being too hesitant in defining themselves).

When I am reflecting solely myself, at the other extreme, as a public role, this too can be interpreted positively or negatively. Here, I manifest myself as decisively resistant to the model communicated by the sanctioning instance. In a negative interpretation, I am sanctioned for incorrigibility or for character corruption. But all sanction will be fended off if that interpretation gives way to a successful narrative program of someone showing 'backbone.' Yet that can function only on a temporal and exceptional basis. Certain 'conservative hierarchs' have lost their reputation in this way.

The intermediate range constitutes the bulk of public self-realization. While 'imitation' is less than mirroring reflection, it is still rather symmetrical between the Me and the model Self. When stars and celebrities are public opinion's way of modelling, this normally creates the expectation that pragmatic subjects correspond to their fitting public role ideal. 'Cool' pupils and 'successful' managers are as much a task of public self-realization as the role of an 'open' priest. With imitation, the Self is not considered stable and firm, but rather still in need of being formed in a certain style. Lifestyle, in that sense, refers more to style than to life. This explains the prominence of celebrities: they demand, rather sublimely, that we become what they display. Counselling in life and sex problems, in particular, has become a sort of television genre (life 'coaching TV') and makes extended use of this pressure. The dictates of fashion with their similarly oriented meanings are much more harmless. The obligation (relating to the alter of ego) is normally not moral; it is more a hedonistic model (relating to alter ego). It is supposed to be fun. What is fun is good, and it is a duty to realize the good of fun in the personal development of the subject. Such meaning could otherwise not be generated as a teleological effect. Only an obligation to self-realization makes people susceptible to a predetermination through a model. In the absence of a middle symmetrical relation, the balance sometimes shifts towards either the model predetermination or resistance to change. The former is realized in phenomena such as stardom and cult movies; the latter, antisymmetry, turns polemical, so that the model is imposed on a recalcitrant Me in inimical intention.

This range, in a Pragmaticist view, corresponds only to the amount of corrective in determining a subject. Logically, the type of corrective matters more. If a subject lets itself be determined by brute fact, then it is subject to a 'method of authority.' However, public roles of 'realized selves' offer little to that type of imagination. Dictates of fashion or 'political correctness' are as close as they can get. Campaigns, especially at their zenith, pressurize much more openly than in a Noelle-Neumann 'spiral of silence.' If the corrective impact on subjects, instead, is a pure generality, then this corresponds to the metaphysical *a priori* method of making ideas clear. Fanaticism, sheer patriotism, as definitions of one's self, are certainly public identities that time and again can be observed 'in the wild.' This is ridiculed in the final scenes of *Wag the Dog* – here, explicitly as a PR product.

A subject correlate for the 'method of science,' Peirce's desirable ideal, would certainly fit, but its existence is doubtful here. There is an inkling of this method in Habermas's Ideal Speech Situation. Does this scientific subjectivity stand a chance of occurring in the public sphere? Habermas has already sacrificed it to the system's constraints on mass media. One might concur, for in this domain it is precisely a corrective for a teleology of truth that is completely lacking. In Peirce's synechistic metaphysic this would correspond to 'the agapastic theory of evolution' developed in 'Evolutionary Love' (CP 6.295). The predetermination of purpose and goal in public opinion arrives in the theatrical way (*tamquam deus ex machina*, respectively θεολογεῖον), as a social consensus or bourgeois ideology. The public subject, therefore, is essentially eristic: only being right matters *per fas et nefas* (as Schopenhauer writes).

Legitimization being the idea behind the metatext I of power, competence, the can-do, must correspond to expected performance. We have already identified a conflict in principle between public opinion and the other divine mandate. In this primordial scandal, public opinion subjected the ecclesial (§5.7). Once metatext I has established sanction and destination firmly, the process can proceed to self-realization, the idea of the subject in metatext II. For public opinion, ministries are identities of power; for the Church, functional identities ('*munera*,' ministries and magisteries) are gifts of the Holy Spirit (see §5.7). Since media apply their public meaning universally, an ecclesial identity is also treated with their means – that is, as a text function with only certain producible meaning positions. Due to the Church's claim, a conflict potential arises between two meaning products of diverse origins, but with an identical object. Ministry$_C$ (service) and ministry$_P$ (power), share hardly any common material content except for the term; but each side might think of targeting with its own term the content of the other as well. With the power-metatext, self-realization also penetrates everywhere through the media of public opinion, and also succeeds in affecting internal ecclesial discourses.

The second metatext fits into the mythological universe of the θέατρον. In the mimetic conflict framework, according to René Girard, it connects intimately with the power-founding myth. He describes this as the myth of romanticism, of the complete feasibility of my happiness, which, therefore, creates also the responsibility for my total happiness.

We have seen how subject competence as an idea involves a real subject's transformation towards a model or ideal goal. As with legitimization, the question of principle arises: Why is an identity not good enough as it is? Why must an 'I' change, why is it still to be realized? What happened that my situation is not permitted to remain as it is? Why am I forced to think of myself in the comparative, to become happier, richer, more 'realized' than I am? With which better self must the real self be compared? Either one goes the way of Mead and sees the genesis of identity as an increase in generality, until the singular I becomes the social Self,[30] or theorizing is done in Girard's (ultimately probably psychoanalytic) style. A Pragmaticist approach can cope better with an increase in generality when identities develop, because this teleology is built into cognitive behaviour and thus into the sign process.

The point of metatexts is not so much their logic, pragmatic, or semiotic, but the presupposed fact that the non-logical constraint of public opinion imposes this teleology. Various discourses are derived from the identity metatext – for instance, cliché feminism, as much as cliché 'dropout' narratives, are unthinkable without the feasibility of realizing one's happiness. If my interiority were not mobile, I could not think of comparative happiness (and of me as the less happy). At the same time, we pay this price: we must take literally the 'comparative,' referring constantly to the other. This comparison robs us of our autarky.

Which is the fitting role in the Θέατρον model for this second metatext? The romanticist myth is not as dependent on a classical role as is public opinion on the κορυφαῖος for its legitimization of power. Nevertheless, it also constructs meaning by means of a role. In a mimetic conflict, this role would inevitably be the beloved other, from whose fascination originates the comparative with the proper I (cf. also Thompson 2004). How does the comparative feedback with one's own Self occur in the typical *vis-à-vis* of the spectators in the θέατρον framework? Spectators, as we have seen, are a necessary part of the Dionysian ritual, a meaning construction around a quasi-divine knowledge of the whole, manifest as pragmatic goal. The relationship of this to the modern mass media of public opinion accounts for the semiotic fact that this teleology cannot logically be strictly justified. When we approach identity in pragmatic terms, one cognitive type or identity corresponds to each of the four pragmatic methods. If the metaphysical *a priori* method (Peirce, CP 5.381–3) were realized in the θέατρον, identity could at best be an 'aesthetic'[31] one (in the sense of an arbitrarily taste-based holding of something).

The theatrical identity formation is not foreign to contemporary media reality. A quite important creation of the media industry is the star system. We are not interested here in the historical question so much as in the economic factors that motivated the Hollywood studios to invent this system. A more interesting question is this: Why can there be stars (celebrities,[32] glamour ...) in the first place? The industrial reality at play here is the production of a machine; indeed, Gamson likens the process to the cross-breeding of vacuum cleaner and sausage machine. Gamson (1994, 15): 'It sucks people in – it processes them uniformly – it ships them briskly along a mechanical assembly line – and it pops them out at the other end, stuffed tight into a shiny casing stamped "U.S. Celebrity."' Nowadays, this applies not only to personalities but also to companies which construe their own prominence by means of media (Rindova, Pollock, and Hayward 2006). Turner describes the enormous industrial effort behind the construction of celebrities (2004). It is not so much that stars were needed to promote the film products of Hollywood studios,[33] for cinema *in se* could have thrived just as well with completely unheralded actors, as Robert Bresson, Éric Rohmer, and the Dogma group have proven.

What exactly is taking place in stardom, then, and why is it possible? Though Gamson writes expansively on the 'celebrity text,' he does not account for the functioning mode of the text itself, but merely for the history and strategies of the enormous studio PR machine. This is, however, an especially visible case of the 'role of happiness' as media construct. According to Turner (2004), its causes are neither the stars and their happy lives, nor the greed of the consuming audience, with whom idols share their power.[34] On the contrary, the entire cause lies in the relation between the two, with the stars becoming the identity models for the real spectators. It is not so interesting how real human beings with grown identities turn into the product 'star,' as Dyer (1986, 5ff) describes in great detail in his examination of three stars (Robinson, Monroe, Garland). What is the condition of the possibility of stardom? At the constitutive act, the 'star-for,' in exercising a goal or purpose predetermination of public competence, identity of being a public person, this question becomes virulent. Dyer (1986, 9): 'Stars articulate these ideas of personhood, in large measure shoring up the notion of the individual but also at times registering the doubts and anxieties attendant on it. In part, the fact that the star is not just a screen image but a flesh and blood person is liable to work to express the notion of the individual.' The genesis of the star persona and the unmasking of its character as an industrial product bring us ask us further: How can it happen that this sparks over into the modelling of public roles? Weiskel (2005) offers an explanation for the cognate effect of the public role of the American politician and how it developed into an instrument of distraction by means of the star system. But why should this not obtain for all other roles as well, for the sole reason that they are public – that is, that their privacy is not accepted by public opinion.

Public opinion is theatrical in the original sense of the term: the spectator-I opines something on the action of an alter ego and in this way becomes the spectator-self. This is what Aristotle's *Poetics* means with its κάθαρσις through ἐλεός καὶ φόβος in pathetic identification with the actors.[35] Through this opining, which is necessarily reflexive, spectators gain a general opinion about themselves. Because the reflexive cognitive behaviour is oriented towards the model (on the stage), and not towards its own acting, it is opinion and not cognition. It is true generality gained from the sanctioning judgment. What cultural studies describes in the rituals of 'fandom,' its classes, its identificatory modes of behaviour – down to the killing of the idol (Gamson 1994, 129–85; Hills 2002, 2004) – is precisely the social behaviour whose possibility is explained here in pragmatic terms. The idea that fandom is a quasi-religious or narrative-performative ritual is often acknowledged in cultural studies (Hills 2002, 158ff). The entertainment industry itself understands that it has produced 'cult movies' (after *Casablanca* the canonical cult movie *per se* was *The Rocky Horror Picture Show*) and 'cult television' (*The X-Files, Star Trek, Doctor Who, Buffy the Vampire Slayer*) – indeed, it tries to replicate the cult status through sequels and so on.

With stars, the positive side is only half the model effect. From a mimetic conflict perspective, enmity and aggression are the downside when stars enable identification, suggesting hope, through an object of imitation. Stars and demons as products are identical in the fascinated or horrified reflexive judgment of the spectator. Not only stars, but also dictators (from Alexander the Great to Saddam Hussein and Osama bin Laden), must be 'made' by means of congruent meaning effects. A dictator (examples would be consummate media artists such as Stalin and Hitler) first has to construct himself as an object of admiration and of power; this, as we know, is then followed by a secular 'personality cult.' Only after a successful construction can the condemnation of 'all' axe him. (The Roman Senate used to 'erase' unloved deceased emperors by deleting and voiding all traces of them in laws, architecture, and so on; this was referred to as the *damnatio memoriae*.) This always presupposes the previous functioning of an admiration text. Similarly, condemnation resulting from reflexive opining on a model is not specifically the result of cognitive achievement based on one's own experience. In that sense it is very different from the negative self-assurance in contrite self-reflection of one's own life experience or one's experience with others, as in St Augustine's *Confessiones*.

Both metatexts are undoubtedly visible in mass media. We need only investigate what exists exclusively as the manifestation of public opinion in media – that is, how spectacularly, in the political sphere, power is legitimized and delegitimized. Corresponding to this, we have identified two exemplary media genres: investigative journalism and media scandals. In the sphere of entertainment, intrinsically attendant on the political, there exist various cult genres with stars and fans. The intrinsic connection between the two is perhaps nowhere clearer than in scandal. All agree in scandal, despite all the product differentiation in marketing, despite differentiation into serious and scandal press, into information and entertainment, and so on. Scandal, then, seems to be the quintessence of public opinion.

6.4 Deduction of Classes of Scandal

Not everything is called a scandal that is a scandal. Nor is it by being called a scandal in the first place that something becomes a scandal. A scandal is a meaning type generated by public opinion as a necessary by-product. The teleological knowledge of a goal constitutes the core, but only the by-product justifies it (albeit by imposition, not by argumentation). Scandal being more a logic than an object, anything can be scandalized. With the ubiquity of scandal (sex scandal, financial scandal, political scandal, etc., and any combination thereof) in industrial production, it is not reasonable to classify scandals according to content. Lull and Hinerman with their inventorial 'typology of media scandals' (Lull and Hinerman 1997, 19ff) share with Thompson (2000) a focus on diverse loci of scandalization. Contrary to that approach, we will not attempt here to subject the effectively produced media scandal events to a taxonomy of their material content. It is much more interesting to examine how scandalicity appropriates any object you want. A consideration of the logic, the quasi-argumentative rhetoric, in all of these appropriations indicates that it is much more useful to classify scandals logically. Scandal is not arbitrary, but arbitrarily anything can become scandal. The close predetermination of a pragmatic goal circumscribes an area of the possibly scandalizable in the public sphere. We would not want to call this procedure a limitation (which would imply limits on someone's negative feelings in real social life), for in terms of public opinion, real-world indignation is no factor at all in scandal production. Scandal, therefore, exists as typology rather than as social behaviour. Approaching scandals through metatexts of public opining will allow us to classify them along the diverse dimensions of the nature of scandalicity itself. Regarding the possibilities for the production of religious media scandals, we have already briefly mentioned the principles. Below we take a more panoramic look at the entire spectrum of scandalous meaning.

Derived from the θέατρον model, we distinguish (1) the predetermination of a goal or destination, from (2) the action itself or performance, and from (3) competence, the characterization of the pragmatic subject. By this approach, we arrive at three theoretical classes of scandal. Goal predetermination or an imposed teleology is neither theoretically nor practically compelling. This adds, therefore, weight to scandal's source and not just to its goal. It characterizes the complete logical procedure as a predetermination of a goal. Purpose and goal also play an important cognitive role in Peirce's philosophy. He established this in more than one context. The sign, as the fundamental context, has the Interpretant in every single interpretation as the Third Correlate. Through the Interpretant, the sign process then continues from one sign to the next, and it does so with a constant, identical object. That this process is not directionless is something that every concrete sign owes to a 'goal-Interpretant' (in the sense of a *causa finalis* of interpretation). Peirce (CP 8.184): 'But we must also note that there is certainly a third kind of Interpretant, which I call the Final Interpretant, because it is that which would finally be decided to be the true interpretation if consideration of the matter were carried so far that an ultimate opinion were reached.' Public opinion has no centrally important cognitive goal. In lieu of a cognition (spontaneously) oriented towards a goal, however, the goal here is already determined, as if an ultimately true cognition had already been realized. Instead of the final cause, we have a final determination. This lends the source of that finality an effect on meaning.

Publicity has good reasons to differentiate the source quite strictly from the recipient. Press and readership would otherwise be identical, when journalistic practice must keep them sharply separate. Only scientific logic can assume an identity and make no further distinction between the researcher and the recipient (student), because here the logical constraint is universal. This holds at least for the ideal of science, which does not admit final authority.

By applying our θέατρον model of publicity, we arrive at the following classes of scandal in media.

6.4.1 Scandal of Destination

The first class is the destination scandal, corresponding to (1). In our thematic field of religious scandals, this class is semanticized in vocables such as 'usurpation,' 'minister by the grace of God,' 'responsible to nobody,' 'abuse of authority.' The destinator is the one who possesses the knowledge of the 'whole,' a transcendent instance transmitting this knowledge to the public (i.e., public opinion) as expressed by its chorus leaders.[36] The question is this: Can there be destination scandals at all? Where at this level is the sanctioning instance? It is difficult to scandalize destination; indeed, it would be impossible if the force guiding the process were a cognitive (logical) constraint. Here, however, it is merely an imposed teleology inseparably connected to a source. Now, behind this source can always be another source of causality, which in turn predetermines a more general teleology. 'More general' in this context can only mean that someone succeeds in hypotactically subordinating the lower teleology. This happens when institutions judge one another. Every institution has an overarching goal that is foundational to it. It follows that every other goal is a potential scandal if it can be subordinated to one's own goal.

Other than this, there can be no scandal proper around the destinator, for the entire meaning construction would collapse if such a scandalous occasion were not repaired at once. In such a case, the predetermination of the goal would inevitably fall flat – that is, we would not have a clue what this was all about, what the purpose of the text was, what determined as value the pragmatic goals of the represented. With missing goals, we would fall back into real life, where every person acts herself and for herself and where she has to find for herself what is worth desiring (what Schütz described as 'subjective' *vis-à-vis* the 'objective' sense).

Destination media scandals include these possible subforms: scandal of the source (e.g., a press scandal); and scandal at the receiving end (i.e., an audience scandal). Θεολογεῖον scandal: so we might call this class, which derives from the source. Every press scandal is a problem with the qualification of the destination instance's pragmatic competence. Should it turn out that there is no pragmatic competence to veridicality or to veridiction, to saying the truth, such a scandal could be set off. Examples of such scandals include the one surrounding Jayson Blair, the *New York Times* reporter who freely invented reports or plagiarized them from other newspapers (Hindman 2005); or the one that embroiled *USA Today* reporter (and Pulitzer nominee) Jack Kelley, who over the years published quite plastic inventions as observed facts (Smolkin 2006; Wyatt 2007).

Destination scandals are quite rare and can occur only under two conditions: (1) If it is a case of a 'repair mechanism,' where a media institution corrects itself or the news paradigm (Hindman 2005). By doing this, however, that institution reconfirms itself as a destination instance, as confirmed by most strategies on Hindman's list. (2) If it entails critique from outside, levelled in particular against 'partisanship,' lies, and so on. In theory, any appearance of 'self-interest' is deadly for the institution of the 'whole.' *But*, such a critique necessarily comes from another institution, which means that the accusation of self-interest can easily be turned against the critic. One such institution is, for instance, science, *in specie* also communication science. Another could be the Church taking the upper hand over public opinion (see §5.7).

A κοῖλον scandal, instead, originates from the other side (of the orchestra). Who is the recipient of the knowledge of the 'whole'? This knowledge is shared directly by those rallied around the Dionysus altar: the people κοῖλον or 'all,' the people's spokesperson χορός and κορυφαῖος. Here, only the imaginary alliance between the press and the readership takes effect, manifesting itself in the creative fiction of a 'public opinion' as 'that which all opine.'

Can this meaning position imply scandalization of the public, of public's opinion? That something like this happens is conceivable only for partial audiences, never for one's own – when the audience, for instance, of the *Big Brother* series, or of certain Reality TV shows, is qualified as 'primitive' or 'sensation-seeking,' or the audience of televangelist shows is qualified as 'bigots,' or similar. *Big Brother* has caused a major outcry, especially in the quality press, not only as a TV production, but also through accusations that it panders to dangerously indecorous and perverted audiences. While it doesn't happen often, audiences can scandalize, very much so. One might think this is impossible, since the audience instance is always encapsulated in the text. But it *becomes* possible provided that it represents a relation of '(inclusive) we' to 'you' (resp. 'them'). The proper audience in this way remains protected. Scandal means always other 'publics' than the readership directly involved in the act of reading. The right and proper (i.e., serious) audience may look down on the wrong one (the masses), but the audience in its entirety can never be scandalized as incompetent or mendacious.

In the religious area there exist many examples from these two classes of scandal. The primordial scandal remains the destination of the ecclesial ministry. In the context of public opinion, the sanctioning instance, an appeal to divine election is not permissible. For when this is done explicitly, the divinely elected–destinated subtracts from the destinator–publicity as instance of judgment. This kind of verdict on religious pragmatic subjects is frequent and almost inescapable.[37] For the ecclesial *magisterium*, in consequence of the negation of a divine mandate, it is most often a connotation of usurpation of authority that comes into play. This presents itself as shameless 'truth possession,' which is to be fought against, or as the 'last absolute monarchy,' 'non-enlightened despotism,' or similar. In the ultramontanist controversy, in the Prussian '*Kulturkampf*,' in the dogma of infallibility or the *Syllabus Errorum*, this primordial scandal has become historical. 'God not publicity' could be the catchword for this scandal, and even today it is construed around this mutual exclusivity. In this sense, when Boston's Cardinal Law claimed that he was exclusively responsible before God, he was interpreting an obligation to be responsible before the press only as a negation of the very basis of his ministry. Accordingly, his resistance was interpreted by his public opinion antagonists as a concealment attempt – that is, as a rejection of his duty of public responsibility.

In principle, religious mandates are evaluated negatively as scandal when they are seen as usurpation or as charlatanry (or similar semantics). 'Unmasked' religious actors, who are 'only' much too human, are a staple of literature and populate wide universes of the novelistic imagination. This applies also to narrative cinema. Interesting in this regard are disastrous failures of religious roles and problems of credibility with their pragmatic motivations. This is logically distinguishable from failures of religious pragmatic subjects (see below). Divine vocation that is not scandalized can be heroicized and turned positively into 'charisma.' Such events are felicitous PR, 'megahits.' They produce religious stars, gurus of the Rajneesh type, called 'Bhagwan' (i.e., God; and see in this context Jane Campion's deprogramming film *Holy Smoke*). Cases where religious actors subject themselves voluntarily to the destination and sanction instance are interesting. This would happen, of course, in the hope of a glorifying sanction. What began as stardom, though, can tip over into its opposite, as we have seen in televangelism.

6.4.2 Scandal of Action

Λογεῖον or stage scandals would be the term applied to scandal effects carried into the pragmatic goal itself – after its determination. Decisive here is the factual *vis-à-vis*, the opposition of a volitive relation, again distinguished into an object and a subject of the action. It concerns generally meaning alternatives for acting itself – that is, someone chooses to do something, already presupposing permission, obligation, force, and will to do this. This field concerns both competence and performance, ability and execution.

A ὑπόκριτης scandal is, then, the class of meaning when it is found in the actor's person – that is, when it concerns that actor's competence. A πρᾶξις scandal, by contrast, puts the scandal's emphasis on the performance, on the action itself, which is defined by its pragmatic object as goal or motivation. In the religious realm, a religious act can 'overturn' when it strives for a non-religious goal object. The great majority of recent pedophilia scandals, for instance, are a reversal of the pragmatic object: 'pastoral care' turns into 'predation.' The Boston priest Paul R. Shanley had enjoyed considerable fame for pastoral care – before his scandal. Under the headline 'Predator Priests,' the *Boston Globe* wrote: 'The Rev. Paul R. Shanley made his reputation as a Boston "street priest" in the 1960s and 70s – a crusader for runaways and drifters, drug addicts, and teenagers struggling with questions about their sexual identity. But those who turned to Shanley for comfort and guidance often found themselves in the clutches of a sexual predator.'[38] Similar to this is a Belgian scandal relating to a Rwandan nun who took part in slaughtering the other ethnic group. This engaged for some time the international press (in particular the Belgian press) on the occasion of criminal court proceedings relating to a law that allowed Belgian courts to try international crimes against humanity. This law, though, was heavily rewritten following American pressure, because after Abu Ghraib it threatened to implicate U.S. Army generals in crimes against humanity.

Religious subjects are turned into scandals in a corresponding procedure. These scandals generally relate to pragmatic competence rather than performance. Topics calling into question the competency of priestly behaviour were listed in the *Boston Globe* with exemplary clarity: 'Homosexuality and the church: My life as a gay priest. A former priest in the Boston Archdiocese speaks out about secrecy, scandal, and being gay in the church.'[39] Two more examples: 'Should celibacy be reconsidered?' 'The scourge of celibacy: By endowing priests with an aura of discipline and trust, the Catholic Church's policy on celibacy fosters pedophilia and facilitates coverups.'[40] When the performance of a religious subject matters for scandal, it mainly has to do with a more or less failed program of action. A bishop who has failed as a shepherd becomes the object of scandal after his flock deserts him ('statistically proven'; though incommensurate for causal cognition, here statistics are nevertheless useful for this purpose).

Not every 'scandal' is a scandal, however. False scandals are different in their meaning. Even a certain utilitarianism of scandal exists, for sometimes scandals become mere instruments. Thus, gossip columns in the scandal press sometimes serve as pillories for victims, not simply as stages for self-promotion. It is only a short step from this to criminality. This threshold seems to have been crossed recently: Jared Paul Stern, a *New York Post* gossip reporter (Love 2006), allegedly tried to extort money from the billionaire Ron Burkle by 'selling' his not-reporting of invented gossip (i.e., 'protection' from his inaccuracy). A much more serious chapter in scandal criminalization has been opened by the corruption of secret services trying to destroy the reputations of people who are hostile to the government. Here is not the place for a general conspiracy theory. In analytical terms, it is not helpful for an understanding of scandals to approach them through the key question of who stands to gain from them. This is part of the routine of political struggle; and one does not have to suspect scandals as invariably having an author with vested interests. This is oversimplifying the production of teleology. Furthermore, it cannot explain the surplus value of the scandalous, as described earlier. In political life, it is a cherished *topos* and crisis communication strategy to brand scandals as 'staged.' The point in this counterstrategy is to weaken the object of indignation as an immaterial assertion. Such accusations and strategies miss the point of scandal.

It cannot be denied, though, that the scandalous can be and has been produced intentionally (Love 2006). The secret services and political police in totalitarian regimes (and in not so totalitarian ones) even today produce, invent, find, or investigate compromising facts about their enemies. Here we see at least a scandal *threat* (in public opinion, or in government propaganda, for that matter). Not surprisingly, this has led to a general distrust of any representation, not only negative ones (which is again an *e contrario* proof of how indispensible the divine replica of 'all' is in a scandal production). Regarding Church protagonists, it is known that they often end up in sights of totalitarian regimes. There have always been attempts to destroy the reputations of those who are better known in the public. Usually, the tactic of choice has been not to bring them into conflict with the law, but to damage their honour. The simplest methods have consisted in documenting something indecent. In Communist Czechoslovakia, priests and bishops were forced to get drunk and then filmed or photographed. In Nazi Germany, an enemy of the state, Fr Rupert Mayer, was accosted by a naked woman and a group of Gestapo photographers. There are countless variations of drunkenness and nakedness as destroyers of reputation, and all sorts of other compromising human constellations. This, too, is the power of primary definers, or of storytellers, once they own the teleology, which they can then fit to any fact they like.

7 The Course of the Scandal Pro-Gram

The arsenal of instruments, as discussed above, is really nothing but a pro-gram, 'pre-written.' We now turn to the actual course of the programmed, once it has been pre-scribed, prepared, and readied for use. All depends on the event. When we start the event, we are also setting its middle and its end: With this rule, Aristotle's *Poetics* raises an issue that is more than temporal sequence. The beginning of the end is an operator of (*post hoc ergo proper hoc*) logic as much as the turning point towards the end, and the recognition of achievement of the purpose. After a brief reflection on old and new semiotic methods, we settle on a descriptive methodology that does not suppress public meaning production as it is typically practised. In section 2 we analyse the event creation of probably the most famous media scandal story in recent history. This will involve showing how disparate facts were transformed into a single new story, bearing in mind that these 'facts' themselves consisted of various stories of diverse origin. We will describe this narrative achievement as a repositioning of historical, social personalities in (narrative) roles (section 3). Scandalicity, however, can also arise from a different pro-gram, one that is entirely tributary to religious behaviour and its pragmatic logic. This not-told scandal can be reconstructed by examining its proto-stories (see section 4). In the chapter's final section we take up what seems to be the central preoccupation of communications debate: the story and the real. We frame this as an exploration of two recognized news media practices: advocative journalism and satire. We end this chapter by reflecting on how various authorities 'tell' the story of a reality.

7.1 Media Scandal Methods

Empirical research, too, concerns itself with the field (i.e., scandal) we are entering now. While descriptions of that media phenomenon are within the customary limits of such research, the rules of the behaviour being researched are *outside* it. In ethnographic and statistical descriptions, these rules come to the fore as 'theory' of the data, or at least as native general rules for the behaviour being examined. A semiotic-pragmatic method would never deny that rules are embedded in behaviour (*logica utens*); however, it grasps those rules explicitly in terms of the sign. This theoretical advantage was discussed earlier; now it will bear fruit methodologically.

Especially when we deal with social realities as complex as religion and public opinion, it is practically impossible to grasp behaviour directly without the mediation of signs. A strict 'sociology of variables'[1] is misguided. The instruments developed above (θέατρον, metatexts) are thus part of the 'data.' When in his *Grand Logic* (1893) Peirce writes that 'the truth is there are no data' (CP 7.465), he means that what are commonly thought of as data are actually (possibly false) inferences from data. The inference, therefore, is the data material. In the present case, public opinion is the result of logical inference that applies, in every observation of facts, general laws. Here, however, these laws are of a special kind: not subject to any correction and predetermined (v. *supra*). Thus, these laws construct no causalities *ab ovo*, as is sometimes the temptation when social science methods are applied to historical or generally temporal data – including narrative texts – as survival analysis (Büthe 2002; Doreian 2001).

When illustrating the methodological difference, one might cite Hoover's elaborate survey of how religion is treated in American news (1998). Hoover found what we might well have expected – that the news approach leads to a general incomprehension of religion. The Iranian Revolution, American fundamentalism (David Koresh in Waco, Jim Jones in Guyana), Pope John Paul II, and so on all encounter a public discourse that is firm in its axiomatic belief that religion is gradually declining. As a result, journalists are generally helpless when they encounter religious phenomena. When we reflect on the methods and the preconditions of Hoover's and similar research, though, a different helplessness becomes visible. As usual, it is well hidden within hypotheses and in research questions that operationalize unnamed theories. How does religion fit news? The answer to that question was well expressed by Robert Darnton, who recast rather cleverly the *New York Times*'s motto 'All the news that's fit to print' into 'All the news that fit we print'[2] (Hoover 1998, 9). What, though, does 'fit' mean in this context, and how is fitness construed? Empirical perspectives cannot ask how religion can ever be fit for the arena of public opinion. Even if publicity were nothing but facts (which of course is not the case), what is religion as pure fact? We raised this question earlier in the context of investigative journalism. Our historically and culturally contingent answer was developed with the two metatexts.

Journalistic practice pivots around two separate points: first, that 'something' is 'event' and must be treated narratively (§7.2); and second, that 'something' is also a 'fact.' Yet these two points require entirely different linguistic-pragmatic treatments (§7.5). In practice, they are mixed – indeed, they amplify each other. The becoming-news of an event as a narrative necessity, as its narrability, presupposes a transformation;[3] a fact seems to presuppose merely a reference to something exterior. Actually, a fact is preceded by a qualitative determination of what-ness. It is a fact that everything can become news; but by becoming news, it loses its original meaning and a new meaning is imposed. Ritual lamentations[4] about too little, too uncomprehending, too demeaning news about religion (as documented by Hoover) ignore the peculiarities and mechanisms of meaning production in public opinion.

This peculiarity might appear in the semiotic-pragmatic method as deductive reasoning, but semiotic is also an empirical method. In the full sense of 'experience,' however, it is more than the empirical method, as we know from our discussion of sociological 'epistemologies.' It is, furthermore, a method that takes time itself seriously, at its very root. It is not merely a matter of, say, religious scandals as media fact but (better) of the scandal in its course. In surveying religion as fact in news, Hoover's findings are concerned more with journalists' intentions than with what they actually achieved. But the subjective intentions of authors or editors (including their self-glorification) are not relevant in explaining the resulting product. Sometimes they are even contraindicative.[5]

Taking time seriously has profound methodological consequences for our understanding of scandals. It would be reductive to treat scandals as facts that exist or not, or as after-the-facts of facts that 'caused scandal.' It would be more apposite to say that 'it came to a scandal,' because that would at least imply a rudimentary understanding of a scandal's development. Some researchers have concerned themselves with the genesis of scandal, from prenatal to post-mortem life (Burkhardt 2006; Jiménez 2004; Thompson 2000). This genetic aspect can be addressed in various ways. One possible approach would be 'archaeological' in Foucault's sense: a mere series of 'archival' findings. A philosopher's strong configurative effort from outside is required in order to join the visible with an episteme. But this historiographical method is seldom applied radically, especially to media (Schilling 2003). Another theoretical possibility is historiographical in the traditional sense. When researchers 'let the facts speak for themselves,' a sort of (weak) law of history often results. This breaks down a scandal's development into phases that, while predictable, are not 'regular' in the strict sense. Most histories of the media are cast in this broad, mainstream sense. Our semiotic-pragmatic approach goes further than this, in that it does not pretend that the cognitive object is a collection of chance events with a weak law holding them together. Scandal is clearly a production rule of meaning. This cannot be grasped simply through historiographical methods.[6] Our primary approach to the object leads through the sign – not through the intentions that underlie its production, and not through reflections about its consumption. Signs are more objective (i.e., more communicable) than descriptions of subjectivities, which interest us marginally, at most, in the interpretation of signs. It should now be clear that the sign of scandal is a culturally contingent but strong rule. This allows us to take the media scandal as the star discipline of (investigative) journalistic practice (which enshrines the rule). From there, the real events literally make sense of what resulted in a scandal by taking their course in real time. This leads us to a sort of 'rhetorical' analysis of the argumentation logic in temporal procedure – one that contrasts with a numerically quantified content analysis, but also with a semantic one in the sense of Franzosi (1995, 2004).

7.2 Event: How Destination in the Shanley Story Created the Scandal

What the *Washington Post*'s Watergate coverage was to the U.S. presidency, the *Boston Globe* of the CSA scandals has been to the Catholic Church ('even Napoleon had his Watergate,' Yogi Berra once remarked). There had been earlier reports relating to CSA,[7] but they had not swamped the institution of the Church (Cannon 2002a). People, Cannon speculated, first had to wrap their heads around such topics through, for best example, the Clinton–Lewinsky scandal.

The Big Bang of this scandal was Sacha Pfeiffer's (2002) story in the *Boston Globe* ('Famed "Street Priest" Preyed upon Boys' A21 1/31/2002). This 2,049-word story was the igniting spark. In retrospect, it was also prototypical and exemplary, in that it contained the entire teleological predetermination of narrative logic – both the author's and the team's. It manifested *in nuce* the argumentation pattern of other stories – indeed, of the entire scandal. The present aim is not to reconstruct historically the reported events – a non-juridical finding and evaluation of facts. Our sole task at hand is to reconstruct and explain how media produce meaning.

With regard to the events themselves, briefly: On 7 February 2005 the central figure in this story, Paul Shanley, was convicted in a court of first instance, which in 2010 the Supreme Court of Massachusetts confirmed.[8] He was sentenced to twelve to fifteen years in the state prison. The charge for which he was convicted was the double rape of a young boy. Yet the accuser (Paul Busa), who even as an adult requested anonymity, had recovered his memory of these events only when he was twenty, a decade after the incidents of which he accused Shanley, through a questionable therapeutic method that is no longer widely practised: 'repressed memory recovery.'[9] It is interesting to note that all four accusers (there were four at the beginning of the trial) had recovered their memory only after reading the *Globe* story, which seems to have caused this recovery – so it emerged during court questioning. Shanley is an ideal object of inquiry, as the criminal facts have been established by a court.[10] The charges he faced, though, were clearly not those leading to the media scandal. None of the four victims from Pfeiffer's initial story were able to sustain their accusations during the criminal trial.[11] At any rate, beyond doubt the extraordinary moral abjection has been – *nemine contradicente* – recognized. The Vatican has sanctioned it by forcibly dismissing Shanley from the clerical state (canon 290f, *Codex Iuris Canonici*, 'laicization' or defrocking). This allows us to treat all questions of facts, ecclesiastic discipline, and morality as settled, in order to focus on the the scandal *in se*.

Logical predetermination being its foremost operation, the initial story also exemplifies the entire range of ambivalence of the surplus value of scandal and, besides, its ambivalent effects.

Very much in keeping with its logical underpinnings, this famous story begins as the story of a fallen (unmasked) hero, a traitor figure. It then turns into a 'Gothic' narrative (Ingebretsen 2004).[12] This logic proves to be decisive for some of the following pillars of its meaning construction:

Construction of the ideal. Upstream of narration, Pfeiffer's story was clearly concerned with an 'important social ideal' – what we call destination. Downstream, this ideal was then used to construct narratively the ideal aim and the purpose of action in the story, for only after a strong ideal has been established can there then be a clear-cut verdict. Precisely this ideal proved to be quite ambivalent in the present case, in that Shanley had been revered for decades for precisely this behaviour – under a different semantic. The more the destination in ideals must be presupposed in metatexts without any need for explicit retelling, the more difficult it is to accomplish polarity change in an ideal.

The delicate operation that is *polarity change*. For scandalicity to function, ideals must be negatively polarized that otherwise would have been valued positively by public opinion. In the case at hand, the patent criminalization of homosexuality entered into a strong contrast with defending homosexuality. This reversal of values had penetrated Shanley's biography: his positive CV[13] states: 'He openly questioned church teachings, particularly its condemnation of homosexuality ... He created a "ministry to alienated youth" for ... teenagers struggling with their sexual identity.' Now, how does one climb down from such a high pedestal? In the course of the story – in his *criminal* CV – a 'quite normal' homosexual chat-up was reported with a twenty-year-old adult, Arthur Austin. Since this as such could not be incriminated, it became an 'abuse of authority,' changing the frame from a metatext of identity to one of power legitimization. After this change, it became natural that authority of office should become the focus of accusation (and not a moral issue). That Shanley openly attacked church teaching was attributed positively to the pragmatic subject. Yet the same attribute was the chief accusation against bishops for not having taken drastic measures in a timely manner (i.e., measures against insubordination, what exactly was extolled before, following the metatext schema). In addition, in the schema of the other metatext, they should have taken drastic measures against the self-realization of certain unpriestly behavioural liberties. This story mentioned only faintly (though in the course of the scandal it would become much clearer[14]) what exactly he 'openly questioned.' The focus here was turned on public speeches (admirable for some, scandalous for others) that Shanley gave at public forums of the 'Boston/Boise Committee,' out of which a pressure group was formed (in which Shanley did not participate, contrary to widely diffused reports) called NAMbLA (North American Man/boy Love Association).[15] The patron of the New York chapter of NAMbLA, by the way, was Horatio Alger, a pastor and renowned pulp fiction author, coiner of the 'American Dream' but also a notorious pederast – with boys in his own congregation.[16]

Pfeiffer's deheroizing, scandalizing manoeuvre was possible only because of the plausibility of both metatexts, which could be presupposed as known. The result was a coarse, low-resolution picture of fine-grained, humanly complex interactions. This coarsening, these crude generalizations, may well have been intentional – that is, deliberate signs and desired effects of a 'client-oriented' press. As 'explanation,' all of this can be subsumed under the journalistic task of simplifying complex reality. Following our θέατρον model, this is the inevitable consequence of predetermining a single teleology. The Shanley media scandal, however, was not the result of direct experience or first-person 'participant observation.' The journalistic narration here built on other narrations as sources. These sources are now, by and large, accessible electronically, thereby allowing us to reconstruct the editorial effort. When we do so, we find that various antecedent narrations, the proper and sole sources, yield a picture that is remarkably more complex than the journalistic one, which is strongly simplistic and reductive. The principal sources for the news stories were as follows: (1) 'stories' of various kinds in the personnel file of the Archdiocese; (2) personal injury lawyers and their rhetorical case building as *narratio probabilis; and* (3) the witness stories, some of them included in (2), that lawyers folded into their own stories. Over and above the main sources, there are vestiges of historical sources, a result of the PR of the gay scene of the 1960s and 1970s. All of these alien narrative teleologies were to be recast in a journalistic teleology of its own metatexts.

A plethora of Shanley stories, rich in nuances and aspects, had to become a single coherent one. 'Explanation' has always been a journalist's task, and the chief explanatory force is construed through a single coherent story. The one coarse 'authority' relation is like a gavel under which the entire ambivalent, complicated relation becomes crystal clear. Shanley's personnel files, for instance, show traces of considerable tensions among Church officials over pastoral care for young people about to redefine their identities, the 'gay and bisexual communities.' If this were a relation of authoritarian power, ecclesial moral authority would confront repentant humiliation. Evidently, this is the reference frame of Pfeiffer's metatextual schemata, added to which is the abuse of such authority (e.g., in Arthur Austin's victimization tale). This authority infests these schemata so thoroughly that the Bishops' use of authoritarian power was more than plausible. That they failed to use it against priests like Shanley was then held against them; that they covered up such failures amounted to recognition of fault.

Production of scandal is an achievement in itself. In order to comprehend it in this paradigmatic case, we need only look to Shanley's own discourses and their apologetic aims. Unsurprisingly, Shanley saw his relations totally differently[17] – at a time, moreover, when he did not need to defend himself. He saw himself mainly in the 'troubled youth ministry,' the 'sexual minorities ministry,' yet at the same time he did not deny or apologize for his sexual contacts (be they gay or straight) or for what others might call 'seductions.' In such discourses, the reference frame is complex. Pastoral motives surface just as clearly – and outspokenly – as gay self-realization discourses; but this need not interest us further in our context. Of greater interest is that Shanley did not portray himself in black and white, as if to display a reverse picture of the scandal discourse. He saw himself neither as hero nor as scoundrel, but *con sfumature*. After the defensive discourses (which Wypijewski [2004] brings to light from his family, his circle of friends, and his own documents), he is 'sorry beyond telling for the wrongs of my life and for the sorrow and anguish of which I have been the occasion. How I envy those who say in their declining years: "if I had it to do over I would not do anything differently." For me it is the opposite: I would do many things differently. For one, I would never have become a priest and tried to wrestle with mandatory celibacy and the myriad consequences of that folly. But who knew?' He then offers a tale-telling literary interpretation of his life. 'My thoughts run to that beautiful whiskey priest of Graham Greene's novel, the last one left in Mexico, underground, no good, yet he cannot leave' (Wypijewski 2004). Ironically, Wypijewski engages herself in a discourse about Shanley that is entirely in keeping with the 'objectivity' criterion 'balance.'

Another discourse is the court reconstruction of Shanley's actions (with an indictment of 'rape'). Yet not even here was the abuse of professional authority or power a central consideration. In contrast, what Pfeiffer suggests in her public opinion tribunal as her own indictment, never constituted an element of a civil or criminal offence, nor was it tabled as such by the prosecution. The judiciary process, of course, also construes 'stories' with perpetrator, victim, motives, and so on, but with rigorous rules relating to the exclusion and inclusion of causalities. This construction is nowadays so much regulated that it is not truly comparable with other narrativities.

These contrasts demonstrate the achievement of Pfeiffer's scandal construction. In the name of public opinion, her foremost contribution consisted of one decisive element: supposing moral motivation. Through this textual construal she succeeded in streamlining for her own power metatext all those other component narratives with their own heterogeneous respective teleologies. Construing 'wicked motives' ('preying' instead of 'praying'), however, is not as easy as it might seem. Sources have their own narrative aims, which diverge widely. This is aggravated by the fact that those aims must then be attributed to different metatexts. In this story, there was the danger of a collision of two metatexts: 'abused power' and homosexual 'self-realization.' The latter was part of the PR of not just the 'movement,' but specifically of NAMbLA, which was not the least infamous of Shanley's public appearances. Here the perennial journalistic dilemma with sources came to the fore with a vengeance, only this time it was not a problem of access so much as one of ideology. Sources do indeed have their own interests, and when they contact the press, those interests can be decisive. Pfeiffer's sources exhibited irreconcilable and ideologically determined conflicts of interest. Her remedy for this was an ideology of her own, as expressed in the metatexts.

Shanley flaunted his apparently frequent homosexual contacts with youths and young adults. How did the media scandal succeed in seeing these encounters precisely not as (an ideology of) self-realization but as (the ideology of) power abuse? Shanley saw it as his mission to the 'gay and bisexual communities' precisely not to bring peccants to conversion from a peccaminous conduct but to liberate them. This posed an ideo-logical dilemma for the *Globe*. On the one hand, the newspaper perceived this as a matter of conflict with the Church hierarchy, and it explicitly praised Shanley for his fight against the oppressive power of bishops. In this construction, the homosexual discourse would fall on the side of the metatext of identity and self-realization. On the other hand, Pfeiffer could not simultaneously acknowledge the content and cause of this fight against hierarchy – a delicate manoeuvre. The contentious content was precisely 'man-boy love,' a self-realization treated here as abuse of authority, and legally as child abuse.

This dilemma could give rise to speculation on the intrinsic incongruence of social values, either as (homosexual) self-realization or as (authoritarian) power, but this would be to indulge in normative historiography. We are concerned here with the immediately more important and delicate narrative function, which is by the same token a function for the functioning of scandal. Logically, then, it is incompatible when one and the same thing is represented as both a positive value and a negative one. In such circumstances, metatexts become helpful because they function without argumentative justification. Pfeiffer's story accomplished this feat of changing value polarization rather masterfully[18] by confirming the positive value of liberty in (homosexual, antiauthoritarian) self-realization in the Eulogium, and then, however, by negatively recontextualizing it as power metatext. Except that in this latter context, the object was the abuse of professional authority: 'Shanley used his power and authority to prey on those who came to him for guidance and support.'

A single person cannot generate a scandal, unless as *pars pro toto*. Petronius, *Satyricon* XLV, gave this a classical expression: 'Sed qui asinum non potest, stratum caedit' ('he who cannot beat the donkey, beats the saddle'). It is not enough to sanction a lone villain. Scandal only occurs if the individual stands for a greater and more general actor. Had Shanley been a lone villain, public opinion would have taken notice of him at best as a confessing hedonist, at worst as a psychopath. That would have been enough to make a monster of him, the conviction of whom would have been a public spectacle. Yet this is some other genre; it is not scandal. Only through a sort of corporate identity does a villain acquire interest for scandal production. Through the villain – albeit by way of unusually strained or broken relations with, and obedience to, his superiors – the entire institution is dragged into scandal.

Accomplishing this is not terribly complicated, which brings us to the law of series. So, further cases are presented as 'further cases' (of a generality), the implication being that there must be a rule or regularity in play. The same could be done for parents, educators, and psychotherapists, but here the respectively next cases are not further cases – rather, they belong to the white noise, to detrital 'social sediment.' The latter, however, appears already to be quite high in the United States.[19] So, if this had not successfully become a problem of 'the priests' – and *per extensionem* of the institution of the Church – then public opinion would have had no reason to take notice and to deal with it in its own way. Nothing can be done against social sediment, and there is no point in getting worked up about it against anybody. Public opinion treats these constant states, if at all, with the 'monster' schema: constant crime, endemic corruption, and so on. Meantime, whoever succeeds in establishing a series, and then in reducing that series to a single cause, can put into full effect judgment, which is the function mode of public opinion. Here can be applied the truistic equivalent of Leibniz's law of sufficient causality: everything has a cause, especially if it is a series, and especially if in a regulated institution, and especially where the cause must be in the rule and in those who wield that rule.

Pfeiffer's genuine achievement in the narrative construction of the media scandal cannot be appreciated unless her representation of events can be shown to be more than merely referred sources. The law firm of the first four accusers certainly was a source, and that firm's vested interest was in extracting huge compensation from the Church as the responsible institution (it is likely that a mere civil case would not have been so potentially lucrative as a civil case linked to a criminal one). With Pfeiffer, however, the logic of public opinion came into effect and transformed the compensation logic of the source stories at its origin. On the source side, for example, the lawyers tried to thoroughly exploit Shanley's participation in NAMbLA, in the deposition of the former Boston auxiliary bishop, Daily. They tried to prove negligent supervision and management control according to the Church's own management criteria.[20] Yet the result of this deposition – a morally objectionable logic of self-realization and lack of oversight – was not made use of by the *Boston Globe* but its contrary was even explicitly affirmed. It did, indeed, postulate a rather strict behavioural control of subordinate priests through the bishop. The misdemeanour of the one could thus become the failure of the other. But how difficult it is in practice for a bishop to forbid or command or prevent something in or by his priests can be ascertained from the opposite accusation levelled against bishops (Henningsen 2004). According to this blame, the 'fast track' procedures of pure administrative measures and roadblocks practised against suspects – in reaction to the massive media scandal – did not respect fundamental canonical rights and rules of due process. They did, however, achieve almost direct control that amounted to an employer–employee relationship. Such coercive powers and other means are presupposed when mass media make the ordinary bishop – or the Pope in the last instance – responsible for the abuses of individual priests. Over and above the chain-of-command responsibility, indirectly an entire culture is pilloried: celibacy, seminaries, and so forth.

Conflicts of principle between source and journalistic ideology were not fought out in this case and were mere speculation; so a detailed textual analysis of the journalistic final product is more instructive than a historical-critical analysis. This treats the story text as a whole and investigates its coherence and construction principles, as if it were an original production of creative meaning. Many have repeatedly emphasized the narrative achievement of journalism (*v. supra*). This does not mean (and this is something that has been misunderstood repeatedly) that news stories are fictions, self-contained narrative universes. It is merely that a proper narrative causality needs to be construed. This logic concerns us next.

7.3 The Role Structure of the Shanley Story

For an overview of the complicated functional relationship, we need to assemble the roles the text provides and then analyse their argumentative functions. The purpose is not simply to catalogue all appearing actors; rather, it is discursive order. How, then, are we to 'argue through' the ordering of actors?

Only a handful of methods in communication sciences take cognizance of discursive argumentation. The instruments of discourse analysis, for example, could be put to use. Beyond the strictly quantitative, even content analysis takes a perspective similar to, or in the direction of, textual logic. However, each of these and similar methods come with strongly heterogeneous theoretical presuppositions, so it is inadvisable to raid the warehouse of methods without discussing epistemology. The narrative structure in this scandal story, deducible from our θέατρον model, is polemical and not contractual (which it generally is in most genres of journalistic practice). This means that the structure is built around a pragmatic subject and its antisubject. With merely one subject, the narrative structure would be similar to a contract. These kinds of literary structures are used in elaborate coming-of-age novels, but also in banal stereotypical homosexual coming-out stories (which will remain in the thematic realm of our story at hand). Journalistic stories could construct the same topic narratively, also 'without an antagonist'; however – for reasons just mentioned – such stories are typically presented 'with an opponent.' Yet before a polemic can develop, its purpose must be predetermined as aim within the text. With all of this in mind, in Pfeiffer's scandal story, the following actors and functional roles appear:

Metatext level. The recipient of the predetermination of purpose is a purely functional role originating in enunciation itself. Is such a role demonstrable at all, considering that it lies *per definitionem* outside the text? Once we extend the linguistic concept of enunciation marks[21] to the news story's telling, vestiges of its enunciation are also retrievable in the told. In our story at hand, the rationale of enunciation, the reason why news must / ought to / can be told at all, communicates itself, as it were, to the reporter Sacha Pfeiffer and the *Boston Globe*'s Spotlight Team. This solemn duty transpires from every corner of the framework, in particular from the heroization of the team (awards, praise in other papers, etc.). The narrative function of this supreme instance is not to initiate proper action, but to mandate others to act and to sanction. This function works in the context of the omniscient 'all' of public opinion, the meaning locus θεολογεῖον of our θέατρον model and the industrial practice of 'objectivity.'

Text level. The story designates clearly as pragmatic subject Shanley in polemical interrelation with his antisubject, Boston attorney Laurence E. Hardoon (who was probably instrumental in setting the ball rolling in this affair by mentioning it to the reporter – thus, he might surreptitiously have been a mandating instance). Both stand synecdochically for larger institutions – the Church and the juridical system not yet differentiated (later we will see civil and criminal law actors as antisubjects).

The action's pragmatic objects – that is, the objects with which the subject acted – were the four victims (three of them Hardoon's clients for civil damage claims against the Archdiocese of Boston). These cases can be summarized as cases of consensual homosexual relations with youths or young adults, initiated through Shanley's seduction of needy persons:

1. Arthur Austin 'first met Shanley in 1968 at the St. Francis rectory to talk about his breakup with his first gay lover. Shanley made "peculiar" inquiries, Austin said, about his genitalia and the details of his homosexual experiences.' (Gravamen: Shanley made him his 'sex slave' until he was twenty-six years of age.)
2. 'Victim who lives in Boston's Back Bay – the 42-year-old man.' (Gravamen: 'seven-year sexual relationship in which Shanley also arranged sexual liaisons for him with other men.')
3. 'A Stoneham man who died in 1998' (spokespersons: his siblings and mother). (Gravamen: 'After molesting the man, Shanley, despite his public support of homosexuals, would "tell him he was doing the Lord's work to find out who the homosexuals were and tell him he would burn in hell for what just happened," according to the man's brother.')
4. Another Shanley victim, 'who settled with the archdiocese in 1993'

(spokespersons: his sister and mother). (Gravamen: 'Said that when her brother was 11, around 1969, their mother sent him to Shanley at St. Francis after he had run away. She said Shanley abused her brother in his office, but her brother didn't reveal the abuse to her and other family members until the 1990s. "My brother thought it was a sin."'

Further figures are marginal as the helpers of the pragmatic subject and antisubject, without functionally changing anything in the argumentative structure of the tribunal:

5. 'Rev. William F. Murphy, the archdiocesan official who handled sex abuse complaints at the time.'
6. 'Top Church officials.'
7. 'Rev. John J. White.'
8. 'Donna M. Morrissey, spokeswoman for the archdiocese.'

The structure of functional role assignments can now be expanded to the process question. What, in the story text, sets off the process (public opinion tribunal, i.e., the scandal)? How does it come to the accusation at all? Who accuses? And why? These questions need to be answered in terms of narration technique.

The process is initiated with journalistic narrative's attributing of functional roles to real-life social actors. Only through this operation are we no longer astonished that anyone who is not concerned with the events (which goes in the direction of journalistic 'detachment') adopts a foreign cause as her own, in the name of a general principle, becoming accuser (which is then genuine 'attachment'). The lawyer and his clients have a vested natural interest that explains their accusation sufficiently. Their accusation, however, is not taken on simply but is reconstructed as an accusation of institutional failure. In the technical realization of the ensuing narrative, it is now the priests' abusing (sexually and otherwise) systematically, being fully aware of the committed damage, hiding it from those to whom they are responsible, and basking nevertheless in the sun of their public hypocrisy. In Aristotle's *Poetics*, turning into exemplar has been viewed as a narrative requisite. Accordingly, not the singular but the typical (= 'better or worse than the contemporaries') is of interest. In the story at hand, the scandal subject is also a type distinct from its normal contemporaries.

Besides the journalistic construction of the public opinion tribunal[22] and accusation, two further narrative techniques are employed: (1) attribution of roles and (2) typing. A juridical tribunal, by comparison, assigns roles either rigidly, through a juridical idea in applying the law to decidable cases (the principle 'every person has her competent judge' – *habeas corpus*), or variably according to legal interests. Public opinion tribunals, by contrast, must be established *ab ovo* in all their particular details.

In these role attributions, one could object that one is dealing with 'natural' roles, which those concerned would have attracted without this attribution. Victim remains victim and the perpetrator a perpetrator, after all. In the real social world, however, roles are never attributed unambiguously to a person. A determinate text is required in order to connect a person with one of the possibly attributable roles. The social world has available a great number of such texts. Authoritatively, roles are attributed only in courts of law. In the real world of social interaction, attributions are negotiated at best and are accepted or corrected. The fact that legal battles around one's role occur demonstrates the possibility that it could have been another role, at least in the eyes of one party.

How does the order of roles produce a narrative dynamic? With narratively closed texts such as novels, this question is superfluous. For a 'running story' – which is what news stories are by definition – this encapsulates the problem of such a story growing beyond itself: How does a story turn into a scandal, in narrative technique? In order to achieve this, a journalistic author must determine the purpose of the whole in the single story, the general in the singular. Since this is normally the case, anyway, it is not obtrusively clear. Journalistic practice calls this logical operation 'background,' 'further context,' 'explanation' of an event, where the one event at hand is explained by means of a temporally or objectively more general framework. The invention of the 'inverted pyramid' – after abandoning the hitherto usual chronological narrating style – constrained authors to find and determine the general purpose. After that, we can only experiment mentally in our imagination with what such a story would be that merely tells facts, one after another. Certainly it is not a news story we would recognize. In the story at hand, Pfeiffer opens the broader horizon of general purpose by not narrating the Shanley story as a monstrous solitary action but rather as a behavioural pattern of one person and then as the behavioural problem of an entire institution. The 'celibacy problem' explains 'Shanley.'

The development of the role of enunciation instances is also an outgrowth of narrative dynamic. This is the narrative role concretely responsible for purpose predetermination. In Pfeiffer's story, however, this role is complex and involuted. The role's abstract nature is grasped more concretely as an answer to this question: Who can do what? Since a narrative text does not allow arbitrary figures to execute arbitrary pragmatic aims (i.e., by self-control), there is the need for a rule that mandates every single figure to perform certain actions, or (better) that sanctions and therefore mandates according to what the author's plans dictate. Such a supreme plan need not be the only predetermination of purposes. Enunciation instances are not limited to the supreme, journalist's level. In Pfeiffer's story, too, enunciation is realized in steps.

The supreme, metatext level is responsible for a sort of metaplot. It is merely presupposed, is mostly text-transcendent, and – as it were – is a societal mandate to transform institutions (reform). Our Shanley story is almost a perfect example of how this functions without further argumentation. A barrage of undoubtedly exact truths, appearing initially as extremely fact-oriented, reveals a story nevertheless, not only as narrative, but also as tribunal. Facts turn into proofs of fault, which a quasi-legal, almost classical rhetoric then lines up for condemnation purposes. Concordant with those purposes, another element, the rhetorical ritual of legal procedure, is added (i.e., the right to be heard and to defend oneself). We cannot simply presuppose that Pfeiffer's journalistic predetermination is identical to the legal system's purpose. Law certainly also predetermines its purpose – with a millenary history and revolutionary ruptures in its justification, both logically and societally. Even so, the judiciary's built-in checks and balances in the last resort remain foreign to the nature of journalism, which merely borrows from them formally. Journalism could borrow from many other, likewise possible forms; that said, the reason for leaning on the judiciary form can remain obscured, as one of journalism's unfounded foundations. Nevertheless, innocuous textual clues hint at a metaplot: (a) 'Shanley's story is among the most insidious cases of clergy sex abuse found by the Spotlight Team'; (b) the role assignment of pragmatic subjects and objects, which means, here, whom the text casts as perpetrator and whom as victim; (c) the imposition of further roles through the tribunal story structure or the rituals of investigative journalism.

The text level and main plot carry with them a proper mandating figure, albeit in the passive form of the reporter as mandated. The mandating instance itself is a vacuum and must be implied – at any rate, there is no auto-mandate. 'Public opinion,' for which the reporter acts interpretatively, can fill this vacuum. What is the reporter doing in the name of the mandating instance? In claiming to possess knowledge of 'doing the right thing,' she need only make this a binding value for all those bound into the narrative. Both the pragmatic subject, Shanley, and the antisubject, Hardoon, are oriented by this predetermination of purpose – Shanley, however, only by struggling against it (and thereby acknowledging it). A major effort is needed to imagine against the grain of a story and its narratively determined purpose if we hope to reconstruct the discursive representations of Shanley (i.e., not the narrative subject 'Shanley the predator'). Real subjects treated as pragmatic subjects in this way accordingly often feel wrongly interpreted, or – as is the case with Shanley – they view themselves as targets of hate and slander (Cockburn 2005). The pathos of a completely differently motivated imagination, of a quite different ideal, is difficult to reconstruct from Shanley's own discourses. In his own defence, these list time and again his *cursus honorum*, awards, distinctions (cf. *supra*). They also invoke almost ritualistically the 'healing' effect of his 'pastorally bodily' attention to homosexual youths (hinting strongly that such bodily attentions were homosexual encounters).

There is, though, no evidence of Pfeiffer's direct and explicit purpose predetermination in her story; such prescriptive journalism would be extremely unusual. What instead remains true is that the concrete predetermination of a narrative purpose is occurring in the victims, who must have a role attribution not as pragmatic subjects but rather as objects of action, to which role they remain bound. It is thus again very meaning-determinant that referenced real-world actors are mapped to narrative roles. Later, an attempt will be made to reconstruct the purpose of action of those actors who have been assigned the narrative role of objects – as much as this is reconstructable from their own discourses. Even if auto-representing themselves as victims, they act according to their own intentions in their discourses and in their discursive-narrative purpose determination. Yet by being built into the scandal purpose predetermination, they are all uniformly fitted into logical counterparts of power abuse. Only this makes the story coherent (also in a Poetic sense as 'unity of time and place'). Power as an abused one implies powerlessness of the abused ones: seduced, without will ('slave'), incapable of deliberate decisions due to infancy or the like. All four victims, turned into objects of action by the narrative, are characterized in one form or another through this vulnerable powerlessness.

But are these not real-world facts? Except that they are products of narrative construction, it could be objected, is this not the factual constraint of truth outside narrative construction rules? It is beyond doubt that children are incapable of taking decisions in the strict sense of the term, insofar as they would have to be able to judge the consequences of their actions. For argument's sake, let us grant that all the actors mentioned in the story were incapable of decision in the real world. Nevertheless, we are dealing with a narrative function here. Whatever they were in the real world, for this narrative they must be not responsible for their actions (for the legal discourse of a civil damage claim, too, of course). How far these youths were incapable factually and in the real world in their interactions with Shanley can perhaps never be reconstructed. Qualifying this as a 'seducing' (story) or a 'healing' (Shanley) interaction is litigious. In such interaction, this inability to reconstruct is the common destiny of Pfeiffer's story, probably the court's, and even the participants'. The latter have only memories – indeed, 'repressed memories,' which have long dissolved into the personality (Lief 2003). Here remains a personal history with its own episodes and events – or better, into which facts have been metamorphosed as episodes of a whole. As the legal proceedings in and out of court have shown, such personal remembrances – if factual – can almost never be confirmed by another source. When there were documentary vestiges in closer range to the events, these were mostly either defensive or accusatory (and these documents can be reduced to the defensive or accusatory content of Shanley's personnel file). In other words, facts have a slim chance of survival without a story to transform and conserve them.

One can only conclude, then, that Pfeiffer's story follows her own narrative rules – or, as a non-mutually exclusive alternative, that it adopts the point of view of one of the parties. Nowhere would it be possible for her to get to the 'things themselves' (Ranke) and to give a narrative form to her own direct observation of a state of affairs. Instead, standardized narrative forms are employed, into which, in turn, standardized narrative forms of the sources are built, to the extent that they can be reconciled for the purpose of supreme narrative determination. Relative to the more nuanced source material, the effect of the journalistic construction is again coarsening and simplifying, with even the sources simplifying for the sake of their interests' advancement. Without difficulty, then, it can be conceded that authentic pieces of a complex reality have made their way into the journalistic product – passing, however, through a number of purpose-guided filters. This is more a pledge and token of reality than objectivity. News stories make a diligent effort to emphasize the real by elaborating on as many pure facts as possible (such as names, places, if possible times, and public historical data like Shanley's employment record). Almost all of these facts, however, are merely accessories and do not depend on the event.

This story has one further purpose predetermination. Each victim's story has its own narrative structure if we reconstruct it as bits and pieces of its own discourse. In these reconstructions, however, one must carefully separate a vestigial proper discourse from its narrative usage in the journalistic product, for all victim stories exhibit an explicit enunciation instance just as as do the reporter's and the Spotlight Team's. This enunciation is different from the supreme story framework, and these traces cannot be concealed, because this instance predetermines too clearly the purpose as a sexual relationship that ought not to have been (semantically as 'sexual abuse'). There are, however, enough ambivalences in these subplots to allow us to reconstruct that, even in the victims' own discourses, the effective motivation was much more complex. In particular, consent in the sexual relationship, so decisive for Pfeiffer, is all but unambiguous. Especially with homosexual relationships continuing far into adulthood, the victims (and their attorneys) found it difficult to refer to these as authority abuse. This allows the relationship to appear more as a lapse in professional standards (i.e., in the priestly relation) as a result of which the victims claim to have suffered.

'Defence' is another important role that arises almost compulsively in journalistic narrations. In order to satisfy the objectivity norm of 'balance,' before the tribunal of public opinion something resembling procedural justice is construed (*audiatur et altera pars* in Roman law). What must those who are responsible for the demeanour of Shanley and all the others bring forward in their own defence? This is so much an integral part of the pattern 'tribunal' that its mere appearance in a story implies and presupposes the pattern itself. This pattern is so strong that it surfaces ritually after very strong accusations on the very tenuous basis of hearsay (Jacobs and *Globe* staff 2002): 'Shanley's penchant for young boys was no secret, at least not in some quarters of the city, and the word among street veterans was to steer clear of him. Shanley, now in the Middlesex County jail awaiting trial on rape charges, was unavailable for comment. His lawyer, Frank Mondano, did not return repeated telephone calls. So daunting was Shanley's celebrity that some of those who followed his career and had suspicions about him didn't know where to go with their concerns. Boston, after all, was among the most Catholic of cities. Nor was the gay community, struggling to emerge from a shroud of secrecy and condemnation, particularly eager to have one of its most vocal champions linked to sexual abuse.'

The role of defence and its functional value, one could have surmised, is an occasion for a self-reflexive grasp of journalistic practising. After all, at stake is the fundamental construction of the tribunal scheme itself, which is an important cue to the self-understanding of journalistic practice. It spawns non-partisanship, balance, and factuality in the differentiation of fact and opinion. Since the accuser is at the same time judge, though, fairness must be construed into the narrative. This reflexivity does not usually go very deep; it is reduced to providing opportunities to opine about established facts – after, of course, the journalist has authoritatively established those facts. In terms of rhetoric, both the *quaestio elenchi* as much as the *quaestio facti* is already decided long before the adversary is allowed an argumentative contribution ('comment').

To conclude, we have seen that very complex communicative relations in journalistic representation are coarsely simplified even while publicly opined. The closer one takes cognizance of the rich details in various narrative representations of the sources, the more this simplification stands out. It would be far too simple to attribute this to some 'frame.' It is not a frame drawn around a picture detail – to stay within the metaphor – but the picture's granularity itself that is reduced. Now, this is the case with every narrativization, as Hayden White has shown (1984); this is the very craft of historiography (as we discussed earlier). The concrete reduction of public opinion, however, far outpaces historiography (when not practised in a postmodern fashion, in Foucault's sense). The *Boston Globe* and Pfeiffer only fall back on this; the invention itself is much older.

7.4 Two Discursive Scandal Constructions

For scandal, there exists as well a quite different source, again as something relative to an event. The other source for things 'scandalous' is in the religious rather than the public discourse. In the usage of the term 'scandal,' a difference is detectable in how purpose is predetermined: here in the ecclesial community, there in public opinion. Despite its present near-exclusive reference to the media version, there also exist scandals of a different sort. It should not be surprising after what has been explained so far that deceptive misunderstandings can result – in both directions – from the univocal usage of this term. The rights of primogeniture, however, belong to the religious sense of the term scandal, for the entire semantic has its sole source in biblical language.[23] There it surfaces in the context of 'snare,' stumble, and later in the context 'moral offence'; all further usage of the term has been crucially determined by Paul's use of it in 1 Corinthians 1.23, where he speaks of the 'scandal of the cross.' Only later did the term 'scandal' emancipate itself from its original meaning, and only in French and through French to other languages, in which it came to mean 'offence to public opinion.'

The semantic continues to hide conceptual differences in essence. The faith metatext and public opinion have different pragmatic programs and different predetermined goals. 'Causing offence' and 'bringing to a fall' (originally in the sense of the hunter's snare), scandal, all of these concepts refer to the transmission of faith and its opposite. Public opinion, in contrast, sees scandal in the cover-up by a power that is trying to hide its evil intent.

The faith metatext is not directly comprehensible. Why need we be so apprehensive of stumbling blocks, snares, temptations? One of the first 'discoverers' of CSA scandals in the United States, Jason Berry, titles his work with an Our Father quote: *Lead Us Not into Temptation: Catholic Priests and the Sexual Abuse of Children* (cf. Cannon 2002a, 19). This indictment before the tribunal of publicity, however, completely distorts the logic of his quote, for the temptation of the Lord's Prayer does not accuse (it comes right after the petition for forgiveness); rather, it relates to the loss of a redeeming relation to God. Believing is based in witnessing. There is no theory-guided, universal access to the truths of faith, for in that case they were logically necessary truths, compelling for everybody. These truths are thus transmitted by believe-able witnesses. For those who cannot accept these truths, they become stumbling blocks, the 'scandal of the cross,' either as a scandal of foolishness or as a scandal of conscious, free rejection (1 Corinthians 1.23). Is this a preterintentional side effect? If this were so, then even the central tenets of faith would be scandalous: for instance, that there have been only selective resurrection witnesses (Acts 10.41) and no trace of a generally accessible and compelling proof; or the unexplainable election of God, of Joseph instead of his older brothers, of David instead of Saul, and so forth.

Thus scandal – offence or fall – seen from the outside, will always be the other side of faith. 'Becoming a scandal for someone,' in consequence, means leading someone to the outside of faith. Certain Canon Law regulations have been incriminated and interpreted as cover-ups (v. *supra*). From an inside perspective, this must be seen from this argumentation context of scandal avoidance. Canon Law differentiates procedures according to whether something causes scandal or not, and has rules of discretion and secrecy to avoid scandal, including rules to protect a culprit's personal reputation. In this vein, destroying the trust of abused youths (as in the Boston CSA scandal) is one of the gravest possible malfeasances for a priest; this is evident in the severe canonical penalties for such crimes – penalties that apply even for deeds not punishable by criminal law. Indeed, canonically sanctioned crimes are even desirable in public opinion, such as in cases of consenting adult homosexuals.[24] The reason for σκάνδαλον is, however, quite different from those for scandals of public opinion. For example, when diverse discourses discuss such CSA monsters as Geoghan, the defrocked Boston priest since murdered in prison, the scandal's impression derives from different rationales. Different reasons lead to very different consequences that one must draw and to different ways in which an institution reacts (public sphere, legal system, Church). How the Church (which has no coercitive powers) 'punishes' is, in principle, different from how the judiciary system punishes. In extremely scandalous cases, too, the Church is more mindful of the reputation of those involved, at least much more so than public opinion.

So far apart were the ideas regarding adequate sanctions that even a pastoral tone (instead of a stern confrontation) sounded too much like cosying up to evildoers. The *Boston Globe*, writing about letters from Cardinals Medeiros and Law to Geoghan, took exception at the paternal and encouraging tone. Such a tone, however, is the rule for this kind of communication within the Church. 'I am confident that you will render fine priestly service to the People of God in St. Andrew parish'[25] meant for all practical purposes that the priest had been forcibly removed from his previous parish because 'he had allegedly abused at least three victims' (Pfeiffer and Globe Staff 2002). The *Globe* had fully expected severe sanctions against Geoghan for abusing powerless victims. The bishop's reaction to these allegations – providing therapy for the priest – was clearly described as inadequate:

> In one hand-written letter to Medeiros, addressed 'Your Eminence' and dated Nov. 2, 1980, Geoghan reported: 'I have been receiving excellent care on direction from two wonderful Catholic physicians, Dr. John Bren-

nan and Dr. Robert Mullins. They assure me that within a relatively short time I shall be able to return for fruitful years of priestly ministry. I am eager to return and I thank God for his many blessings.' The Spotlight Team reported last week that Brennan was charged in a civil lawsuit with sexually molesting one of his patients, who received $100,000 to settle the suit, and that Mullins is a general practitioner with no experience in psychiatry or psychology.

Readers were meant to be angry about this 'merciful' treatment of troubled priests. This was clear in subsequent reporting as well, which included stories about the mental profiles of seminarians, celibacy as withdrawal from the world, and similar (here also the second identity metatext came into play).

Clearly, Church sanctions diverge sharply from public ones. Public opinion interprets as concealment what ecclesial practice views more delicately as a matter of conscience. This is not simply a matter of 'tone'; it is formally established in the *forum internum,* staunchly separated from all information available outside the confessional. Priestly misconduct is treated as a matter between God and a sinner, which renders social judgment irrelevant. What the Church practises as a pious masking of the sinner's ugliness, public opinion views as a hush-up of criminality ('obstruction of justice'). This approach to sanctioning is underpinned by God's boundless forgiveness and the constant assumption of a will to conversion. In the eyes of public opinion, these turn easily into an inconsequential *laissez-faire* laced with self-protection. The Globe Spotlight Team (2002):

> Even one of the priests whose abuse of children resulted in confidential settlements said he has been troubled at how the church managed to hide his problems, and those of so many other priests, from an unsuspecting public. The priest, who like many others was removed from his parish in the early 1990s, disagrees with the view of many lawyers that Law was seeking to protect his own public image. 'What they were protecting was their notion that the church is a perfect society,' said the priest, who asked that his name not be used. 'If the archdiocese really wanted to protect its other priests from scandal, they would have gotten those of us who abused children out of there much earlier.'

The confrontation of the logics of metatexts shows clearly in the sensational episodes surrounding the publication of an outdated Latin Canonical procedural instruction in cases of abuse by the Holy Office (at that time, still its official name).[26] This was leaked to public opinion by a canon lawyer, yet there was no attempt to interpret this document from the inside. It became immediately, by its very leaking, the *corpus delicti* of a long-running systematic cover-up. In October 2006, this document – buttressed by Ireland's Ferns Report – served as the basis of the conspiracy theorizing in a BBC feature, *Sex Crimes and the Vatican*.

Scandals in public opinion play on a quite different stage. That metatext can be abstractly translated as follows: Power is a (necessary) evil that needs to be contained by the powerless. Containment occurs functionally (according to the idea of separation of powers), temporally (terms of office and legislative periods), quantitatively (absolute power, as dictatorship, is beyond control), and (in particular) in terms of the reversibility of power at any moment (the 'dictatorship of the majority' is only legitimate because the Sovereign, who is not in power, can reverse it at any moment). Public opinion partakes in this transcendent mandate because it is not a proper main actor. According to this pragmatic goal, the uncovering of power's evil side – that is, when it tries to overstep its limits – is the antiprogram of power. The production of scandal is merely the instrument, the visible side of evil. Now, scandal can be seen from two sides – as a result or as a product – but the two belong together. The result, the visible evil, is evil only in the context of this stage and of this dramaturgy; the product, the visibilization, always already knows where the evil is. This evil takes place only in this context. Similarly in another context, the *Ancien Régime*, an absolute monarch could have furthered the commonwealth of the people. Conversely, nothing can hinder a thoroughly controlled power from becoming no more than the enforcement of the particular interests of an empowered clientele against the minority of the depowered. Neither of these thinkable alternatives can have a place in the metatext of public opinion (or such topic is treated as an incomprehensible 'weariness with politics').

7.5 Reality: News Practice between Reality Determination and Satirical Alienation

Goal predetermination, while decisive, does not cover all aspects of media scandals. A mere goal quickly gives the impression of a partisan tract taking reality into account only insofar as it furthers the cause. Dionysian θέατρον and agora complement each other, so rhetoric comes into play as well, since the two loci of meaning share a judgment orientation. Only from our modern perspective does this commonality of judgment appear incommensurate. Yet in ancient times, the judiciary was as sacred as the rite that became the Dionysian theatre. Our juridical practice also preserved the agonistic element as expressed in rhetoric. The latter also had an interest in relegating meaning production practices to the background, while highlighting what was produced. Theatre makes us forget that it is a sacred and earnest Dionysian rite that brings forth a representation of a closed action. Analogously, the jurisdiction rite (in Italian still *si celebra un processo*) obfuscates that it owes to the agonistic representation of a cause as a 'case of ...' the fiction of the ability to state authoritatively what is right (and wrong). Similarly, the rhetoric of modern journalism: advocative journalism as an industry brand suggests that no others are advocating. This is only a useful illusion, though. If representing something as a 'case of' something general – that is, a case of a general norm or abnormity – is the core of advocateship, then it is also an integral part of the profession, the 'write rite of right.'

The discourse appealing to the judging public contains two logically separable truths, different in nature. The first is the *casus* (literally 'fall'), when a case falls under a general law. The second is the existential fact, which must be asserted or negated. In terms of the logic of relations, the latter is a dyadically degenerate sign, the former a genuine triad. In rhetorical terms, the former needs to be treated as a *quaestio juris*, while the latter is a bivalent simple *quaestio facti*, which can have only the two values: true or false. The trick of a false discursive effort to convince (i.e., not adequate to the nature of the question) consists in carrying the truth of the latter over to the former. This turns the proof of a fact that something is or is not, into a proof of the rule that this must be (Walton 1997).

Advocacy journalism dedicates itself with information to a cause (investigative journalism: to a *just* cause). It orders – and selects – information towards a goal in such a way that a case is supported or turned into a *narratio probabilis* of defence or accusation. Though the selective hand is clearly present in the result, it should not appear to be so in the form. What is truly important here is not expounding before a tribunal one of two opponents, but pretending to treat a factual matter rather than a legal one. (This is how, in French etymology, *chose* derives from *causa*.)

For reality to be summoned, it must be foregrounded as task of meaning production. Again, this task can rely on industrial practices condensed into a canon text of rules and prohibitions. The rules of this form, in semiotic generalization, require the elements of Secondness to be relocated into the news story frame. All Seconds satisfy the condition of a common universe of discourse for a proponent and an opponent, author and recipient. Only in the frame is the instance of enunciation allowed to be visible; elsewhere it must step back and refrain from communicating with the role of recipient or reader. Of course, not even then is the communication between enunciation and reception curtailed, yet communication must pretend to be toward a general public. Logically such an 'all,' as we have said, behaves as if it were an all-quantified, unlimited community of researchers that in the long run produces an adequate opinion on a state of affairs. Especially useful for this purpose is the third person singular (of definition), 'we,' which refers to no one in particular. Below this frame, everything else must result from a construed inner causality (following classical rhetorical principles). Journalism shares this with many other discursive practices.

More typical is journalistic enunciation management. Enunciation instances keep themselves at the other end of the enunciated but are never completely separated. This distance from the enunciated, which is achieved in various degrees, is very meaningful in journalism. Here, reality is graded on a 'truth scale.' Everything reported is true, but more or less so depending on the degree to which a reporter assumes responsibility for the reality effect.[27] While we are discussing goal predetermination as the one decisive contribution of journalism, let us remember that journalism is not confined to reality derived from narrative causality. News stories convey plenty of external references generating the impression of a facticity that is independent of the construing journalist. Typically, journalists achieve these gradations by resorting to time-honoured tools such as the provision of unnecessary factual bivalent data (names, times, places, etc.; v. *supra*). However, this arsenal is much richer in professional practice; for example, it includes a strong vein of authoritative speaking truth: 'true-speak' – which by the way can be expressed as a scale. This truth scale is generated by positioning every single speaker in relation to the 'facts.' In practical terms, truth scales mean that not everything in news stories is equally true, or true in the same way. Only when an assertion stands on its own is it marked as absolutely true; this is almost the exclusive privilege of the enunciation instance. When a journalist attributes an assertion to someone else, the quotation marks render it an assertion of a lesser truth. The enunciation instance no longer vouches for it but distances itself, as it were, from the other's statement. Playing with quotes exercises a peculiar charm, though, for it is possible to engineer a veritable disputation through the felicitous arrangement of quotes. Since the journalistic producer of the text stands at some distance from the various quotes, one quote can challenge the truth of the next quote *ad libitum*. These and other similar games presuppose a well-ordered graduation of truth.

Grade 0, the level of enunciation, is exclusively taken by the originary instance of enunciation. This ultimate guarantor, holder of the 'narrative contract,' is the media institution with its internally distributed roles. Not every article or radio or television piece is connected to a visible person (journalist, reporter, et al.). Even completely depersonalized agency or wire news must be covered by the institution's unquestionable guarantee that a true object is being reported on. Most often, however, the enunciation instance is quite visible, as with the *Boston Globe*'s 'Spotlight Team,' Sacha Pfeiffer and colleagues. Audiovisual media add a number of various further practices that serve to grade the truth. Thus, a moderator (host) retains the highest authority, while a reporter 'out there' merely confirms the truth as defined by the moderator. Here we see many redundant truth indices – more than the print media can ever provide. Some are system-related and thus unavoidable (e.g., stand-ups with changing background, including bystanders pushing their way into the picture), and some are staged to a degree (such as hand-held cameras and blurred sounds and images). A felicitous expression for these truth indices is Luhmann's 'systemically built-in resistances to information acquisition' – referring to resistances that prove the reliability of the actually acquired and that are not so much selection achievements. The immediate consequence of this grading is the reality illusion. As soon as reality (as representation thereof, of course) 'is a given,' all alternative representations of the same reality enter into a relation of modalization to the basic representation.

Grade –1, 'expert truth,' can be viewed as the 'unshakeable truth' confirming the moderator's 'unquestionable truth.' On occasion, external voices are implicated not as expressions of opinion but as expert knowledge. Incontrovertibly true knowledge is attributed to these voices, but always in ways that confirm the 'true' knowledge of the moderator, the reporter, and so on. This procedure places a media institution at the head of socially instituted knowledge. Academic pundits often seem more neutral than experts drawn from the power operations of politics or from the private economy. In the latter cases, authority can easily slip into mere opinion (grade 1). This truth scale sometimes translates into an actual program format; think here of 'lifestyle journalism' as encountered in health magazines, investment columns, and sex advice that is short of voyeuristic appeal but is presented laced with 'science.' Owing to this grade's peculiar symbiosis with the authority of the enunciation instance, it is not always easy to decide whether it is a grade of its own with an enhanced truth claim, or whether it serves merely as an endowment of the enunciation instance. Especially with regard to the dialogical preferences of most television formats, the position of the chat partner in relation to the host always depends heavily on the person. In any case, there must never be a constellation where an external voice holds the monopoly of truth without the host or moderator partaking in its authority. The narrative contract needs to be concluded with the enunciation instance. Based on this anchorage, any further concessions to telling the truth are attributed.

Grade +1: To express an opinion, one must have the enunciation instance's permission. By this point, the direct relation to reality is already broken, and an opinion on true objects can only be one of many possible opinions one could entertain. It is the enunciation instance's competency to collect these opinions. Gathering is not for completeness's sake but for two functional reasons. First, opinion pluralism veils the obvious fact that the truth of the enunciation instance is merely one of many possible selections. Through gradation, however, one opinion turns into truth and the rest into mere opinion. Second, the clever composition of outside opinions allows for a miniature edition of an ideal social composition – social engineering *en miniature*. Obviously, this can occur only reductively. This means that from the many possible opinions, enunciation identifies two positions: 'left' and 'right.' Whatever either of these positions stands for substantially, one of them becomes the leftist position with the enunciation instance's permission (liberal, progressive, enlightened, or similar), the other the rightist position (conservative, reactionary, or the like). Since all of this is no longer a truth, and since with opinions the plural is essential, it is *ad libitum* which positions are reflected onto the two functional positions. The only requirement is that an antagonism somehow be generated between opinions. For journalism, of course, it is helpful if this packaging is available off the peg. The notoriety effect brings about the assignment of a determinate opinion onto one of the available positions almost 'naturally,' without bespeaking the enunciation instance's selective and typifying hand.

A notable subgroup of this grade is satire. In a general context we have already encountered this genre as an appendix to (or in some cultures, an *admixture* to) investigative journalism (see §6.2). In the journalistic universe of the true, satire has acquired its own place, mostly in the form of caricatures. Some caricatures are so legendary that a newspaper's comprehensive style is condensed in their caricaturist. Evidently, in many North American papers this is not possible, as the cartoon pages are bought from syndicates. At best, such cartoons carry general political references or social criticism; but they cannot contrast the daily news with a satirical commentary. On television, satire is practised in various forms, and not only in entertainment programs (which are left to comics). Such programs are apparent attempts to replicate audiovisually the journalistic caricature, either in dedicated program blocks or in continuance of news broadcasts. In the Britain of the Thatcher era, *Spitting Image* did pioneering work in commenting on current events in a caricatural way. But it seems that the Germans actually invented this format, with RTL's *Explosiv!*

The German branch of RTL garnished its news magazines for some time with the satirical interlude *Explosiv!* One interesting and typical example: At the 1992 national convention of Catholics (*Katholikentag*), in the format of a reportage (or a 'mockumentary' *avant la lettre* or *avant* Michael Moore), the producers sent a passionately kissing couple – of a heavily pregnant nun and a priest – into the convention's crowd. The 'news story' represented the angry reactions of the participants in the same objective manner as the *agents provocateurs*. In mock interviews, genuine nuns were quizzed about their reactions. The satire form made it evident that these were roles highly representative of the Catholic Church (signalled by subtitles, just to make sure for pagans ...). Then a doubly illustrated intertitle made a reality proposition: first the real nuns, then the fake nuns in roles mirrored through supporting identical garb. This kind of 'theatre within the theatre' was intended to trigger a reaction of the 'real' nuns to their mirror by means of the re-presentation. This brought about a further re-presentation: the subject of the satire not only showed the real nuns their (caricatural) mirror, but also showed *us* the 'true' nuns – that is, nuns as they truly are. However, the 'nuns' not only were present factually as the true, but also were carried over into a metadiscourse of self-realization (which is the germ of another story). Not only were they shown (or better, displayed) to us explicitly, but they were also equipped with pragmatic competence – though a competence to be judged negatively, precisely because they were lacking the competence for sexual action, whereas they had more than enough competence in the sanctimonious keeping up of appearances.

Irony in *Explosiv!* suppresses the difference between the demonstrating and the receiving instance, author and audience, in favour of an exclusive *we* (in opposition to the *you* of the Church): *we* laugh about *you*-there! *We* produce the laughter effect by comparing *you*-there with an ideal human, by judging before an imaginary tribunal of ridicule. But it always takes two to laugh: *I* together with the ideal other laugh at the ridiculous other (see Jauß 1977). Just to make sure and to leave nothing to chance, this laughter effect is replicated in the represented. When the reaction of a woman laughing at the heavily pregnant nun is demonstrated (after editing), no ambiguity can arise as to what is meant by all this. In exactly the same way, *we* have to laugh about *you*-there. To theatre-within-theatre corresponds the correctly reacting spectator-within-theatre; the doubling of the mirror is in this way perfect. At this point, the entire role construction is in danger. The intention is to showcase an unmasked railing Catholic woman (which indeed succeeds, on the surface); what, however, can also happen through this massive anger (against the intentions of the satirical program) is a genuine metacommunication. The woman herself becomes an enunciation instance by re-presenting *us*. Since she is addressing *us* so massively, the representation effect may crumble (such an effect is still there during the nun's response to the interviewer; v. *infra*). Now, however, the woman enters *our* metalevel and addresses *our* behaviour, which she characterizes as voyeurism and so on. There is a chance that the instances may change (especially if the salvage operation in the signing off does not work): one still can understand an interviewer who is asking provocative questions about the represented 'position on sex' as being part of the representational universe. But will it be credible when this angry woman breaks out of the constraints of her assigned representational universe (limited to answering the interview questions about her reaction to the nun and priest couple) and unmasks the real game of making fools of honest people? At that point she would be addressing *us* directly, thereby bypassing the enunciation instance.

Explosiv! takes precautions against metacommunication, however. In the real world, the subject of the satire may have consisted of the interviewer and the *agents provocateurs* (who might be objects of anger, at least in the context of editing). In the world of *us*, the subjects of satire play a completely different game of irony (of those who 'know and are better,' in the sense of the definition of comedy in Aristotle's *Poetics*). The real-world participants apparently understood the theatre-in-theatre of pure provocation (as far as one can reconstruct this). *We* satire subjects, however, see unmasking, exposure, sarcastic irony – in other words, *we* also see the reacting onlookers. The spectacle, then, is slightly different. Now the real-world woman cannot know in which other play she was to appear. She is thus defending herself merely against the fact, not knowing that *we* have laughed at her already. She cannot see *us* laughing, but thinks to catch *us* with serious provocation, ridiculing, sheer aggression. The journalistic meaning repair succeeds when the woman's 'deviation from the subject' lets her effectively not communicate with *us*, but only with the interviewer, in an angry exchange. If the real spectator is addressed without the mediating enunciation instance, then a real communication between *me* as ironic voyeur knowing better, and an object of satire rejecting this communicative relation, will take place. From this mishap, however, the enunciation instance has a duty to protect *me*; that is the narrative contract.

Satire is not simply clowning; it occupies a position on the truth scale. The subject, however, needs to be differentiated from the object, for those who produce caricatures, meaning, are entitled to direct their *vis comica* against others, are detainers of truth in a sense quite different from that of their victims. Victims lose their masks through comical unmasking, but at the same time they hold an extrinsic truth: in laughing about themselves, they appropriate the truth about themselves. If not, if they merely feel hurt, they reject this truth, which always remains truth in the satire context. As an alternative, only insult is left. By insulting, the victim reverses the direction of the satirical communication, destroys the comic effect, and suspects the satire subject, in non-comical earnestness (or libel action), of malicious intent.

Grade 3, the lowest level, can accommodate merely ridiculous targets of satire, for there is no possibility of possessing less truth than this. *Monty Python, Spitting Image,* and look-alikes preside haughtily over the objects of their comicality. This power position has become so attractive that some have tried to style it as the essence of journalism. In this spirit, *Jullands Posten*'s cultural editor could invite the contestants in a caricaturist contest to target 'Mohammeds ansigt' (Hussain 2007). (Said that editor: 'It does not mean that religious feelings should be made fun of at any price, but that is of minor importance in the present context.') That the targets of this did not find it comical at all, but took it as libellous or blasphemous, shows the power of this truth position. Which proves, by the way, that journalists are not willing to renounce this power to define 'natural' truth, even for their own sake. That renunciation would amount to giving up the power to subordinate (hypotactically) other truths to positions of mere opinion. Should someone refuse this game, a war of truths can break out, whose stage can shift from paper to the streets, its weapons from pen to stones or bombs. In the area of religious scandal, a number of more or less comical works utilize the power of satire – if not actually seizing the power of grade 0 truth. Examples of this run from satirical entertainment (Almodovar's *La mala educación*) to seriously accusatory, angry caricature.

Grade 2 contains the testimony of those directly concerned but also mirrors the truth situation of the interview. With this grade, journalism marks a truth that is less than a legitimate opinion about something true but more than an unmasking of a truthless liar in satire. Witnesses and interviewees are entitled to own not a proper opinion but a singular and non-generalizable truth. In journalistic composition, they cede the right to a general truth to the enunciation instance. Also, interviewees do not just express their opinion about the truth owned by the journalist (otherwise, that expression would be a statement instead of an interview), but express a singular truth. In staying within the bounds of their singularity as the concerned, they remain outside the danger zone. If they try to turn their singular into a generally valid truth, however, they risk entering onto a collision course with the journalistic enunciation instance. In that event, the entire journalistic arsenal of interviewing prowess can be brought to bear, described by Jucker (1986) as the face-threatening scale. Applying Geoffrey Leech's politeness maxims, the confrontational interview can reach from absolute polite respect to the direct threat of losing one's face. These are only the instruments of linguistic pragmatic, though, shaping the peculiar authority distribution of interviews. They determine nothing yet about the reasons for face threatening or granting. The central reason relates to the sovereignty over who can say the truth. The initiative to investigate states of affairs through the interview situation is asymmetrically distributed and clearly tilted towards the enunciation instance. Despite appearances of dialogue form, the journalist keeps enunciating the whole and never leaves the definition of the truth to the interviewee, let alone to a Socratic dialogicity. With this procedure, the enunciation instance also sets the topic for the interview. The interviewee, then, is left with the choice between embarking on this subject or dodging it. Yet obfuscation is interpreted as having something to hide. Interviewees, therefore, contribute to the definition of truth only in a complementary way. By overstepping this role, they would be directly attacking the definition authority of the enunciation instance, which is the foundation of all the real in this discourse. This need not preclude journalists from being oriented at the very few commonplaces, which in their opinion allow the *we* of public opinion to construe public meaning in its entirety. That this gives rise to the δυνατόν and εἰκός of the *narratio probabilis* (see Poetica Aristoteles, 51b31f) of the story is not in contradiction with the reality definition of the enunciation instance.

Returning to newspaper caricature, its status encapsulates the problem nature of grading truth validity. Obviously, such drawings are not placed in a medium of public opinion as aesthetic objects. An enunciation instance intention, therefore, determines a cartoon's meaning. If it were the simple opinion of an individual fully responsible for the communicative interaction, the caricature would not be attributed such a moral weight; indeed, some cartoons exude morality (Mooney and Fewell 1989). Only a moral claim can justify violating political correctness and generally accepted good manners. If it were not for the intended ambivalence between moralism and the caricaturist's subjective mood, one would have to describe caricatures as offensive and libellous (Dias 2002; Jones 2001; Jones 2003; Naron 1990; Winchester 1995). In many cultures, the liberty of caricature is not accepted, though as an art form it has existed for a long time and in many places. What is lacking, as it were, is the 'bracket' of higher moral purposes – that is, the bracketing of the offence with disengagement from rules of social conduct. Since the sixteenth century, a bizarre form of moralizing drawing has spread from Italy, the *caricatura*, and this has fitted wonderfully – in particular since Hogarth in England – into the production of public opinion. Caricatures, especially political, class struggle, and racial caricatures (Delporte 1995; Green 1998), have always been at their zenith during times of social crisis, as during the Weimar Republic and the Nazi era, under totalitarian Socialism, and in times of war. Nowadays they are ordinary instruments of public opinion.

Despite this spread, in some societies some groups have succeeded in being taboo as targets of caricature and satire. We certainly owe it to feminism that certain types of caricature against women no longer exist (Lisenby 1985). Similarly, homosexuals and lesbians have succeeded in doing *le pas du ridicule au sublime* (paraphrasing Napoleon, who with this sentence, in inverse order, departed in 1811 from Moscow). In the present climate of political correctness, some stereotyped discourses have succeeded in disentangling themselves from the victim role: besides women (Bradley, Boles, and Jones 1979), there have been Afro-Americans (Brown-Nagin 2003) and the Jews as a social group, though not as a religion (anti-anti-Semitism). The Muslim world community's radical reaction against the Mohammed caricatures sparked a debate about the right of moralizing public opinion to stand above others, in particular when it resorts to these intentionally exaggerated means. In the past, one might have considered religion to be a taboo subject, above the fray; today, however, one might claim with better probability that any parodistic blow against religion is allowed. One can hit the sack and mean the donkey, as a Kuwaiti proverb says.

The research on caricature goes beyond Mohammed caricatures. What are caricatures, at all? How can we grasp them theoretically (Coupe 1969; Streicher 1967)? Theory sees the importance of physiognomy as paramount. Also, the historical links between caricature, political situation, and recipient reaction can be established. These approaches, however, do not concern caricature itself as a sign. Here we avail ourselves of a semiotic comprehension of publicity with its logic of goal predetermination. Clearly, all caricatures are stereotypes, inasmuch as the intention behind the stereotyping is spitefulness. For caricatures to be comprehended, this determinate goal of enunciation must be always in force. In the same way that the drawing reduces facial traits to the essential, exaggerating this essence into the grotesque, the identification operates a boundlessly crude oversimplification. We have already discussed the oversimplification of delicate communication constellations in news narratives of the Shanley scandal. In caricatures, that same simplification is made even cruder, but now with a clearly derogatory intent. Caricatures thus become the means of choice for morally higher positions (against the lower ones), as much as for any kind of propaganda. The spectrum runs from the educatory wagging finger (as against women in the past) to the sheer racist hatred of a Julius Streicher and his ignoble satirical magazine *Der Stürmer* (notorious for its caricatures of Prussia's Jewish police chief, for instance).

8 Effect and Reality of Scandal

Not without reason, previous chapters of this book bracketed the thematic complex 'reality' as much as possible, in order to treat it explicitly at the conclusion of narrative meaning. At first sight, the fact that the 'reality' concept is so ambiguous makes it useless as a simple point of reference, without critically discriminating analysis. Thus, when 'real' refers to truth claims proffered in media scandals ('a true story'), this refers to past reality. When we consider the political use of media scandals, we are referring to a future reality, which we distinguish here by calling it 'effect.' Asking whether scandals are 'true' or 'objective' is a meaningless question in this simple form, as we have seen. That being so, there is an increased interest in the second, political question: What purpose does 'reality' serve in scandal production?[1] At this stage, it is already obvious and presupposed that scandals are not free to choose whether they are objective or fictive: they *have* to be true. Though scandal stories almost always flaunt their pretensions to objectivity, this much is certain: scandal is not a real-world (physical) object or state of affairs that can be clarified entirely by inspection.[2]

When objects of scandal are referred to as 'objective,' external reality as objective is used as a pretext for ejecting the onus of proof from scandal reality, which is properly social (seen in itself and taken for itself). This was discussed earlier as part of the narrative strategy. No serious newspaper, of course, would want to be accused of fabricating or inventing scandals. The 'feeding' component is nevertheless sometimes criticized for spin doctoring, though the 'spin' also ends up in the press. One way or another, reality is at the core of scandal, and this raises two questions without even indulging in naive or ideological realism. The first of these questions has already been discussed in terms of narrative technique: (1) How is the impression of objectivity produced? The second question is, on the other hand and above all: (2) To which real-world states of affairs is a reference supposed to be established? These two questions are not tautological. One concerns media strategy, the other the social nature of the real world.

The next two sections of this chapter address those two questions respectively. Then the third section takes the findings of the previous one – that real scandal effects concern institutions rather than individuals – as a conclusive critique of 'moral outrage' theories of media scandal. This critique is also applied to the opposite (i.e., functionalist) approach, which needs to suppress all actors' perspectives. Then in the fourth and fifth sections we discuss a comprehensive semiotic theory of institutional reality and change, first as a recovery of actors' perspectives (section 4), then as an investigation of the semiotics of institutions (section 5), capitalizing on our previous discussions of the sign of society. This is of course no Rawlsian look-alike institution behind a veil of ignorance, but a fully operative cognitive sign in the real pragmatic world. The final section of this chapter takes up normativity and its challenge in scandal.

8.1 Scandal as Objectivity Effect

Let us briefly summarize what our previous analyses contribute to the first question. Reality indices, leaning on different techniques in different media, purvey some redundant information without contributing anything to narrative development in the strict sense – from the story point of view, they are mere distractions. At the same time, they hint at the real genesis of the story, serving to put forward an impression of reality. From this platform, the story aims upstream at a reality that is supposed to be factual and unquestionable. Inserting the narrative object of the story (scandal) into checkable and checked facts generates a series of the same, a serial truth effect. It is typical of the genre that we encounter a mixture of facts accessible to all, radically judgmental adjectives, and encapsulated subjectivisms. That encapsulation is operated not only as a quotation or original sound, but also as hypotaxis, as is typical of 'objectivity.' This allows it to apply truth modalities both linguistically and audiovisually from the superordinate to the subordinate text, thus qualifying the dependent text as true, subjective, mendacious, sceptically as possibly true, possibly false; or – in particular with audiovisual media – through further personality traits (hysterical, authoritative, vulgar – whatever the camera chooses to show directly or through context).

Undoubtedly, an existential fact is cogent as a state of affairs: *contra facta non valent argumenta*. Yet no narrative configuration can ever be factual, for it regulates a series of events as temporality towards a goal (time *per se* is not oriented towards a goal). The rule of the series is the goal. A goal can never be objective, because *per definitionem* it does not yet exist, but an action keeps it permanently in mind. Such a de-existentialized predetermination has also been conceived as the 'social imaginary,' meaning simply the superindividual – and the communicable – in pragmatic goals. The 'trick' of objectivity in news stories is based on the idea that a constellation of single facts, in combination with redundant facts, can *all* be existentially true. This truth is then transferred incorrectly onto the rule constituting the ordered series. A story, therefore, is neither true nor false, only credible or not (this is what *narratio probabilis* means in rhetoric and in poetic).

In the initial *Boston Globe* story of the CSA scandal, what produced the main effect of objectivity was in the first place the series of witnesses served up to underpin objectivity. These witnesses appeared in just the same manner that the lawyer fighting for their indemnification claims brought them into position before the court of justice and in his litigation PR (Roschwalb and Stack 1992). Each of these witness accounts followed exactly the rhetorical type for this narrative genre, which is well established, but each also had an accusatory narrative purpose. Before the accusation came the damage representation, and the sole responsibility for the damage was attributed to the defendant. By adopting this form, the news genre clearly turned into a *j'accuse*. Only in this way could information mutate into a scandal.

As a tribunal, the CSA story internally imitated the model of fair process, corresponding to the Roman law principle *audiatur et altera pars* that the accused must have the opportunity to be heard. When the strategy is to shift responsibility to higher instances, the truly accused are not single defendants or offenders, but the institution for which they stand. Only because of this textual strategy could the approach taken by the spokesperson for the Archdiocese, Donna Morissey, become a PR mistake of battle-decisive proportions. By stonewalling, she missed the last chance to give a 'spin' to the story. Such silence is usually interpreted as a 'cover-up' on behalf of the accused.

8.2 Objective Scandal Effects

The second, more important question in the context of objectivity inquires about objective effects. We can forgo discussing effects in an economic sense. Scandal is a product that sells extremely well because it is entertaining; thus the economic success of a media enterprise can hinge on it. At the same time, 'tabloidization' mass-produces scandals without pretending to affect anything. The most ineffective but still highly profitable scandals target stars and celebrities. In a revealing interview about the 'fame game' of celebrities, the *Mirror*'s editor-in-chief, Piers Morgan, in the *Media Guardian* listed the rules of the game.[3] This industry professional sees a sort of tacit agreement between the two sides. The private sphere of a star or celebrity, revealed in the form of a voyeuristic intrusion, is actually part of star promotion and is carried out by a celebrity handler.

Nevertheless, media scandals certainly have effects besides economic ones. Scandals are not purposeless. A Pragmaticist approach recognizes this effect of scandals, which occurs when we start to behave in this meaning. If the pragmatic goal of a scandal also predetermines the behavioural goal in real social interaction, genre and social institution (as a rule of conduct) interweave. This sort of reality is not simple; it 'is' indeed only an in-between, an interstice that brings individuals together into a *we*. Everything in this reality exists, therefore, in connection with how it brings *us* together. If the true object of scandal is understood as the reality of a qualified *we*, it might as well be vested in reifying semantics. Someone crying out 'this is a scandal!' intends by the scandalous thing *us*, or appeals to something general behind *us*. It does not matter much whether one goes so far as Ricoeur with his concept of refiguration. This is an attempt by philosophical anthropology to identify beyond historically contingent humanity a kind of timeless, perennial justice, the plenitude of being human. Let us note here a relation to the same generality, both in a media scandal and in the 'scandal' of historical injustice. This generality is comprehensible as a general rule in society, one that varies according to the purpose of actions. In the religious sphere, for example, the Almighty God, who is capable of doing everything and whose conduct is not subject to human limits, represents this generality.

Now the question of the real, of the scandal factor's 'objectivity,' of the very fact that has originated the scandal, arises in a much more specific way. For the media scandal in particular, the reality question comes before the purpose's generality. That scandals have a peculiarly proper way to become reality has already been asserted by the 'moral panic research' school, which approached scandal in the first place in terms of its effects. This began with the Birmingham School of British media sociology (Cohen 1972; Young 1971). Their research thesis was that scandals have political effects, despite being produced by media. This is a peculiar kind of reality effect. Typically, for the sociology of such effects, research topics have been formulated as drug consumption, the sexual behaviour of celebrities, and crime incidence. Suddenly, the discourse of public opinion has convinced itself, in a wave of collective consciousness, that criminality is on the rise and has become a menace to collectivity. Recently, one might add a belief that suddenly there are too many foreigners, to whom a xenophobic society ascribes all kinds of jeopardy. However, is this only a sociologically padded out version of the well-known Thomas theorem?[4] Addressing scandals as media products insinuates that 'objectively' this effect is not necessary. In terms of effective causality, in other words, the same social reality could also have caused other, different effects. The school of British media sociology in this way objectively stirred up the hornets' nest of causal effects in society. Though media are a reasonably limited case to which effective causality can be applied, nevertheless, media effects research is notoriously problematic and a bone of contention. Despite its symbolic-interactionist aspiration, even Lull and Hinerman's (1997) media scandal theory is still indebted to this approach and does not go really far beyond it. Here the share of the 'symbolic' is still not adequate, leading to an underexposition of the sign nature of media. According to the schemata of the sociological wars of religion, one can only choose one's camp between the empirical truth and semiological structuralism. Taking cognizance of the sign nature of media, however, is not as simple as switching camps.

The magical links between media and social reality are the 'norms.' With Pragmaticism we emphasized this in the deeper sense of Thirdness in the social sign (see §4.4). That sociality construes precisely a sign relation indicates that 'social reality' is never reducible to a factual *vis-à-vis*. Otherwise, how would it be possible to establish 'social norms reflecting the dominant morality' (Lull and Hinerman 1997)? If it is established through media-produced scandals, then sociality's realization commences as narrative form and thus as the ἦθη of a narration community (according to Aristotle's *Poetics*). This is implied by narration itself. What Cohen and Young earlier described as 'moral panic'[5] has now been brought into clearer perspective. In particular, it has been causally linked much more to media texts themselves (McRobbie and Thornton 1995, 560):

> Although both the original model of moral panics and the reformulations which introduced notions of ideology and hegemony were exemplary interventions in their time, we argue that it is impossible to rely on the old models with their stages and cycles, univocal media, monolithic societal or hegemonic reactions. The proliferation and fragmentation of mass, niche and micro-media and the multiplicity of voices, which compete and contest the meaning of the issues subject to 'moral panic,' suggest that both the original and revised models are outdated in so far as they could not possibly take account of the labyrinthine web of determining relations which now exist between social groups and the media, 'reality' and representation.

Fiddling with 'norms' as if they were a material something and thus investigable 'objectively' quickly brings us to insurmountable barriers. This also obtains for the creation, based on the collective illusion, of a new normativity or, in particular, sanction.

Representation in signs is not a negligible transitory stage of communication, cancelled out of the equation once the sender has attained the effect on the receiver.[6] Signs are determinant in and by themselves, because without representation there is nothing (*quoad nos*). Peirce's well-known anti-intuitionist arguments against Descartes need not be taken up again here (cf. Ehrat 2005a, 95ff), but we should remember them. How is social causality thinkable without signs? Why should media, or any other social *abstractum*, have an influence on real social interrelations? Here we are in the crossfire of the debate with postmodernism, which on these questions takes an radically anti-empirical position. Taking a position seems inescapable, not only when choosing a sociological method for investigating this problem, but also by the very problem definition. Those who with postmodern methodology thus investigate the relationship between media and society, between media scandals and social condition, will certainly not find any effect in the causal sense. Media effects research, instead, assumes a completely different ontology. If, and as far as, it were reflected at all, such ontology could be categorized as nominalistic realism – that is, as a nominalism that believes only in the existence of singular facts and that pushes everything else into ultimately arbitrary, non-real, theoretical hypotheses.

At this juncture, we can avail ourselves of the critical realism of semiotics and Pragmaticism, and this as a response to the effects question. Since signs[7] are triadic relations, everything 'is' sign, yet not in a simple way, but in three modes. Sign is no longer a discriminating concept, as one can no longer indicate anything that is not-sign. Here, effect is already part of the relation, as discussed earlier (§4.2).

Our reflections of public opinion showed us highly complex sign relations in the Θέατρον model. While there is always the relation to reality in the sign, the question is this: Which reality? What exactly does the sign of public opinion relate? A weathercock sign has a direct relation to the wind (to use Peirce's favourite example for the simple direct relation of sign to outside reality). The investigation of public opinion (the genesis of which is historical practice) proved it to be a sign of goal predetermination. Now a goal is, *per definitionem*, not yet a fact but a *futurum*, or more precisely a *facturum*. To what can public opinion refer, therefore, in the realm of goals? What exactly is the effect of a scandal (our initial question)? We now know which semiotic means scandal makes use of for its effects, and of what kind are the industrial practices in which these signs have found their systematic usage. Since semiotic describes signs as cognitive behaviour, signs are practice. Effects are describable as determinate effects of a determinate practice. This allows us to catch up with research traditions that are not semiotically inspired.[8]

8.2.1 Scandal as Effect

Any investigation of scandal effect might start from the oxymoron 'empirical text effect.' Reality and effects of scandals are observed from three sides – that is, three different communication practices, each with its own semantic field (which, however, tends to obfuscate their connections):

1. Spin (upstream)
2. Text (the media product itself)
3. Audience (downstream)

All three aspects shed light on one common narrative production; each aspect is a necessary (or necessarily implied) part of a single produced meaning. Even when 'empirical' (i.e., non-comprehending) methods are employed in their investigation, narrative meaning unifies these three fields. Thus, 'audience research' (downstream) researches interpretative conduct – and *not* the social psychology of a social group of media consumers. Spin has the richest semantic – 'public relations,' 'crisis management,' 'media campaign,' 'corporate communications,' 'propaganda,' 'communicator research' – but involves nothing more than making a narrative goal seem meaningful. Spin is not a power holder's 'strategic action' against an inferior (since this action already makes use of this logic). At the core of spin doctoring is the ancient craft of *inventio*, in eristic, dialectic, or sophistic rhetoric (Schopenhauer 1983). These three perspectives on the one meaning precisely do *not* constitute actors, agents, or social agencies. Esser and Hartung's 'micro-level perspective' (2004, 1043f), for example, understands scandal as the cooperation, or the coeffect, of four actions: the *denunciatum*, the denunciated, the denunciator, and the judge. That is, an *evil action* of a *wrongdoer* is revealed by a *denunciator* to a *normative sovereign*. Here are meant concrete human beings, who act differently in a shared social context. This instrument would doubtlessly allow the description of a court scandal, if the describer were directly involved and thus ethnomethodologically 'accounted for' the social behaviour of all other participants. A notorious historical figure of scandal, Lola Montez, whose real name was Elizabeth Rosanna Gilbert, the lover of King Ludwig I of Bavaria, succeeded in sparking the Munich Revolution of 1848. However, when the historical Lola Montez ends up in Max Ophüls's film (*Lola Montès*, (1955) – and from there perhaps becomes the model for a White House media scandal (or Marie Antoinette, etc.), then meaning is construed only by autonomous textual rules. No further foundation in genuine human indignation is either necessary or effective. The question then can only be specified as follows:

1. How far, if at all, does a media scandal need an effective social reality – for example, a civil scandal or any other social experience – for its meaning production?
2. How is the relation of imitation generated (as *simulacrum*)?
3. From where does the media product draw its meaning potential beyond social behaviour?

If scandal is not an objective, mundane state of affairs, if it is not subjective imagination, but if, however, noeither is it is fully comprehensible as a mere textual construction, then what 'is' it? In other words, which traits make media scandals recognizable by all – as generality rather than as sum? We can grasp scandal reality as scandalous effect upon 'all' (general, not sum). If scandal is more than cognitive effect – if it is also social conduct or effectuation – then how is it (empirically) measurable as that effect? To answer this question, we must first ascertain where – and on whom – this effect is produced and where it can be measured as effect.

A simple communication model of the sender–message–receiver type, or a variant of the 'hypodermic needle,' would doubtlessly be too simple. Such anthropomorphic patterns cannot do justice to the complex nature of media, since they necessarily reduce any social effect to psychological effects. Communication models that include different levels of abstraction degrees – for example, systems theory or the generativism of semionarratology – are more suitable. Where an adequately abstracted level is lacking, the tripartite division is at least a practical heuristic for research and communication. With the proper abstract theory, however, spin–text–audience serves as a basis for two higher levels of abstraction and one lower: the θέατρον model of public opinion, being more abstract, is still anthropomorphic, whereas a level of pure pragmatic logic represents the highest level of abstraction. On that level only can a reasonable choice be made as to whether an actantial, or systemic, or phenomenological, or Pragmaticist logic is the most adequate. All sociological or social-functional analyses are less abstract, or on a lower level.

In 2003 the *Boston Globe* was awarded, for its successful *mise-en-scène* of the CSA scandal in the Boston Archdiocese, the most prestigious of all Pulitzer Prizes ('for meritorious public service') 'for its coverage of sexual abuse by Roman Catholic priests.' The Pulitzer board's official recommendation highlighted the *Globe*'s '"courageous, comprehensive coverage," which "pierced secrecy, stirred local, national, and international reaction, and produced changes" in the church' (*Boston Globe*, 8 April 2003, A1). This institutional transformation was probably what the publisher, Baron ('speaking before a packed newsroom'), saw as radical world improvement of historical dimensions: 'You made history this past year. And you made the world a better and safer, and more humane place' (oddly reminding us of G.W. Bush's simultaneous characterization of a world after Saddam). On page A19, the same edition described the achievement of imposing profound change on a powerful institution despite its resistance:

> Coverage of the scandal that rocked the Roman Catholic Church to its

very core, and that earned *The Boston Globe* a Pulitzer Prize yesterday, began on Jan. 6, 2002, with a story about the archdiocese's failure to prevent the Rev. John Geoghan's abuse of children. A year later, Boston's powerful church had lost its leader and was mired in a deep crisis. And the Globe's reporting, which included some 800 stories in 2002, helped lead to scrutiny of clergy sexual abuse throughout the United States and the world.

This assessment was then independently confirmed by a series of outside authorities:

> 'The scandal, in all of its dimension, has really shaken the church … in an unprecedented way,' said Tom Roberts, editor of the *National Catholic Reporter*. 'We're just beginning to come to grips with the fact that this is corruption and it is, in fact, systemic. In the countries where it is being dealt with openly, the church will come to health more quickly.' 'There is no respected institution that I can recall in my lifetime that has been as devastated as the church has been,' said Walter V. Robinson, editor of the *Globe* Spotlight Team, which led the reporting on the story. 'The impact could not have been anything other than enormous … given the extraordinary influence and moral authority that the church and particularly the cardinal archbishop of Boston have long held.'

On 7 July 2002, on page D3 of the *Globe*, columnist Andrew Greeley had summarized the *Globe*'s reporting of the story for the past five months, in a review of the work of an investigative *Globe* reporter titled 'Betrayal: The Crisis in the Catholic Church':

> A Honduran cardinal, who a lot of people think will be the next pope, has accused the American media (this paper included) of persecuting the Catholic Church as did the Nazis, the Communists, Nero, and Diocletian. The poor man doesn't have a clue. In fact, the investigative staff of *The Boston Globe* has done the Catholic Church an enormous favor. It has forced reform on a reluctant Catholic hierarchy. It has revealed to the Catholic laity the ignorance, arrogance, stupidity, and insensitivity of the hierarchy. It has bared a pattern of sinfulness that has been a cancer eating at the church and has forced the bishops to excise it. If it had not been for the *Globe*'s investigation, the bishops would never have enacted the 'Charter for the Protection of Children and Young People' at their Dallas conference in June. Much less would they have appointed a lay supervisory board to assure compliance in the respective dioceses.

Media scandals, empirically, transform the behaviour of institutions, not audiences. How are we to empirically describe this behavioural change? To do this, we need to accurately describe an institution's behaviour *ante quam* and *post quam* and then compare the two. *Not* relevant here is the entire apparatus of a functionalist description of an institution's systemic behaviour. It is perfectly sufficient to describe a strictly behavioural conduct in a determinate interaction relationally. As interaction, the powerful (λογεῖον) must live under the impression of having lost their access to 'all' (the κοιλόν) except when it is already mediated by the media (χορός). Institution stands exactly for such interaction, which is impossible to fight, since the κοιλόν is the sanctioning instance. This sets limits to eristic. Empirically, a scandal effect is sufficiently defined as a transformation of institutional behaviour. 'Crisis communication' describes itself well as remediating professional practice,[9] since its instructions for communication strategies contain the relational behavioural changes of the institution receiving the consultation. Because everything empirical in scandals is historically contingent (methodological access is thus ideographic-biographical), there is scant methodological purchase for (nomothetical) stochastic abstraction. On the other hand, generalization *de facto* occurs in finding rules and recipes for strategic behaviour. For the consultancy industry, such cognitive competency is foundational.

Besides crisis communication, which is occasion-driven, there exists a permanent industrial practice that focuses on institutional behaviour. This practice has always been tempted to institutionalize itself, parallel to the political institutions of Montesquieu's division of powers. Altschull (1984) and especially Schultz (1998) have identified the peculiarity of 'investigative journalism' in this quasi-institution. Schultz proposes almost a theory of parallel statehood (Fourth Estate) with a division of powers that leaves to journalism one of its branches ('to act as one of the checks on the exercise of power'; 1998, 232). In reality, this industrial practice has been more of a fad, as Schultz himself recognizes: 'The heady optimism of the possibility of journalists reclaiming responsibility for the Fourth Estate ideal lingered well into the 1990s. A backlash was nonetheless building, which, by the end of the decade, had debased many of the principles that propelled the earlier movement. Audiences grew weary of disclosure and moral certainty, managements tired of the high costs and journalists found their attentions directed towards small-time shysters, and populist campaigns designed to "name the guilty man," and swamp public figures with saturation coverage' (ibid., 230). This decline describes more pertinently industrial ideology rather than an institutional behaviour. The historical fate of this institutional imposture has thus been predictable: 'Just as had happened at the beginning of the century when the popularity of the American muckraking magazines reached into the mainstream before disappearing, the investigative journalism popularised in the 1980s progressed along a similar path. At the beginning of the 1990s there was a plethora of programs and publications with an overtly watchdog agenda, most notably in commercial television current affairs' (ibid., 230).

Media scandals, then, had to become a mass product despite their apparently exceptional character. The 'regular scandal' as an everyday outflow of a textual practice is indeed much more than the occasional barking of the watchdog: 'The focus moved back towards consumer rip-offs, small crimes, law and order, the century-old standbys of popular journalism ... As news and current affairs had become the key to television's profitability, popular audience appeal in news, not just entertainment, was crucial. Television news and current affairs chewed up stories like a hungry beast, with an insatiable preference for personalities, glamour, goodies and baddies, once the line of soap operas and television dramas' (ibid., 230). However, if all of this mutates into an institutional gesture, it becomes a way of making politics, as Tiffen (1999) has emphasized. At that stage, the reality of scandal has turned emphatically into effect, consisting not so much in that a narrated event was real. A scandal's genuine aim, rather, lies in the possibility of using permanent presentations of such selected events in order to further similarly selected political aims. Its form is especially appropriate for such aims because it produces 'crisis.' This translates into institutional pressure to act on the actor who is the scandal object.

A further step beyond institution, or the Fourth Estate, is to elevate a quite banal – albeit for some time rather profitable – industrial practice to the level of normativity. McQuail (2003) provides a sterling example for the communication ethical hypostasization of an ideological self-justifying hypostasization. This transforms genre roles and their social effects into 'several principles of rights and responsibilities that both satisfy essential requirements of society and also command wide acceptance by the mainstream media institution' (ibid., 298). Then comes the list of ethical norms satisfied by the best practices in that industry: 'As much freedom to communicate as possible should be available to as many as possible, including a public right to receive information' (ibid.). Furthermore, 'the use of this freedom brings with it a responsibility to adhere to truth, in the widest sense, including informativeness, openness, integrity, honesty, and reliability. The media have solidaristic obligations as collective participants in social life. This includes expressing and supporting the needs and interests of component groups in the society as well as meeting the essential informational, social, and cultural needs of society. The media can legitimately be held to account for the use they make of their power of publication' (ibid.). Ethicizing, however, is merely the last consequence of research options further upstream, which regularly underrate textual production in favour of an overemphasizing of the subjective experience of the scandal.

8.3 Critique of Subjectivity Approaches and Functionalism

Nothing seems more effectual in scandal than indignation. Rather than an institutional or political effect, indignation is a subjective experience. If sociological research can be interested in individual experience, it can be so only on the condition that it amplify the individual effect of scandals to a disturbance in 'normal life.' This posits (as do Lull and Hinerman 1997) conservative morals regulating normal life, thereby yielding a natural contrast to everything 'not normal.' What is not normal, however, is not defined except in terms of whether it causes moral indignation. In this way, circularity arises.

It seems natural to experience indignation, yet it is easy to overlook the construed nature of the scandal. The text as much as the scandal is construed by the predetermination of the goal; so, too, is scandal effect construed. One can think of this effect as a communicative goal that, while distinguishable from the textual goal, is not without inner connection to it. For a subjectivity approach it seems irrelevant that we are dealing with media scandal, because such an approach assumes that the social scandal evocation of moral indignation is the same as with media. Semiotic, however, cannot overlook that a scandal has its origin in public opinion, a political facility for the extrapolitical control of power. Perhaps it applied certain patterns of social scandals, but the social goals have been completely replaced. Whereas reputation is at stake in the social domain, with publicity comes into play how far the coercive power of an institution can encompass the populace at large. Media scandals destroy or least disturb the legitimization of power possession. Raw power turns into power built on a legitimization by 'all,' despite its established administrative capacity to coerce every individual. Social reputation, in contrast, is diffuse and by no means coercive. Those who lose it may be obstructed in their interactions; that said, what a social scandal sanctions is *per definitionem* not justiciable.[10] This kind of scandal thus also evidences traits of sanctions based not on rules but rather on the discretion of 'all' (i.e., of the social class that sees itself concerned by such scandal).

Regarding media scandals, semiotic considers goal determination as built into the scandalous meaning itself. A goal concerns not so much the indignation of 'all' – which is only the instrument – but the sanctioning of the scandal object. One might object that, for instance, the sanctioning of 'celebrities' does not fit with this, as there seems to be no negative, delegitimizing consequence. But what is the object proper of this kind of media scandal? That celebrities are the focus here does not imply that they are the scandal's object proper. We showed earlier how complicated it can be to mount a sanction in the metatext of identity. Ideal goals are posited here, as well, but the emphasis here is on *posited*, because these goals are not *found* as they are in morals, which orient the actions of concrete human beings (this is what Lull and Hinerman suggest). Positing means construing a goal as textual predetermination (and this idea is as old as the ἤθη in Aristotle's *Poetics*, since the 'customs' are also functions of a narrative diegesis). It is likely that what determines meaning in the case of celebrities is not concern for their moral welfare. On the contrary, here we are dealing with 'all,' for whom stand the larger-than-life celebrities, and to whom on these occasions an ideal is given that constitutes their general identity. One would be mistaken, then, to search for the scandal effect in the sanctioning of celebrities. Nor should we look for it in the moral indignation of the audience. Neither is really the focus of our concern. Because they are not object, they are instrument at best for the true purpose, which is to construct 'all' as an ideal identity.

The relation of a media scandal to the real social world is far from obvious. Assuming real-world causes of media scandals is difficult because in real social life there exist countless well-known norm transgressions, committed by wilful specific transgressors. Since very few of these turn into scandals, the transgression alone does not bring out the proper specificity of media scandals. Lull and Hinerman say of media scandals 'that they have to be turned into a narrative' (1997, 13), among other criteria. In reality, one would be more correct if this definition were turned on its head so that it could then be said hyperbolically: 'A narrative has to be turned into events in order to become a scandal.' Narration stands causally at the beginning of a media scandal, and this, as we have seen, first as the construction of a teleology, from which follows sanction. Only then does a media scandal also become an experience in reality. For the rest, Lull and Hinerman's definition[11] is completely in keeping with the normal narrative rules: attribution of motives (third and fifth criteria), mixed with sanction (fourth and sixth). In order to function in a scandal story, narrating would have to be parametrized in greater detail, and also be determined syntagmatically, since it is not the disposition of roles that generates a scandal but rather the typified course of the story. This is quite often overlooked (ibid., 1997). The most conspicuous characteristic of scandal is that it begins with the end – that is, with the sanction. One starts with the verdict, and *then* one proceeds to construct the ideal, which is roughly identical to the 'dominant morality' (ibid., 11).

Narrativity of the media scandal, as not only comprehensive of the technique but also mindful of the cultural contingency of publicity, is summarized in the θέατρον model. Relative to Lull and Hinerman's rudimentary narrative awareness, it need fall back neither on the hypostasis of a society's morality, nor on a subjective experience of indignation.[12] Lull and Hinerman (1997) explain too much and too little about scandals. In our analysed cases, they leave too many questions open: How did the massive eruption of the church scandal occur, and how could it have been so sudden and unexpected? Of what did the church scandal really consist? Here we come to a quasi-anthropological response that was intended to be a narratological one. Others tend to respond in terms of political economy – that is, it proved to be profitable for a new form of news, even the Internet. Tumber and Waisbord: 'In the 1990s, the Internet emerged not only as a far-flung media technology but also as a forum for scandal. The Net is flooded with scandalous information. Web sites such as the Drudge Report, which had a crucial role in the unfolding of the Clinton/Lewinsky affair, have become forums for rumor and sensation.' Yet the Internet has less authority than the watchdog press (see Ehrat 2003), and this has greatly minimized its sanction potential.

To recapitulate: downstream indignation cannot explain why something turned into a media scandal.[13] It is *upstream* norm infraction that holds the key to that process. The only explanation is the most immediate one: it must involve interpretation or internal text mechanism, the beginnings of which are also seen by Lull and Hinerman. Indignation intends to be *explanans* of the effective cause of scandal, yet it has no purchase on its real effect, which is the effect on institutional change.

Only the text explains media scandal intrinsically from its purposiveness, and that purpose is also instrumental for a transformative effect on institutions.

This raises again the spectre of functionalism, which seems such a straightforward and facile explanation of society that constrains itself to change. This vests scandals, like organisms, with functions for the whole and explains them functionally. Functionalism would also explain scandal's purpose *and* effect. This would elegantly allow us to comprehend 'effect' as much broader than the moral indignation of scandal consumers. Moreover, the action perspective of social actors could safely be jettisoned. This perspective postulates purposes that need no longer be demonstrable in any concrete human actor's pragmatic aim. But from where do we obtain such knowledge of a universal purpose of society? Would we – at best – become engulfed in a sort of sociological transcendentalism? Even when the source of such knowledge is disguised behind the organism metaphor, and even if this releases us from the intellectual labour of transcendental thought in the social domain (as Georg Simmel explicitly suggests), the fundamental problem remains: social purposes cannot be experienced. The ideas of organistic functionalism have existed ever since the exordium of sociology (Maryanski and Turner 1991, 107):

> Durkheim's functionalism was distinguished by its emphasis on the problem or requisite of social integration and on the mechanisms for meeting this one master requisite. In this regard, Durkheim stood directly in a long line of French thinkers, starting with Montesquieu, proceeding through Condorcet, Turgot, and Rousseau, and then moving on to Saint-Simon and Comte. Over his career, Durkheim posited four basic types of mechanisms for resolving integrative problems: 1) cultural (collective conscience, collective representations), 2) structural (structural inter-dependencies and subgroup formation), 3) interpersonal (ritual and the ensuing sense of effervescence and social solidarity), and 4) cognitive (classification, modes of symbolization).

We have since then lived with the ghost of functionalism, because the basis of such knowledge has been questioned. C. Wright Mills's 'grand theory' label stuck to Parsons's functionalism, together with the suspicion that all of this was irrelevant for observation-based social analysis and research.

Some found the shortcoming of functionalism in the fact that the systemically interacting partial functions of society cannot be re-enacted from the perspective of social actors. While functionalist systems theory defines scandal emphatically as being beyond any actor's perspective (Hoffjann 2001), neofunctionalists like Alexander recognized the need to supplement functionalism with action theory (Schwinn 1998, 76): 'Parsons worked with a "problem-solving model" ... [Smelser] in which society is treated as an instrumentally oriented, purpose-directed enterprise. After a certain sequence is gone through, systems tensions that emerge at a certain state of differentiation are resolved on a new level of differentiation.' That 'extension,' however, remained a foreign body in the functionalist approach, since the transfusion of system function into pragmatic motivation remained inexplicable. This would have been decisive exactly for the scandal subject.

8.4 Scandal Effect as Semiotic

We have concluded that a scandal effect emanates uniquely from a purpose, produced by a text. It is not a learning experience, where an impact of reality changes cognition, but the imposition of a goal. Its effect, however, is indeed real – that is, it changes reality. The question discussed above merely concerned the locus of change – whether this is in feelings of indignation or in the 'indignation' of a societal institution (also favoured by functionalism, which had to sacrifice the actor perspective for this). While semiotic achieves a supra-individual logic without suppressing the actor's perspective, the relevant question becomes this: Who uses this logic, and for what reasons? According to the methods in Peirce's 'How to Make Our Ideas Clear,' these reasons can reflect tenacity, authority, or an *a priori* idea. The most primitive of these methods is the one of quality taken absolutely. Here society would simply be affected by a feeling of security, which a scandal can only shake up. Scandal, as long as it remains on this pragmatic level, has no clear social purpose proper, only the aim of singular assurance. In a certain sense, the feeling of indignation amounts to the method of tenacity, provided there is also a social variant of 'indignation' (its rich semantics could comprise everything from jingoism to political correctness).

In the realm of public opinion, however, the societal purpose can no longer consist of a mere logic of assurance. According to the metaphysical *a priori* method, clarity of belief is attained on the basis of a beautiful idea. Public opinion is this kind of 'beauty idea.' Since it is not owed to an experience of reality, it is shielded from acquiring knowledge or learning. A historian of the French Revolution baptized the Enlightenment ideology of Reason's invisible hand as the imagined 'inviolate state' of a consensus relying not on truth but rather on the manifold of diverging opinions and interests. Such ideology is capable of concealing effectively unbridgeable conflicts of interest, oppositions, but also the ultimately coercive basis of power, both being real experiences (Baker 1990). That this *a priori* logic can also contain authoritarian traits does not contradict the distinction between metaphysical and authoritarian methods. Since the former are categorically higher than the latter, they comprehend the authoritarian methods. In the sign relation, authority, then, is a Second Correlate standing in a determinate relation to the two other correlates, under the determination of the Third.

In the social domain, a 'beautiful idea' is of course not the product of a beautiful mind or soul, but a collective idea. Our social life is replete with useful fictions besides those of publicity. Basic legal ideas (e.g., property) are as intangibly common an imaginary as basic forms of statehood (cf. Kevelson 1988); neither can be the cognitive result of experience. They are, therefore, rule, but not laws (of nature). 'Beautiful ideas' are exchangeable at will, even though in social life this arbitrariness is checked by inertia, whereas experience is only replaceable by a more adequately understood experience. Social 'ideas' are not individual fancies, but are of the sort of institutions.

It is clear how far public opinion is a predetermination of a goal, and thus logically teleology. This is not so clear with social institutions. Not all of them can be as easily traced back to a precise historical constellation as public opinion can be to the *Ancien Régime*. Not all institutions, therefore, so clearly express their ideological basis. Yet there exist a sufficiently large number of historical investigations of all major social institutions, enough that they can be seen in their present form against a background of imaginable alternatives. To imagine such an institution in a different form needs no effort of fantasy, merely some historical imagination. Semantic constancy merely insinuates more stability. As Paul Veyne (1971) justly remarked, we apply 'state,' 'law,' 'family,' and similar concepts as if they designated things, in a univocal way and to our present-day institutional reality in much the same way as to, say, the Roman. That semantic usage, however, is no proof that the Roman state (i.e., the *senatus populusque Romanus*) was the 'same' (*même*) as a contemporary state system. Besides, historical imagination has also been lost – for example, comprehension of the ancient institution of slavery.

If all societal institutions have contingent logical foundations, then in certain constellations these impinge on one another as ideologies. Institutions as 'beautiful ideas' do not develop under logical constraints in the way that scientific cognition does when confronting its own errors (cf. Peirce's Pragmatic Maxim). Societal institutions can only be stabilized and maintained (through 'metaphysical' if not authoritarian methods). Yet this method can still become the guiding principle of our (controlled) behaviour, because it also allows the fixing of our beliefs – with an idea, that is, a sign.

Even with institutions, the actors' perspective is maintainable. With institutional scandals, we do not have to assume that actors direct their attention to the proper purpose of scandals. Yet attention is only one, the Second, of the Correlates, and it is always completed by a Third of a generality. This Third Correlate can indeed be the purpose of a scandal, which predetermines a societal institution's goal other than the scandal source's. If scandals are interpretations of signs and not functional operations, then they constitute interpretations that are virulently different from the proper interpretations of the targeted institutions. On this basis, we obtain the possibility of an institutional quasi-dialogue. The 'virulently different interpretation' is in reality a relatively fixed pattern, which is typical of public opinion. Nevertheless, the force of scandal puts another institution in *Zugzwang*.

How does (de)legitimization function as a logical operation? It is important that the actors' perspective be more than subjective and that it be a logical generalization that makes it social and communicable. Since teleology generates media scandals, the development of a generality presenting itself as 'all' in public opinion needs to be explained in further detail. The historical fact that this 'all' existed in the *Ancien Régime* cannot suffice, for it must appear as a quasi-logical constraint. It must be viewed as logically necessary and not as an arbitrary imposition.[14]

One could be tempted to solve the generating of an 'all' through an organistic or systemic functionalism. This, however, has the downside of either breaking up the one society as a community of interpretation, or giving up the actor's perspective (as we have seen). Even with legitimization, there is a coherent interpretation at work in one living society, not a suprasystem mediating between closed social systems. Yet in the one society there are still actions of different types. There are, therefore, also pragmatic connections of different types, with their respective logics. Behavioural control is still conceivable in the meaning of concepts, which need not be abandoned; only now, an entire class of behaviour is controllable. For example, the rich content of concepts – such as 'economy' or 'money' – makes 'all conceivable consequences' of this class of behaviour clear (and can be activated in the counterfactual conditional), so much so that they constitute a coherent 'logic.'

At this point, however, it is important that this not be the end of interpretation. Even such a 'logical' behaviour (of, say, the economy) can be further generalized. Then one draws the conceivable consequences wider and further – for example, of behaviour *per se* as it changes the world – and then 'economy' relativizes itself in reference to that more general behaviour. 'Economy' and 'money,' in this instance, become merely a special case of the class of rational conduct – that is, opportunistically egotistic conduct (according to prevailing economic theories). From this interpretation hierarchy one would expect to immediately draw the conclusion that there must be a single *most general* behaviour that is the highest. Peirce avoids precisely this Hegelianizing snare, for it suffices for the sign, in which we are thinking, that there be a relatively more general correlate in the Relation (i.e., that it is the Thirdness of a Firstness) relative to a less general and therefore qualitative correlate.

If everything must legitimize itself before everything else when it is interpreted, this makes a semiotically conceived pragmatic freer than a functional-structural system. Legitimizing means, quite literally, in this context, 'to be brought under the rule of a law.' In the case of a historical constellation, if some classes of general behaviour exist under the control of substantial general concepts, these have already legitimized a broad domain of behaviour. However, these behaviours can still further interpret one another. These interpretations can never develop into 'rationalities' aporeticly excluding one another, for this would mean that the Interpretant had found no further rule. Such rationalities have still been an important concept in nominalist sociologies – for example, in Simmel and Weber. When we share neither the philosophy of history nor methodology on a nominalistic basis, the problem of synthesizing the manifold is much less acute. In addition, the smallest unit is no longer the individual subject that must be brought into a societal synthesis. On the contrary, every thought is already dialogic in nature, whether it takes place in one subject or is taken up by the sign process in another subject and then continued in its interpretation.

8.5 Institutions as Pragmatic Predetermination of Purpose

Do institutions exist in reality, and if they do, what exactly are they? The classical question of social institutions arises also in the pragmatic context. Classes of behaviour based on their proper logic are, if they exist, not constantly inventible and reinventible; rather, they need a certain lasting existence. Classical institutionalism – for example, that of Jean-Jacques Rousseau – shows a certain tendency to reify institutions and to uncouple them from concrete behaviour. Semiotic has no difficulties with such logics that have developed historically.

There is little to be gained from the etymology of the word *institutio*, for it is, first of all, merely the instruction of future jurists by Gaius. This is also the reason why the *institutiones*, according to the *proeomium* of the *Codex Justiniani* – later known as *codex juris civilis* – is dedicated *'cupidae legum juventuti.'* The idea of institution, ever since, has been linked with rules and has also retained its connection with its jurist origins.[15] Institution as idea has great consequences for any social theory. To accept it as an idea means to oppose in principle all theories that are intrinsically egotistic or even solipsistic. This would exclude, say, behaviourism as much as the more utilitarian rational choice theory of a *Homo economicus*. Such implications may have induced neo-institutionalism to rediscover the institution and to make it bear fruit for social theory. The far too strong influence of economic theories has defined the rational in human action as opportunistic striving for one's own profit. This is clearly incompatible with any Pragmaticist definition of action, as we have seen. At the very least, *Homo economicus* constitutes an intense constriction of acting to one single type.

If human acting occurs in or through institutions, this means that this action is controlled. Control means, however, not only that the volitive act encounters the resistance of the real, but also that it is under a rule that is more general than proper interest. An invisible hand, the 'market,' regulates behaviour, geared towards *Homo economicus'* opportunistic interest. The market turns all his opportunism into rational behaviour, against his subjective intention.[16] For behaviour regulated through institutions, however, rational and reasonable generality is explicitly predetermined.

It is facile to conceive action reductively as a volitive act and then to develop it into interest-guided motivation. From an actor's perspective, such a view imposes itself almost as natural. It is much more difficult to understand how to think generality in connection with volition, because volition merely needs the dyadic polarity of Subject and Object. How this can be thought from an actor's perspective was seen in our discussion of the Pragmatic Maxim. At any rate, introducing controllability into action is connected with an ethic of truth – that is, with the value 'truth.' How does this relate to the institution? Institutional behaviour can only surpass the complexity of truth-guided behaviour, since institutional goal predeterminations are different from the ideal of truth guiding cognition. This is not only caused by the former's coercive nature, but also by the logical nature of its predetermination as 'beautiful idea.' Institutions regulate behaviour, but without the force of logical necessity as is the case with cognition. There is so much inherent contingency that they also need physically coercive force for their regulative effect. This is true of law, in the first place, and then – derived from law – of lesser forms of behavioural regulation with lesser mechanisms of coercion. The free constraint of logic and cognition, which corresponds to Peirce's 'scientific method,' is lacking in institutions, but their contingency is more than compensated for by the imposition of purpose and sanction.

Institutions are better comprehended (and more easily and with less onus) in the form of problems that a society defines for itself. Social institutions, then, are the solution, because they present themselves as the goal of the purpose. Both problem and solution are re-enactable from the actors' perspective, which is a further advantage. This is feasible without first introducing an 'agency' *à la* Giddens or a *habitus à la* Bourdieu; sign and interpretation are enough. Much more than a practical life matter, defining a problem is a logical procedure of casting something into doubt, thus entering a doubt–belief cycle. Doubt is simply there, as an existential fact or problem. It is bivalently true and areality resistance. A problem is, therefore, ideally suited to being an object of individual volition, whereas an institution subsequently offers itself as a solution to this problem if it can posit the solution as its goal. It is only that the problem must exist (in the factual sense of existence). The goal – that is, the institution – can remain a generality, and thus, as action, a *futurum*. On the basis of a factual problem, institutions posit themselves logically as teleology.

This procedure, albeit complicated to describe in a pragmatic key, fits perfectly into the relational operations of the sign. Institutions emphatically are signs for the simple reason that they consist of 'nothing' except the factual problem – that is, they merely represent general pragmatic goals. Their correct interpretation is determined, as with any other sign, by usage – that is, the existential context of the sign use, which for institutions is the here and now of an experienced problem. Without the experience of some kind of 'disadvantage' (here, or remembered or imagined), the institution of right, for example, cannot be interpreted; it remains an empty sign without significance. As with other institutions, an experienceable fact defines the unique problem connected with this institution.

How far is public opinion an institution? Which problem is defined in such a way that it can be solved by public opinion? Though this is probably a very old problem, there is a very modern character to power as a determinate constellation of asymmetric distribution. In this constellation, the power of the One (the absolute Monarch) is experienced as the opposite of the total deprivation of power from the many. The solution is the invention of 'all' as the highest instance of sanction, also in a typical institutional role distribution. The Church, too, must in a certain way possess a character of social institution, if she can be delegitimized by other institutions. The problem definition, which could be the institutional foundation, is, in this case, difficult to recognize. The prevailing antagonism suggests a moral institution, a social problem defined by discursive treatment of situations of ethical doubt. We merely have to resist the temptation of being ensnared by a sort of substitute functionalism through understanding problems as social functions.

But problems and their complementary institutional solutions are not left to the free evolution of the cognizing thought. They remain characterized as arbitrary. Conflicts among teleologies, therefore, are not to be excluded because no unconstrained societal metateleology exists that is analogous to the fallibilistic self-correcting process of cognition 'in the long run.' By contrast, every teleology must pose as the ultimate one, for its validity is not limited by its nature. They owe such boundlessness to their arbitrary imposition. Teleologies represent nothing other than a coherent intentional will that imposes itself on the recalcitrant real. Therefore reality *as a problem* is the crystallization point of a dyadic volition, which *then* receives an 'arbitrary general' rule from an institution.

The genesis or production of the rule, however, is not necessarily the volitive result of an individual will. It would be daring to claim that the institution of right sprang from the experience of Solon or the mythical *nomothetai*, the primordial legislators of the Athenian polis. Social contract theories, too, stress not just the individual will but the consensus of *all*. This entails a logical question regarding the origin of the general (which Greek political theory also conceals behind the 'rule of law'). The contingency of its genesis can be treated as a question of historical fact but is not relevant to the sign relation as such.

8.6 Delegitimization of an Institution as Purpose of Media Scandals

Institutions stand for legitimacy, and conflicts between institutions are fought as contradictions of legitimacy. In such a contradiction, one institution can only delegitimize the other – for instance, the delegitimization of religion by public opinion through a media scandal. The delegitimizing effects can reach as far as the problem definition, which founds an institution.

This problematic occurred in media scandals that involved various televangelists, for instance. Here, part of the collective problem experience is a determinate dualistic world view. The separation of evil from good leads to a point where illness is interpreted as the tug of war between the devil and God. Only against this menacing background can the purpose of institutionalization stand out – that is, that of a graced mediator, the televangelists surrounded by their flock of believers. In such an extreme personalization, the person of the televangelist becomes the antagonist of the antagonist. All is centred on the televangelist, to whom the assembly is merely attached. In the television format this institutionalization comes to the fore as spatiotemporally concrete (cf. §5.3). This dualistic world can become delegitimized, in turn, by public opinion – for example, as 'unhealthy' or 'fundamentalist.' Once this happens, even the televised staging has a different effect. This turns a mediator figure into a sick fanatic and a hypocritical, fallen moral bloodhound, whose menaces sound empty. Public opinion has already sanctioned this person. Some sanction-aware televangelists who have been targeted by media scandals have tried to save what they can, sometimes in extremely emotional public confessions of sin, complete with tears and whining. Staged very telegenically – in, for example, extreme close-ups – this turns the televangelist subject into the show's only content. Scandal targets stand a chance of redefining reality only at a very early stage in public opinion's sanctioning process. If this fails, all that is left are fallen stars – televangelists staring at their wounds, either whining or aggressively backbiting.

An institution or its actors can try to evade delegitimization by another institution through a strategy of 'stealing thunder' (Williams,

Bourgeois, and Croyle 1993, 597): 'Stealing thunder is defined as revealing negative information about oneself (or, in a legal setting, one's client) before it is revealed or elicited by another person.' Five reasons are given for why this strategy is useful: 'framing' (i.e., defining by contextualizing); 'credibility' increase of the accused; 'counterargument formation'; 'old news is no news' (i.e., destroying the surprise moment); and 'change of meaning' (i.e., harmonizing with expectations about the statement's author). A later study considers the last of these the most important (Dolnik, Case, and Williams 2003, 267): 'Stealing thunder refers to a dissuasion tactic in which an individual reveals potentially incriminating evidence first, for the purpose of reducing its negative impact on an evaluative audience.' At the same time, Dolnik and colleagues see this tactic's effect as a function of its stealth. It is certainly not new. As an old rhetorical strategy, its main purpose is to redefine one's own weakness, at least partially, by means of an anticipatory confession. Redefinitions occur at different levels, starting from the *quaestio elenchi*, which makes the very value of valuation questionable. This tactic was originally practised successfully in the courts. A scandal target can thus salvage its problem definition on which the proper institution is based, for the provided information not only confesses, but also constructs a favourable context.

Arpan and Pompper apply this tribunal tactic to public relations (2003, 295): 'The stealing thunder strategy ... may reduce journalists' likelihood of using default crisis news frames consistent with the enduring journalistic values of conflict or disorder. Thus, practitioners may stand to enhance credibility among journalists and favorably shape the meaning of news texts.' The 'default crisis news frames' materially stand for those reporting stereotypes that are instrumental in mechanically reducing richly differentiated events into customary event types (which we have conceptualized as metatext). The most interesting result – apart from the speaker authority – is a redefined reality of the reported, compared with the way it would be treated in an adversary text with the probability of sanction. Since this treatment is delegitimizing, a targeted institution that successfully steals thunder, reaffirms a new legitimacy, despite a proven failure. Because a sanction of the adversary institution is still possible, the tactic needs to be used with discretion. 'Hence, when stealing thunder is perceived as an earnest attempt at frank and timely communication, the result could be journalists' perceived credibility of the practitioner and acceptance of the message. On the other hand, if the practice is perceived as manipulative, the result might be greater antagonism of reporters toward public relations practitioners and their organizations' (Arpan and Pompper 2003, 296).

While postmodernism is inclined to stress the diversity of reality definitions (Tyler 2005), an antagonistic interpretation is more adequate in the context of public opinion. Legitimacies are not arbitrary. The idea of a *lex* indicates the goal (or at least the possibility of its imposition). Though there exist any amount of stories, each one construes only one pragmatic purpose, a teleology. If the teleology crashes, or even the problem leading to the goal, the entire story will collapse and will give way to a different story. The Boston CSA scandal has shown this with all desirable clarity. In analysing the stories of the story, we can still find their various origins with a recognizable autonomous discursivity, subordinated under the main 'scandal' discourse. This also subsumes their different problem definitions, institutional solutions, proper legitimization, under the public opinion's legitimacy to unmask.

There probably exists an entire arsenal of tactics to evade the merciless machinery of media scandals, or even to turn that machinery to one's advantage by successfully turning the tables. In all these tactics, all participants know what is at stake, for behind the legitimacy of the delegitimization of an institution there is the reality of brute facts, not merely a constructivist 'reality.' At stake is the possibility or impossibility of acting habitually as a collective under the control of rules. Scandals do indeed have effects on social reality, in a real change of a behaviour, by changing its rules. Reality is defined as the rule for a behaviour – in Pragmaticism, a rule enabling acting. This lets us concentrate on the rules proper without forgetting reality. A 'conductible' reality is rational, for rationalities are nothing other than classes of behaviour that can be reinterpreted, and thereby legitimized, differently. Public relations, as much as scandals, are such reinterpretations. Both connote misunderstanding and deception from the standpoint of a further interpretation instance. Through its 'true' interpretations, journalism distances itself from PR products, through its capacity to better interpret what PR could only represent too narrowly owing to vested interests.[17] Similarly, scandals are interpretable. Some can interpret soberly, not giving in to excitation, while others indignantly overinterpret with a blown-up teleology. Both interpretations produce real effects in opposite directions, but also these go against reality changes and institutional delegitimizations.

Reality, conceived pragmatically, is re-enactable in an actor's perspective; therefore, sanctions also constitute reality, because they impede behaviour. Beyond the institutional framework, this also applies to individual intentionality. Reality changes for pragmatic subjects under public judgment, and publicity passes verdicts on a number of undesirable action outcomes, the results of evil intentions, and so forth. Very little of this would reach scandal status, but scandal colossally amplifies all negative interpretations. Not only does scandal interpret a pragmatic subject as being responsible for a negative result, but it also negatively generalizes the subject's competency. A real effect is thereby obtained through the pragmatic regulation of the behaviour of the individual actor and beyond. This occurs as an interpretation, precisely as an attribution of pragmatic responsibility. In media scandals this is so central that without recognizable bearers of responsibility the scandal can be nipped in the bud (see Pujas 2002). Responsibility is not difficult to allocate in political systems, as a rule, because someone is always responsible, or is taking credit for something. In case real responsibility for a real behaviour is attributable only to a real individual, scandal dimensions need to be scaled up by relocating responsibility to higher places. This occurred in 2002 during the Boston CSA scandal, where the sick individual perpetrators increasingly lost the interest of the media, which identified the Bishops as the 'systemic perpetrators.' These, in turn, reacted in the traditional way by refusing to take any legitimacy from human instances (see §5.7).

The question of the purpose of the media scandal is not exhausted by the institutional reality; it also reaches deep into the individual actor's perspective. Nevertheless, media scandals are the only way to affect institutions. This was demonstrated with crystalline clarity in the Boston scandal; and some have seen Watergate and Zippergate as redefining the U.S. Presidency (Schudson 2004; Thompson 2000).

In conclusion, scandals, in their effects, are real – as we have seen. But are they also real in the sense of being occasioned by real causes? This question lies behind assertions of 'objectively scandalous' acts. While no one doubts the objectivity of an event, an objective event's scandalous nature is not remotely as objective.

In considering this question, it helps to extend the line of argument for the reality of effects in the opposite direction – towards causes. The founding act of an institution is the definition of a problem to which the institution offers a solution. Scandal, in this causal chain, is no more than a virulent means of posing the question, defining the problem. This characterizes scandal as a transitory form arising from pressure towards a solution. Its formative capacity, its meaning-shaping potential, is still decisive, but this is not meant as a permanent state. Only institutions offer permanency, which can turn into sclerosis. When sclerosis develops, scandals challenge the institution's logic from the outside.

This is not a repackaging of Lau's 'realism' in journalism research (cf. §6.2), for two reasons: first, it does not deny the meaning-formative potential of the narrative news product; and second, we do not indulge in a naive concept of facticity. Facts are not something that scandals that hit upon 'out there' and that they need only pick up and pass on to the targeted institution. The 'facts' of scandal are not a plain state of affairs in the physical or social world; rather, they are tailored to the scandal.

Yet jumping to the conclusion that the news industry is merely an entertainment industry would be a total misunderstanding. The conclusion is not that there is no 'serious reporting.' It is not that newspapers spin fairy tales. It does not even mean that the same kind of meaning production does not also exist outside the media industry.

It is not unheard of for scientific research to strive to turn into a public debate. Epidemological studies, for instance, of the distribution of determinate cancers in determinate areas are conducted routinely. But the point of these studies – the methods of which have no means to even suggest causal relationships – is not to produce a colourful map of variations from the normal distribution of the means. While this unexciting picture might prevail in almost all cases, the mapping's practical significance shines when it can visualize, for example, a wedge profile with an incinerator at the cone's tip. Said Yogi Berra: 'In theory there is no difference between theory and practice. In practice there is.' Even without causal support, such a finding cries out for political action. The ingredients to be added are certain patterns of power delegitimization, such as powerful corporations taking advantage of powerless ordinary folks, as well as a hero whose task it is to defend them. Robin Hood is Greenpeace's role model, for appropriate reasons. These additions turn a science report into a public opinion piece. A news story might even have a reporter's research as its basis, or a sort of precision journalism with information collected from other primary sources such as databases, public records, and other data collections. Even when a journalist uses secondary data, such as texts containing others' conclusions about their primary data, there is still a collection aspect.

However, journalists would not complete their task if they did not write a story, if they did not use these data for a story, if they did not select and order these data for the purpose upon which they were founding their story. The story is a logical creation of a teleology, as we have demonstrated, not a truth predication of facts; but it also *orders* facts towards its purpose. This logical difference, once recognized, is also the basis for acknowledging the genuine contribution of meaning, which arises wholly in journalism. From a broader cultural perspective, there is also a crucial role for the meaning of publicity in our society.

With regard to the cultural-historical constellation 'publicity,' we can ask: Is power indeed such a pressing problem that it needs a permanent solution? It is, evidently, a cultural-historical contingency of the bourgeois, post-absolutistic era that power is permanently in danger of being abused and that there is an ontological divide between those holding power and the dispossessed. Furthermore, is identity such a permanently pressurizing problem? For publicity to function it must at least be kept alive. What, however, is the social reality that is a condition for scandals to function? Is the condition of the possibility of scandals the existence of 'liberal democracies' (Tumber and Waisbord 2004a), because here corruption destroys trust, which rests on public accountability? Mistrust is, from this angle, the new problematic reality pressing for a new institutional solution, at least in the domain of power.

Power is conceivable – indeed, most of the time it has been exercised – without any public accountability at all. Presently, it is extremely accountable, over and above the public sphere. Refined control mechanisms abound in contemporary state apparatuses as a model of transparency: *ombudsmans*, consumer protection centres, parliaments, and an apparatus of justice. This all suggests a general suspicion of power abuse, power as essentially seductive. On the other hand, power must be exercised only in responsibility before those over whom it is exercised. This is the reality pressure at the root of publicity. Historically, however, liberal democracies have been mere exceptions. Power in monarchies, and in medieval republics such as Florence and Venice, was not accountable. In these statehoods, the normal situation was what we metaphorically call 'corruption,' belonging to power as a natural *paraphernale*. An increase in political power used to correspond to an increase in material and juridical influence. Breach of trust was not even possible, because power did not lean on trust but rather on violence of all sorts. Machiavelli's *Il Principe* provides all the details, but it speaks to a completely different problem consciousness that he did not advocate for accountability but for a greater efficiency of power (and he was personally its victim).

The scandals we have analysed, instead, show a very successful definition of power as highly problematic. Was it the experience, say, of a counselling priest and therapist abusing the confidence and trust of his young adult Boston clients, that triggered a reality pressure that could be turned into a scandal? Do the experience of power and the imagination of its possible abuse really matter? Do scandals or media scandals develop only then? Are scandals, in consequence, congruent social reactions to certain experiences of power? Experiences causing scandal are, on close examination, not mere facts but *factura* or, even better, *facienda*. We certainly do experience facts, as painful, as annoying; but we do not experience them as causes of scandal. The real in scandal causes comes in the form of a 'to-do,' not a 'did.' As a consequence, intention and aim penetrate the depths of the factual. They constitute conclusions within facts, turning a constative into an appellative experience. Without these conclusive facts, we experience only a non-directive suffering under something, an aimless *malaise*. What, however, constitutes a problem, even in its virulent form as scandal, is a mixture of factual reality and cognitive purpose. Institutions are, then, founded on such problems.

Coming specifically to publicity, the reality that causes it cannot be a mere *malaise* and a general suffering under prepotency and the powerful, a schoolyard bullying experience writ large. Power becomes a problem, and a cause for scandal, only when an aim is adduced to the fact. This aim can take the form of a simple ideal, or of a planned reaction to crisis, or any other form of appeal, including taboo.[18] Turning a fact into a problematic fact does not even require an actual intensive level of suffering or pressure. It is only important that it ought to exist, following the integrated ideal; but that it exist in actuality, sporadically, is also not excluded. Moralizing prohibition effectively joins pure facticity with a deontic, a factual malaise with the task of overcoming or preventing it. The uninterrupted chain of scandals keeps providing this pressure at points where it can crystallize. But there also exists a systemic anaesthesia for this suffering under power. Power conflicts find their permanent solution in the form of positive law, which is endowed with absolute power over all and everyone, including power holders and legislators.

One would be mistaken, therefore, if one looked for simple experiences as realist scandal causes. Power is always a social institution based on a defined problem, and not the physical experience of brute force (suffering under it) and weakness. The two experiential objects, institution and media scandal, both contain teleologies, and allow us to ascertain, in principle, how teleologies are experienced with facts. In analogy to Secondness and Thirdness in the sign of public opinion (discussed above), social reality becomes a cause for scandal. This enables us to avoid the trap of reductively understanding experience as dyadic facts. Triadic Thirdness is also an experience. It is typical of media scandals that two fundamentally different types of experience are mixed and connected: facts and generality. The experience of social institutions – logically a general – is thus enriched by the experience of facts, which can only be bivalently true or false. Pure facts are never sufficient conditions for the possibility of scandals. Teleology, or deontic, must also be experienced.

Now we can consider this situation as a sign relation. In a scandal, the relation to facts is in the Second Correlate and need be extended no further than this. Under the heavy weight of a teleological Thirdness, in other words, the Second Correlate is reduced to a mere example. Something must be demonstrable. This 'something' is more than pure fact; it is also an instance of a general law. In this sense, the fact designated by the Second Correlate must not be false, because this would lead to the temporary suspension of the law and would spark another round of the doubt–belief cycle. In scandal especially, this law, teleology, is so broad (in principle) that it can never be falsified under finite conditions. An example of teleology: The universe has been expanding constantly since the Big Bang. This assertion supposes not only a general law of the universe, but also a generality constituting a goal. This goal need not necessarily determine the behaviour of every single element, for it remains undetermined how the goal is reached. An element, for example, that does not contribute to the goal would not falsify the general law. In particular, a goal can also be attained – *salva veritate* – in a non-direct way, with contradictions, deviations, retrogressions, and nevertheless remain in force. It can, in fact, only finally be confirmed if it is itself reached, or rejected, if another goal is logically contradictory to the first. Final causality is not composed of effective causes.

Exactly the same logic applies to goals of public opinion, and the control of power is just such a permanent task. While the semiotic, logical scaffolding remains the same, the justification of that pragmatic goal is interchangeable. Some would on principle declare power an evil kraken whose curtailing can never match its growth. At the other extreme, others justify power as an endowment of God's omnipotence, the control of which can only obstruct God's grace. Still others have argued against divine right from the position of corruption, which seems to be the logic behind Waisbord's approach: that the blessing of the effecting act has been corrupted by human weakness or sinful self-interest. Final causality is equally supported by diverse and even contradictory true facts, regardless of any substantializing theory. There exists a classical philosophical debate regarding social finality. The question is whether there is a common good (*bonum commune*), or whether there are only egotistical private interests (which in their sum according to the utilitarian view increase the benefits of all). Of semiotic relevance in this entire complex is merely the logical nature of goals, in contrast to the logical nature of facts. Public opinion enjoys the privilege of not ultimately being subject to the falsification of its goal. At the same time, facts built into the sign relation insinuate that the goal is falsifiable and that power is controllable, as objective scandals prove every day. Who would dare contradict this when we look at history books?

9 Conclusion

This study addressed two central topics, neither of which, as we stated in the introduction, is self-evident or even generally accepted in the discipline. We argued, first, that how publicity constructs meaning must be grasped theoretically and historically; and second, that there is an intrinsic relation of publicity to religion. Regarding the first argument, some would pass over endeavours to determine the theoretical nature of publicity as an exercise in futility and explaining the obvious; while the second, bringing religion into this picture, may seem adventurous or artificial to others. Once the range of what they encompass became apparent, however, it turned out that both theses cloaked deeper challenges. If the nature of publicity is not a theory-free, pure fact of opinions, an empirical aggregate, in which way is it (as we have argued) a meaning construct, one masked as an inalienable individual right to think whatever one pleases? The first challenge was that publicity must be understood as meaning, not stated as fact. If it was possible to discern public opinion and publicity as precise forms of meaning with a universal claim, albeit contingent historically and culturally, the next challenge could only be to identify competing universal forms of meaning. While the law and political power have long been recognized as logics that are often in conflict with or in dangerous collusion with publicity, we have argued that publicity, properly understood, enters into a peculiar relation to religion. Through their respective nature as meaning constructs they relate to each other with a peculiar force of logical necessity, yet through their respective claims they cohabit in a particularly uneasy manner. Those analogous claims can lead to two opposite effects: either a conflict resulting in disintegration, or metatextual hypotactical subordination. The latter is the case with scandal. If it is granted that our explanation of the underlying meaning constructs and their competitive relation is valid, this would constitute a novel theory of public scandal. As a semiotic theory of meaning, the novelty of this scandal theory consists also in the absence of all psychological *explanantia*.

Is it important to concern oneself with the nature of publicity? It is certainly not a novel insight to deconstruct the pretended validity of public opinion research, among the critics of which we have already mentioned Bourdieu with his well-known essay (Bourdieu 1980). Surveys done by 'public opinion research' companies pretend to target the 'public opinions' of their sample in order to create a statistical abstraction. However, publicity is not an empirical content of consciousness ('opinion') that is identical for a determinate part of a group or mass. The bulk of the survey industry continues to base its practice nevertheless on a consciously simplified model of meaning, as Bourdieu showed in strikingly practical examples. As a sociologist, Bourdieu was fighting for research methods that are less destructive of social meaning, but social meaning is different from public meaning. The media, in contrast, present an altogether different situation and are not simply social meaning of a particular kind. Media that produce public opinion create their meaning through texts, and can thus be much more stringent and definite than social behaviour *tout court*.

Delimiting publicity negatively in opposition to the practice of public opinion surveys is not yet a theory of an entity in its own right. Such a theory could succeed only through a thorough critique of, and in contrast with, important competing theories, mainly those of Luhmann and Habermas. Furthermore, it was important to theorize the entire context of society in order to attain a grasp on normativity, not as such, but as a social production, a general sign. Only then would the peculiar ideal norm of publicity have a theoretical grounding in a pragmatic-semiotic theory of society and not come as a postulate out of the blue. As norms, public opinion and scandal revealed themselves as a very peculiar normative logic, and as a social practice with limited but precise scope. This effort to arrive at a theory was necessary because publicity is intangible, not empirical, a pure configuration of meaning, from inside a logic of societal cognition. Compared to publicity, we comprehended and analysed society as a vast domain of meaning, comprising all three categorical modes of being. Against this wider background of societal cognition, it was important to emphasize the limits of publicity: it is by no means a necessity of thought. There is, strictly speaking, no necessity at all that it exist, either cognitively or socially. It has surreptitiously and parasitically, as it were, attached itself to societal mechanisms; at the end of that historical development it exists epiphytically upon other social institutions, as a quasi-institution.

This cannot be without consequences for the form of public meaning. Philosophy used to concern itself, canonically, solely with cognition as such, inasmuch as it was true cognition. Philosophical theories of cognition have run into problems since Aristotle and Plato when they have had to deal with rhetoric, to which they can concede at best a less stringent form of cognition, of minor dignity – at least up until now. With Nietzsche, and through him certain postmodern attitudes that have gained popularity, there has come a thorough rhetorization of truth and cognition. Since then the discipline of philosophy has seen itself compelled to invent various equivalents that could replace true cognition. One such truth equivalent has been found in publicity, which was introduced with forceful argument by Habermas as a philosophical-societal category (however, having done so he once more attempted to reattach it to the cognitive process of truth). As a matter of fact, in the present state of affairs in the philosophical reflection on truth, there is no denying that it is a process that is never concluded but must nevertheless be directional (towards an end). Truth can no longer be defined substantially. The only alternative is to abolish the concept of truth altogether and admit only certain truth effects, as we discussed in the debate with radical constructivism. If publicity, therefore, is not deemed a lesser philosophy, of scant cognitive value, then there is only one alternative – namely, to comprehend it as a cognitive process of a determinate kind, a kind that takes account of its historical contingent form.

Such a determination is not as easy to accomplish as it might seem, for even though it is pure meaning, publicity is not simply cognition. We determined this using the full apparatus of semiotic theory, in which Pragmaticism is expressed in the purest and most abstract form. The practical advantage of this lies in the fact that semiotic analyses not only deductively necessary forms of thought but also any form of meaning. Habermas's language-analytical reconstruction of meaning is the clearest demonstration that his method is merely capable of detecting in public meaning a defective form of 'real meaning' (the fully discursive justification of all three validity claims). This defect he calls 'strategic, i.e. non-rational, acting.' Also for semiotic the first reference point is cognition, based on experience. Peirce saw this realized in the scientific method, which alone is constrained by an unlimited and illimitable cognitive progress without being under a guarantee of being always true. However, other types of meaning also effectively fulfil the pragmatic function of settling real doubt and compelling a new belief. Purely historical contingent configurations of meaning also fall under this heading; Publicity and public opinion are a very important instance of such a configuration. In this conception, public opinion is still a far cry from that statistical abstraction of survey research, which merely attempts to create an aggregate from the total of individual opinions in order to suggest that there exists in fact something like a factual public opinion (often differentiated into a reduced number of broader groups of public opining). No one in particular, however, entertains this opinion in fact; it is a pure abstraction. What manifests itself in the media of public opinion, though, is of a totally different kind and bears no relation to the singular opinions of individual persons. We clearly demonstrated from the birth and historical development of this genre of meaning, and from its everyday textual evidence in the media of public opinion, the decisive difference: here, a reality *sui generis*, namely, public opinion or that which 'all' opine, is constitutive for the meaning and the effect. This is no longer a matter of objective facts in narrative representation (as the trade myth of 'objectivity' suggests), but constitutes the altogether different subject of 'all' judging what was represented as fact. The expression of the opinion of 'all' does not necessarily occur explicitly, however. Already the narrative form (of factual representation) is oriented towards a normative judgment and is not purposeless.

An adequate instrument was needed to grasp something that exists only as meaning. In view of the inadequate reach of the usual survey practices and constructivist philosophical-sociological approaches, such an instrument is even more imperative. Semiotic, the abstract form of sign relation, is, on the one hand, the maximally possible abstraction of meaning as such inasmuch as it comprises the three universal categories of every possible meaning in the course of cognizing the experienceable real. On the other, however, this universal categorical analysis of meaning enables also the analysis of very contingent, historical meaning. It is not unreasonable to question the real symbolic (not physical) existence of a pure meaning entity such as publicity. It would never be more than a rather vague ideology: a collective one, if held by a group such as investigative reporters, or an individual one, if merely the political world view of a single operator. Semiotic has allowed us to prove its existence and to qualify it at the same time. Such a proof proceeds by two steps. First, we must demonstrate that such a sign is possible in principle, that the abstract form of that kind of meaning is thinkable in the first place. Second, and equally important, is the factual historical existence of such a meaning practice (which cannot be proven as necessary but can only be shown as existing). Sign nature (the First Correlate) determines its meaning (the Third Correlate in the sign relation), the particular type of its interpretation. With regard to publicity, the particular nature of its sign makes teleology the hallmark and the central process of its meaning. In precisely this feature, then, lies its difference from cognition based on experience. While it is thus determined in abstract general terms as teleological, this meaning is not uniquely realized in publicity. It will also exist in comparable form in other historical configurations, such as, for example, the idea of growth at the root of economic thought. However, it has also become historically concrete as public opinion, and that historically determined meaning can only be described. The combination of an abstract type of meaning and its historical configuration in different genres of narrativity and theatrical representation guided us in the analysis of the *Boston Globe* articles as much as it did in the description of the apparatus of ancient theatre. Only the sameness of meaning allowed us to identify them as instances of the same thing, however far apart they are in time and as practice.

With tragedy, ancient Occidental culture brought forth a very peculiar religious form of representation, stemming originally from the Dionysos cult. It is certainly not unique to tragedy that it consists of the sacred ritual participation of all in a re-enactment of a deadly salvific event. This character is shared by other cultic forms and exists also in other cultures. In most cases it is performed in a faithful, sometimes even slavishly identical, repetition of a foundational event. For René Girard this is the mimetism of an originary collective murder. Uniquely in the case of tragedy, however, this event is fate, the entanglement of human beings in a divine destiny, and the punishment of the gods that is beyond any measure. This literally incommensurate fate became the rite, and therefore became the rightly (*rite* in Latin) represented action.

It is far from obvious why the cult of Dionysos, and the culture based on this cult, should have chosen and produced exactly this form of representation, together with its orgiastic element. We leave it to Nietzsche, though, to speculate about the birth of tragedy, discovering in it the abolishment of difference and identity. We can limit ourselves to taking tragedy simply as a historical fact. The fact itself can only be described, that in the depth of the core of European culture a uniquely singular pattern of meaning was born. Then we can follow the history of how this pattern was preserved, transformed, and cultivated in the deeper cultural strata. So deep was the protoplasmic effect that public opinion could use it as a 'matter of fact' to give itself a form. On the one hand, the Dionysian has been preserved without interruption in theatrical praxis and continues to be developed. On the other hand, it is also intimately connected, through its very origin, with narrating as such, for entanglement of destiny can only bring forth a temporal form of meaning that tends towards an end, which is as irreversible as a sanction.

It should not surprise us that this meaning form, with all its constancy, has changed since antiquity. It should therefore not be expected from present-day theatrical practice that it still be consciously aware of being a Dionysian cult representation. While within our contemporary theatres the comprehensiveness of Dionysian cultic aspects may no longer be felt, the Dionysian has split up into niches of meaning where some of these aspects can indeed be felt. One such niche is public opinion. Here, in particular, the inexorability of theatrical sanction comes to bear. Contemporary theatrical performances, in contrast, go off quite harmlessly. They are still play, of course, but they are not serious – that are not a *sacred* play. They are still a representation of actors for spectators, but all attempts to involve spectators in the play and to elicit their reactions (*pace* Berthold Brecht) give the impression of being forced. They no longer succeed in getting the spectators/θεαταῖ out of the woolly comfort of their aestheticism. All of these terrifying effects were present in antiquity, in particular in the early Dionysian stages, and have there been a central part of the meaning of theatre. At a minimum, the viewing, θεωρία, should have led to catharsis (κάθαρσις) for those who on either side of the play shared in the terrifying experience of it. This core of the ancient theatre had to be exiled, in the contemporary world, to those loci where there is still serious sanction, an inexorable punishment for acting the wrong way, and this even when the wrong was committed subconsciously or was not known to have been committed. Hyperbolically we could say that the deepest nature of ancient tragedy subsists in modern public opinion, precisely because it is not a mere opinion but serious sanction with a reality effect.

If public opinion were the only case where our culture has inherited meaning from the ancient theatrical form, one could have some doubts about the origin. The logic of theatre, however, is also continued in simple narrativity. Narrative genres have preserved an Occidental style that is distinct from other styles (e.g., 'mythical' styles) in other cultures. The news story in particular has especially emphasized and leaned on the most typical feature of this Occidental style: its strong orientation towards a teleology. Through the 'inverted pyramid,' this practice (μία πρᾶξις), enshrined in Aristotle's *Poetics* (59a.19), has become the dominant feature of the news story genre. One could probably not exaggerate the depth and the variegation of the penetration of this theatrical pattern of meaning into Occidental culture. When finally, in the eighteenth century with its widespread dissemination of pamphlets, wars were fought against absolutist monarchs over the legitimization of power, it almost seemed natural to choose for this astonishing reversal the metaphor of 'tribunal of public opinion.' The tribunal, however, was a permanently concomitant one and not the strictly regulated court procedures in reconstructing past factual elements of an offence; neither was this tribunal a process according to a previously established law. For that public opinion form of tribunal, though, there existed only one model of meaning: the Dionysian. Only here is there the logical meaning locus of an orchestra as the mediation of action and judge, and only here is there an instance of explanation subsisting in the leader (κορυφαῖος) and the chorus, whose function it is to issue serious moral warning. Moreover, only here can we find the provision that an instance was in possession of the knowledge of the whole. Only in this way could public opinion set itself up as a tribunal over the power holders, as the voice of the god.

We might expect from the modern practitioners of public opinion that in their own practice they would reject this transcendent function. Even communication science refuses to take seriously the astounding arguments with which investigative journalists justify and immunize their own practices. Journalists do indeed warrant profound reflection. What is the rationale behind that self-serving slogan of 'loyalty towards the people' (scil. justifying any disloyal behaviour against trusting sources) – a slogan so frequently proffered by exaggerating investigative journalists? In investigative contexts, at least, no one claims seriously to follow the practice of 'detached journalism.' Detachment is abandoned along with loyalties of any kind, especially when such loyalties are being switched. Investigative reporting instead appeals clearly and deliberately to a normativity in order to bring it to bear (to enforce it) against those at the receiving end of sanction. However, there is no need to take literally – and to bank on – the proclaimed self-understanding of investigative practitioners (a self-understanding that does not automatically and in principle coincide with the praxis itself). In this matter, we can avail ourselves of the more secure method of semiotic by demonstrating, in the product itself, the operation of teleology in the news story. When in the representation of action the logical constraint of teleology is very strong, this is demonstrated chiefly as taking actors to task or as sanctioning them. Here the *telos* itself is no longer negotiable and often needs not even be thematized or mentioned. In its concrete use, this logical constraint is of course much more complex. We have made such complexity analysable in the form of two metatexts, which are the concrete forms of normativity. They in particular and concretely comprise all the vestiges of the Dionysian theologion (θεολογεῖον) on the textual level.

With a little creativity and effort, one could perhaps even muster arguments supporting the thesis that public opinion constitutes a form of theology. Indeed, public opinion has all the traits of speaking for a god. By connecting the dots between the patterns of meaning used by public opinion, we can spot a form of theological knowledge, a transcendent mandate. However, such an argument is (mildly) hyperbolic, even though it has technically the support of solid semiotic textual analysis uncovering all the tacit presuppositions for the functioning of the very meaning of publicity. What is more important, though, is the constellation – and it is a highly confrontational one – with the 'other' theology, the other way of speaking in God's name and mandate. Only once we understand this meaning confrontation, the shocking similarity, can we grasp the procedure of scandalizing religion. Religious media scandals are thus unlike other scandals. A political scandal follows the same meaning procedure of delegitimization, but it lacks the fundamental challenge to public knowledge itself. It does not defy the public cognition of the whole, including the roles implied by this cognition, as religion does – indeed, as religion *must* for the sake of its own identity. How religion as religion reacts to its (now) secular (but originally quite sacred) pendant public opinion is another discourse – it is a theological reflection, and this has not been our concern here. Suffice it to refer to the classical theological works of Hans Urs von Balthasar for a thorough reflection on the Judaeo-Christian reaction to tragedy and ancient theatre (Balthasar 1937, 1973). We remain on the other side, on the side of the reaction of public opinion to religious claims, on the side of media scandal.

This study has concerned itself with the media scandal around religion, with religion existing in the universe of the media, under their subordination. The inner workings of that conflict relation, the technique of a highly complex meaning construction, with the danger of self-exposure of publicity and its ideological basis, was our real subject. The analysed CSA scandals were the location. On the surface, the media reported content of a general nature that had no intrinsic relation to priesthood and religion – before they successfully established such relation, that is. For sexual abuse of children as such is a general social problem. (It has been investigated in thousands of research papers and projects in a plethora of specialized scientific journals dedicated only to this problem; we mentioned, or quoted from, some of them. Their evidence points to the family as the prime neuralgic locus of this vast social problem and sad human reality, in combination with physical abuse or violence.) Now we have analysed a novel media genre with a clear proper identity, CSA by priests. Here CSA is no longer a social problem, but a clerical, religious one. What is especially irritating about clerics is their claim that they can avail themselves of a special divine remit. From the clerics' own perspective, this establishes their identity that they act not from personal motives and in their own interest, but from a received mandate. This characterizes their role and is reflected in their behaviour, and thus it yields the proper criteria for evaluation and sanctioning. Foremost, however, this divine mandate guarantees that other secularly mandated instances of destination are prohibited from sanctioning. But not only is there an immunity effect on the side of the religious claimant. The same meaning construction of religious scandal produces as well a corresponding effect on the side of public opinion. We have analysed this as the effect of a textual hypotaxis, when some matter comes under the logical domination of one of the metatexts. By performing a sanction, which has no other justification than the metatext's normativity, public opinion can posit at the same time and by the same token that it also rightly destinates this action. The inherent plausibility of a sanctioned wrong makes it appear much more convincing that public opinion, a metatext, assumes this destination role over whatever action it chooses to mandate. With this established right, public opinion has the same right to do with religion as it does with the legitimization of political power.

Notes

Preface

1 Throughout this text, the term 'publicity' will be equivalent to the concept of *'Öffentlichkeit'* cf. (Adorno, Perrin, and Jarkko 2005; Adorno and Tiedemann 1995; Habermas 1962) which is translated sometimes as 'public sphere' and sometimes as 'publicness.' This usage is wider than in common parlance, where it tends to be restricted to the public display of public personalities. Public opinion in our sense of the term is a product of publicity/'Öffentlichkeit.'
2 There is no commonly used designation for this research tradition, which also goes under the names *École de Paris* (Coquet 1982) or *sémiotique* (which could, however, give rise to misunderstandings and confusion).
3 For instance, when an Italian minister resigned after being caught spying on his rivals, *La Repubblica* (11 March 2006, 1) referred to this as *'spia-gate.'*

1. A Theoretical Approach to the Nature of Media Scandal

1 We prefer to speak abstractly of objects of scandals instead of moralizing with 'real world' terms such as *culprit* or *victim*. Here, consider Esser and Hartung (2004, 1043): 'the culprit, that is, the person or group that can be blamed rightfully or wrongfully for the defect – keeping in mind that it is not necessary for the defect to actually exist and that the "culprit" can be quite innocent.'
2 We are used to saying 'there is a scandal,' which sounds like 'there is thunder'; however, the implied facticity is not a given in the case of a scandal, which is not strictly a datum.
3 A quite interesting example of a systemic conflict of mutually exclusive re-

constructions was a scandal relating to a Nigerian adulteress. Kalu (2003) argues that according to *sharia*, this adulteress could and should have been punished in a way other than lapidation. The international media scandal over the public stoning to death of a divorced out-of-wedlock pregnant woman could not shake the logic of this legal system with all its peculiar rules of reconstruction (evidence hearing, attribution of responsibility and guilt). Public opinion 'procedures' remain foreign to *sharia*. Except for the pure fact of a pregnant woman, there were no overlaps at all between these two reconstructions. On the contrary: here, the meaning pressure of a media scandal was reinterpreted as a result immanent to *sharia*, where the article 'explore[d] the interior of the *sharia* laws on adultery. The international community hailed the power of global communications and of the media when the woman was acquitted on appeal. Many Muslims, however, contended that sharia is both just and merciful and that 'critics are blinded by ignorance' (ibid., 389). Kalu closes his argument with this rhetorical flourish: 'The point remains as to whether the Prophet had a revelation that commanded killing for adultery. Even more distressing, can anyone appeal against a divine law in a common law court?' (ibid., 408). This is exactly the point we will be making in our own context regarding the originary media scandal of religion (cf. §5.7)

4 'Scandals result from the publication of information about corruption' (Tumber and Waisbord 2004a, 1032), and 'wrongdoing is not sufficient for scandals to break out; instead, the revelation of corruption is a necessary condition. Scandals broke even though courts later proved that suspects were innocent. Scandals do not need legal proof of corruption but mainly allegations that wrongdoing existed. Making corruption public is the defining element of scandals' (Waisbord 2004, 1077). Yet one might ask: What is the point of defining scandal through corruption, if effectively there is no corruption? It would be much more interesting to uncover the process by which an arbitrary action is placed in the pillory.

5 Thus Tumber and Waisbord do not conclude that in scandal we are dealing with a social reality in its own right; even so, they cut the ties with the remainder of the social real: 'Once corruption then becomes widespread, everyone in politics and the media realizes that if you examine more closely and for long enough, damaging information can be found on almost anyone. In this way, the hunt begins; advisors prepare ammunition to attack or defend, and journalists attempt to fill their roles as investigative reporters finding stories to increase both audience and sales.' But then, quite correctly, they continue: 'The proliferation of scandals requires

the study of the conditions for publicity rather than the conditions for corruption' (Tumber and Waisbord 2004a, 1034).
6 A contraction of *tangente,* which means bribe, and *monopoli* (after the board game Monopoly).
7 See Roodhouse (2002, 384–411).
8 'Scandals encapsulate the dynamics of accountability in liberal democracies' (Tumber and Waisbord 2004a, 1035).
9 This trait (along with others) was widely perceived as heralding the dawn of a 'new political culture,' as if it were a novel feature of the Clinton presidency, soon to be imitated by Blair and Schröder (Clark 2002). History has since run its course and shredded yet another new culture. Even so, it is beyond dispute that political office holders must somehow take on an aura of universal credibility; but here we argue that this is of the logical nature of a pragmatic ideal.
10 Those caustic manifestos – affixed by night on the stele of an ancient marble figure, whom the Romans nicknamed Pasquino, near the bottom end of Piazza Navona – that ridiculed the excesses of the Papal court.
11 In media theory, there is no prejudged determination as to whether this constitutes a symbolically generalized system function or a discursively justifiable validity claim. At this point, we are still at the stage of closer observation of a textual product of meaning, and not yet deep into theory.
12 This may differ slightly from the constant stream of news emanating from press agencies – whose approach, it must be said, is oriented towards thematically processing or reutilizing factual stories.
13 A metaphor coined by Walter Lippmann; for scandals, it really should be recast as 'flood light.'
14 Lawrence and Bennett (2001, 443) write: 'This narrative or dramaturgical aspect of the Lewinsky scandal is entirely overlooked in traditional approaches to political communication and public opinion. But we believe it is crucial to understanding how the public made sense of the scandal, precisely because the media do not simply provide the public with free-floating, disembodied bits of information but arrange that information into stories. These stories embody narratives of how events happen, why they occur, and what they mean, as well as socially-constructed symbols representing who is involved, what they are up to, and what is at stake.'
15 Sanskrit स्कंदति (*skādati*): 'he leaps, jumps, bursts.' (See Apte 1963, 617.) The word is cognate as well with the Latin *scandere,* 'climb, rise, clamber' (see Lewis et al. 1955, q.v. 'scandit fatalis machina muros' Aeneis), which survives in English as 'ascend' and 'descend.'

16 We use the term 'social scandal' for events involving real actors in a merely social context without any media contribution. Such scandals are often referred to as 'localized,' which carries the suggestion that the media can shift readers into a transcendent textual media universe. See Thompson (2000, 31ff).
17 In particular, a voluminous literature exists regarding scandals at court. A turn towards the media was evident as early as Jacobean England, as shown by Bellany (2002). Purely social scandals are an even broader field, one that has been investigated both anthropologically and ethnographically. See, for instance, a highly descriptive social-anthropological investigation of family scandals (without media) in a village in socialist Hungary (Hollos 2001).
18 It is interesting that scandal as a form of political struggle in Jacobean England developed from 'libels' and 'pasquils' – that is, from manuscripts (often in verse) that anonymous authors 'forgot' in public places and that then were copied and spread as news. 'From London, copies of libels could reach the provinces along developing channels of information distribution … Professional and amateur newsletters helped to spread these verses into the provinces' (Bellany 1994, 29; 2002).
19 This saves us from entering into unending Habermasian debates about 'colonialized life worlds' and antagonistic 'communicative liquefaction,' where versions of purer societies than the existing one are hypostasized.
20 Real-world family scandals are the object of intervention discourses in journals such as *Child Abuse and Neglect*, *Journal of Interpersonal Violence*, and *Child Abuse Review*.
21 Kitzinger (2000) describes this string of news reports on child abuse in a family and aberrant intervention by the social assistance bureaucracy as a pattern applicable to all similar instances of overblown bureaucratic social assistance.
22 Related terms use a different base metaphor. The journalism of exposure (German: *Enthüllungsjournalismus*) suggests that veils are being lifted. However, what it actually involves is circulating information against the interests of those whom one is writing about; information is snatched from these people in the same manner as the police snatch secrets from criminals. This is a good reason to keep the more neutral designation 'investigative.'
23 A general presentation of Peircean sign theory, with an explanation of the most important terms, can be found in Ehrat (2005a). No attempt will be made to replicate that work here.
24 I have developed this further and in greater detail ibid. (287–314).

25 Cf. Esser and Hartung (2004, 1042), who utterly reverse this connection: 'The fact that scandal is socially selected – or constructed, if you like – is also the basis for the application of the reflection hypothesis on scandal. This hypothesis holds that societal and cultural entities are reflected in media content and art [...] Many authors believe – rightly so, we think – that by looking at scandals, one may learn something about the normative and cultural bases of a society.'

26 See Sagay (2002, 110–11): 'Moreover, a cross-national study of media representations of the same social problem – like sexual harassment – provides the social scientist with analytic leverage for understanding how media reporting is influenced by structural and cultural factors that vary cross-nationally, such as the relative dependence of the media on corporate interests or the state, the political perspectives of journalists and editors, laws governing reporting, laws concerning the object of journalistic inquiry, journalistic traditions, and the relative clout of different social actors as news sources.'

27 See Manning (2001, 50): 'Journalists still often reveal a fondness for the idea that their work is about faithfully reflecting "what happens out there" to their audiences; one still hears journalists describing their "mission to explain" or their achievements in "opening a window upon the world."'

28 Liebes and Blum-Kulka (2004) attempted to categorize anomalous source/journalist interactions that pivot around the central concept of trust. In our context, though, only the quite different degrees of interpretation involved are of interest. Their four types of communication anomalies ('shortcircuiting or subversion of communication between reporters and their sources') (2004, 1154) are actually located in quite different degrees of interpretation. 'Whistle-blowers,' the first degree, interpret themselves; but the journalists who 'trap' them operate on the basis of their own value idealization. 'Spotlighting' investigators and 'mainstreaming' sounding boards shed a different light on what is already generally known; or they make something about which not enough is known, more known – with the intent of negative interpretation. This damages no trust; it merely personalizes and interprets behaviour (of 'others,' the powerful), in the worst case as the failure of an entire society (cultural criticism). The journalistic mandate for this is derived from a higher loyalty – if the case be, a mandate from history – and can be grasped as metatext, which needs no further legitimization.

29 See Roeh (1989); see also the 'objectivist' objection in the ensuing debate over Roeh's article in Liebes (1989).

30 Bird, however, shows that by sharing narrativity, broadsheet and tabloid journalism also share ritual style effects such as objectivity and credibility:

'[Tabloid] writers maintain that the sharp line journalists like to draw between "real" journalism and "sleaze" simply does not exist. Tabloids are entertainment that also informs; newspapers are informational, according to traditional journalistic standards, but they must also entertain to survive' (1990, 378).

31 Luhmann's theory of mass media recognizes the sense-generating impact of narration only for entertainment (Luhmann 1995), where the free play of imagination is fed by the metabole of narration. News is uniquely based on positive and negative codes of actuality, but it must address the suspicion connected with selectivity and interest. Relief against this selectivity is provided by entertainment (even though for entertainment applies the same selectivity code 'actuality,' but here as, the surprising variation of narrative patterns, actuality combined with narration. The decisive factor for relief through entertainment is that here actuality is joined with its opposite, memory (viz., of genre patterns). It is ultimately of no importance – except for theory construction itself – whether the positive code, actuality, or the negative code, memory, is needed in order to achieve system closure. Thus, narrativity plays a mass media key role in Luhmann as well.
32 Treated in much greater detail in Ehrat (2005a, 471–4).
33 Metaphor may well serve, provided that meaning as such can be adequately illustrated as a horizon – that is, as the correlate of an act from a ground or loft, Husserl's *'Boden.'* Beyond metaphoric plausibility and utility, it is by no means certain that something like 'The Meaning' exists as *singulare tantum* or uncountable noun. This must be demonstrated, not simply presupposed.

2. What Is Publicity, the Public Sphere?

1 See Geiger (1962, 179f): 'In weniger aufgeklärten Zeiten ... unterwarf man sich als demütiger Untertan den Anordnungen einer von Gott eingesetzten Obrigkeit oder beugte sich vor einer Tradition, derzufolge "das immer so war." Der im Vorstellungskreis demokratischer Selbstbestimmung aufgewachsene Zeitgenosse aber bäumt sich gegen ein solches Geschobensein auf, und seine Empörung sucht hinter dem unpersönlichen System, das seine Selbstbestimmung und Bewegungsfreiheit einengt, die das System verantwortlich lenkenden Personen, die Machthaber.'
2 Greimas's 'social imaginary' roughly corresponds to this and also to the horizon of Schütz's life world. Being horizon, this can no longer become a topic; rather, it will always be presupposed by all as the 'normal' world. The 'normal' means–end rational behaviour in our present society might be, for instance, 'to pursue happiness,' as the Constitution of the United

States expresses it. Those who are not 'normal' in this sense must drop out or be psychically ill. By these means a society gives itself a horizon of values, which are valu-able – that is, unquestionably desirable to all. It must be assumed that this horizon is quite different across different societies. One need only consider ideologically overcoded confrontation discourses between a 'native culture' or spirituality, and a 'colonialist capitalistic culture of exploitation.'

3 For this subject, the entire second volume of Habermas's *Communicative Action* (1981, esp. II:171–293) is important.
4 The philosophical concept 'substance,' *respectively* 'subsistence,' is fraught with ambiguity and has a long and complex history of philosophical thought behind it. Simulacrum, for its part, has no precise origins except those that derive from the Latin *simul* (e.g., simulation).. Our use of the term here leans on the metaphor, which can be derived from its etymology.
5 In principle, therefore, it is 'comprehending sociology.' Correspondingly, 'semiotic' is listed in handbooks of methodology as a 'qualitative research method.'
6 All of the central concepts of the Paris School of semionarratology are exhaustively described in Greimas's authoritative dictionary (Greimas and Courtés 1972, 1979, 1986).
7 These are also important for the British cultural studies tradition, which is a syncretism of methods, in this instance through extensive borrowings from semiology.
8 Textual ambivalence prepares the ground for standard media practice and is designed as genre convention. Various semantics of concealment seem to rob television of reality. In talking of entertainment (fiction, games), one means the imaginary. In talking of 'transmission,' one means a transparency for the mediation instance. In talking of advertisements, one means a lie with a wink. This is nothing other than the ambivalence built into the genre. Whenever television becomes 'real' (i.e., in the sense of becoming responsible for its enunciations, as an explicit instance of enunciation), someone outside seems to vouch for the meaning. Television 'reports' when its intention is to display some antecedent meaning as the genuine real, in such a way that the matter to be related stands 'objectively' by itself. Then the perceived meaning appears to be – for example – 'politics,' or 'the economy,' or a foreign 'society.' Objectivity is meant to prevent any subjective falsification of the original meaning. This sort of obfuscation papers over the ambivalence that television is not simply a transitory station for foreign meaning; rather, it produces its own meaning and transforms meaning as raw material from outside sources in a way that is specific to

television. With regard to our main thematic emphasis, of course it is not only religious meaning that is treated in this sense. Politics, too, outside of media, is in itself different from within media, once it has been transformed through public opinion in the television medium. This incongruence is quite obvious in the case of the juridical system (we will analyse this below in an interesting triangular case). In Luhmann's systems theory, that intersystemic communication is a key topic, but the matter can also be shown and theorized independently of functionalist systems theory. In our discussion of media theory, we will be avoiding functionalist assumptions such as the one that says the environment places adaptive pressure on the media system. This need not result in a less plausible theory – but one, rather, that is free from other systems theoretical impositions, like the deduction of meaning as such, and that has the advantage of focusing on texts or signs that really exist.

9 Deleuze (1973) makes it clear how difficult it is to grasp the nature of generativism. He tells us that the decisive places contain only metaphors – produce, generate – which acquire meaning only as metaphors of birth. Why this is so remains a mystery, however.
10 'Subsistit hoc quod non indiget alio,' says Boëthius. This term has been chosen in an effort to avoid too close an association with the Kantian category of substance.
11 I have discussed this in greater detail elsewhere; see Ehrat (2005a, 346–71).
12 Luhmann (1996) subjected this concept to sharp and radical criticism. He objected especially to the fleet-footed usage of this concept in contemporary sociology so that – robbed of its phenomenological foundation – it turned into an empty catch-all term for the self-evidence of the ordinary world.
13 As Habermas (1981, II:196ff) criticizes (cf. Kelly 1981).
14 On this point there is an interesting discussion in Luhmann of the modern social constitution of the individual from a systems theory perspective (1981, 252ff).
15 Simmel (1968, 24): 'Das Bild, das ein Mensch vom anderen aus der persönlichen Berührung gewinnt.'
16 Compared with the breadth of the Peircean sign relation, Austin's locutionary forces are restricted to some natural languages; in particular, they exclude all non-linguistic signs. How does Habermas arrive at exactly three + one validities and the corresponding three universes (taken from Popper)? This remains his secret. The three speech acts do not allow us to deduce an ontology; moreover, it is impossible to prove the completeness even after these ontologies have been deduced. So Habermas is very wise

to emphasize the contingent in his theory. On this point, the critique of McCarthy (1985) is indicative, if only because it points out how this theory leans solely on a subset of (European) natural languages.

17 As human nature used to be defined in olden times as an « *être mixte* » of body and soul (cf. Eisler 1904, I:653).

18 And Oehler (1995) is correct – or at least has a good point – in his fundamental criticism of Habermas's fundamental pragmatism (1995, 204–16)

19 Habermas, then, is much more optimistic than all those others – such as Simmel and (following him) Lukács and Adorno – who apparently assume a hopelessly inescapable tragedy of culture. In these latter works, any attempt at a 'global vision' for the philosophy of history is more than suspicious: it is intrinsically irreconcilable and adverse to Habermasian assumptions. If, indeed, such a collapse of culture had ever taken place, he could not hope to ever be able to combat the 'colonisation of the lifeworld' (cf. Habermas 1981, II:489–547).

20 This sort of devaluation of certain types of action as 'strategic,' as impervious to rational discourse, becomes completely superfluous once we recognize the relevance of non-scientific methods 'of making our ideas clear.' This cognitive capacity is formally rendered in the functions of the three correlates of the social sign (§4.3). Yet at the same time, the (albeit convoluted) Peircean lineage of Habermas's *Fundamentalpragmatismus* provides for the not so complete suppression of these pragmatic methods. However, the 'more rational' validities do not integrate the lower methods, and the lower methods cannot be comprehended as degenerative signs of the higher, genuine sign relation.

21 By means of his existential graphs theory of probability and possibility, as Max Fisch reconstructed the complete proof for pragmatism (Fisch, Ketner, and Kloesel 1986).

22 Regarding this point, see Ricoeur's interesting discussion of historical understanding – in particular, of Weber's view of the historical uniqueness of particular events (Ricoeur 1983, 256–69).

23 This by no means amounts to a rejection of 'comprehending' (*verstehende*) sociology in the phenomenological–Weberian tradition. In a number of variants, we find formalisms there as well, albeit in the guise of the 'typicity' of projects of action in the effort of understanding the other. But how do types of action come into being? For Schütz, Luckmann, and others, the first answer is that they are found in ego's empathy with the project of action of alter ego, where a first generalization of an individual plan of action takes place. However, ego acts according to its own life plan, which is therefore not to be generalized. The *typos* is thus of a different nature, which ultimately is pregiven in precisely the same manner as the individ-

ual action. This pregivenness of public action – of ego and alter ego – is, in Schütz as well, ultimately a form – namely, language (etc.).

24 This makes it difficult to discuss world views, because their comparability is so artificial. These macroforms of meaning vary hardly at all, and this leads to highly general statements about them. In the domain of communication sciences, this is shown quite plainly by the classic scholars of the Toronto School such as McLuhan, Innis, and Ong, and even more in their less distinguished followers (Carpenter 1974; Nevitt 1982). Every foreign world view, of course, compares with ours, but this somewhat presupposes that we have appropriated our own reflexively, which is hardly provable. The meaning of 'text grammars,' compared with world views, is much easier to show in their products, because the product itself is already a choice.

25 Without question, such an abstract form of meaning never exists concretely in this pure form. It is usually already mixed with decidable meaning, which can also be based on personal insights. Merely for analytical purposes, it is useful to differentiate meaning into levels of abstraction. In fact, it is not so difficult to concretely isolate meaning at these levels because they constitute different logical operations. This is what in involved in the classification of signs into classes of logical relations, as Peirce undertook it. For more details, see Ehrat (2005a, 116–35).

26 From a logical perspective, this constitutes a relation of an (almost pure) knowledge of a generality. In practical consequence, everything is seen as a 'case of' something that has always been known – or, in this context, of something that is provided for through narrative teleology. Such knowledge of the τύπος, which constitutes narrativity in the first place, is never able to learn. This is in complete contrast to the unforeseeable outcome of many developments in real life. Unpredictability in this sphere can only be predicted with horoscopes and the like. Aristotle described this in his *Poetics* as a requirement that tragedies be oriented not towards actual events but towards the probable (εἰκός) and the possible (δυνατόν, [i.e., according to the standards of the mores of a given society].

27 We need not consider here whether to use Foucault's irrational historical epistemes or Habermas's rational discursive validity claims. In the first, the internal mechanism would be a sheer power relation; in the second, it would be the self-controlling and cognizing subject enlarged to intersubjectivity. If semiological methodology is an option, then functionally, only a mechanism of differentiation is described, which produces meaning, leaving open the question of its anthropological and ontological foundations.

28 But the reader then rightly asks: So what? Did one not always already

know this banal surprise through one's plain common sense as a participant in those interactions? This debate we can leave to Garfinkel and his critical discussion of empiricist social sciences.

3. Semiotic of Publicity

1 This early historical-sociological analysis of civil society has been corrected considerably and conceptualized in a new way as 'validity' in 'communicative action' (in Habermas 1992).
2 In their understanding, two universes come up: one of things that are 'social,' and a second of 'physical' things. That is quite misleading, because it perpetuates the dualistic ontology of Descartes and at the same time takes out the very *clou* of semiotic, which had succeeded in uniting mind and matter into one universe in its Pragmaticist foundation. For example, it is a favourite game to address fashion as social signs (Leeds-Hurwitz 1993). Jensen's treatment of 'symbols' (1995, 162–79), albeit in a more reflected way than others do, is representative for similar inquiries. Almost in the manner of a demiurge generating a creation, these 'semioticians' create a universe of countless 'codes,' the charm of which lies in the suggestion that 'code' proffers a codified law. However, the code-theoreticians approach the establishing of such law as mere fact (i.e., as a social convention); and the same holds for the countless number of codes. From a philosophical perspective, this is an enormous regression to pre-Kantian theories, in which even attempts to generate tables of categories were explicitly abandoned (e.g., by Eco). How the single codes relate to one another remains incomprehensible – at any rate in terms of general to specific, and certainly in terms of ultimate general concepts (the idea of category). Thus, ideas such as those of an 'encyclopedia' or even of a 'rhizome' must serve as substitutes; but this yields not more than ad hoc explanations.
3 Peirce (CP 5.487): 'Moreover – here is the point – every man exercises more or less control over himself by means of modifying his own habits; and the way in which he goes to work to bring this effect about in those cases in which circumstances will not permit him to practice reiterations of the desired kind of conduct in the outer world shows that he is virtually well-acquainted with the important principle that reiterations in the inner world – fancied reiterations – if well-intensified by direct effort, produce habits, just as do reiterations in the outer world; and these habits will have power to influence actual behaviour in the outer world; especially, if each reiteration be accompanied by a peculiar strong effort that is usually likened to issuing a command to one's future self.'

4 This is, therefore, incomparable with a Habermasian 'fundamental pragmatic reconstruction,' to which the criticism mentioned above might well apply.
5 For a more detailed discussion, see Ehrat (2005a, 129–35).
6 This assumption does not deny that there is uncontrolled spontaneous action. As we saw in our previous discussion, this was so important to Schütz that he attributed an 'objective sense' to action that was more the result of an exceptional requirement, in contrast to the normal case of subjectively sensible acting. The consequences of this were enormous, for what can be known about the subjective sense that is not communicable? How is it possible to satisfactorily reduce eidetically what, by its very nature, is interaction, common sense? Schütz and his pupils were forced by these difficulties to borrow and integrate more and more foreign approaches, from Bergson to G.H. Mead.
7 This is the value involved in any conduct that is cognitively controlled, not any other predetermined value, or even one obtained (semiotically thus 'to be obtained') by convention or 'agreement.'
8 ... and this, by the way, neither upwards nor downwards. Not upwards, because an increase in cognition attains an ever higher generality (as discussed earlier). Not downwards, because every sign can be analytically decomposed. This 'degeneration' (which is a term in the logic of relations, the opposite of constructivity in higher-adic relations) can, first, isolate the First Correlate in a triadic sign relation as being – in turn – a sign in itself. Instead of rescinding the interpretation, the First Correlate remains first and is only 'taken as' sign in itself. In this manner, the 'as' in 'taking as' can degenerate to any less complex level of interpretation, also as a mere feeling. The First, then, is always less complex than the Third of a triad (in contrast to a triple, which is only a collection of three elements).
9 (Platon 1578) Theaet 170.b.8 ΣΩ. Οὐκοῦν τὴν μὲν σοφίαν ἀληθῆ διάνοιαν ἡγοῦνται τὴν δὲ ἀμαθίαν ψευδῆ δόξαν.
10 In a semionarratological context, this must sound banal, since the basic assumption is that of the double illusion of enunciation – *l'illusion énonciative* – and reality – *l'illusion référentielle* (see Greimas and Courtés 1979, s.vv.) This self-evidence is solely the result of radical nominalistic origins; for a realist sign theory, this goes not by itself.
11 Peirce's original wording was as follows: 'It appears, then, that the rule for attaining the third grade of clearness of apprehension is as follows: Consider what effects, that might conceivably have practical bearings, we conceive the object of our conception to have. Then, our conception of these effects is the whole of our conception of the object' (Peirce, CP 5.402).

Later, he commented: 'The word pragmatism was invented to express a certain maxim of logic, which, as was shown at its first enouncement, involves a whole system of philosophy. The maxim is intended to furnish a method for the analysis of concepts. A concept is something having the mode of being of a general type which is, or may be made, the rational part of the purport of a word. A more precise or fuller definition cannot here be attempted. The method prescribed in the maxim is to trace out in the imagination the conceivable practical consequences, – that is, the consequences for deliberate, self-controlled conduct, – of the affirmation or denial of the concept; and the assertion of the maxim is that herein lies the whole of the purport of the word, the entire concept. The sedulous exclusion from this statement of all reference to sensation is specially to be remarked. Such a distinction as that between red and blue is held to form no part of the concept. This maxim is put forth neither as a handy tool to serve so far as it may be found serviceable, nor as a self-evident truth, but as a far-reaching theorem solidly grounded upon an elaborate study of the nature of signs' (Peirce, CP 8.191).

12 Hyperbolically speaking, the inverted pyramid – as invented in the American press around the time of the Civil War (Mindich 1998) – in truth always continues upwards towards still more general interpretations until it becomes comprehensible to the respective historical common sense.

13 'Eristische Dialektik ist die Kunst zu disputieren, und zwar so zu disputieren, daß man Recht behält, also per fas et nefas' (Eristic dialectic is the art of disputation, viz. dispute in such a way that one prevails in being right after all, that is, *per fas et nefas*) is the incipit of Schopenhauer's essay under the homonymous title in his *Nachlaß*.

14 That journalistic surplus value crystallizes in buzzwords. Examples: 'greenhouse effect,' 'nuclear – no thanks,' 'Hubble,' 'conquest of Mars.'

15 This very general term includes 'documentary film' as well as psychosomatics and the *objets trouvés* of Dadaist painters. We must also include here journalistic 'pure facts' – style features of the sort that decorate central propositions with completely useless numbers, information items, and so on. This can produce an aura of needlessly precise truth for a fuzzy proposition.

16 Peirce intended and planned this as a major work; unfortunately, the Collected Papers edit it in a totally piecemeal fashion.

17 It means to import rationality into action if the act of 'object manipulation' is the basis. Then only communication, or as Habermas calls it, 'action coordination,' provides for a connection of mind with matter. Since it is not the mental will (this is just one of the necessary parts) that imposes itself

on matter, every action is already towards the individual. It follows that not even a reconstruction of a generalization of meaning in fundamental pragmatic is necessary (this is how Habermas reconstructs Mead). Not even the greatest imaginable collection of empirical expectations to be anticipated covers the leap into their generalization. Again, generality is of a different nature. Individual acts participate in action through signs.

18 'Doxa' or the diverse *idola* of Francis Bacon, v. *supra* §3.1.

19 This does not mean that it could not appear as such. When surveying institutions assume the role of authentic interpreters of the voice of the people, they create this appearance explicitly in contraposition to the power wielders. They can enact the ruse of this 'publicly opining subject' by endowing themselves with characteristics suggesting that 'reality itself' is speaking. The result is a hidden enunciation instance. A compelling illustration is a survey that became notorious: 'What do Germans believe?' *Der Spiegel*, at the time an influential magazine in the Federal Republic of Germany, commissioned it from Emnid on the occasion of the 1992 Catholics' Convention (*Katholikentag*). Here, the survey had the effect of a triple rhetorical envelopment: First, the magazine did not directly argue that 'we see a reality which you do not see and which evidences your incompetence,' posited against the Church hierarchy. Second, this claim to privileged knowledge inevitably contorted the simplest act of communication: the direct accusation 'you are inept, swindling hypocrites!' (and so forth). Third, when presenting the survey, it vested the communication with 'reality itself.' Reality itself accused the hierarchy of being inept administrators of faith or driven by bigotry. Reality, however, is incapable of confronting the hierarchy. To the contrary – as a construct, it is based on someone's interest in representing his selected aspect of society in more or less recognized and replicable conditions. What 'is' was this society? In reality, it was variables: age, East or West German, but mainly Catholic or non-Catholic (the rest of the demographic descriptors served only to consolidate the impression of representativity). 'Any selection is subjective,' apologized the letter accompanying the mailing of this survey – and right that was. These Catholics were what interested the survey commissioners and what came to their mind when they were conceiving of 'faith' – a notoriously ungraspable social concept. Further operationalized more or less aptly into 'valid constructs,' their conception became 'faith'-ful questionnaire items. The result was underwhelmingly ironic: expected replies that their construct correlated positively with 'faith' and that theologically amounted to heterodox or false beliefs. The survey completely missed the object, though granted its execution was impeccably professional. It overlooked

the construct partisanship in the interested (commissioner, researcher, survey or administrative institute). The appearance – in any case, 'the reality' – communicated with the hierarchy in a reproachful manner.
20 Though we do not forget the cogency of those theories which analyse the functional conditions of public opinion by relating a construction of society (in a system theory framework) to the corresponding mass media. This has been critiqued already.
21 Not in the private sphere or in groups, then, where other texts produce other meaning effects. This is shown clearly in the ethnomethodology of the Philadelphia School of Garfinkel and Labov. There are conversational variables signalling positions of power, or differentiating in general. These, however, are different from public texts. At best, one can identify conversational variables that signal 'I want to be seen!' This presents the action, thus signalled, as a public action and therefore explicitly suspends the rule 'I do not want to be disturbed!' In this context it relates to my 'Skopic Apparatus' (cf. §4.6).
22 This extends to 'high society,' or celebrities, depending on which topic the mass media consider viable in the market situation at hand. For instance, it seems that the death knell for gossip columns in newspapers and in television is already audible – and some American newspapers have abolished them as a consequence. They have been perfectly superseded by blogs.
23 Etymology does not provide any purchase on the meaning of public in 'public opinion.' The Latin term *publicus*, which in the eighteenth century found its way into English – having passed through the French *'publique'* (as opposed to *'privé'*) – is merely an adjectival form of the noun *populus*, which in turn is related to *pleo, plebs, plenus* = full (which shares its Indo-Germanic roots with folk, *Volk*). Note, however, that in ancient Rome, the contrast between *Senatus* and *populus Romanus* (SPQR) existed, and *privatus* was also used in Latin as the opposite of state affairs ('an vero vir amplissimus, P. Scipio, pontifex maximus, Ti. Gracchum mediocriter labefactantem statum rei publicae privatus interfecit'; Cicero, *in Catilinam* I:3). But all of this does not quite allow us to read into it the bourgeois life form of public opinion.
24 Or, if tackles were used, αἰώρημα. This is, besides, a logical as well as an architectonic *topos* – and one that Landowski forgets entirely in his theatre model of public opinion (1989, 30).
25 The word itself is probably derived from (f)ἔργον (to do), ἔρδω (sacrifice), ῥέζω (perform [a rite]).
26 After all, Bourdieu also argued that public opinion does not exist (in the sense of opinion polls). Here, he applies three unreflected assumptions

on which the practice of polling is based: (1) everyone does in fact have an opinion; (2) all opinions have the same weight; (3) by putting the same question to all participants, a consensus about the problem itself can be developed (Bourdieu 1980).

27 Griffin sees tragedies less in the 'collectivist' context of 'democratic virtues' and Athenian state ideology and more as an expression and exaltation of the real human life and suffering (1998): This sets him in a sharp contrast to others, who see many typically Athenian central issues – for example, the conflict between democracy and oligarchy – as central to the tragedies' interest (Goldhill 1987; Seaford 2000). Of interest in this book's context is the emphasis Seaford places on the unifying impact of the hero's death, as if that character serves as a scapegoat (φάρμακος) (Seaford 2000, 40f)

28 'Framing,' for example, has been utilized to analyse discourses of abortion in the United States and Germany. In these analyses, different frames (e.g., 'fetal right to life' versus 'self-determination') have been found that lead to different political consequences (Marx Ferree et al. 2002). The same situation could be replicated with states of affairs that, for example, sometimes are 'framed' as scandal and sometimes are 'framed' as crime.

29 Landowski calls this τό κοῖλον: (1989, 30f), which more closely resembles a back-formation of *cavea*. In fact, the tiers of spectators were generally called the θέατρον or simply the spectator seats θέαι.

30 This obtains quite literally. Media history tells us that the 'facts only' news product exists only because of news agencies, especially the one founded by Paul Julius Freiherr von Reuter (né Israel Beer Josaphat). These agencies had to shape their product in such a way that it could be sold to diverse publication organs. The result was a style that signalled 'objectivity' and that eventually became relevant for literature through the former newspaper reporter Ernest Hemingway (see Desmond 1978).

31 δι' ἐλέου καὶ φόβου περαίνουσα τὴν τῶν τοιούτων παθημάτων κάθαρσιν (Aristoteles, *Poetica* 1449b 27).

32 On the contrary, perhaps today's theatre practice suffers under the stigma of the unreal; if so, the political stage is the place where something is really going on (or really something is going on).

33 Semionarratology used to claim as its very own domain being able to abstract the narrative configuration (as Ricoeur called it) into 'actantial roles.' Since this abstraction process is purely differential – always constructed from binary contraries and contradictions – it is not really feasible to adjust this so that it constitutes a semiotic sign process. All attempts in this direction are highly unsatisfactory and cannot really convince. On the other hand, the basic principles of narrativity, generally known since the Aristo-

tle's *Poetics*, can be represented semiotically without difficulties. The Aristotelian *telos* – referred to as 'destination' in semionarratological parlance – logically amounts to teleology. In the sign relation this requires, as the Third Correlate, a representation of time as goal. The semionarratological reduplication – destinator (sender) and destinatee (receiver) – is logically superfluous and arises merely from the binary differentiation. Admissible as Object in the Second Correlate – which always implies its dyadic opposition – the Subject is no arbitrary something, but only what can become a teleological object. In the sign classification of the second trichotomy, this is a Symbol. For reasons of principle, Semiotic cannot follow the dualism of Greimas. This begins with the conjunction/disjunction (*copula*) of a property (*objet*) with a subject (*sujet*) (cf. Greimas 1983a, 67–91 'Pour une théorie des modalités'); this is not how predication actually works. For Peirce, predication is a relation between two logically unequal elements; a more general element is the predicate ('is black'), which enters into a relationship with a quantifiable singular element, the subject ('this stove,' 'all stoves').

34 For this, see Ehrat (2005a).
35 That is, we would then say it modalizes itself as a competent pragmatic subject in different ways.
36 For example, in the predication. As mentioned briefly, in the predication 'the stove is black,' blackness is the more general element, and 'this stove here' is the indexical element. The stove, of course, can be analysed further into qualities, but this would constitute another, further sign relation. Often, the relationality is hidden in the semantic: 'acceleration,' 'sale,' and 'father' all contain three or more relates, which are of different natures.
37 In semionarratological theory design, this set-up is much more complex – without changing its nominalist nature – especially when modalities are concerned. These proceed from the virtualizing (*devoir, vouloir*) to the actualizing (*pouvoir, savoir*) and to the realizing (*faire, être*: the first element is always exotaxic, the second endotaxic) (see Greimas and Courtés 1979, s.v. 'modalité').
38 I have expanded on the details of this operation elsewhere; see Ehrat (2005a, 287–314).
39 This is the tragic ἀνάγκη.
40 This practice is described in historical detail by Schudson (1978).

4. Publicity in Media Theory

1 Let us remember, against all post-metaphysical thinkers, that Semiotic also does not relapse into metaphysics conceiving of reality in substance think-

ing. That said, there is no justification for falling by default into nominalistic thinking. Granted, nominalism is somewhat easier to handle because it can spare itself the trouble of addressing the thorny question *how* raw reality relates to thought. Simmel's social form was radically nominalistic, and rationality – both in the Weberian sense and as adopted by Schütz and Habermas – is still a historical nominalism. The semiotic idea of the sign relation comes closer to reality, but for that reason it cannot offer impressive configurations such as 'world views,' 'rationalities,' and 'social forms of exchange value.' It reaches as far as cognitive steps, as contingent common sense; however, it becomes a 'critical common-sensism' when the procedure is treated as 'doubt/belief' cycles and thus, as we saw, becomes the application of one of the different methods of 'how to make our ideas clear.'

2 If the term 'systems theory' is not to be taken as referring to 'no clear meaning' (see Luhmann 1984b, 15), one should follow the rough distinctions among various systems theories (as per Willke 1989, 5ff): (a) structural-functional (Parsons); (b) system-functional (Buckley); (c) functional-structural (Luhmann); functional-genetic, and (e) self-referential systems: *autopoiesis* (Maturana) and radical constructivism.

3 I treated this more extensively elsewhere; see Ehrat (2005a, 8–111).

4 Even Habermas seems to accept this premise, as McCarthy has criticized (1991, 169). However, he does not reach the same consequences, and he is not even referring directly to Luhmann's system theory, but to Parsons's. Media remain 'colonisations of the life world'; they must still be legitimized discursively, especially the non-monetary media. For Habermas, it still must be possible to criticize society; this is no longer a possibility in Luhmann.

5 Luhmann (1981, 9–44). does not explicitly reject this option; rather, he interprets ends ateleologically, merely as an 'interruption of interdependence,' while maintaining self-reference. 'Zwecke dienen auf der Grundlage unaufhebbarer Selbstreferenz der semantischen Verdichtung von Interdependenzunterbrechungen. Sie sind, mit anderen Worten, Interdependenzunterbrechungen zweiter Stufe. Eine Zweckformel macht im Normalfall von Temporalisierung, Kausalität und Externalisierung Gebrauch. Sie wird zuweilen auch als Reflexionsformel benutzt' (35).

6 Cf. Luhmann (1984b, 9–44), where the relation to Schelling and Fichte is established but not discussed.

7 Habermas and Luhmann (1971, 11): 'Alles, was über Systeme gesagt wird ..., läßt sich ... funktional analysieren als Reduktion von Komplexität. In dieser Form kann die Systemtheorie ... sich jenem transzendentalen

Problem der Kontingenz der Welt nähern, und d.h.: Ausgangspunkt einer Theorie der Gesellschaft werden, sie muß dazu nur Kontingenz in Komplexität umdefinieren. Die soziale Kontingenz sinnhaften Erlebens ist nichts anderes als ein Aspekt jener unermeßlichen Weltkomplexität, die durch Systembildungen reduziert werden muß.'

8 In Welker, ed. (1985, 38f): '[In ihrer selbstbewußten Situierung als Subsystem der Gesellschaft] die Relativität jeglicher Bestimmung so heilig, daß sie diese mittels heimlicher Chiffrierung unbedingt gegen den Verdacht auf triviale Beliebigkeit zu verteidigen sucht.'

9 It is comparable only with the secular religious historical transformation of religious experience into the sacred/profane difference or into morality/immorality.

10 In almost his final work (1997), Luhmann added a new twist to Spencer-Brown's Law of Form, which seems to skirt the problem of how systems are ultimately constituted by simply admitting the circularity and the impossibility of assuming a third position – the distinguishing itself – between the distinction of 'marked' and 'unmarked space.' In a footnote (186n255) referring explicitly to that critique, Luhmann thus rejects the very possibility that 'society' (which is indeed the last system) could still reflect the unity of its system difference. This means there is no possibility of seeing society as 'rational.'

11 At the Cambridge Conferences of 1898, *Reasoning and the Logic of Things*, Peirce stated: 'I stand before you an Aristotelian and a scientific man, condemning with the whole strength of conviction the Hellenic tendency to mingle philosophy and practice' (CP 1.618). 'And it is precisely because of this utterly unsettled and uncertain condition of philosophy at present, that I regard any practical applications of it to religion and conduct as exceedingly dangerous. I have not one word to say against the philosophy of religion or of ethics in general or in particular. I only say that for the present it is all far too dubious to warrant risking any human life upon it. I do not say that philosophical science should not ultimately influence religion and morality; I only say that it should be allowed to do so only with secular slowness and the most conservative caution' (Peirce, CP 1.620).

12 Metaphysic, therefore, is no longer the first or proto-science, but the last one as it were, explicitly derived from the modes of experiencing, which in turn it comprehends as logical operations. 'Experience' in the Peircean context always means 'conduct' or 'habit of behaviour.' Any aspiration to deduce a metaphysic from experience needs first to ascertain the types of goals in these conducts – that is, the most general types of values. By means of these values, conduct orients itself towards modes or types of

reality, which can then be developed in a metaphysical key. This is quite different from Schütz's and Berger and Luckmann's constructivism, which, despite its Meadean inspiration, remains firmly anchored in an egological attitude of subjectivity.

13 Peirce (CP 1.191f): 'Normative science has three widely separated divisions: i. Esthetics; ii. Ethics; iii. Logic. Esthetics is the science of ideals, or of that which is objectively admirable without any ulterior reason. I am not well acquainted with this science; but it ought to repose on phenomenology. Ethics, or the science of right and wrong, must appeal to Esthetics for aid in determining the summum bonum. It is the theory of self-controlled, or deliberate, conduct. Logic is the theory of self-controlled, or deliberate, thought; and as such, must appeal to ethics for its principles. It also depends upon phenomenology and upon mathematics. All thought being performed by means of signs, logic may be regarded as the science of the general laws of signs. It has three branches: 1, Speculative Grammar, or the general theory of the nature and meanings of signs, whether they be icons, indices, or symbols; 2, Critic, which classifies arguments and determines the validity and degree of force of each kind; 3, Methodeutic, which studies the methods that ought to be pursued in the investigation, in the exposition, and in the application of truth. Each division depends on that which precedes it.'

14 Post-metaphysical metaphysics is not so unusual in sociology. For example, Berger and Luckmann (1967) developed a relativistic metaphysic from their egological theory of society (without calling it so). Even in systems theory, there is an equivalent to ontology when systems operations constitute the real as their product.

15 This classification of signs, at which Peirce arrived in this very late manuscript (MS 318), constitutes a new approach to considering the relation between an inner and an outer world (Peirce, CP 5.474). The object relation is viewed as having an immediate, a dynamic, and a logical object; to these, the emotional, the energetic, and the logical Interpretant correspond.

16 How complex and differentiated this and other socially highly relevant behaviours can be was evinced convincingly for the southern American states in the extensive descriptions of Birdwhistell (1970, 39–46).

17 By no means has this limitation prevented music from being theoretically conceived, starting with Pythagoras and continuing up to his contemporary academic successors. The iterative character of the sign relation, the unlimited chain of interpretations, covers this. Though one can express it mathematically, harmony has its originary locus in musical behaviour, in particular in performance practice – not in thought but in the ear, that is, in a sensory kernel that no one can ever strip away.

18 Peirce (CP 5.538): 'In the formation of habits of deliberate action, we may imagine the occurrence of the stimulus, and think out what the results of different actions will be. One of these will appear particularly satisfactory; and then an action of the soul takes place which is well described by saying that that mode of reaction "receives a deliberate stamp of approval." The result will be that when a similar occasion actually arises for the first time it will be found that the habit of really reacting in that way is already established. I remember that one day at my father's table, my mother spilled some burning spirits on her skirt. Instantly, before the rest of us had had time to think what to do, my brother, Herbert, who was a small boy, had snatched up the rug and smothered the fire. We were astonished at his promptitude, which, as he grew up, proved to be characteristic. I asked him how he came to think of it so quickly. He said, "I had considered on a previous day what I would do in case such an accident should occur."'

19 By becoming worldless and thus negating the specific reality constraint, systems theory has, as noted, shed an onus of proof. Freed, the double contingent communication system can commit itself arbitrarily. In postmetaphysical theory designs, this allows us to rid ourselves of any central social governance. What remains as an alternative is only an arbitrary contingent constellation.

20 Durkheim (1985, chapitre Ier): « Un fait social se reconnaît au pouvoir de coercition externe qu'il exerce ou est susceptible d'exercer sur les individus; et la présence de ce pouvoir se reconnaît à son tour soit à l'existence de quelque sanction déterminée, soit à la résistance que le fait oppose à toute entreprise individuelle qui tend à lui faire violence. »

21 Even though the biblical use is deliberately metaphorical, applying the economic term ὀφείλημα (Matthew 6:12 or, even more explicitly, Luke 7:41 χρεωφειλέτης, 'someone owing debt, loan') to the moral concept of 'sin.'

22 Whereas Habermas has already addressed the system constraint of the mass media in his critique of Luhmann's functionalism.

23 McLuhan (1962, I): 'Any technology tends to create a new human environment. Script and papyrus created the social environment we think of in connection with the empires of the ancient world. The stirrup and the wheel created unique environments of enormous scope. Technological environments are not merely passive containers of people but are active processes that reshape people and other technologies alike.'

24 Ricoeur, and Greimas in a quite different way, have much more to say to this point. For Ricoeur, with his phenomenological tying of any mimesis of action to the existential I of the Reader, the authentic expression of myself needs to be understood as my entanglement into my own history. This is

inherent in every existence as soon as it represents itself (be it only before oneself). Since Habermas bases his approach on analyses of propositional logic, he sees only the results of validities with atemporal characteristics. Histories instead, except for propositions, must take their time from somewhere. In contrast, for Greimas the expression of interiority is a question of the technique of representation, which evolves from narrative grammar and the social imaginary. In that context, there exist no privileged accesses, only different (actorial and thematic) investments of syntactic roles. One of these stands as the basis of meaning as such, the all-important destination role, which in the case of the representation of interiority must be modally invested with a special competence of 'knowing.'

25 Cf. Habermas (1981, I:497), following Horkheimer and Adorno.
26 For Peirce the logic of sign relations is also expressed in the diversity of the roles of proponent and opponent (cf. CP 3.481 and 5.47) and also with regard to 'vague' and 'general' signs. Our Theatron model of public opinion has tried to apply this division of roles, inherent in the sign relation, to some advantage.
27 Hitchcock (1995, 343): 'Significantly, Williams eschews technological determinism and any attempt to isolate technology as a cultural form. Yet this approach also entails the restoration of intentionality ('purposes and practices') to the process of research and development, which certainly entertains a dangerous determinism all its own.'
28 The problem is mainly a methodological one: How can the connection between an aesthetic and a social form be proven? With Simmel's amalgamate *'Soziale Form'* applied to the form of television, the advantage consists, on the one hand, in the ahistoricity of the form of socialization, and on the other, in the historicity of the contingency of that form. The fundamental ahistoricity of the historiographical construction of causality can be assumed to be fundamental to causality construction in news production and also in any other text form. So far, television appears as a medium of narrative formation of society in that it self-monitors in the form of events. On the other hand, Simmel's social form permits us to conceive of the historical contingency of socialization as a form of communication typical of modernity. The modern construction of individuality, in interaction with its form of socialization, found its congenial medium in television, mass individuality. Television – in particular in its entertainment form – suggests, in representation, an interactive form of socialization. Entertainment, after all, is derived from *entre-tenir, tenir entre – that is*, 'to hold the between' exactly where it has been most lost. Simmel's analyses are highly instructive – generally, they are microanalyses of the little things of eve-

ryday life. They show how individuality depends on social typification. Without types there would be no individuals, but we would still be in the age of orders and we would be defined by our being part of our estate or guild.
29 Cf. the cogent critique of geniality aesthetics in Gadamer (1960).
30 For greater detail, see Ehrat (2005a, 435–57).
31 Butler (2002, 335): 'The initial academic theories of television were particularly attentive to the impact of TV on the viewer. The hypodermic needle concept, which television research inherited from post–World War I studies of propaganda in newspapers and magazines, is one of the earliest of so-called effects theories. In this model, we are directly affected by what we see on TV as if we were injected with a hypodermic needle. Or, to borrow a metaphor from Pavlovian psychology, the bell rings and we salivate.'
32 Which is promptly and energetically rejected by Schiller (1989) in the controversy with Thompson (1995), who argues against 'a too uniform view of the American media culture and their global dominance.'
33 Cf. Odin (1990) regarding the entire problem complex of the language paradigm in film theory.
34 In a Greimasian context, one could call this the modalization of the roles by the actantial enunciation role, the embedding of a narration into a framing narration, which has its independent role positions.
35 Uncoupling means that from the I-now-here a dependent not-I, not-now, not-here universe is produced. Textual methodology involves adopting a number of linguistic concepts. The nominalist generativism of the Paris School is not embraced; even so, important insights are drawn from it. These are epitomized in Greimas and Courtés (1979). That insights from Benveniste and Weinrich are extremely useful for audiovisual enunciation analysis is demonstrated by (Carontini 1986; Casetti 1986).
36 There is no need to follow Greimas in his « parcours génératif » of subject modalization, which is merely a sort of pragmatic based on meaning understood as pure difference. From depth to surface, generative grammar modalizes subjects from virtual to realized to acting subjects: wanting-to (*vouloir*), being able-to (*pouvoir*), knowing-to (*savoir*), having-to (*devoir*). The combination of its four modality positions realizes (semionarratologically) a subject as meaning. Taking into account that the pragmatic 'object' of display is an audience, this also needs to be modalized though it is not evident as what, in the modalities of being or of doing. The combination of all positions is a covariation of the four positions of the four modalities, 4×4 squares with $4 \times 4 \times 4 - 3 = 61$ possible meanings (position A is identical for all four modalities). Now if the object of interest is not just one subject

of the communication axis, but the two complementary subjects of enunciation, the formal description of enunciational meaning becomes so complex (61 × 61 = 3721) that it is comprehensible only as a combinatory, but not as an effective meaning with assignable discriminating semantic labels.

5. From Jubilation to Scandal

1 Albeit with a long tradition of theoretical reflection in sociology (Durkheim, Marx, Weber, Fromm), anthropology and ethnology (van Gennep, Turner, Otto), and of course theology and religious studies, with all its highly speculative discourses about the unspeakable, apophatic in the experience of God (in such formulas as Lateran Council IV, 'Quia inter creatorem et creaturam non potest tanta similitudo notari, quin inter eos maior sit dissimilitudo notanda' [DS 806], Cusanus' *conincidentia oppositorum*, and Barth's *totaliter aliter*).
2 For instance, in the centre of the storm over 'fundamentalist' military chaplains trying by rather 'rough' methods to proselytize other soldiers (Goodstein 2005a, 2005b).
3 This made the Guyana Tragedy and *The Handmaid's Tale* religious in genre, since they represented religion. This meaning had to be displayed convincingly; otherwise, the entire story could not have been understood. Religious meaning is here represented, though negatively valuated.
4 Mittell (2003, 36): 'One way to explore the talk show genre is to examine the ways in which audiences use the generic category of talk shows to ground their own cultural assumptions and locate the genre within a set of extant hierarchies and power relations ... More specific questions arise: How do audiences define the talk show genre? What interpretations do they foreground in understanding the talk show? What cultural evaluations and hierarchies do audiences draw on? What other assumptions and linkages does this generic category activate for audiences? How do audiences view the talk show genre in relation to other genres? How do divisions and categories of social identity relate to the talk show genre and its audience? What divisions, categories, and hierarchies do audiences construct within the genre itself? How do audiences locate particular programs within this generic framework? How do visions of the talk show audience itself intersect with these generic assumptions? ... a site of cultural hierarchies and identity formation for television audiences.'
5 From a famous article by Carey (1989, 20f): 'A ritual view of communication will focus on a different range of problems in examining a newspaper. It will, for example, view reading a newspaper less as sending or gaining

information and more like attending a mass: a situation in which nothing new is learned but in which a particular view of the world is portrayed and confirmed. News reading, and writing, is a ritual act and moreover a dramatic one ... Under a ritual view, then, news is not information but drama; it does not describe the world but portrays an arena of dramatic forces and action; it exists solely in historical time; and it invites our participation on the basis of our assuming, often vicariously, social roles within it.'

6 It is known, however, that the Swiss author Friedrich Dürrenmatt gave his novel *Grieche sucht Griechin* (Once a Greek) two different endings, one for lending libraries; and Beethoven might have had difficulty imagining that his Ninth Symphony could also be watched on television lying in a bath tub.

7 For more detail, see especially §2 in Ehrat (2005a).

8 Very instructive with regard to the semantic investment of *sanctum*, *sacrum*, and *profanum* is Benveniste and Lallot (1969).

9 From this sacral combination a psychoanalytic thesis has been construed. See Schroeder (2004, 3): 'This book on utilitarianism and romanticism is an encounter with Hegelian philosophy and Lacanian psychoanalysis, and an exploration of the erotics of law and the market using metaphors drawn from classical mythology. I argue that the utilitarian-romantic analysis of the law and the market is incorrect for two interrelated reasons. First, Hegelian philosophy shows us that, far from being anti-erotic, market relations are the most basic and primitive form of eroticism. Meanwhile, Lacanian theory reveals that the feminine is the primal commodity; money is Juno Moneta.' Schroeder does not acknowledge, however, that Juno also warns us about dangers – an attribute historically connected to the Gallic invasion under Brennus and the Capitoline sacred geese, which were kept in the *auguraculum* of an oracle goddess from Cumae. Cf. Dury-Moyaers and Renard (1981, 165–7): 'Consequently, the utilitarian is correct in seeing a fundamental similarity between erotic and economic behavior, but wrong in thinking that the former can be reduced to the latter. Rather, it is the latter that can be explained in terms of the former. Venus triumphs over the market. To put this another way, both the utilitarian and the romantic see desire as external to law. In contradistinction, the Hegelian and Lacanian, following a Western philosophic tradition reaching back to Aristotelian virtue ethics, posit that law operates at the level of desire.'

10 As very impressively described in Certeau (1980, chapter XIII).

11 As a religious rhetorician, she works absolutely visually, in the very strong opening shots 'From heaven high ...' (as a Luther hymn says literally), when the Führer's airplane approaches through white clouds, with the

Imperial Nuremberg Castle as the first meeting point on earth for the new messiah. The symbolism is clearly intended as well as too obvious to be missed by any contemporary, and it obviously worked quite well for some time.

12 Within the range of vertical vectorization, one should also be able to show differences between the forms of social communication of the installation of divine power. In one case, the proxy person becomes the centre; in another, that centre is the sacrament, in the monstrance – a strong spatial symbolism of eucharistic devotion in a concentric-vertical form. We might note here that different understandings of the Eucharist must also entail differences in the construal of space. Sacramental devotion in orthodox churches emphasizes the mystery so clearly that there is no point in showing the sacramental species. Iconostases conceal the essential but at the same time enhance the image as an especially powerful form of representation of the divine nature.

13 War reporting has contributed much to recent television: the First and Second Gulf Wars; death in front of live cameras during the siege of Sarajevo; and race riots broadcast by satellite in real-time, such as the pogrom in Rostock-Lichtenhagen, against Vietnamese asylum seekers and a TV team (22–26 August 1992) (Landtag Mecklenburg-Vorpommern 1993).

14 Weber (1920b) distinguishes sects from churches by applying the criterion of personal decision (i.e., in contrast to being born into a church). If decision is the *conditio sine qua non* of appurtenance, this has strong consequences for rules of life and conduct following that decision.

15 Jim and Tammy Baker of the Praise The Lord Club (PTL) made this very evident; but elsewhere, too, an entire large family would handle a televangelist show, in venues sometimes as large as Madison Square Garden. Schuller bestowed his ordination powers on his son in a carefully staged ordination as a Reformed pastor.

16 Peters places a question mark beside the media's general ability to witness: 'One of the most daring things in media events theory [i.e. Dayan and Katz's] is the question: just when can media be agents of truth or authenticity instead of prevarication and ideology? In other words, can the media sustain the practice of witnessing? The notion that home audiences could be witnesses is one of those apparent category mistakes whose elaboration the media events movement has made its task ... Presence-at-a-distance is precisely what witnessing a media event claims to offer ... In media events, the borrowed eyes and ears of the media become, however tentatively or dangerously, one's own' (2001, 717).

17 Weber, Parsons, and Giddens (1992, 60): 'In its extreme inhumanity this

doctrine must above all have had one consequence for the life of a generation which surrendered to its magnificent consistency. That was a feeling of unprecedented inner loneliness of the single individual. [Footnote: The deepest community (with God) is found not in institutions or corporations or churches, but in the secrets of a solitary heart,' as Dowden puts the essential point in his fine book *Puritan and Anglican* (p. 234). This deep spiritual loneliness of the individual applied as well to the Jansenists of Port Royal, who were also predestinationists.]'

18 Max Weber in 'The Protestant Sects and the Spirit of Capitalism' (Weber 1920b, I:223ff) reports a number of events in the history of Calvinism, including one episode (Kuyper's Schisma) in the Dutch Herformde Kerk, where a Church split over the question of whether sinners could be admitted to the Last Supper.

19 Pierre Lacroix became a victim of televangelist's scandal when he was dragged mercilessly into the public sphere, indicted for homosexual relations. Before this demise, he had increased his celebrity status by staging a megademonstration against abortion legislation on Ottawa's Parliament Hill with Mother Theresa of Calcutta. There he used his televangelist skills of stridently judgmental rhetoric and condemnation to hell. This was the last straw, for it left him ripe for a public unmasking; indeed, public opinion succeeded perfectly in 'shooting him down.'

20 The 'higher loyalty' of investigative reporting or journalism, as described above, belongs in this context.

21 Rather, before the 'heavenly choirs' of the cherubim (fire carriages, four-headed winged beings in the Temple) and the seraphim (dragons).

22 Propaganda is a genuine Christian endeavour in the original sense of the term. It simply means that faith is to be spawned (from *pangere*, to 'plant or set out layers'). Hence the name of the *Congregatio de propaganda fide*. But after the term was abducted by political discourse, propaganda – and its intensive form, agitprop – became instruments of boundless power.

23 And even then they are mostly revealed as frauds or impostures, as in the case of Leni Riefenstahl's *Triumph des Willens*, which tried to convey this divine instrument role, bestowing it on Hitler (cf.§5.3).

24 Hoffjann (2001), for instance, has developed these useful misunderstandings for every intersystemic relation in the forum of public opinion.

6. Judgment: Bringing into a Scandal-Position

1 It is not by chance that Peirce also referred to Semiotic as Speculative Grammar (i.e., theoretical grammar).

2 Cf. Peirce's *'The Logic of Mathematics; An Attempt to Develop My Categories from Within.' (1896):* 'The triadic clause of the law of logic recognizes three elements in truth, the idea, or predicate, the fact or subject, the thought which originally put them together and recognizes they are together; from whence many things result, especially a threefold inferential process which either first follows the order of involution from living thought or ruling law, and existential case under the condition of the law to the predication of the idea of the law in that case; or second, proceeds from the living law and the inherence of the idea of that law in an existential case, to the subsumption of that case and to the condition of the law; or third, proceeds from the subsumption of an existential case under the condition of a living law, and the inherence of the idea of that law in that case to the living law itself. Thus the law of logic governs the relations of different predicates of one subject' (CP 1.485).
3 It was Schütz' 'Choosing among Projects of Action' that used these two connectives in order to differentiate two types of action ('projects') and motives (Schütz 1973, I:67–96).
4 The different modes of enunciation are discussed in detail in Ehrat (2005a).
5 There have been various attempts (cf. Lau 2004) to differentiate in the journalistic production process 'external' constraints from 'internal' news values. Obviously, in our view these factors are irrelevant if they do not show up concretely as meaning in the news product. The distinction between text and metatext, therefore, is not between an outside and an inside of whatever, be it organization, culture, political economy, or news values (and so forth). Effectively, its reach beyond the text from within the text extends to an ancient model of spectacular meaning.
6 This highly consequential fiction – a purified conception of politics in its 'inviolate state,' before it enters a stage of insurmountable conflict and strife – is addressed by Luhmann and Kieserling (2002a, 274–82).
7 Schudson wanted to turn this antagonism into a distinction of essence between an 'information' and a 'narrative (i.e. story) journalism' (1978, 88–120). The real boundaries, though, were always somewhat more fluid, if we discount stylizations in the respective editorials of their own and the others' 'true identity.'
8 In concrete reality, though – for example, in the nascent Chinese economic bourgeoisie – the watchdog function needs to be taken *cum grano salis*. Zhou (2000, 594): 'Watchdogs may continue to bark but they may carry a privileged accent, and attack selectively in their own political and commercial interests or in the interest of advertisers' favored audiences.' According to Gitlin, this is also true for Washington journalism: 'Contrary to

the profession's conventional wisdom, I would say that during most of the past forty years, American journalism has been more amplification system than watchdog' (2006, 5).
9. Tettey (2001, 6): 'In this analysis, I see the media and democracy as symbiotically related. I, therefore, share Suarez's [...] view that "democratization and journalism influence each other's advances and setbacks."'
10. However, with the anarchic Internet culture, this monopoly could also cease to be exercised in the hitherto known fashion (see Ehrat 2003)
11. The concept of 'viability' in the reality theory of systems theory involves the relativism of the one system, but even more the relativisms of another second system. Thus viability postulates merely the ability to communicate between two reality constructs. As we have already discussed, this frees systems theory from the onus of realism, as it arises in semiotic Pragmaticism as a problem.
12. Bell, a BBC journalist, while reporting on the Bosnian conflict, counterposed to that an 'attached' journalism (i.e., emotional involvement). While this might function in rare individual cases, especially where the general indignation of 'all' can be presumed, the opposite danger looms that journalists will ride subjective hobbyhorses or even advocate for their own individual causes. With the demise of party journalism, the industry credited itself with overcoming partisanship through a 'consensus on the facts' *supra partes*, and that achievement would be in danger.
13. Joseph Pulitzer, the press baron of the then scandal press, established 'moral journalism' in this classic motto: 'Above knowledge, and above news, above intelligence, the heart and soul of a newspaper lie in its moral sense, in its courage, its integrity, its humanity, its sympathy for the oppressed, its independence, its devotion to the public welfare, its anxiety to render public service' (Mencher 2003, 621).
14. Explicitly, in this sense, de Burgh (2000, 66) brings a plethora of anecdotal evidence to the self-comprehension of the investigative journalism industry. More extensively, Clayman (2002, 199): 'Thus, far from being a simple manifestation of unadulterated professionalism, this practice is best understood as a mode of selfpresentation – a style of questioning employed methodically to achieve a defensible professional posture at particularly sensitive moments in the course of an interview.'
15. Baker (2003, 21): 'Jayson Blair used the cover of unidentified sources to make things up. Miller allows sources to hide their identities in order to advance a self-serving agenda. Using unnamed sources is a common and necessary technique in journalism. But sources should not be allowed to remain unnamed when the information they are imparting serves to di-

rectly advance their own and their employers' objectives. In other words, a reporter needs a very good justification for not naming a source – usually because a source is saying something that could get him or her in big trouble with some powerful entity. But what kind of trouble could befall some unnamed Pentagon source who is leaking material in accord with the objectives of the current Administration? The principal motive for remaining under cover in such circumstances, besides preserving deniability, is to gain greater currency for the leaked material, as something that has received the imprimatur of our internationally recognized "newspaper of record," the New York Times.'

16 As Mindich (1998, 64–94) discovered.
17 www.guenter-wallraff.com
18 Berlau (2006) quotes Section 806 of the Sarbanes-Oxley Act: 'No publicly traded company, or any officer, employee, contractor, subcontractor or agent of such company may discharge, demote, suspend, threaten, harass, or in any other manner discriminate against an employee in the terms and conditions of employment because of any lawful act done by the employee.' However, this law is limited to companies listed on stock exchanges; also, it relates principally to internal control and does not directly concern media contacts. That said, it seems to have played a role in the process against Mathew Cooper and Time Inc. concerning the handing over of interview notes, as well as in accusations of 'obstruction of justice' arising from Karl Rove's 'outing' of CIA agent Valery Plame-Wilson.
19 Searle (1983, 1): 'Intentionality is that property of many mental states and events by which they are directed at or about or of objects and states of affairs in the world. If, for example, I have a belief, it must be a belief that such and such is the case; if I have a fear, it must be a fear of something or that something will occur; if I have a desire, it must be a desire to do something or that something should happen or be the case; if I have an intention, it must be an intention to do something. And so on through a large number of other cases.'
20 Even 'phenomena of nature' – Gauthier's first of seven classes of 'brute facts' that he claims to have found in the *New York Times* – almost never remain facts. One can, for example, find some culprit even for snowstorms or for hurricanes like Katrina – for instance, by identifying preterintentional pragmatic goals of energy-wasting politicians and national economies. While as assertion this can be relegated to the realm of mere speculation, it is still the most virulent part of a news story. In recent years we have seen elections won or lost as a result of hurricanes (United States) and floods (Germany).

21 Baym (2004, 281f): 'Packages are defined here as stories in which the reporter's voice track is matched with corresponding visual imagery and often intercut with sound-bites and reporter stand-ups. Packages also include live lead-ins and often on-camera tags. The package is distinguishable from other common news formats such as readers or voice-overs, in which the anchor reads short stories either with or without accompanying full-screen imagery.'

22 'Bias' is in any case an incommensurable qualification for the use of true, objective, factual assertions in a story. Its 'obliqueness' connotation refers to a level *status ante quam*. But what is level in a story? If it is not oriented as closely as possible towards its pragmatic goal, it fails in its purpose. An example of a perfectly level story is a list of true numbers alphabetically ordered, such as stock quotations; but those numbers become narratively comprehensible only as a crash, a bull or bear market, a reaction to a crisis or bubble, or similar.

23 D'Angelo (2002) tries to remedy the core's lack, replacing the lacunar theory with a metatheoretical 'research programme' as proposed by Lakatos. Once a common paradigmatic research landscape exists, it can accommodate different theories. He provides three theories for 'framing theory': cognitive, constructivist, and critical. All of these, though, are independently viable and need no frame theory to be plausible.

24 Entman (1993) identifies the four 'locations' into which communication is usually broken down: sender, receiver, text, culture. Text content is framed with devices that are both different from and outside the text. Frames originate in social causes, movements, and interest groups. Also, they are thought to have cognitive and behavioural effects. The fourth location – and the most interesting – relates to how frames shape various forms of social life. Most of this is common sense, but it would be interesting to have theoretical explanations of these assumptions.

25 These are also the two formal aspects that semionarratology distinguishes in acting: the forms make–be (*faire être*) and make–make (*faire faire*), with a change of state of being and the manipulation of another subject.

26 Two famous examples: the one paid for by *Der Spiegel* in 1992; and the one paid for by the *Boston Globe*. Both found the bishops (also) responsible for secular events.

27 In 1997, various European TV channels, including *arte*, showed a series on popes and the Vatican, apparently inspired by the Vatican series developed by Sir Peter Ustinov. Analysing these series with regard to the meaning that holds them together, we find that precisely the destination situation described here is in effect. For instance, in both series it is John Paul II who

brought about the fall of communism. What is insidious here is that it is not quite wrong, but only if one has construed the story with a quite determinate narrative causality. Once stories are told, they are always plausible because of their historical causality. That causality, however, is nothing one can see. It needs to be construed, and thus the pope is acting in two different plays without having to change his wardrobe. Only the scenery and the script have been exchanged.

28 The *illusion référentielle* is the cogent result of the nominalistic approach of semionarratology, as Coquet (1982, 19–30) demonstrates in his polemic against the real as such.

29 Kitzinger (1995), for example, examined the genesis of sexual roles and the public reputations that result. Her subjects were girls in Glasgow. Her study is limited to negative reputations, mediated by Scottish *epitheta ornantia* such as 'slag,' 'tart,' and 'slut' (187 and passim); also, it focuses on the sustained effects of negative reputations for those concerned. It would have been at least as interesting if she had investigated the construction of reputation as such, especially in terms of the public reputation of high-calibre stars like Madonna. Kitzinger concerns herself with how the reputations of stars like Madonna and Kylie Minogue impact young Scotswomen, that is, on 'why Madonna is not a slag – sexually attractive but powerful' (192–3). In this study, Madonna is an elaborate product, or an ideology, whom Kitzinger uses in her interviews as a positive model of femininity: 'The day-to-day business of being female is fraught with pitfalls, and these young Scottish women were acutely conscious of the dilemma they face when trying to attract men without "going too far." One interviewee explained how it was possible to appear "tarty" simply in the normal course of being feminine' (190).

30 In a broader sense, identity transformation is a standard topic of social science. Turner's (i.e., van Gennep's) concept of liminality is an equivalent of this metatext with regard to societies having fixed positions; for it expresses the only mobility of social identity. Weber's ideas about the genesis of modernity also belong in this context. A merciless 'particularism of grace' destroyed universalism – and brought individuals down with it – by proving themselves, demonstrating their election, which in consequence brought about the 'spiritual virtuosoship.'

31 Peirce (CP 5.382): 'Systems of this sort have not usually rested upon any observed facts, at least not in any great degree. They have been chiefly adopted because their fundamental propositions seemed "agreeable to reason." This is an apt expression; it does not mean that which agrees with experience, but that which we find ourselves inclined to believe.'

32 Boorstin (1961, 58): 'The celebrity is a person who is well-known for their well-knownness.'
33 Today, most of the big stars are 'handled' by one of three big agencies (CAA, MCA, William Morris). Their image is groomed systematically, with output constantly provided for the gossip press and the fan clubs, including usenet groups and blogs.
34 Turner (2004, 135): 'What I described as the demotic turn in media content was explicitly disconnected from an intrinsically democratic politics, but it was seen to hold possibilities for the exercise of a greater degree of popular sovereignty over media content – and a greater degree of media access for ordinary people. Where I treated the consumption of celebrity as a potentially productive social activity it was because, through their consumption of the celebrity-commodity, the consumer accessed some forms of power.'
35 For more detail, see Ehrat (2005a, 360–71).
36 Esser and Hartung (2004) wrongly presume a social legitimate expectation, instead of comprehending it as the construct of the scandal itself. 'Generally speaking,' they write, 'the defect – real or alleged – at the center of a scandal requires some form of injury to a social norm ... This norm can be a law, a value, a rule of conduct, or a legitimate expectation – in the sense of something generally considered legitimate' (1041). They also refer to realities in society when it comes to qualifying the subject's competence, instead of the product generated by the scandal itself as meaning effect (which can then be expected by all scandal 'participants' as adequate interpretative behaviour). 'It needs more than tastes, aesthetical judgments, idiosyncratic normative conceptions, or group values to do this successfully,' they continue. 'If a claim that a norm no longer be breached does not meet general approval, at least of this norm, the person to propagate the claim either will not be listened to, if he or she is lucky, or will be considered a lunatic if not' (ibid.).
37 At the lowest level, this manifests itself as incomprehension. For instance, how can 'holy warriors,' future 'martyrs' (*shuhada' al-ma'raka*) in the party of God ('*hizb Allah*'), appeal to a direct divine mandate? Also, how is it possible for someone to kill in the name of God? This incomprehension is not another view of God, accepting no partisan God, and *a fortiori* no God who is a party against his creatures. On the contrary, public opinion has a general incomprehension of claims that there can be actions 'in the name' of God, that someone could have a mandate from God to do something.
38 *Boston Globe* (2004b).
39 *Boston Globe* (2004a).
40 *Boston Globe* (2004c).

7. The Course of the Scandal Pro-Gram

1. Abbott (1997, 1152) does his best to dissect this research attitude in a slightly polemical article from a pragmatic perspective: 'Social facts are located. This means a focus on social relations and spatial ecology in synchronic analysis, as it means a similar focus on process in diachronic analysis. Every social fact is situated, surrounded by other contextual facts and brought into being by a process relating it to past contexts. An immediate corollary is that not only do variables not exist in reality, they are misleading even as a nominalist convention. For the idea of a variable is the idea of a scale that has the same causal meaning whatever its context: the idea, for example, that "education" can have "an effect" on "occupation" irrespective of the other qualities of an individual, whether those qualities be other past experiences, other personal characteristics, or friends, acquaintances, and connections. Within variable-based thinking, one allows for a few "interactions" to modify this single causal meaning contextually, but the fundamental image of variables' independence is enshrined in the phrase "net of other variables" and in the aim to discover this net effect, whether through experimental or statistical manipulation. The Chicago view was that the concept of net effect was social scientific nonsense. Nothing that ever occurs in the social world occurs "net of other variables." All social facts are located in contexts. So why bother to pretend that they are not?'
2. The origin of which seems to be in a gents' toilet graffito at that paper (cf. Silk 1995, 49).
3. This is an explicit subject matter; that, or it must be contributed as a meaning foundation. Accordingly, the biggest imaginable transformation is a revolution-in-the-act. The minimum is that nothing occurred, but narrativity must presuppose that something should have occurred (that did not occur). Between the two comes the crisis, with a balance between virtual and actual.
4. An old hand at religion reporting, Peter Steinfels of the *New York Times*, sees a repetition of this shortlist of little stories: 'Religious leader reveals feet of clay (or turns out to be scoundrel); Ancient faith struggles to adjust to modern times; Scholars challenge long-standing beliefs; Interfaith harmony overcomes inherited enmity; New translation of sacred scripture sounds funny; Devoted members of a zealous religious group turn out to be warm, ordinary folks' (Silk 1995, 54). This would be confirmed by investigations starting from the enunciation instance, public opinion. With that instance, we would understand why this is so and must be so, but

also how widely this can vary. Systemic resistance of religious discourse is easier to imagine.

5 Meaning that journalistic practitioners are deluding themselves regarding the nature of their meaning construction; see Ettema and Glasser (1988).

6 Moreover, by the nature of the matter, historiography must be more or less anecdotal, in spite of the relatively systematic historiographical efforts (Kaplan 2002; Mindich 1998; Schudson 2001).

7 Which is a rather general phenomenon, with 104,000 estimated cases per year in the United States; see Satcher (2001).

8 D'Entremont (2008): 'On November 9, 2007, a new trial motion was filed at Middlesex Superior Court in Cambridge, Massachusetts, on behalf of Paul Shanley, 77, a former Roman Catholic priest now serving a 12- to 15-year sentence for sexual crimes he is said to have committed in the 1980s. In one of several affidavits supporting the ex-priest's motion for a retrial, Dr. R. Christopher Barden, a Utah-based psychologist and lawyer, states that in his opinion, "the record in *Commonwealth v. Shanley* documents the most egregious case of gross negligence, incompetence, and greed that I have seen in practicing law in several dozen jurisdictions over many years."'

9 Cockburn (2005), the editor of the 'muckraking newsletter *Counterpunch*,' writes: 'This case is a throwback to the high 1990s, when people were put behind bars for lifetimes on the basis of memories elicited by the leading questions of psychotherapists. Ultimately, after years of patient effort by a few journalists, psychoanalysts, psychological researchers and advocates for justice, "recovered memory" as a tool of the latter-day Inquisition fell into well-deserved disrepute. In the state that gave us Salem in the 17th century and the Amiraults in the 20th (all wrongly sent to prison on charges brought by Middlesex county District Attorney Martha Coakley), Shanley's conviction has reintroduced "recovered memory" to the courtrooms of the 21st century.' There is considerable controversy over 'repressed memory' theory (Kihlstrom et al. 2005; McNally 2004, 2005a, 2005b; McNally and Clancy 2005; McNally, Ristuccia, and Perlman 2005). The state of New Hampshire does not admit repressed and recovered memories in court (*Hungerford v Susan L. Jones*), unless eight criteria have been met. In other jurisdictions, enormous awards have been granted against psychotherapists whose recovery techniques led to false accusations. As early as 1999, Lief (1999, 1) had averred: 'The flood of accusers suing their alleged perpetrators is now a mere trickle. There are several reasons for this reduction. For example, the increasing recognition by the courts that many accusations were based on pseudomemories rather than on historically accurate memories led to a marked decrease in such cases. This change in the

position of the courts has in large part been due to both the marshalling of evidence that the accusations were false and to the replacement of the Frye decision by the Daubert decision ... Thus, a trial judge can throw out testimony purporting to establish the validity of recovered memory therapy because its rate of falsifiability cannot be established. Recovered memory therapy cases were based on the concept of repression and the development of psychogenic amnesia. Since the percentage of cases in which recovered memories are false cannot be established, the theory lacks scientific validity.' Cf. Loftus (1997); McHugh et al. (2004).

10 The world press widely circulated a '10,000 abuses' number in the context of Pope Benedict XVI's visit to the United States and his apology. This is apparently a received wisdom in the media world, one that is no longer deemed worth verifying. Yet the sole source is a research finding of a comprehensive – not merely representative – inquiry among all American Ordinaries in the name of the U.S. Bishops' Conference. Of the 10,667 complaints (from frivolous jokes to rape) to bishops or major superiors (between 1950 and 2003), very few were denounced to the police. There are certainly a number of reasons for this, one of them being that not every moral trespassing is a statutory offence. Of the few who *were* denounced, most were investigated, but very few investigations led to prison sentences for different crimes. John Jay Report (§3.2): 'About one in three priests were charged with a crime. Overall, few priests with allegations served criminal sentences; only 3% of all priests with allegations served prison sentences. The priests with many allegations of abuse were not more likely than other priests to be charged and serve prison sentences.'

11 Three of them are victims represented by the law firm Greenberg & Traurig, who set out to extract considerable amounts of money from the Archdiocese of Boston in civil court proceedings. They succeeded in doing so. Note that the rest of the victims have been found by a handful of law firms specializing in indemnities – that is, not through police investigations.

12 Ingebretsen (2004, 22) shows the meaning effect of the Gothic genre on CSA scandal stories, which applies very well to the trajectory of Shanley stories in the *Boston Globe* and elsewhere: 'The "discovery" of priestly abuse of children collapses at least two, and possibly more, pre-existing formulas, the first the extensive use of priest sex as narrative and the second involving a rediscovery, as it were, of a Victorian model of the innocent child.'

13 Shanley's *cursus honorum* is even more impressive. The National Young Adult Reporter (1997) of the U.S. Catholic Conference writes: 'Father Paul Shanley has been engaged in youth work for over 20 years and has received numerous awards for his work in mental health: the Mayor's Citi-

zenship Citation in Boston, the Distinguished Service Award for "lasting contributions to the community and nation," and the 1960 citation from the Eastern Massachusetts Mental Health Association. In addition to lecturing at Harvard, he is a former campus minister at Boston State College and currently teaches graduate courses there. Assigned by Cardinal Medeiros to a "ministry to the gay and bisexual communities" he is perhaps the first priest to be so assigned by a Bishop. Sensitive, yet forceful, Father Shanley brings understanding to this issue. With a team of doctors he has lectured throughout the archdiocese of Boston, and has been elected to the Priests' Senate for three terms.' A photocopy of this article was found in Shanley's personal file, which was made public by a court decision. Its content is now available on the Internet: (National Young Adult Reporter 1977).

14 This fact was central to the courtroom interrogations of Bishop Daily on 22 August 2002 in New York in the civil proceedings against Paul Shanley. The resulting transcripts have been published. From an AP article printed in the *New York Times* on 6 May 2004, 'Boston Priest Is Defrocked in Abuse Scandal': 'Among the records were documents indicating that he was transferred from parish to parish after allegations surfaced, and that he had attended a forum with other people who later went on to form the North American Man-Boy Love Association, or NAMBLA. Hailed as a hero and crusader in the 1960s and 1970s for his street ministry working with disenfranchised youth, he worked with the permission of former Cardinals Richard Cushing and Humberto Medeiros but with little oversight from the archdiocese, and became known as the "street priest" or the "hippie priest." He frequented the city's Combat Zone red-light district, alleys, bus stations and gay bars where troubled and confused youth gathered. And even though the Catholic church condemned homosexuality, Shanley preached that it was OK and even advocated for gay rights. He called himself a "sexual expert" and advertised his counseling services in the alternative press. Even as city officials hailed his work, allegations were surfacing of sexual contact with some of the young boys he was supposed to be helping. As far back as 1967, a priest at LaSalette Shrine in Attleboro warned the archdiocese that Shanley had had inappropriate sexual contact with a boy. The documents included revelations that Shanley attended the 1978 forum in Boston that predated NAMBLA. Shanley also wrote in frank language about having venereal disease. His comments at that meeting were reported in a publication for gays, and forwarded to the archdiocese. Early in 1979 Medeiros wrote to the Vatican, "I believe Father Shanley is a troubled priest."'

15 The motto of their home page is the often quoted: 'Freedom is indivisible. The liberation of children, women, boy-lovers, and homosexuals in general, can occur only as complementary facets of the same dream' (NAMBLA 2005). In the context of a further speech: 'Our movement today stresses the liberation and empowerment of young people. Instead of pedagogy, democracy. Rather than a Greek love mentor-relationship, the companionship of independent and autonomous individuals. In place of male supremacy, a vision of sexual, economic, and political liberation for all' (Thorstad 1998).
16 Cf. Huber (1971, 45f).
17 Wypijewski (2004): 'By 1977 anyone wanting to report molestation could call an anonymous tip into a hotline instituted by the Boston D.A. Innuendo poured in about hundreds of gay men. It was a year of panic that set the stage for Shanley to articulate his most "deviant belief." In nearby Revere, a police dragnet implicated 25 men and 64 youths in an alleged sex ring. Police detained the young people, or enlisted psychiatrists and priests, to coerce them into cooperating. A group called the Boston/Boise Committee was formed to defend civil liberties. Ultimately none of the men did time, and the district attorney responsible for the scandal was swept from office. Afterward, the committee held a conference to discuss sex between men and teenage boys. Shanley was among the clerics, ethicists, lawyers, activists, and psychologists invited to speak. He told the story of a gay teenager, rejected by his family, who took up with an older man. When the boy's parents found out, they called the police and the man was imprisoned. "He had loved that man," Shanley said of the boy. "And when he realized that the indiscretion in the eyes of society and the law had cost this man perhaps 20 years ... the boy began to fall apart. We have our convictions upside down ... the 'cure' does far more damage." At his 2002 PowerPoint show, MacLeish projected a sentence from a 1979 account from *Gaysweek* that read, "At the end of the conference, 32 men and two teenagers caucused and formed the Man Boy Lovers of North America." The suggestion or assertion that Shanley was among the 32 has been repeated in the press many times since. But Shanley wasn't part of that group, say a Catholic priest and Protestant minister who were.'
18 The ambivalence of this polarity change in both values was recognized later, and attempts have been made to correct this. Some have diagnosed the church crisis in this way: 'Priesthood became a homosexual profession.' Considering that 80.9 per cent of the 10,667 victims of alleged abuse relating to 4,392 priests (149 of whom accounted for 26 per cent of all reported events) between 1950 and 2003 were male (see John Jay Report),

this is not totally implausible. Yet at the same time, public opinion has been accusing the Church of fear and hatred towards homosexuals. This battle of public opinion continues against the Vatican instruction – an explicit reaction to the scandal, combined with an Apostolic visitation of all seminaries in the USA, – that no homosexuals be admitted to Holy Orders. The value at the root of the power metatext has in the meantime become a scandal-scandal, for the bishops' administrative reaction against abuse has been condemned as glaring injustice and arbitrariness. Such reactions have mainly involved dismissing the accused from office. According to Henningsen (2004), 'the thugs [i.e., bishops] are in charge.'

19 John Jay Report (2004, §3.5): '[For] adolescents ages 12 to 17 across racial and ethnic groups, the lifetime prevalence for sexual assault is 8.1%.' This figure is from a 2003 U.S. Department of Justice inquiry, half of all raped women are girls under 18 (Kilpatrick, Saunders, and Smith 2003, 1).

20 Under the right of free speech, of course, the mere expression of an opinion – even about an indecent act – is not a statutory offence. Only people who do what they have said face a possible prison sentence. The severity of Catholic morals makes it easier to infer that as consequence there must be severe supervision.

21 Better known under designations such as Benveniste's *marques d'énonciation*, or Weinrich's speech attitudes dichotomy narrating/commenting.

22 Schudson (1995) demonstrates this for the journalistic construction of politics, which he encapsulates as politic in stories about the politic. A by-product of this process is journalists' construction of their own role. 'A study of reports of the State of the Union message … demonstrates that these conventions [narrative techniques: summary lead and inverted pyramid, president most important actor, single event not pattern, quote speeches, meaning of event], among others, incorporate into the structure of the news story vital assumptions about the nature of politics and the role of the press' (Schudson 1995, 56). This role is not partisanship so much as analytical expertise: 'Although as journalists they hold to principles of objective reporting, they nevertheless view their role as involving some fundamental translation and interpretation of political acts to a public ill-equipped to sort out for itself the meaning of events' (ibid.). Schudson then comes to the journalistic technique employed in our case as well: 'Further, these conventions institutionalize the journalists' view that meaning is to be found not in the character of established political institutions, but in the political aims of actors within them. The journalist's responsibility, as they see it, is to discover in the conscious plans of political actors the intentions that create political meaning' (ibid.).

23 According to Thayer in *A Greek-English Lexicon of the New Testament*, s.v. 'σκάνδαλον' Most of the time this term, which occurs twenty-five times in the Septuagint, translates as the Hebrew מוֹקֵשׁ (snare) or מִכְשׁוֹל (stumbling stone, meaning 'the movable stick or tricker ['trigger'] of a trap, trap-stick; a trap, snare; any impediment placed in the way and causing one to stumble or fall.' Outside the Septuagint, the closest correspondence in profane Greek usage, Σκανδάληθρον, meaning 'snare,' occurs only once in Aristophanes' Acharnians.

24 As we saw, this connection was made when the media scandal was in danger of running out of control. Even Cannon, the protagonist against CSA, very cautiously dared to establish a connection between the homosexuality problem and the fact that over 80 per cent of the abused were boys. 'In the mid-1980s, theologically conservative church officials were trying to avoid The Conversation: that is, a candid discussion of the subculture of homosexuality in the priesthood and the related issues of whether celibacy – and an all-male priesthood, for that matter – are still sustainable. For their part, liberals in the media had a Conversation that they were avoiding as well: Why do the vast majority of these priest molestation cases involve boys or male teenagers? To admit this was, in some quarters of the press, tantamount to giving ammunition to homophobes' (Cannon 2002a, 25).

25 It seems that this formula was used as a blueprint for form letters whenever priests were transferred into other parishes, as can be seen from the fact that in the files published by the *Boston Globe* alone, it is found *verbatim* at least six times.

26 Normally, an accusation is made in the name of a general consensus in public opinion. Then scandals constitute the moral discontinuity, as with the CSA monsters Shanley, Geogan, and Paquin. 'General consensus' often hides the PR of the conflict partners. These are mostly law firms with their PR agents (hired or directly employed). Such interventions, however, cannot explain a scandal, for so far they have strengthened positions in juridical conflicts, not social ones. For a time, it was customary practice to 'solve' these conflicts out of court with indemnifications. But at least since 1995, news stories have appeared sporadically reporting such accusations. In parallel to this peculiar 'court beat,' interested insider parties have gone into operation whose strategy has been to force the Church to deal with this grave matter.

An example is Dominican Father Thomas Doyle, who worked in a leading position in the U.S. Bishops' Conference and as a canon law counsel for the Washington Nunciature. He failed to get the attention he wanted for his much-warranted warnings (the Doyle-Mouton-Peterson Report); indeed, it seems that for his efforts, he was exiled to the Siberia of military chaplaincy. It became publicly known (Walsh 2003) that he provided to Daniel Shea of Houston an in its time rather severe secret instruction of the Holy Office under Cardinal Ottaviani (albeit superseded in 2001 by *De delictis gravioribus*). The instruction, *Crimen sollicitationis* (16 March 1962), regulates the canonical process sanctioning abuses of the Sacrament of Penitence through *sollicitationes ad turpia*, under the direct responsibility of the local Ordinaries (Bishops, Patriarchs). What caused consternation evidently was §11, which imposed secrecy on those officially involved in the canonical process. But this secrecy excluded witnesses and accusers (who in §15 are explicitly obliged to denounce the solicitation to the Ordinary, and who of course were always free to initiate criminal or civil procedures in non-canonical tribunals). Secrecy did not cover the verdict itself. This regimen of secrecy is evidently stricter than *in camera* rules obtaining in civil trials, which, however, are operating under the premise of public hearings. Canonical trials, instead, always must protect the reputation of both accuser and defendant. 'Quoniam vero quod in hisce causis tractandis maiorem in modum curari et observari debet illud est ut eadem secretissime peragantur et, postquam fuerint definitae et executioni iam traditae, perpetuo silentio premantur; omnes et singuli ad tribunal quomodocumque pertinentes vel propter eorum officum ad rerum notitiam admissi arctissimum secretum, quod secretum Sancti Officii communiter audit, in omnibus et cum omnibus ... inviolabiliter servare tenentur.'

Shea was one of the lawyers with a strong personal economic interest in suing the U.S. Catholic hierarchy, not only in civil indemnity cases, but also in criminal cases of 'criminal conspiracy.' ('[*Crimen sollicitationis*] shows that the Vatican has been providing instruction to all bishops in the United States to obstruct justice ... That's called a criminal conspiracy.') In this scenario, the provided document should have been 'not just a smoking gun, but a nuclear bombshell,' as Shea told *Washington Post* reporter Alan Cooperman in an interview on 25 August of that year. Probably this must be seen as an attempt to take up the role of 'whistle-blower' and so to move the counter-role, investigative journalism, up a gear.

27 This seems to reflect Potter's discourse-psychological constructivism; see Potter (1996, 97–121). In fact, the conversational determination as to which degree of truth one intends to attach to a statement is also a journalistic technique.

8. Effect and Reality of Scandal

1 Waisbord (2004, 1082): 'The adoption of a media-centered approach to understanding scandals has important shortcomings, however. It runs the risk of being insufficiently political, of subsuming all scandals to media operations and decisions without addressing the politics that generate events and processes for media coverage. It minimizes the actions of a myriad of institutions that make scandals possible.' Contrary to this opinion, there is no intrinsic impediment to a media-centred approach that is fully aware of real scandal effects but that also rejects a simplicist model of an objectively originated media scandal. This ability depends, however, largely on an adequate sign theory.
2 *Le Monde* – in particular, its former director and investigative reporter, Plenel (1999) – « Le journalisme tel que je le conçois est l'amour des petits faits vrais » – has been accused of not being prepared to face openly uncovered truths about itself and of taking legal action against those who *have* proof (cf. Hunter 1997; Péan and Cohen 2003). An out-of-court settlement was reached containing the clause that the 'defamatory' book could not be reprinted or quoted. But it did not expand on the merits of the contentious matter itself, which concerned the methods of investigative journalism (cf. Hunter 2003).
3 Media Guardian (2003). 'Tears for poor, downtrodden celebrities don't naturally well up inside me – particularly when you see someone like Catherine Zeta-Jones celebrating her ludicrous "privacy" win against a magazine that dared to try to spoil her £1m deal with another one. Moral: how dare you invade my privacy when I am making so much cash invading it myself?'
4 Thomas and Thomas (1928, 571–2): 'If men define situations as real, they are real in their consequences.'
5 McRobbie and Thornton (1995, 559): '"Moral panic" is now a term regularly used by journalists to describe a process which politicians, commercial promoters and media habitually attempt to incite.'
6 This type of communication theory is quite ancient. If one chose, one could also call it with Peters (1999) the 'spiritualist tradition,' and through this concept try to connect it to Plato's *Phaedrus*.
7 In the usual semiological investigations one would customarily consider that the question of a real connection between signs and the outside world could reasonably arise; it would, at the most, be a question of reference codes. In this school, 'signs' stand for particular 'things' that differentiate themselves from other things in this world. In semiotic, this is completely different.

8 'Investigative journalism' has been investigated as an industrial practice, with 'scandal' as its congenial form (Saguy 2002). In this practice, Watergate was the almost unreachable high-water mark, since Zippergate no longer had any unmitigated scandalous effect, as Clinton had a better grasp on spin.
9 Crisis management's self-perceived purpose is well illustrated by a familiar anecdote. In thick fog, an aircraft carrier sees an object on its radar and radios it to change course. The object refuses. When the collision seems unavoidable, the carrier's ultimatum again receives a negative reply: 'This is the lighthouse! Your call!' This little story is employed in many expensive training seminars for corporate management. Despite all the paraphernalia of veracity (names, time, place), it is pure legend (but *[se] non è vero [ma] è ben trovato*, as the Italian saying goes).
10 One could classify social scandals as very mild forms of the mimetic conflict in René Girard's sense. This description corresponds roughly to this impression: 'The discourses of the moral panic and the scandal require that a societal moral baseline is challenged. Their very discussion in the media assures that conventional morality is once again asserted as normal' (Lull and Hinerman 1997, 5). Here we enter a logic that can be thought only from the basis of a corporative subject, which reacts in exactly the same way as a moral person. Politicians are representative actors (as Girard had shown in detail with moral monsters and other capital offenders).
11 Lull and Hinerman (1997, 11) as summarized in Tumber and Waisbord (2004b, 1146) and Saguy (2002, 137n): 'The transgressions must be performed by (2) specific persons who carry out (3) actions that reflect an exercise of their desires or interests. So real persons must do (not just think about) something where their selfish interests override social norms and dominant moralities. Further, individual persons must be (4) identified as perpetrators of the act(s). They must be shown to have acted (5) intentionally or recklessly and must be (6) held responsible for their actions. The actions and events must have (7) differential consequences for those involved.'
12 Regarding the crucial difference between a social and a media scandal, let us remember what we have already discussed. The moral actions of real subjects in the social world are quite unlike those of pragmatic subjects in a teleologized text (cf. §7.4). In addition, sanctions differ significantly. The pragmatic subject in a media scandal is condemned as the subject *forever* – that is, the subject's competence becomes negative: the subject must disappear from the stage (in tragedies, they die). This contrasts with social scandals' demonizations, which in reality are no more than negative

fascinations. Furthermore, pragmatic subjects are always more than individuals. They become exemplaries of certain types of actions. The interpretation of behaviour takes place in terms of generalities; thus it is always legitimate in the semiotic sense (as discussed in §4.4). The rules governing this behaviour are not simply logically general; they correspond to the rules governing institutional behaviour, or at least to the rules governing a long-established social megalogic. Their competence, therefore, is that of a corporative action; they act *for* (e.g.) an institution. This negative competence then becomes the institutional not-being-able-to-act.

13 Explanation involves an entirely different approach that departs from the medium itself. Otherwise, we would concern ourselves not with the media scandal, but rather with the original religious indignation, which then becomes a stumbling block, a σκάνδαλον, to other believers. Even for a Symbolic Interactionist, a simple extrapolation from religious intersubjectivity is insufficient as an explanation of the phenomenon of media scandal. No real-world being-scandalized can be blown up to an 'indignation' of public opinion, for then public opinion would again be reduced to the identical opinion of all individuals. Not even media representations of a scandalized person are enough to generate a media scandal. Even if some have managed to carry their indignation into the media, this does not involve public opinion being indignant.

14 This logical constraint is strictly denied by the functionalist perspective of autopoietic social systems. A superordinate governance is denied by which heterogeneous systems could have been governed according to a central plan. Nevertheless, not even functional-structural systems theory can deny that – in public opinion, for instance – this impression is in effect and is necessary for its functioning.

15 von Savigny, the classical historian of law, systematizes 'institution' in Roman law: 'So wie aber das Urtheil über einen einzelnen Rechtsstreit nur eine beschränkte und abhängige Natur hat, und erst in der Anschauung des Rechtsverhältnisses seine lebendige Wurzel und seine überzeugende Kraft findet, auf gleiche Weise verhält es sich mit der Rechtsregel. Denn auch die Rechtsregel, so wie deren Ausprägung im Gesetz, hat ihre tiefere Grundlage in der Anschauung des Rechtsinstituts, und auch dessen organische Natur zeigt sich sowohl in dem lebendigen Zusammenhang der Bestandtheile, als in seiner fortschreitenden Entwicklung. Wenn wir also nicht bey der unmittelbaren Erscheinung stehen bleiben, sondern auf das Wesen der Sache eingehen, so erkennen wir, daß in der That jedes Rechtsverhältniß unter einem entsprechenden Rechtsinstitut, als seinem Typus,

steht, und von diesem auf gleiche Weise beherrscht wird, wie das einzelne Rechtsurtheil von der Rechtsregel' (Savigny 1840, 10).
16 So-called agency theory, in management studies, theorized this pragmatic option. Fong and Tosi (2007, 161–2): 'Agency theory ... deals with the motivation of human behavior, which is aligning principal (the "buyer" of a good or service) and agent (the provider of that good or service) interests through the use of agency controls (i.e., incentives or monitoring). Based on microeconomic principles of utility maximization, human behavior in agency theory is usually reduced to simplifying assumptions such as opportunism in the form of shirking as the default behavior when agency controls are not present.' Critics have objected that 'motivation as strictly opportunistic overlooks complex environmental and individual factors associated with human nature' (ibid.). 'Conscientiousness' plays a decisive role, which is nothing other than 'the agent' (control/management) sharing the same goal with 'the principal' (owner). It is therefore a matter of pragmatic teleology.
17 In the meantime, the intimate relationship between PR and news production is no longer as neglected as stated in Turow (1989, 206): 'The scholarly neglect is curious.'
18 What are the social 'taboos' that Lull and Hinerman describe as if they were facts causing scandals? Taboos were originally prohibitions from sacred texts. They could not exist without such texts because prohibitions must be justified. In this manner, one can reduce social reality again to teleology solidified into an institution. As a condition for 'moral indignation,' taboo is tautological: something is taboo because someone is indignant about it (Lull and Hinerman 1997, 11).

Bibliography

Abbott, Andrew. 1997. 'Of Time and Space: The Contemporary Relevance of the Chicago School.' *Social Forces* 75, no. 4, 1149–82.
Abelman, Robert. 1988. 'The impact of the PTL scandal on religious television viewers.' *Journal of Communication and Religion* 11, no. 1, 41–51.
Abrams, Herbert L. 2004. 'Weapons of Miller's descriptions.' *Bulletin of the Atomic Scientists [Chicago]* 60, no. 4, 56–64.
Achbar, Mark, and Jennifer Abbott. 2003. 'The Corporation.' 145 min. Canada.
Adorno, Theodor, and Albert, Hans, eds. 1969. *Der Positivismusstreit in der deutschen Soziologie*. Neuwied.
Adorno, Theodor W., Andrew J. Perrin, and Lars Jarkko. 2005. 'Opinion Research and Publicness (Meinungsforschung und Öffentlichkeit).' *Sociological Theory* 23, no. 1, 116–23.
Adorno, Theodor Wiesengrund. 1964. *Jargon der Eigentlichkeit. Zur deutschen Ideologie*. 1.10. Tsd. ed. Frankfurt am Main: Suhrkamp.
Adorno, Theodor Wiesengrund, and Rolf Tiedemann. 1995. *Soziologische Schriften I*. [2. Aufl.] ed. Frankfurt a.M.: Suhrkamp.
Akerman, Chantal. 1974. 'Je, tu, il, elle.' 86 min. France–Belgique.
Aldridge, Meryl. 1998. 'The Tentative Hell-Raisers: Identity and Mythology in Contemporary UK Press Journalism.' *Media, Culture, and Society* 20, no. 1: 109–27.
Altheide, David L. 2004. 'Media Logic and Political Communication.' *Political Communication* 21, no. 3: 293–6.
Altheide, David L., and Robert P. Snow. 1979. *Media Logic*. Beverly Hills: Sage.
Altschull, J. Herbert. 1984. *Agents of Power: The Role of the News Media in Human Affairs*. London and New York: Longman.
Anderson, Douglas R. 1990. 'Three Appeals in Peirce's Neglected Argument.' *Transactions of the Charles S. Peirce Society: A Quarterly Journal in American Philosophy* 26, no. 3: 349–62.

– 1995. 'Strands of System: The Philosophy of Charles Peirce.' West Lafayette: Purdue University Press.
Anon. Editorial. 1998. 'Sex, Lies, and Audiotape: Sorting out the Latest Clinton Scandal.' *New Republic* 218, no. 32: 7–8.
Apte, Vaman Shivaram. 1963. *The Student's English Sanskrit Dictionary*. Delhi: Shantila.
Aristoteles. 1836. 'Aristotelis opera :.../ ex recensione Immanuelis Bekkeri ed. Acad. Regia Borussica. – Ed. altera / ...'. Berolini: de Gruyter.
Arpan, Laura M., and Donnalyn Pompper. 2003. 'Stormy Weather: Testing "Stealing Thunder" as a Crisis Communication Strategy to Improve Communication Flow between Organizations and Journalists.' *Public Relations Review* 29, no. 3: 291–308.
Baker, Keith Michael. 1990. *Inventing the French Revolution: Essays on French Political Culture in the Eighteenth Century*. Cambridge: Cambridge University Press.
Baker, Russ. 2003. 'Scoops and Truth at the Times: What Happens When Pentagon Objectives and Journalists' Needs Coincide.' *The Nation* 276, no. 24: 18–21.
Balthasar, Hans Urs von. 1937. *Apokalypse der deutschen Seele: Studien zu einer Lehre von letzten Haltungen*. Salzburg: Pustet.
– 1973. *Theodramatik*. Einsiedeln: Johannes Verlag.
Baym, Geoffrey. 2004. 'Packaging Reality: Structures of Form in U.S. Network News Coverage of Watergate and the Clinton Impeachment.' *Journalism* 5, no. 3: 279–99.
Bazin, André. 1985. *Qu'est-ce que le cinéma?* Paris: Cerf.
Bednarz, John, Jr. 1984. 'Complexity and Intersubjectivity: Towards the Theory of Niklas Luhmann.' *Human Studies* 7, no. 1: 55–69.
Beetles, Andrea C., and Lloyd C. Harris. 2005. 'Consumer Attitudes Towards Female Nudity in Advertising: An Empirical Study.' *Marketing Theory* 5, no. 4: 397–432.
Behrens, Georg. 1995. 'Peirce's "Third Argument" for the Reality of God and Its Relation to Scientific Inquiry.' *The Journal of Religion* 75, no. 2: 200–18.
Bellany, Alastair James. 1994. '"Raylinge rymes and vaunting verse": Libellous Politics in Early Stuart England, 1603–1628.' In *Culture and Politics in Early Stuart England*, ed. Alastair Bellany, Kevin Sharpe, and Peter Lake, 285–310. Houndmills: Macmillan.
– 2002. *The Politics of Court Scandal in Early Modern England: News and the Overbury Affair, 1603–1660*. Cambridge: Cambridge University Press.
Benveniste, Émile, and Jean Lallot. 1969. *Le vocabulaire des institutions indoeuropéennes. 2, Pouvoir, droit, religion Le sens commun*. Paris: Éditions de Minuit.

Berger, Peter Ludwig, and Thomas Luckmann. 1967. *The Social Construction of Reality: A Treatise in the Sociology of Knowledge*. New York: Doubleday.

Berlau, John. 2006. 'Sarbanes–Oxley vs. the Free Press.' *Reason* 37, no. 8: 48–51.

Beuchot, Mauricio. 1997. 'Le carré de Saint Anselme et le carré de Greimas.' In *Lire Greimas*, ed. Eric Landowski, 15–27. Limoges: Presses universitaires de Limoges.

Bieber, Margarete. 1961. *The History of the Greek and Roman Theater*, 2nd ed. Princeton: Princeton University Press.

Bird, Antonia. 1994. *Priest*. UK.

Bird, S. Elizabeth. 1990. 'Storytelling on the Far Side: Journalism and the Weekly Tabloid.' *Critical Studies in Mass Communication* 7, no. 4: 377.

Birdwhistell, Ray L. 1970. *Kinesics and Context: Essays on Body Motion Communication*. Philadelphia: University of Pennsylvania Press.

Boorstin, Daniel J. 1961. *The Image: or What Happened to the American Dream*. London: Weidenfeld and Nicolson.

Bordwell, David. 1985. *Narration in the Fiction Film*. Madison: University of Wisconsin Press.

– 1989. *Making Meaning: Inference and Rhetoric in the Interpretation of Cinema*. Cambridge, MA: Harvard University Press.

Bordwell, David, and Noel Carroll, eds. 1996. *Post–Theory: Reconstructing Film Studies*. Madison: University of Wisconsin Press.

Boston Globe. 2004a. 'Homosexuality and the Church.' http://www.boston.com/globe/spotlight/abuse/extras/gays.htm, accessed 20 December 2006.

– 2004b. 'The Shanley Case.' http://www.boston.com/globe/spotlight/abuse/shanley, accessed 20 December 2006.

– 2004c. 'Should Celibacy Be Reconsidered?' http://www.boston.com/globe/spotlight/abuse/extras/celibacy.htm, accessed 20 December 2006.

Bourdieu, Pierre. 1980. 'L'opinion publique n'existe pas.' In *Questions de sociologie*, ed. Pierre Bourdieu. Paris: Éditions de Minuit. 222–35.

Bradley, Donald S., Jacqueline Boles, and Christopher Jones. 1979. 'From Mistress to Hooker: 40 Years of Cartoon Humor in Men's Magazines.' *Qualitative Sociology* 2, no. 2: 42–62.

Bratton, Michael. 2003. 'Briefing: Islam, Democracy and Public Opinion in Africa.' *African Affairs* 102, no. 408: 493–501.

Bresson, Robert. 1950. *Journal d'un curé de campagne*. France.

Brier, Søren. 1996. 'From Second-Order Cybernetics to Cybersemiotics: A Semiotic Re-entry into the Second-Order Cybernetics of Heinz von Foerster.' *Systems Research* 13, no. 3: 229–44.

– 2003. 'Cybersemiotics and the Question of Semiotic and Informational Thresholds.' *World Futures: The Journal of General Evolution* 59, no. 5: 361–80.

- 2005. 'The Construction of Information and Communication: A Cybersemiotic Reentry into Heinz von Foerster's Metaphysical Construction of Second-Order Cybernetics.' *Semiotica* 154, nos. 1–4: 355–99.
Brown-Nagin, Tomiko. 2003. 'Race as Identity Caricature: A Local Legal History Lesson in the Salience of Intraracial Conflict.' *University of Pennsylvania Law Review* 151, no. 6: 1913.
Brown, Gwen. 1991. 'Jerry Falwell and the PTL: The Rhetoric of Apologia.' *Journal of Communication and Religion* 14, no. 1: 9–18.
Burkhardt, Steffen. 2006. *Medienskandale Zur moralischen Sprengkraft öffentlicher Diskurse*. Köln: Halem.
Büthe, Tim. 2002. 'Taking Temporality Seriously: Modeling History and the Use of Narratives as Evidence.' *American Political Science Review* 96, no. 3: 481–93.
Butler, Jeremy G. 2002. *Television: Critical Methods and Applications*, 2nd ed. Mahwah: Lawrence Erlbaum Associates.
Calame, Byron. 2005. 'Anonymity: Who Deserves It?' http://www.nytimes.com/2005/11/20/opinion/20publiceditor.html, accessed 20 November 2005.
Cannon, Carl M. 2002a. 'The Priest Scandal: How Old News at Last Became a Dominant National Story ... And How It Took So Long.' *American Journalism Review* 24, no. 4: 18–25.
- 2002b. 'Sex, Lies, and Censorship: Why It Took So Long for the US Paedophile Priests Scandal to Hit the Headlines.' *Index on Censorship* 31, no. 4: 40–8.
Canteñs, Bernardo. 2002. 'Peirce and the Spontaneous Conjectures of Instinctive Reason: A Neglected Argument for the Reality of God.' *Proceedings of the American Catholic Philosophical Association* 76: 89–101.
- 2004. 'Overcoming the Evidentialist's Challenge: Peirce's Conjectures of Instinctive Reason and the Reality of God.' *Transactions of the Charles S. Peirce Society: A Quarterly Journal in American Philosophy* 40, no. 4: 771–86.
Carey, James W. 1975. 'A Cultural Approach to Communication.' *Communication* 2, no. 1: 1–22.
- 1989. *Communication as Culture: Essays on Media and Society*. Boston: Unwin Hyman.
- 2007. 'A Short History of Journalism for Journalists: A Proposal and Essay.' *Harvard International Journal of Press/Politics* 12, no. 1: 3–16.
Carontini, Enrico. 1986. *Faire l'image. Matériaux pour une sémiologie des énonciations visuelles*. Montréal: UQAM.
Carpenter, Edmund Snow. 1974. *Oh, What a Blow That Phantom Gave Me!* New York: Holt, Rinehart and Winston.

Carroll, Noël E. 1988a. *Mystifying Movies: Fads and Fallacies in Contemporary Film Theory*. New York: Columbia University Press.
– 1988b. *Philosophical Problems of Classical Film Theory*. Princeton: Princeton University Press.
– 1996. *Theorizing the Moving Image* Cambridge: Cambridge University Press.
Casetti, Francesco. 1986. *Dentro lo sguardo. Il film e il suo spettatore*. Milano: Bompiani.
Caspar, Ruth. 1980. 'The Neglected Argument Revisited: from C.S. Peirce to Peter Berger.' *Thomist: A Speculative Quarterly Review* 44: 94–116.
Cavell, Richard. 2003. *McLuhan in Space: A Cultural Geography*. Toronto: University of Toronto Press.
Certeau, Michel de. 1980. *L'invention du quotidien. 1, Arts de faire*. Paris: Union générale d'éditions.
Chalaby, Jean K. 1996. 'Journalism as an Anglo-American Invention: A Comparison of the Development of French and Anglo-American Journalism, 1830s–1920s.' *European Journal of Communication* 11, no. 3: 303–26.
Cherribi, Sam. 2006. 'From Baghdad to Paris: Al-Jazeera and the Veil.' *Harvard International Journal of Press/Politics* 11, no. 2: 121–38.
Cissé, Souleymane. 1987. *Yeelen*. Mali/Burkina Faso/France/West Germany.
Clam, Jean. 2000. 'System's Sole Constituent, the Operation: Clarifying a Central Concept of Luhmannian Theory.' *Acta Sociologica* 43, no. 1: 63–79.
Clark, Terry Nichols. 2002. 'The Presidency and the New Political Culture.' *American Behavioral Scientist* 46, no. 4: 535–52.
Clayman, Steven E. 1990. 'From Talk to Text: Newspaper Accounts of Reporter–Source Interactions.' *Media, Culture, and Society* 12, no. 1: 79–103.
– 2002. 'Tribune of the People: Maintaining the Legitimacy of Aggressive Journalism.' *Media, Culture, and Society* 24, no. 2: 197–216.
Clem, Lloyd, and Walton Paul. 1999. 'Reporting Corporate Crime.' *Corporate Communications: An International Journal* 4, no. 1: 43–8.
Cockburn, Alexander. 2005. 'Back to Salem: Shanley Prison-Bound.' *The Free Press: Speaking Truth to Power*, 16 February 2005. http://www.freepress.org/columns/display/2/2005/1067, accessed 2 May 2006.
Cohen, Stanley. 1972. *Folk Devils and Moral Panics: The Creation of the Mods and Rockers*. London: MacGibbon and Kee.
Colapietro, Vincent Michael. 1989. *Peirce's Approach to the Self: A Semiotic Perspective on Human Subjectivity*. Albany: SUNY Press.
Coquet, Jean-Claude. 1982. *Sémiotique, l'École de Paris* Langue, linguistique, communication. Paris: Classiques Hachette.
Corner, John. 1997. 'Television in Theory.' *Media, Culture, and Society* 19, no. 2: 247–62.

Costa-Gavras, Constantin. 2002. *Amen*. France.
Couldry, Nick. 2004. 'Theorising Media as Practice.' *Social Semiotics* 14, no. 2: 115–32.
Coupe, William A. 1969. 'Observations on a Theory of Political Caricature.' *Comparative Studies in Society and History* 11, no. 1: 79–95.
Curran, James. 2002. *Media and Power*. London: Routledge.
Curran, James, and Jean Seaton. 1981. *Power without Responsibility: The Press and Broadcasting in Britain*. London: Fontana.
D'Angelo, Paul. 2002. 'News Framing as a Multiparadigmatic Research Program: A Response to Entman.' *Journal of Communication* 52, no. 4: 870–88.
D'Entremont, Jim. 2008. 'Any Prayer for Shanley?' *Guide* 28, no. 3: 8–9.
Daniel, Sharan Leigh. 2002. 'Rhetoric and Journalism as Common Arts of Public Discourse: A Theoretical, Historical, and Critical Perspective (Fred Newton Scott, Ida M. Tarbell).' PhD diss., University of Texas at Austin.
De Albuquerque, Afonso. 2005. 'Another "Fourth Branch": Press and Political Culture in Brazil.' *Journalism* 6, no. 4: 486–504.
de Burgh, Hugo. 2000. *Investigative Journalism: Context and Practice*. London: Routledge.
De Tienne, André. 1996. *L'analytique de la représentation chez Peirce. La genèse de la théorie des catégories*. Bruxelles: Publ. Fac. univ. S. Louis.
Deleuze, Gilles. 1973. 'À quoi reconnaît-on le structuralisme?' In *Histoire de la philosophie*, ed. François Châtelet. Paris: Hachette. 299–33.
Delporte, Christian. 1995. 'Images d'une guerre franco-francaise: la caricature au temps de l'Affaire Dreyfus.' *French Cultural Studies* 6, no. 2: 221–48.
Desmond, Robert William. 1978. *The Information Process: World News Reporting to the Twentieth Century*. Iowa City: University of Iowa Press.
Deuze, Mark. 2005a. 'Popular Journalism and Professional Ideology: Tabloid Reporters and Editors Speak Out.' *Media, Culture, and Society* 27, no. 6: 861–82.
– 2005b. 'What Is Journalism?: Professional Identity and Ideology of Journalists Reconsidered.' *Journalism* 6, no. 4: 442–64.
Dias, Monica. 2002. 'Parody Ruling Threatens Political Commentary, Attorney Says.' *News Media and the Law* 26, no. 3: 50–1.
Dolnik, Lara, Trevor I. Case, and Kipling D. Williams. 2003. 'Stealing Thunder as a Courtroom Tactic Revisited: Processes and Boundaries.' *Law and Human Behavior* 27, no. 3: 267–87.
Donsbach, Wolfgang. 2006. 'The Identity of Communication Research.' *Journal of Communication* 56, no. 3: 437–48.
Doreian, Patrick. 2001. 'Causality in Social Network Analysis.' *Sociological Methods and Research* 30, no. 1: 81–114.

Duke, Daryl. 1983. *The Thorn Birds*. USA, Australia.
Durkheim, Emile. 1895. *Les règles de la Méthode sociologique*. Paris: Alcan.
Dury-Moyaers, Geneviève, and Marcel Renard. 1981. 'Aperçu critique de travaux relatifs au culte de Junon.' In *Aufstieg und Niedergang der römischen Welt: Geschichte und Kultur Roms im Spiegel der neueren Forschung*, ed. Hildegard Temporini and Wolfgang Haase, 2. Principal, Bd. 17, 1, 142–202. Berlin, New York: de Gruyter.
Duvall, Robert. 1997. *The Apostle*. USA.
Dyer, Richard. 1986. *Heavenly Bodies: Film Stars and Society*. New York: St Martin's.
Eberlein, Gerald L. 1994. 'Logik der Sozialwissenschaften – 150 Jahre nach J. St. Mill's System of Logic.' *Protosoziologie* 6: 229–40.
Ehrat, Johannes. 2003. 'Gott im Netz: Religiöse Kommunikation im Internet.' *Communicatio Socialis* 36, no. 3: 244–70.
– 2005a. *Cinema and Semiotic: Peirce and Film Aesthetics, Narration, and Representation*. Toronto: University of Toronto Press.
– 2005b. 'The Logic of Subjectivity: Subjectivité en mouvance.' *RSSI. Recherches sémiotiques. Semiotic Inquiry* 25, no. 3–1: 107–29.
– 2005c. 'St. Francis Xavier, a Pioneer in Communication.' *Studia Missionalia* 54: 213–30.
– 2007. 'Die Semiotik der Gesellschaft: Skizze einer semiotisch-pragmatischen Theorie der Gesellschaft.' *Gregorianum* 88, no. 3: 619–42.
Eisler, Rudolf. 1904. *Wörterbuch der philosophischen Begriffe. Historisch quellenmässig bearbeitet von Dr. Rudolf Eisler*. 2 vols. 2nd ed. Berlin: Mittler und Sohn.
Ekström, Mats. 2000. 'Information, Storytelling, and Attractions: TV Journalism in Three Modes of Communication.' *Media, Culture, and Society* 22, no. 4: 465–92.
Elliott, Richard, and Christine Elliott. 2005. 'Idealized Images of the Male Body in Advertising: A Reader-Response Exploration.' *Journal of Marketing Communications* 11, no. 1: 3–19.
Entman, Robert M. 1993. 'Framing: Toward Clarification of a Fractured Paradigm.' *Journal of Communication* 43, no. 4: 51–8.
Esser, Frank. 1999. '"Tabloidization" of News: A Comparative Analysis of Anglo-American and German Press Journalism.' *European Journal of Communication* 14, no. 3: 291–324.
Esser, Frank, and Uwe Hartung. 2004. 'Nazis, Pollution, and no Sex: Political Scandals as a Reflection of Political Culture in Germany.' *American Behavioral Scientist* 47, no. 8: 1040–71.
Ettema, James S. 2005. 'Crafting Cultural Resonance: Imaginative Power in Everyday Journalism.' *Journalism* 6, no. 2: 131–52.

Ettema, James S., and Theodore L Glasser. 1988. 'Narrative Form and Moral Force: The Realization of Innocence and Guilt through Investigative Journalism.' *Journal of Communication* 38, no. 3: 8–26.

Ettema, James Stewart. 1990. 'Press Rites and Race Relations: A Study of Mass-Media Ritual.' *Critical Studies in Mass Communication* 7, no. 4: 309.

Fan, David P., Robert O. Wyatt, and Kathy Keltner. 2001. 'The Suicidal Messenger: How Press Reporting Affects Public Confidence in the Press, the Military, and Organized Religion.' *Communication Research* 28, no. 6: 826–52.

Felling, Matthew. 2002. 'Sex, Lies, and Vaticangate.' *The World & I* 17, no. 12: 60.

Ferguson, Marjorie, ed. 1990. *Public Communication: The New Imperatives: Future Directions for Media Research*. London: Sage.

Fisch, Max H., Kenneth Laine Ketner, and Christian J.W. Kloesel. 1986. *Peirce, Semeiotic, and Pragmatism: Essays*. Bloomington: Indiana University Press.

Fishman, Mark. 1980. *Manufacturing the News*. Austin: University of Texas Press.

Fong, Eric A., and Henry L. Tosi, Jr. 2007. 'Effort, Performance, and Conscientiousness: An Agency Theory Perspective.' *Journal Of Management* 33, no. 2: 161–79.

Ford, John. 1947. *The Fugitive*. USA.

Frank, Joseph. 1991. *The Idea of Spatial Form*. New Brunswick: Rutgers University Press.

Frankl, Razelle. 1987. *Televangelism: The Marketing of Popular Religion*. Carbondale: Southern Illinois University Press.

Franzosi, Roberto. 1995. *The Puzzle of Strikes: Class and State Strategies in Postwar Italy* Cambridge: Cambridge University Press.

– 2004. *From Words to Numbers: Narrative, Data, and Social Science*. Cambridge: Cambridge University Press.

Friedman, Lisa. 2006. 'Unshielded.' *American Journalism Review* 28, no. 4: 12–13.

Gadamer, Hans Georg. 1960. *Wahrheit und Methode*. Tübingen: Mohr.

Gamson, Joshua. 1994. *Claims to Fame: Celebrity in Contemporary America*. Berkeley: University of California Press.

– 2001. 'Normal Sins: Sex Scandal Narratives as Institutional Morality Tales.' *Social Problems* 48, no. 2: 185–205.

Gamson, William A., and Andre Modigliani. 1989. 'Media Discourse and Public Opinion on Nuclear Power: A Constructionist Approach.' *American Journal of Sociology* 95, no. 1: 1–37.

Gauthier, Gilles. 1993. 'In Defence of a Supposedly Outdated Notion: The

Range of Application of Journalistic Objectivity.' *Canadian Journal of Communication* 18, no. 4: 497.
- 2005. 'A Realist Poinnt of View on News Journalism.' *Journalism Studies* 6, no. 1: 51–60.
Geiger, Theodor. 1962. *Arbeiten zur Soziologie Methode, moderne Grossgesellschaft, Rechtssoziologie, Ideologiekritik*. Neuwied am Rhein: Hermann Luchterhand.
Gennep, Arnold van. 1909. *Les rites de passage étude systématique des rites de la porte et du seuil*. Paris: E. Nourry.
Gerhardt, Volker. 1979. 'Transzendentale Theorie der Gesellschaft: Philosophische Anmerkung zu einem soziologischen Programm.' *Zeitschrift für Soziologie* 8, no. 2: 129–44.
Gibreel, Gibreel. 2001. 'The Ulema: Middle Eastern Power Brokers.' *Middle East Quarterly* 8, no. 4. http://www.meforum.org/article/105, accessed 24 May 2010.
Gitai, Amos. 1999. *Kadosh*. Israel.
Gitlin, Todd. 2006. 'Miller's Malfeasance and Woodward's Folly: The Crisis in Access Journalism.' *Harvard International Journal Of Press/Politics* 11, no. 3: 3–6.
Goddard, Peter. 2006. '"Improper Liberties": Regulating Undercover Journalism on ITV, 1967–1980.' *Journalism* 7, no. 1: 45–63.
Goddard, Peter, John Corner, and Kay Richardson. 2001. 'The Formation of World in Action: A Case Study in the History of Current Affairs Journalism.' *Journalism* 2, no. 1, 73–90.
Goldhill, Simon. 1987. 'The Great Dionysia and Civic Ideology.' *Journal of Hellenic Studies* 107: 58–76.
Goodstein, Laurie. 2005a. 'Air Force Chaplain Tells Of Academy Proselytizing.' *New York Times*, 12 May 2005, A16.
- 2005b. 'Evangelicals Are Growing Force In the Military Chaplain Corps.' *New York Times*, 12 July 2005, A1.
Graham, William A. 1980. *Guyana Tragedy: The Story of Jim Jones*. USA.
Grant, Audra, and Mark Tessler. 2002. 'Palestinian Attitudes toward Democracy and Its Compatibility with Islam: Evidence from Public Opinion Research in the West Bank and Gaza.' *Arab Studies Quarterly* 24, no. 4: 1–19.
Green, Garrett. 1982. 'The Sociology of Dogmatics: Niklas Luhmann's Challenge to Theology.' *Journal of the American Academy of Religion* 50, no. 1: 19–34.
Green, J. Ronald. 1998. 'Oscar Micheaux's Interrogation of Caricature as Entertainment.' *Film Quarterly* 51, no. 3: 16–31.
Greimas, Algirdas Julien. 1970a. *Du sens: essais sémiotiques*. Paris: Editions du Seuil.

- 1970b. 'Éléments d'une grammaire narrative.' In *Du sens: Essais sémiotiques*. Paris: Editions du Seuil. 157–83.
- 1983a. *Du sens II: essais sémiotiques*. Paris: Editions du Seuil.
- 1983b. 'Pour une théorie des modalités.' In *Du sens II: Essais sémiotiques*. Paris: Editions du Seuil. 67–91.

Greimas, Algirdas Julien, and Joseph Courtés. 1972. *Semiotics and Language: An Analytical Dictionary*. Bloomington: Indiana University Press.
- 1979. *Sémiotique: Dictionnaire raisonné de la théorie du langage*. Paris: Hachette.
- 1986. *Sémiotique: Dictionnaire raisonné de la théorie du langage II (compléments, débats, propositions)*. Paris: Hachette.

Griffin, Jasper. 1998. 'The Social Function of Attic Tragedy.' *Classical Quarterly* 1: 39–61.

Grosbard, Ulu. 1981. *True Confessions*. USA.

Grossberg, Lawrence, Ellen Wartella, and D. Charles Whitney. 1998. *Mediamaking: Mass Media in a Popular Culture*. Thousand Oaks: Sage.

Gup, Ted. 2004. 'Covering the CIA in Times of Crisis: Obstacles and Strategies.' *Harvard International Journal of Press/Politics* 9, no. 3: 28–39.

Habermas, Jürgen. 1962. *Strukturwandel der Öffentlichkeit. Untersuchungen zu einer Kategorie der bürgerlichen Gesellschaft*. Neuwied: Luchterhand.
- 1981. *Theorie des kommunikativen Handelns*. 2 vols. Frankfurt: Suhrkamp.
- 1985. *Der philosophische Diskurs der Moderne. Zwölf Vorlesungen*. Frankfurt am Main: Suhrkamp.
- 1992. *Faktizität und Geltung. Beiträge zur Diskurstheorie des Rechts und des demokratischen Rechtsstaats*. Frankfurt am Main: Suhrkamp.

Habermas, Jürgen, and Niklas Luhmann. 1971. *Theorie der Gesellschaft oder Sozialtechnologie*. Frankfurt am Main: Suhrkamp.

Hadden, Jeffrey K. 1993. 'The Rise and Fall of American Televangelism.' *Annals of the American Academy of Political and Social Science* 527: 113–30.

Hagen, Ingunn, and Janet Wasko. 2000. *Consuming Audiences? Production and Reception in Media Research*. Cresskill: Hampton.

Hay, James. 2001. 'Locating the Televisual.' *Television New Media* 2, no. 3: 205–34.

Heider, Fritz. 2005. *Ding und Medium. Hrsg. und mit einem Vorwort versehen von Dirk Baecker*. Berlin: Kulturverlag Kadmos.

Henderson, David. 2002. 'Norms, Normative Principles, and Explanation: On Not Getting Is from Ought.' *Philosophy of the Social Sciences* 32, no. 3: 329–64.

Hennig, Boris. 2000. 'Luhmann und die Formale Mathematik.' In *Die Logik der Systeme zur Kritik der systemtheoretischen Soziologie Niklas Luhmanns*, ed. Peter-Ulrich Merz-Benz. Konstanz: UVK Universitätsverlag Konstanz. 157–98.

Henningsen, Catharine A. 2004. 'The Second Wave of Abuse: The Fate of Our Accused Priests.' http://www.bishop-accountability.org/resources/resource-files/timeline/2004-02-05-Henningsen-SecondWave.htm, accessed 14 June 2010.

Herbst, Susan. 1993. 'History, Philosophy, and Public Opinion Research.' *Journal of Communication* 43, no. 4: 140.

Hesse, Mary. 1978. 'Theory and Value in the Social Sciences.' In *Action and Interpretation: Studies in the Philosophy of the Social Sciences*, ed. Christopher Hookway and Philip Pettit. Cambridge Cambridge University Press. 1–16.

Hills, Matt. 2002. *Fan C.ultures*. London: Routledge.

– 2004. 'Strategies, Tactics, and the Question of Un Lieu Propre: What/Where Is "Media Theory"?' *Social Semiotics* 14, no. 2: 133–49.

Hindman, Elizabeth Blanks. 2005. 'Jayson Blair, The New York Times, and Paradigm Repair.' *Journal of Communication* 55, no. 2: 225–41.

Hitchcock, Peter. 1995. 'Information in Formation: Williams/Media/China.' In *Cultural Materialism: On Raymond Williams*, ed. Christopher Prendergast. Minneapolis: University of Minnesota Press.

Hoffjann, Olaf. 2001. *Journalismus und Public Relations. Ein Theorieentwurf der Intersystembeziehungen in sozialen Konflikten*. Wiesbaden: Westdeutscher.

Hollos, Marida. 2001. *Scandal in a Small Town: Understanding Modern Hungary through the Stories of Three Families*. London: Sharpe.

Hondrich, Karl Otto. 1989. 'Skandalmärkte und Skandalkultur.' In *Kultur und Gesellschaft*, ed. H.J. Hoffmann-Nowotny, M. Haller, and W. Zapf. Frankfurt: Campus. 575–86.

Hookway, Christopher. 2000. *Truth, Rationality, and Pragmatism: Themes from Peirce*. Oxford: Clarendon.

Hoover, Stewart M. 1998. *Religion in the News: Faith and Journalism in American Public Discourse*. Thousand Oaks: Sage.

Horsfield, Peter G. 1984. *Religious Television: The American Experience*. New York: Longman.

Howley, Kevin. 2001. 'Prey TV Televangelism and Interpellation.' *Journal of Film and Video* 53, nos. 2–3: 23–37.

Huber, Richard M. 1971. *The American Idea of Success*. New York: McGraw-Hill.

Hunter, Mark. 1997. 'Ethical Conflict and Investigative Reporting: Le Monde and the Contaminated Blood Affair.' *Harvard International Journal of Press/Politics* 2, no. 2: 77–95.

– 2003. 'When Mondes Collide: Has the Watchdog of France Gone Mad?' http://markleehunter.free.fr/lemonde.html, accessed 14 June 2010.

Hussain, Ali J. 2007. 'The Media's Role in a Clash of Misconceptions: The Case of the Danish Muhammad Cartoons.' *Harvard International Journal of Press/ Politics* 12, no. 4: 112–30.

Ingebretsen, Edward J. 2004. 'Reading Scandal: Civic Gothic as Genre.' *Journal of Media and Religion* 3, no. 1: 21–42.

Iser, Wolfgang. 1972. *Der implizite Leser*. München: Fink.

– 1976. *Der Akt des Lesens. Theorie ästhetischer Wirkung*. München: Fink.

Jacobs, Sally, and Globe Staff. 2002. '"If they knew the madness in me": A Search for the Real Rev. Paul Shanley Suggests He Was Part Hero, Part Horror.' http://www.boston.com/globe/spotlight/abuse/stories2/071002_shanley.htm, accessed 23 May 2006.

Jacoby, William G. 2000. 'Issue Framing and Public Opinion on Government Spending.' *American Journal of Political Science* 44, no. 4: 750.

Jahraus, Oliver, and Nina Ort, eds. 2001. *Bewusstsein–Kommunikation–Zeichen Wechselwirkungen zwischen Luhmannscher Systemtheorie und Peircescher Zeichentheorie*. Tübingen: Niemeyer.

Jauß, Hans Robert. 1977. *Ästhetische Erfahrung und literarische Hermeneutik I*. München: Fink.

Jensen, Klaus. 1995. *The Social Semiotics of Mass Communication*. Thousand Oaks: Sage.

Jiménez, Fernando. 2004. 'The Politics of Scandal in Spain: Morality Plays, Social Trust, and the Battle for Public Opinion.' *American Behavioral Scientist* 47, no. 8: 1099–121.

Joas, Hans. 1999. *Pragmatismus und Gesellschaftstheorie 2. Aufl*. Frankfurt am Main: Suhrkamp.

Johnson, Paul C. 1997. 'Kicking, Stripping, and Re-dressing a Saint in Black: Visions of Public Space in Brazil's Recent Holy War.' *History of Religions* 37, no. 2: 122–40.

Jones, Arthur. 2001. 'Pen-and-Ink Prophet.' *National Catholic Reporter* 38, no. 1: 12–13.

Jones, Ken. 2003. 'Whipping the Tribune.' *St Louis Journalism Review* 33, no. 255: 11.

Joußen, Wolfgang. 1990. *Massen und Kommunikation. Zur soziologischen Kritik der Wirkungsforschung* Weinheim: VCH.

Jucker, Andreas H. 1986. *News Interviews: A Pragmalinguistic Analysis*. Bd. 7. Amsterdam: Benjamins.

Kalu, Ogbu. 2003. 'Safiyya and Adamah: Punishing Adultery with haria Stones in Twenty-First-Century Nigeria.' *African Affairs* 102 no. 408: 389–408.

Kaplan, Richard L. 2002. *Politics and the American Press: The Rise of Objectivity, 1865–1920*. Cambridge: Cambridge University Press.

Katz, Elihu, Lazarsfeld, Paul Felix, and Columbia University. 1964. *Personal Influence: The Part Played by People in the Flow of Mass Communications*. New York: Free Press of Glencoe.

Kauffman, Louis H. 2001. 'The Mathematics of Charles Sanders Peirce.' *Cybernetics and Human Knowing* 8, no. 1–2: 79–110.

Kelly, John. 1981. *A Philosophy of Communication*. London: Centre for the Study of Communication and Culture.

Kevelson, Roberta. 1988. *The Law as a System of Signs*. New York: Plenum.

Kihlstrom, John F., Richard J. McNally, Elizabeth F. Loftus, and Harrison G. Pope. 2005. 'The Problem of Child Sexual Abuse.' *Science* 309, no. 5738: 1182–5.

Kilpatrick, Dean G., Benjamin E. Saunders, and Daniel W. Smith. 2003. 'Youth Victimization: Prevalence and Implications.' Washington: National Institute of Justice.

Kitzinger, Jenny. 1995. '"I'm Sexually Attractive but I'm Powerful": Young Women Negotiating Sexual Reputation.' *Women's Studies International Forum* 18, no. 2: 187–96.

– 2000. 'Media Templates: Patterns of Association and the (Re)Construction of Meaning over Time.' *Media, Culture, and Society* 22, no. 1: 61–84.

Knight, Myra G. 1999. 'Getting Past the Impasse: Framing as a Tool for Public Relations.' *Public Relations Review* 25, no. 3: 381–98.

Knox, Andrea. 1999. 'Busted! Sex, Lies, and Red Tape: Do Political Scandals Affect International Trade?' *World Trade* 12, no. 4: 57–63.

Koker, Tolga. 2004. 'The Political Economy of Turkish Islamism and Secularism: The Role of Preference Falsification in the Establishment of Kemalist Secularism and the Polarization of Turkish Public Opinion on the Public Role of Religion.' PhD diss., University of Southern California.

Kuhn, Thomas S. 1970. *The Structure of Scientific Revolutions*, 2nd ed. Chicago: University of Chicago Press.

Kurosawa, Akira. 1950. *Rashômon*. Japan.

Landowski, Eric. 1989. *La société réfléchie: essais de socio-sémiotique*. Paris: Seuil.

Landtag Mecklenburg-Vorpommern, 2. Untersuchungsausschuß. 1993. 'Beschlußempfehlung und Zwischenbericht 16. Juni 1993.' Drucksache 1/3277. Schwerin.

Langman, Lauren. 2002. 'Suppose They Gave a Culture War and No One Came: Zippergate and the Carnivalization of Politics.' *American Behavioral Scientist* 46, no. 4: 501–34.

Lau, Raymond W.K. 2004. 'Critical Realism and News Production.' *Media, Culture, and Society* 26, no. 5: 693–711.

Lawrence, Regina G., and W.L. Bennett. 2001. 'Rethinking Media Politics and

Public Opinion: Reactions to the Clinton-Lewinsky Scandal.' *Political Science Quarterly* 116, no. Seas Aut: 425–46.
Leeds-Hurwitz, Wendy. 1993. *Semiotics and Communication: Signs, Codes, Cultures*. Hillsdale: Lawrence Erlbaum Associates.
Legg, Karen L. 2009. 'Religious Celebrity: An Analysis of Image Repair Discourse.' *Journal of Public Relations Research* 21, no. 2: 240–50.
Lehmann, Ingrid A. 2005. 'Exploring the Transatlantic Media Divide over Iraq: How and Why U.S. and German Media Differed in Reporting on UN Weapons Inspections in Iraq, 2002–2003.' *Harvard International Journal of Press/Politics* 10, no. 1: 63–89.
Lewis, Charlton Thomas, Charles Short, E.A. Andrews, and Thomas Leiper Kane Collection (Library of Congress, Hebraic Section). 1955. *A Latin Dictionary; Founded on Andrews' Edition of Freund's Latin Dictionary*. Oxford: Clarendon.
Liebes, Tamar. 1989. 'But There Are Facts: Comments on Roeh.' *American Behavioral Scientist* 33, no. 2: 169–71.
– 2000. 'Inside a News Item: A Dispute over Framing.' *Political Communication* 17, no. 3: 295–305.
Liebes, Tamar, and Shoshana Blum-Kulka. 2004. 'It Takes Two to Blow the Whistle: Do Journalists Control the Outbreak of Scandal?' *American Behavioral Scientist* 47, no. 9: 1153–70.
Lief, Harold I. 1999. 'Patients versus Therapists: Legal Actions over Recovered Memory Therapy.' *Psychiatric Times* 16, no. 11.
– 2003. 'Questions Raised by the Controversy over Recovered Memories of Incest.' *Journal of the American Academy of Psychoanalysis and Dynamic Psychiatry* 31, no. 2: 381–95.
Lisenby, F. 1985. 'American Women in Magazine Cartoons.' *American Journalism* 2, no. 2: 130–4.
Loftus, Elizabeth F. 1997. 'Repressed Memory Accusations: Devastated Families and Devastated Patients.' *Applied Cognitive Psychology* 11, no. 1: 25–30.
Love, Robert. 2006. 'Shakedown! The Unfortunate History of Reporters Who Trade Power for Cash.' *Columbia Journalism Review* 45, no. 2: 47–51.
Loyal, Steven, and Barry Barnes. 2001. '"Agency" as a Red Herring in Social Theory.' *Philosophy of the Social Sciences* 31, no. 4: 507–24.
Luhmann, Niklas. 1977. *Funktion der Religion*. 1. Aufl. – ed. Frankfurt am Main: Suhrkamp.
– 1981. *Gesellschaftsstruktur und Semantik. Studien zur Wissenssoziologie der modernen Gesellschaft Bd.II*. Frankfurt am Main: Suhrkamp.
– 1984a. *Religious Dogmatics and the Evolution of Societies*. New York: Mellen.

- 1984b. *Soziale Systeme: Grundriß einer allgemeinen Theorie*. Frankfurt am Main: Suhrkamp.
- 1995. *Die Realität der Massenmedien*. Opladen: Westdeutscher.
- 1996. 'Die Lebenswelt nach Rücksprache mit Phänomenologen.' In *Protosoziologie im Kontext: 'Lebenswelt' und 'System' in Philosophie und Soziologie*, ed. Gerhard Preyer, Georg Peter, and Alexander Ulfig. Würzburg: Königshausen und Neumann. 268–89.
- 1997. *Die Gesellschaft der Gesellschaft*. 2 vols. Frankfurt am Main: Suhrkamp.
- 2000. *The Reality of the Mass Media*. Cambridge: Polity.

Luhmann, Niklas, and André Kieserling. 2002a. *Die Politik der Gesellschaft*. Frankfurt am Main: Suhrkamp.
- 2002b. *Die Religion der Gesellschaft*. Frankfurt am Main: Suhrkamp.

Lull, James, and Stephen Hinerman, eds. 1997. *Media Scandals: Morality and Desire in the Popular Culture Marketplace*. Cambridge: Polity.

Manning, Paul. 2001. *News and News Sources: A Critical Introduction*. Thousand Oaks: Sage.

Martin-Kratzer, Renee, and Esther Thorson. 2007. 'Use of Anonymous Sources Declines in U.S. Newspapers.' *Newspaper Research Journal* 28, no. 2: 56–70.

Marx Ferree, Myra, William Anthony Gamson, Jürgen Gerhards, and Dieter Rucht. 2002. *Shaping Abortion Discourse: Democracy and the Public Sphere in Germany and the United States*. Cambridge: Cambridge University Press.

Maryanski, Alexandra, and Jonathan H. Turner. 1991. 'The Offspring of Functionalism: French and British Structuralism.' *Sociological Theory* 9, no. 1: 106–15.

McCarthy, Thomas. 1985. 'Complexity and Democracy, or the Seducements of Systems Theory.' *New German Critique*, no. 35: 27–53.
- 1991. *Ideals and Illusions: On Reconstruction and Deconstruction in Contemporary Critical Theory*. Cambridge, MA: MIT Press.

McHugh, Paul R., Harold I. Lief, Pamela P. Freyd, and Janet M Fetkewicz. 2004. 'From Refusal to Reconciliation: Family Relationships after an Accusation Based on Recovered Memories.' *Journal of Nervous and Mental Disease* 192, no. 8: 525–31.

McLuhan, Marshall. 1962. *The Gutenberg Galaxy: The Making of Typographic Man*. Toronto: University of Toronto Press.

McNair, Brian. 2003. *News and Journalism in the UK*. London: Routledge.

McNally, Richard J. 2004. 'Is Traumatic Amnesia Nothing but Psychiatric Folklore?' *Cognitive Behaviour Therapy* 33, no. 2: 97–101.
- 2005a. 'Debunking Myths about Trauma and Memory.' *Canadian Journal of Psychiatry / Revue canadienne de psychiatrie* 50, no. 13: 817–22.

- 2005b. 'Troubles in Traumatology.' *Canadian Journal of Psychiatry / Revue canadienne de psychiatrie* 50, no. 13: 815–16.
McNally, Richard J., and Susan A. Clancy. 2005. 'Sleep Paralysis, Sexual Abuse, and Space Alien Abduction.' *Transcultural Psychiatry* 42, no. 1: 113–22.
McNally, Richard J., Carel S. Ristuccia, and Carol A. Perlman. 2005. 'Forgetting of Trauma Cues in Adults Reporting Continuous or Recovered Memories of Childhood Sexual Abuse.' *Psychological Science: A Journal of the American Psychological Society / APS* 16, no. 4: 336–40.
McQuail, Denis. 2003. *Media Accountability and Freedom of Publication*. Oxford: Oxford University Press.
McRobbie, Angela, and Sarah L. Thornton. 1995. 'Rethinking "Moral Panic" for Multi-Mediated Social Worlds.' *British Journal of Sociology* 46, no. 4: 559–74.
Media Guardian. 2003. 'Tabloid Editor: "I Was Wrong."' *Media Guardian 2003*, 14 April.
Mencher, Melvin. 2003. *News Reporting and Writing*, 9th ed. Boston: McGraw-Hill.
Mermin, Jonathan. 2004. 'The Media's Independence Problem.' *World Policy Journal* 21, no. 3: 67–71.
Mindich, David T.Z. 1998. *Just the Facts: How 'Objectivity' Came to Define American Journalism*. New York: NYU Press.
Misak, Cheryl. 1994. 'Pragmatism and the Transcendental Turn in Truth and Ethics.' *Transactions of the Charles S. Peirce Society* 30, no. 4: 739–75.
Mittell, Jason. 2003. 'Audiences Talking Genre: Television Talk Shows and Cultural Hierarchies.' *Journal of Popular Film and Television* 31, no. 1: 36–46.
Mittell, Jason Scott. 2000. *Telegenres: Television Genres as Cultural Categories*. Madison: University of Wisconsin Press.
Molotch, Harvey. 1999. 'Spilling Out.' *Critical Sociology* 25, nos. 2–3: 247–60.
Molotch, Harvey, and Marilyn Lester. 1974. 'News as Purposive Behavior: On the Strategic Use of Routine Events, Accidents, and Scandals.' *American Sociological Review* 39, no. 1: 101–12.
- 1975. 'Accidental News: The Great Oil Spill as Local Occurrence and National Event.' *American Journal of Sociology* 81, no. 2: 235–60.
- 1999. 'Accidents, Scandals, and Routines: Resources for Insurgent Methodology.' *Critical Sociology* 25, nos. 2–3: 247–59.
Mooney, Linda A., and Carla-Marie Fewell. 1989. 'Crime in One Long-Lived Comic Strip: An Evaluation of Chester Gould's "Dick Tracy."' *American Journal of Economics and Sociology* 48, no. 1: 89–100.
Moore, Michael. 1989. *Roger & Me: A Humorous Look at How General Motors Destroyed Flint, Michigan*. USA.
- 2002. *Bowling for Columbine*. USA.

- 2004. *Fahrenheit 9/11.* USA.
Mujani, Saiful, and R. William Liddle. 2004. 'Politics, Islam, and Public Opinion.' *Journal of Democracy* 15, no. 1: 109–23.
NAMBLA (North American Man/Boy Love Association). http://216.220.97.17, accessed 30 November 2005.
Naron, Gregory R. 1990. 'With Malice Toward All: The Political Cartoon and the Law of Libel.' *Law and the Arts* 52, no. 1: 93–116.
National Young Adult Reporter. 1977. *Young Adult Personalities.* Washington: United Stated Catholic Conference. http://www.bishop-accountability.org/docs/boston/shanley/RCAB_00771-2.pdf, accessed 1 May 2006.
Nevitt, Barrington. 1982. *The Communication Ecology: Re-presentation versus Replica.* Toronto: Butterworths.
New York Times. 2004a. 'Confidential News Sources.' www.nytco.com/company/business_units/sources.html, accessed 20 November 2005.
- 2004b. 'New York Times Ethical Journalism Guidebook.' http://www.nytco.com/pdf/NYT_Ethical_Journalism_0904.pdf, accessed 20 November 2005.
Newman, Jay. 1996. *Religion vs. Television: Competitors in Cultural Context.* Westport: Praeger.
Odin, Roger. 1990. *Cinéma et production de sens.* Paris: Colin.
Oehler, Klaus. 1995. *Sachen und Zeichen: Zur Philosophie des Pragmatismus.* Frankfurt am Main: Klostermann.
Olmi, Ermanno. 1988. *La leggenda del santo bevitore.* Italy.
- 1994. *Genesi: La creazione e il diluvio.* Italy.
Ophüls, Max. 1955. *Lola Montès.* France.
Ostling, Richard N. 1987. 'Raising Eyebrows and the Dead.' *Time*, 13 July 1987.
Pape, Helmut. 1986. 'Einleitung' zu *Charles S. Peirce. Semiotische Schriften Bd 2.* Frankfurt am Main: Suhrkamp.
Péan, Pierre, and Philippe Cohen. 2003. *La face cachée du Monde. Du contre-pouvoir aux abus de pouvoir.* Paris: Mille et une nuits.
Peirce, Charles S. 1960. *Collected Papers* (**quoted as CP**), ed. Charles Hartshorne and Paul Weiss. Cambridge: Belknap.
- 1976. *The New Elements of Mathematics* (**quoted as NEM**). The Hague: Mouton.
Peirce, Charles S., Nathan Houser, and Christian J.W. Kloesel. 1992. *The Essential Peirce: Selected Philosophical Writings.* 2 vols. Bloomington: Indiana University Press.
Peters, John Durham. 1999. *Speaking into the Air: A History of the Idea of Communication.* Chicago: University of Chicago Press.
- 2001. 'Witnessing.' *Media, Culture, and Society* 23, no. 6: 707–23.

Petrilli, S. 2004. 'Semioethics, Subjectivity, and Communication: For the Humanism of Otherness.' *Semiotica* 148, nos. 1–4: 69–91.

Pfeiffer, Sacha. 2002. 'Famed "Street Priest" Preyed upon Boys.' http://www.boston.com/globe/spotlight/abuse/stories/013102_shanley_spotlight.htm, accessed 19 November 2006.

Pfeiffer, Sacha, and Globe Staff. 2002. 'Letters Exhibit Gentle Approach toward Priest.' http://www.boston.com/globe/spotlight/abuse/stories/012402_letters.htm, accessed 19 July 2005.

Pickard-Cambridge, Arthur Wallace. 1953. *The Dramatic Festivals of Athens*. Oxford: Clarendon.

Platon. 1578. *Platonis Opera quae extant omnia: Ex Nova Ioannis Serrani Interpretatione, perpetuis eiusde[m] notis illustrata: quibus et methodus et doctrinae summa breviter et perspicue indicatur = Πλάτωνος ἁπάντα τὰ σωζόμενα / eiusdem annotationes in quosdam suae illius interpretationis locos, Henr. Stephani* ... s.l.: Stephanus.

Plenel, Edwy. 1999. *L' épreuve*. Paris: Stock.

Potter, Jonathan. 1996. *Representing Reality: Discourse, Rhetoric, and Social Construction*. Thousand Oaks: Sage.

Pujas, Véronique. 2002. 'Explaining the Wave of Scandal: The Exposure of Corruption in Italy, France, and Spain.' In *Political Journalism: New Challenges, New Practices*, ed. Raymond Kuhn and Erik Neven. London: Routledge. 149–67.

Ranke, Leopold von. 1824. 'Geschichten der romanischen und germanischen Völker von 1494 bis 1535.' Leipzig: Reimer.

Real, Michael. 1977. *Mass-Mediated Culture*. Englewood Cliffs: Prentice-Hall.

Real, Michael R. 1989. *Super Media. A Cultural Studies Approach*. Newbury Park: Sage.

Ricoeur, Paul. 1983. *Temps et récit. I*. Paris: Seuil.

Rindova, Violina P., Timothy G. Pollock, and Mathew L.A. Hayward. 2006. 'Celebrity Firms: The Social Construction of Market Popularity.' *Academy of Management Review* 31, no. 1: 50–71.

Roberts, Don D. 1981. 'Peirce's Proof of Pragmaticism and his Existential Graphs.' *Graduate Studies* 23: 301–6.

Roeh, Itzhak. 1989. 'Journalism as Storytelling, Coverage as Narrative.' *American Behavioral Scientist* 33, no. 2: 162–8.

Roodhouse, Mark. 2002. 'The 1948 Belcher Affair and Lynskey Tribunal.' *Twentieth Century British History* 13, no. 4: 384–411.

Roschwalb, Susanne A., and Richard A. Stack. 1992. 'Litigation Public Relations.' *Communications and the Law* 14, no. 4: 3–23.

Rosenbaum, John, and Heather Duncan. 2001. 'When the Watchdog Sleeps: Investigative Journalism in the Czech Republic.' *Communications* 26, no. 2: 129–48.
Roth, Robert J. 1965. 'Is Peirce's Pragmatism Anti-Jamesian?' *International Philosophical Quarterly* 5: 541–63.
Rousseau, Jean-Jacques. 1782. *Collection complète des oeuvres.* Genève: Société typographique de Genève.
Ruggerone, Lucia. 1999. 'Da Husserl a Schutz: La fenomenologia e le scienze sociali.' *Studi di Sociologia* 37, no. 2: 167–91.
Sagar, Ramanand. 1986. *Ramayana.* India.
Saguy, Abigail C. 2002. 'Sexual Harassment in the News: The United States and France.' *Communication Review* 5, no. 2: 109–41.
Salmon, Andrew. 2005. 'Celebrity Dirt Report Shocks Korea.' *International Herald Tribune,* 24 January 2005.
Salvatore, Armando, and Mark Levine, eds. 2005. *Religion, Social Practice, and Contested Hegemonies: Reconstructing the Public Sphere in Muslim Majority Societies.* Basingstoke: Palgrave Macmillan.
Satcher, David. 2001. 'The Surgeon General's Call to Action to Promote Sexual Health and Responsible Sexual Behavior: A Letter from the Surgeon General.' http://mentalhealth.about.com/library/sex/blletter.htm, accessed 24 May 2010.
Savigny, Friedrich Carl von. 1840. 'System des heutigen römischen Rechts.' vol. 1. Berlin: Verlag von Veit.
Saxer, Ulrich. 1983. 'Systemtheorie und Kommunikationswissenschaft.' In *Kommunikationswissenschaft*, ed. Roland Burkart. Wien: Böhlau.
Scheibmayr, Werner. 2004. 'Niklas Luhmanns Systemtheorie und Charles S. Peirces Zeichentheorie zur Konstruktion eines Zeichensystems.' Überarbeitete Dissertation Ludwig-Maximilians-Universität München, 2002.
Schiller, Herbert I. 1989. *Culture, Inc.: The Corporate Takeover of Public Expression.* New York: Oxford University Press.
Schilling, Derek. 2003. 'Everyday Life and the Challenge to History in Postwar France: Braudel, Lefebvre, Certeau.' *Diacritics* 33, no. 1: 23–40.
Schiltz, Michael. 2007. 'Space Is the Place: The Laws of Form and Social Systems.' *Thesis Eleven* 88, no. 1: 8–30.
Schlöndorff, Volker, and Margaret Atwood. 1990. *The Handmaid's Tale.* USA / Germany.
Schmidt, Rosemarie, and Joseph F. Kess. 1986. *Television Advertising and Televangelism: Discourse Analysis of Persuasive Language.* Amsterdam: Benjamins.
Schopenhauer, Arthur. 1983. *Eristische Dialektik, oder, Die Kunst, Recht zu behalten in 38 Kunstgriffen dargestellt.* Zürich: Haffmans.

Schroeder, Jeanne Lorraine. 2004. *The Triumph of Venus: The Erotics of the Market*. Berkeley: University of California Press.
Schudson, Michael. 1978. *Discovering the News: A Social History of American Newspapers*. New York: Basic.
– 1989. 'The Sociology of News Production.' *Media, Culture, and Society* 11, no. 3: 263–82.
– 1995. *The Power of News*. Cambridge, MA: Harvard University Press.
– 2001. 'The Objectivity Norm in American Journalism.' *Journalism* 2, no. 2: 149–70.
– 2004. 'Notes on Scandal and the Watergate Legacy.' *American Behavioral Scientist* 47, no. 9: 1231–8.
– 2006. 'Was Objectivity Killed in Action?' *Critical Studies in Media Communication* 23, no. 2: 171–2.
Schultz, Julianne. 1998. *Reviving the Fourth Estate: Democracy, Accountability, and the Media*. Cambridge: Cambridge University Press.
Schütz, Alfred. 1973. *Collected Papers*. 3 vols. *Phaenomenologica*. The Hague: Nijhoff. 11, 15, 22.
Schütz, Alfred, and Thomas Luckmann. 1975. *Strukturen der Lebenswelt*. Neuwied.
Schütz, Alfred, Richard Grathoff, Hans-Georg Soeffner, and Ilja Srubar. 2003. *Werkausgabe: ASW*. Konstanz: UVK.
Schwinn, Thomas. 1998. 'False Connections: Systems and Action Theories in Neofunctionalism and in Jurgen Habermas.' *Sociological Theory* 16, no. 1: 75–95.
Scott, Linda M. 1994. 'The Bridge from Text to Mind: Adapting Reader-Response Theory to Consumer Research.' *Journal of Consumer Research* 21, no. 3: 461–80.
Seaford, Richard. 2000. 'The Social Function of Attic Tragedy: A Response to Jasper Griffin.' *Classical Quarterly* 1: 30–44.
Searle, John R. 1983. *Intentionality: An Essay in the Philosophy of Mind*. Cambridge: Cambridge University Press.
Shapiro, Samantha M. 2004. 'All God's Children.' *New York Times Magazine*, 5 September 2004.
Short, T.L. 2007. *Peirce's Theory of Signs*. Cambridge: Cambridge University Press.
Silk, Mark. 1995. *Unsecular Media: Making News of Religion in America*. Urbana: University of Illinois Press.
Simmel, Georg. 1968. *Soziologie. Untersuchungen über die Formen der Vergesellschaftung*. 5. Aufl. Berlin: Duncker & Humblot.

Smith, Tom W. 1992. 'The Polls: Poll Trends: Religious Beliefs and Behaviors and the Televangelist Scandals of 1987–1988.' *Public Opinion Quarterly* 56, no. 3: 360–80.
Smolkin, Rachel. 2006. 'Too Transparent?' *American Journalism Review* 28, no. 2: 16–23.
Soderbergh, Steven. 1989. *Sex, Lies, and Videotape*. USA.
Spencer-Brown, George. 1973. *Laws of Form*. New York: Bantam.
Streicher, Lawrence H. 1967. 'On a Theory of Political Caricature.' *Comparative Studies in Society and History* 9, no. 4: 427–45.
Sullivan, Denis F. 1979. 'Instinct and Dogmatism.' *Transactions of the Charles S. Peirce Society: A Quarterly Journal in American Philosophy* 15: 61–7.
Tarde, Gabriel. 1989. *L' opinion et la foule*. Paris: Presses Universitaires de France.
Tejera, Victorino. 1996. 'Has Habermas Understood Peirce?' *Transactions of the Charles S. Peirce Society* 32, no. 1: 107–25.
Tettey, Wisdom J. 2001. 'The Media and Democratization in Africa: Contributions, Constraints, and Concerns of the Private Press.' *Media, Culture, and Society* 23, no. 1: 5–31.
Thomas, William Isaac, and Dorothy Swaine Thomas. 1928. *The Child in America: Behavior Problems and Programs*. New York: Knopf.
Thompson, Deborah. 2004. 'Calling All Fag Hags: From Identity Politics to Identification Politics.' *Social Semiotics* 14, no. 1: 37.
Thompson, John B. 1995. *The Media and Modernity: A Social Theory of the Media*. Stanford: Stanford University Press.
– 2000. *Political Scandal: Power and Visibility in the Media Age*. Cambridge: Polity.
Thorstad, David. 1998. 'Pederasty and Homosexuality. Speech to the Semana Cultural Lesbica-Gay, Mexico City, June 26, 1998.' http://www.nambla.org/pederasty.htm, accessed 14 June 2010.
Tiffen, Rodney. 1999. *Scandals: Media, Politics, and Corruption in Contemporary Australia*. Sydney: UNSW Press.
Timmerman, D.M., and L.D. Smith. 1994. 'The World According to Pat: The Telepolitical Celebrity as Purveyor of Political Medicine.' *Political Communication* 11, no. 3: 233–48.
Toulmin, Stephen Edelston. 1969. *The Uses of Argument*. Cambridge: Cambridge University Press.
Toulmin, Stephen Edelston, Allan Janik, and Richard D. Rieke. 1979. *An Introduction to Reasoning*. New York: Macmillan.
Trier, Lars von. 1996. *Breaking the Waves*. Denmark.

Tuchman, Gaye. 1972. 'Objectivity as Strategic Ritual: An Examination of Newsman's Notions of Objectivity.' *American Journal of Sociology* 77, no. 4: 660–79.
– 1978. *Making News: A Study in the Construction of Reality*. New York: Free Press.
Tufte, Thomas. 2000. *Living with the Rubbish Queen: Telenovelas, Culture, and Modernity in Brazil*. Luton: University of Luton Press.
Tumber, Howard, and Silvio R. Waisbord. 2004a. 'Political Scandals and Media across Democracies: Introduction volume I.' *American Behavioral Scientist* 47, no. 8: 1031–9.
– 2004b. 'Political Scandals and Media across Democracies: Introduction volume II.' *American Behavioral Scientist* 47, no. 9: 1143–52.
Turner, Graeme. 2004. *Understanding Celebrity*. London: Sage.
Turner, Victor Witter. 1969. *The Ritual Process: Structure and Anti-Structure*. London: Routledge and Kegan Paul.
– 1974. *Dramas, Fields, and Metaphors: Symbolic Action in Human Society*. Ithaca: Cornell University Press.
– 1979. *Process, Performance, and Pilgrimage: A Study in Comparative Symbology*. New Delhi: Concept.
Turow, Joseph. 1989. 'Public Relations and Newswork: A Neglected Relationship.' *American Behavioral Scientist* 33, no. 2: 206–12.
Tyler, Lisa. 2005. 'Towards a Postmodern Understanding of Crisis Communication.' *Public Relations Review* 31, no. 4: 566–71.
United States Conference of Catholic Bishops. 2004. 'The Nature and Scope of the Problem of Sexual Abuse of Minors by Catholic Priests and Deacons in the United States: A Research Study Conducted by the John Jay College of Criminal Justice.' http://www.nccbuscc.org/nrb/johnjaystudy, accessed 20 December 2006.
Veyne, Paul. 1971. *Comment on écrit l'histoire. Suivi de Foucault révolutionne l'histoire*. Paris: Seuil.
Villaseñor, Juan Gonzalo. 2001. 'For Entertainment Purposes or Ad Majorem Dei Gloriam: Televangelism in the Marketplace of Ideas.' *Vanderbilt Journal of Entertainment and Technology Law* 3, no. 2: 145–68.
Voigt, Stefan. 2005. 'Islam and the Institutions of a Free Society.' *Independent Review* 10, no. 1: 59–82.
Waisbord, Silvio. 2002. 'The Challenges of Investigative Journalism.' *University of Miami Law Review* 56, no. 2: 377–95.
Waisbord, Silvio R. 1994. 'Knocking on Newsroom Doors: The Press and Political Scandals in Argentina.' *Political Communication* 11, no. 1: 19.

- 2004. 'Scandals, Media, and Citizenship in Contemporary Argentina.' *American Behavioral Scientist* 47, no. 8, 1072–98.
Walsh, Andrew. 2003. 'Instructions from the Vatican.' http://www.trincoll.edu/depts/csrpl/RINVol6No3/instructions%20from%20vatican.htm, accessed 10 December 2006.
Walton, Douglas N. 1997. *Appeal to Expert Opinion: Arguments from Authority.* University Park: Penn State University Press.
Weber, Max. 1920a. 'Die protestantische Ethik und der Geist des Kapitalismus.' In *Gesammelte Aufsätze zur Religionssoziologie*, Bd I, 17–206. Tübingen: Mohr.
- 1920b. *Gesammelte Aufsätze zur Religionssoziologie*, Bd III. Tübingen: Mohr.
Weber, Max, Talcott Parsons, and Anthony Giddens. 1992. *The Protestant Ethic and the Spirit of Capitalism.* London: Routledge.
Weinrich, Harald. 2001. *Tempus besprochene und erzählte Welt.* 6., neu bearb. Aufl. ed. München: C.H. Beck.
Weir, Peter. 1985. *Witness.* USA.
Weiskel, Timothy C. 2005. 'From Sidekick to Sideshow – Celebrity, Entertainment, and the Politics of Distraction: Why Americans Are "Sleepwalking Toward the End of the Earth."' *American Behavioral Scientist* 49, no. 3: 393–409.
Welker, Michael, ed. 1985. *Theologie und funktionale Systemtheorie. Luhmanns Religionssoziologie in theologischer Diskussion.* Frankfurt am Main: Suhrkamp.
West, Harry G., and Jo Ellen Fair. 1993. 'Development Communication and Popular Resistance in Africa: An Examination of the Struggle over Tradition and Modernity through Media.' *African Studies Review* 36, no. 1: 91.
White, Hayden V. 1984. 'The Question of Narrative in Contemporary Historical Theory.' *History and Theory* 23, no. 1: 1–33.
Wilcox, Clyde. 1989. 'Evangelicals and the Moral Majority.' *Journal for the Scientific Study of Religion* 28, no. 4: 400–14.
Williams, Kipling D., Martin J. Bourgeois, and Robert T. Croyle. 1993. 'The Effects of Stealing Thunder in Criminal and Civil Trials.' *Law and Human Behavior* 17, no. 6: 597–609.
Williams, Raymond. 1974. *Television: Technology and Cultural Form.* London: Fontana.
Willke, Helmut. 1989. *Systemtheorie entwickelter Gesellschaften. Dynamik und Riskanz moderner gesellschaftlicher Selbstorganisation* Grundlagentexte Soziologie. Weinheim: Juventa.
Winchester, Mark D. 1995. 'Litigation and Early Comic Strips: The Lawsuits of Outcault, Dirks, and Fisher.' *INKS: Cartoon and Comic Art Studies* 2, no. 2: 16–25.

Wyatt, Wendy. 2007. 'American Carnival: Journalism under Siege in an Age of New Media.' *Journalism and Mass Communication Quarterly* 84, no. 3: 629–31.

Wypijewski, JoAnn. 2004. 'The Passion of Father Paul Shanley.' http://www.legalaffairs.org/issues/September-October-2004/feature_wypijewski_sepoct04.msp and http://www.counterpunch.org/jw01292005.html, accessed 20 November 2005.

Young, Jock. 1971. *The Drugtakers: The Social Meaning of Drug Use*. London: MacGibbon and Kee.

Zelizer, Barbie. 1990. 'Achieving Journalistic Authority through Narrative.' *Critical Studies in Mass Communication* 7, no. 4: 366.

Zhou, Yuezhi. 2000. 'Watchdogs on Party Leashes? Contexts and Implications of Investigative Journalism in Post-Deng China.' *Journalism Studies* 1, no. 4: 577–97.

Index

abduction, 130f, 150, 153
actantial role, 299, 348, 355
Akerman, Chantal: *Je, tu, il, elle,* 27
Alger, Horatio, 263
'All,' ixf, 82, 91, 93f, 96, 101, 269
Almodovar, Pedro, *La mala educación,* 288
anonymous sources, 226
Anselm of Canterbury, 174
antethics, 129f
appresentation, 106, 111, 115, 124
Aristotle: *Categoriae,* 59; *Poetic,* 7, 15, 54, 90, 97, 177, 183, 206, 248, 286, 304; *Rhetorica,* 82; Περί ἑρμενείας (*de interpretatione*); 174
Auctoritas, 209, 224, 226
Augustinus Hipponensis, *Confessiones,* 183, 201, 203, 205, 249
Austin, Arthur, 262f, 269
autopoiesis, 55, 84, 105, 110, 116, 150, 172, 350, 377
Axel, Gabriel, *Babettes gaestebud,* 178

Bakker, Jimmy: Heritage USA Christian Theme Park, 201; *Praise the Lord!* 175, 184, 191, 195, 199f, 205, 358

Bird, Antonia, *Priest,* 179
Boetius, 174
Bourdieu, Pierre, 1, 312, 324, 347
Bresson, Robert, *Journal d'un curé de campagne,* 178
Busa, Paul, 261

caricature, 285
Carré sémiotique, 56, 174
Carter, Chris, *The X-Files,* 248
celebrity, 3, 8, 17, 41, 149, 182, 191, 197, 200, 203, 207, 220, 229, 234, 243f, 247, 249, 294f, 304, 347, 375
Cissé, Souleymane, *Yeelen,* 183
colonization of the life-world, 87, 162, 341
continuity, 140
Costa-Gavras, Konstantin, *Amen,* 212
Crimen sollicitationis, 373
Curtiz, Michael, *Casablanca,* 248

David–Uriah story, 177
Delegitimization, televangelists, 314
democratic principle of truth, 86
desarrollismo, 88
Dionysia, 90, 92, 94
Dionysos, 92f, 95, 183, 212

Doyle, Thomas, 373
Dreyer, Theodor, *Ordet*, 208
Duke, Daryl, *The Thorn Birds*, 179
Duvall, Robert, *The Apostle*, 178

egology, 111
Energetic Interpretant, 143
entitative graphs, 123
enunciation, 26, 52, 56f, 74, 94, 97ff, 120, 166ff, 172, 190, 220, 238, 268, 272, 275, 282, 284, 286ff, 339, 344, 346, 355f, 367; act, 44; instance, 55, 168, 209f, 283f; in journalism, 101, 282; marks of, 170; modes, 360
ethnomethodology, 40, 64, 187, 347
existential graphs, 123f, 341
Explosiv! 285f

First Correlate, in public opinion, 99
Ford, John, *The Fugitive*, 179
frame analysis, theatre logic, 95
frame theory, 236
framing, stealing thunder, 314
functionalism, 64, 76, 83, 86, 122, 156, 211, 306, 313, 353

Garfinkel, 342, 347
Geertz, Clifford, thick description, 133
Geoghan, John, 278, 300
Giddens, Anthony, 312
Gitai, Amos, *Kadosh*, 179
Graham, William A., *Guyana Tragedy – The Story of Jim Jones*, 120, 183, 356
Grosbard, Ulu, *True Confessions*, 179

Habermas: ideal formalism, 64; Ideal Speech Situation, 50, 63, 168, 245; *kommunikative Verflüssigung*, 67; media theory, 45, 49; *Öffentlichkeit*, 43; Reason, 63; speech act theory, 64f; systems constraints, 64; therapeutic discourse, 32
Hardoon, Laurence E., 269, 273
Hochhuth, Rolf, *Der Stellvertreter*, 212
hope in research, 86
hypotaxis, 170, 172f, 211, 219, 221, 237ff, 292

identity display, 3 transformations, 173
illusion énonciative, 56, 168, 344
illusion référentielle, 56, 168, 344, 364
indignation, 303
individuality, 143
inquiry, hope, 86
institution: class of behaviour, 309; transformation, 301
interpretation, chain of, 99
interview, 288; face-threatening, 288
inverted pyramid, 16, 220, 224, 227, 271, 345, 371
inviolate state, 308, 361

journalism: advocative, 82, 221, 227, 233, 257; attached, 227, 361; construction of 'All,' 93; critical, 73; enunciation, 101; exposure, 230; Fourth Estate, 102, 223, 301f; gossip, 24, 217, 255, 347, 365; investigative , 24, 31, 77, 216f, 222f, 225ff, 229f, 233f, 236, 249, 259, 272, 281, 285, 301f, 336, 362, 374f; – methods of investigation, 231; – satire, 229; – whistle blowers, 231; muckraking, 223, 302, 367; opinion, 230; public, 233; realist theories, 232; watchdog, 224f, 302, 305, 361; – 'bonk,' 233

Katholikentag, 285, 346
Kulturkampf, 253
Kurosawa, Akiro, *Rashômon*, 28

Lacroix, Pierre, 208, 359
Legisign, 58, 148
Levinson, Barry, *Wag the Dog*, 43, 245
litigation PR, 293
Logical Interpretant, 143
Lola Montez, 298
Luhmann, Niklas: God-Chiffre, 117, 120, 171; and Law of Form, 122; mass media, 119; medium theory, 105; medium theory vs relation, 106; reflexivity of knowledge, 114; sociology of religion, 117, 171, 180; system re-entry, 77, 106, 109, 114ff; world society, 117

medad, 138
media sign: First Correlate, 147; Second Correlate, 151; Third Correlate, 157
metatext: and frame theory, 236; as interpretation, 236; as modalization, 239; I, 239; II, 239, 242; II – in the Theatron model, 246; II – mimetic conflict, 245; II – Pragmaticist view, 245; II – stardom, 249; II and pragmatic truth theory, 243; II and range of variability, 243f; institutional practices, 238; performance of being, 241; performance of having, 241; sign relations, 237; specific difference and complementarity, 239
method: a priori, 128, 134, 147, 246, 307; of authority, 82, 86, 91, 102, 127f, 133f, 221, 244, 308; of science, 80f, 112, 128, 134f, 152, 217, 245; of science, hope, 86; of tenacity, 128, 133, 307; mockumentary, 32, 285
moral sentiment, 5f

Newman, Sydney, *Doctor Who*, 248
North American Man/Boy Love Association (NAMbLA), 262, 265, 267, 369f

Olmi, Ermanno: *Genesi – La creazione e il diluvio*, 179; *La leggenda del santo bevitore*, 178
organism, functionalism, 306

Peirce, C.S.: abduction, 130; antethics, 130; entitative graphs, 123; existential graphs, 123f; medad, 138; Pragmaticism, 41, 54, 65, 68ff, 76, 78, 81, 84ff, 101, 103f, 112, 127, 130, 135, 138, 141, 146, 155f, 216, 228, 243, 295, 297, 316, 325; sign of illation, 125; Synechism, 126; 'sign of itself' and Spencer-Brown's 're-entry,' 125
percept, perceptual judgment, 28
Pfeiffer, Sacha, 261ff, 271ff, 283
Practices, 129f
Pragmatic Maxim, 10, 43, 50, 77, 83, 100, 137, 141, 151, 154, 309, 312
pragmatic truth theory from the subject perspective, 243
preaching, 182
privatization of religion, 182
PTL, 176
public opinion: First Correlate, 99; Rhetoric, 89; role relations, 91; Second Correlate, 98; Third Correlate, 99; two conditions, 91
public relations, stealing thunder, 314

public sphere and religion, conflict of rationalities, 159
publicity: truth equivalent, 87; unity of action, 96

Qualisign, 58
quidditas, quiddity, 99, 129

religion: private and public, 182, 218; and public sphere, rationalities, 159
religious communication: as entertainment, 179
Representamen, 28, 32, 144, 147
Roberts, Oral, 207, 209
Roddenberry, Gene, *Star Trek*, 248
Rousseau, Jean-Jacques: *Confessions*, 31, 202, 205, 237, 306, 311; *volonté générale*, 82

Sagar, Ramanand, *Ramayana*, 183
satire, 284; and investigative journalism, 229
scandal: construction of an ideal, 13; definition: – compared with law, 8; – from industry practice, 6; – from social behaviour, 4; etymology, 18; function in society, 306; Gothic genre, 369; in religious not public discourse, 276; indignation, 303; industrial rhetorical form, 16; institutional transformation, 301; journalistic form, 233; litigation PR, 293; media / social scandal difference, 25; moral acts, 6; objectivity, 234; real corruption or ideal construction, 13; reality vs effect, 291; research method and approach, 9; semiotic of effect, 296; 'turned into a narrative,' 304; σκάνδαλον, 6, 13, 19, 278, 372, 376; – τοῦ σταυροῦ, scandalum crucis, 18
scandal, *CASES:* abuse by priests, 20; Argentinean military chaplains, 20; Belcher, 9; Boston Church, 38, 82; Cleveland scandal, 24; Enron, 24; Lola Montez, 298; Michel Friedman, 40; O.J. Simpson, 24; Rwandan nuns, 20; Tangentopoli, 9; Televangelists, 20; Valerie Plame, 225; Watergate, 24, 260, 317, 375; Zippergate, 10f, 20, 25, 229, 260, 305, 317, 335, 375
scandal, *CLASSES:* audience (κοῖλον) scandal, 252; destination scandal, 254; source (θεολογεῖον) scandal, 251; stage (λογεῖον) scandal, 254; performance (πρᾶξις) scandal, 254; actor (ὑπόκριτης) scandal, 254
Schlöndorff, Volker, *The Handmaid's Tale*, 179, 183, 356
Schopenhauer, Arthur, eristic logic, 86, 245, 345
Schuller, Dr Robert, 359; *The Hour of Power*, 197
Second Correlate, in public opinion, 98
semio-narratology, 40, 56ff, 75, 162, 299, 339, 344, 348f, 364
semiology, 55ff, 71, 100, 107, 111, 146, 162, 186, 339
Sex Crimes and the Vatican, 280
Shanley, Paul, 37, 254, 260ff, 290, 367, 369ff
Sharman, Jim, *The Rocky Horror Picture Show*, 248
Shea, Daniel, 373
Sign: body, 141; constructiveness, 87; degeneration, 87, 138, 143, 149, 153, 166, 188, 281; Energetic

Interpretant, 143; Legisign, 58, 148; Logical Interpretant, 143; Qualisign, 58; Representamen, 144, 147; Sinsign, 58; theory, 139; relations in metatexts, 237
sign degeneration, 344
Sinsign, 58
skopic apparatus, 174, 176f
society: as feeling habit, 146; individuality, 143; as organism, 306; reacting to reality, 146; selfishness, 143
Soderbergh, Steven, *Sex, lies, & videotape*, 26, 28
spectacularization, 178, 209
Spencer-Brown: Law of Form, 106, 122; 're-entry' and Peirce's 'sign of itself,' 125
Spiegel, 97, 346, 364
stardom, 249
stealing thunder, 314
summum bonum, 130, 132, 352
Swaggart, Jimmy, 198
Syllabus Errorum, 253
Symbolic Interactionism, 128, 156, 295
Synechism, 126, 140, 245

technological determinism, 164
teleology, undecidable, 96
televangelists, delegitimization of, 314
television news format, 232
theatre, ancient: θεαταί, 92; θέατρον, 36, 92, 96f, 134, 161, 180, 212f, 215, 220f, 226, 228, 233, 236f, 245f, 250f, 258, 63, 268f, 280, 299, 305, 348; θεολογεῖον, 92, 245, 269; κορυφαῖος, 95, 102, 246; κήρυγμα, 182; κοιλόν, 301; λογεῖον, 92, 95, 102, 301; ὑποκριταί, 95, 102; χορός, 92, 95, 252, 301; in public opinion, 99; role differentiation, 91; thick description, 133; Third Correlate; tribunal rite, theatre, 90
Trier, Lars von, *Breaking the Waves*, 179
truth, democratic principle, 86
truth equivalent, 87, 216, 239
truth-speaking scale: grade −1, expert truth, 283; grade 0, enunciation, 283; grade 1, opinion, 284; grade 1, satire, 284; grade 2, testimony and interview, 288; grade 3, ridicule, 287

unity of action, 96

Wallraff, Günter, 230f
Weber, Max, *Protestant Ethic*, 184f, 195f, 198f, 201ff, 205, 218f, 359
Weir, Peter, *Witness*, 179
Whedon, Joss, *Buffy the Vampire Slayer*, 248
whistle blowers, 231